Balthasar and Anxiety

Balthasar and Anxiety

by
John R. Cihak

t&t clark

Published by T&T Clark

A Continuum imprint

The Tower Building
11 York Road
London SE1 7NX

80 Maiden Lane
Suite 704
New York NY 10038

www.continuumbooks.com

British Library Cataloguing-in-Publication Data
A catalogue record for this book is available from the British Library.

ISBN-13: 978-0-5670-0047-7

Typeset by RefineCatch Limited, Bungay, Suffolk
Printed and bound in Great Britain by the MPG Books Group

For while we are still in this tent, we sigh with anxiety.
(2 Corinthains 5.4)

Fear is already God's daughter, redeemed on the night of Good Friday.
(Georges Bernanos)

Dedicated to

My Grandmother

Antoinette Lillian Janda
(1910–2005)

Requiescat in pace

and to

Those who are anxious
yet cling to the words of our crucified and risen Lord,

In this world you will have tribulation, but take courage, I have overcome the world. (John 16.33)

Contents

Preface and Acknowledgements

I was first introduced to the theology of Hans Urs von Balthasar back in 1992 as a philosophy undergraduate at the University of Notre Dame. Then Fr. Robert Morlino (now Bishop of Madison, Wisconsin), had given a Lenten mission to the students of Alumni Hall where I lived. After the mission I was invited out to dinner with him and the priest, Fr. John Conley, CSC, who had hosted him. During the meal, Fr. Morlino spoke about the richness of Balthasar's theology and handed me a little book entitled, *Does Jesus Know Us, Do We Know Him?* The reading of this text began my study of this great theologian. My interest in Balthasar was encouraged after I entered Mount Angel Seminary by Fr. Jeremy Driscoll, OSB and then Fr. Rino Fisichella (now auxiliary bishop of Rome and Rector of the Pontifical Lateran University) who was guest lecturing at the seminary that semester. I continued my studies at the Pontifical Gregorian University in Rome and wrote my licentiate thesis on Balthasar under the direction of Fisichella. After ordination and assignments as a parish priest and faculty member at Mount Angel Seminary, I went back to the Gregorian to study for the doctorate. My experience in the parish impressed upon me the need for theologians to be writing about suffering; I also wanted to continue my abiding interest in Balthasar's theology. Fr. Jacques Servais, SJ agreed to direct the thesis and suggested that I write on the theme of anxiety. I was surprised to find out in the preliminary research that very little had been written on this topic within Catholic theology. It seemed opportune to write on such an important topic. I am very grateful to all those in my life who have helped me to appreciate Balthasar's theology.

I also wish to thank Archbishop John Vlazny, for sending me to obtain the doctorate, and to Abbot Nathan Zodrow, OSB of Mount Angel Abbey for helping to finance the studies. A special debt of gratitude is owed to my dear Family who first brought me to the knowledge and love of Jesus Christ and his Church. Special thanks to my brother, James, for helping to proofread the manuscript and who has now begun his own theological studies for the priesthood at the Gregorian.

Since this work is intended to extend beyond the realm of theology to engage the other sciences which treat anxiety, I am thankful to those scholars and experts who gave invaluable feedback on various aspects of this thesis: Lynne Bissonnette, MD, PhD, Fr. Donath Hercsik, SJ, Rodney Howsare, PhD, Aaron Kheriaty, MD, and Stephen Loughlin, PhD. I am grateful to my brother priests of the Casa Santa Maria, Rome for their priestly example and fraternity, and to the members of the Casa Balthasar for the access to their library, for stimulating discussions and even occasional musical *divertimento*. Finally a special note of thanks is given to Monsignor Gerard O'Connor, SLD for his friendship, his patient suffering in proofreading the initial drafts, and for his encouragement, sometimes with a cricket bat, to keep working.

Abbreviations

Below is a list of abbreviations used in this work. Full titles and information are provided in the bibliography. Whenever possible, I have referred to published English translations of texts from Hans Urs von Balthasar. For other authors, I have referred to extant translations or made my own.

1. The Works of Hans Urs von Balthasar

AA	*Der antirömische Affekt*
B	*Gelebte Kirche. Bernanos*
BG	*Das Betrachtende Gebet*
CA	*Der Christ und die Angst*
Cœur	*Au Cœur du mystère rédempteur*
CS	*Christlicher Stand*
EB	*Erster Blick auf Adrienne von Speyr*
HI-VII	*Herrlichkeit, vols. 1–7*
HW	*Das Herz der Welt*
K	*Klarstellungen*
KB	*Karl Barth. Darstellung und Deutung seiner Theologie*
KL	*Kosmische Liturgie*
Kw	*Kreuzweg*
PI	*Pneuma und Institution*
RS	*Nochmals. Reinhold Schneider*
SC	*Spiritus Creator*
SV	*Sponsa Verbi*
SwG	*Schwestern im Geist*
TDI-V	*Theodramatik, vols. 1–5*
TDT	*Theologie der drei Tage*
TG	*Theologie der Geschichte*
TLI-III	*Theologik, vols. 1–3*
UA	*Unser Auftrag*
VC	*Verbum Caro*
WdK	*Wenn ihr nicht werdet wie dieses Kind*
ZSW	*Zu Seinem Werk*

2. Other Abbreviations

a(a).	article(s)
AAS	*Acta Apostolicae Sedis*, Romae (1909)
BDAG	W. Bauer, *A Greek-English Lexicon of the New Testament another Early Christian Literature*, rev. and ed. by F. Danker,

	based on Walter Bauer's *Griechisch-deutsches Wörterbuch zu den Schriften des Neuen Testaments und der frühchristlichen Literatur*, sixth edition, ed. K. Aland and B. Aland, with V. Reichmann and on previous English editions by W. Arndt, F. Gingrich and F. Danker, Chicago 1957, 2000[3]
c.	*circa*
CCC	*Catechism of the Catholic Church*
Cf.	Confer
Dr(s).	Doctor(s)
DS	H. Denziger and A. Schönmetzer (eds), *Enchiridion Symbolorum, Definitionum et Declarationum de Rebus Fidei et Morum*, Freiburg 1937[23]
DSM-IV-TR	*Diagnostic and Statistical Manual of Mental Disorders*, 4th edition, text revision
e.g.	*exempli gratia*, for example
ed.	editor(s)
EDNT	H. Balz and G. Schneider (eds), *Exegetisches Wörterbuch zum Neuen Testament* (vol. 2; Stuttgart: Verlag W. Kohlhammer GmbH, 1978–1980); English trans., *Exegetical Dictionary of the New Testament* (vol. 2; Grand Rapids: Eerdmans, 1990)
Eng.	English translation
et al.	*et alii*, and others
etc.	*et cetera*
f(f).	following page(s)
i.e.	*id est*, that is
Ital.	Italian translation
LW	*Luther's Works*
n.	note/number
nn.	numbers
orig.	original
p(p).	page(s)
q(q).	question(s)
rev.	revised
RSV	Revised Standard Version
sol.	solution
St(s).	Saint(s)
STh	*Summa Theologica*
trans.	translation, translator
WA	*Martin Luthers Werke. Kritische Gesamtausgabe*

Introduction: A Tale of Two Gardens

The contemporary situation of western civilization is marked by a profound anxiety. Several factors have converged to create and intensify this anxiety. These factors include the rise of atheism, the speed of technological advance, the annihilation of hope in human progress, especially with the devastation of the two World Wars and the loss of hope in human reason in post-modern philosophy. We can also think of the unexpected, tragic and continued threats of natural disasters, terrorism (whose very name indicates its intention to spread anxiety), nuclear disaster now in the form of a 'dirty bomb' and the continued social and political destruction of core institutions like the nuclear family which are so necessary to instill in people a sense of security. In the United States, for example, anxiety is second only to drug abuse as the most common mental health problem affecting approximately 25 per cent of the population.[1] Historians observe that at the end of an age, as the dominant civilization declines, the level of anxiety felt in that people increases. As in the waning days of the Roman Empire, the twenty-first century in the West is also aptly termed an 'age of anxiety'.[2]

The etymological roots of anxiety convey, first and foremost, the sense of a *constriction* in the throat or heart.[3] Perhaps the greatest attention given to this universal human phenomenon in recent decades is, from what might be termed in a broad sense, the psychological sciences, which would include psychiatry, psychoanalysis and psychology. In order to obtain a grasp of the phenomenon under consideration for this study where we explore Hans Urs von Balthasar's theology of anxiety, we first briefly present psychiatry's description of the phenomenon. This brief treatment is done in the manner of

1. Anxiety is a factor in drug abuse, and also plays a role in many other mental illnesses (cf. A. Sims, *Symptoms in the Mind: An Introduction to Descriptive Psychopathology* [London: Saunders Ltd., 2003], p. 335).

2. Cf. E.R. Dodds, *Pagan and Christian in an Age of Anxiety: some Aspects of Religious Experience from Marcus Aurelius to Constantine* (Cambridge: Cambridge University Press, 1963).

3. Cf. J. Ritter (ed.), *Historisches Wörterbuch der Philosophie* (vol. 1; Basel/Stuttgart: Schwabe, 1971), p. 310. The root word in Greek is ἄγχειν and in Latin *angor* meaning 'to choke', or 'to throttle' and 'to feel oppressiveness or apprehension'. The Latin word *angustiae* means 'narrowness, crampedness or tightness', and *angere* meaning 'choking in the throat', or 'an oppressiveness in the heart' (H.J. Sandkühler [ed.], *Europäische Enyzklopädie zu Philosophie und Wissenschaften* [Hamburg: F. Meiner, 1990], pp. 134–35). The term is related to anguish, fear (*timor, Furcht*), and terror (*Schreck*).

'descriptive psychopathology' which seeks to avoid theoretical explanations for psychological events.[4]

The Phenomenon of Anxiety According to Psychiatry

In general

Anxiety can be described in general as 'a diffuse, unpleasant, vague sense of apprehension, often accompanied by autonomic symptoms such as headache, perspiration, palpitations, tightness in the chest, mild stomach discomfort and restlessness, indicated by an inability to sit or stand still for long'.[5] The characteristic feeling of anxiety is constriction, and the person may feel 'restless, uncertain, vulnerable, trapped, breathless, choked. As well as feeling frightened and worried, hypochondriacal ideas and even feelings of guilt are often prominent'.[6]

Many, but not all, in psychiatry make a distinction between 'anxiety' and 'fear' with fear being the response to an identifiable danger while anxiety is the response to an unidentifiable threat.[7] In such an understanding, fear is

4. Cf. Sims, *Symptoms in the Mind*, 3. It is admitted from the beginning that constructing such a phenomenological sketch is difficult because of the wide variance within psychiatry on basic definitions and first principles. A primary reason for this variance is historical. Psychoanalytic schools of thought, rooted in Freud's approach, tend to focus on a person's early developmental history and current unconscious conflicts rather than precisely describing the phenomena themselves. Another significant tradition, exemplified by E. Kraepelin and the 'Heidelberg school', pays very careful attention to the phenomena as they appear to the therapist and experienced by the patient. The *Diagnostic and Statistical Manual*, so influential in psychiatry in the United States, reflects these two traditions. The *DSM-II* took a more psychoanalytic, psychodynamic approach, while the *DSM-III* and current *DSM-IV* took a more Kraepelinian approach. This second approach provides operational definitions based on clusters of symptoms, while trying to remain 'theory neutral' about the origins of these symptoms, or the reasons why symptoms tend to cluster in these specific ways. The following description attempts to follow in the line more of the second tradition while recognizing that even supposedly neutral scientific observations are influenced by theory. I am grateful to Aaron Kheriaty, MD (psychiatry) and Lynne Bissonette-Pitre, MD, PhD (psychiatry and neurophysiology) for their invaluable assistance on the psychiatric portions of this study.

5. B. Sadock and V. Sadock (eds), *Kaplan and Sadock's Synopsis of Psychiatry* (Philadelphia: Lippincott Williams & Wilkins, 2002), p. 591.

6. Sims, *Symptoms in the Mind*, pp. 329–330. Cf. A. Colman (ed.), *A Dictionary of Psychology* (Oxford: Oxford University Press, 2003), p. 46; R. Corsini (ed.), *The Dictionary of Psychology* (Philadelphia: Taylor & Francis, 1999), p. 58.

7. Cf. Sadock and Sadock (eds), *Kaplan and Sadock's Synopsis*, pp. 591–92; A. Kazdin (ed.), *Encyclopedia of Psychology* (vol. 1; Oxford: Oxford University Press, 2000), p. 209. Freud indicates this fundamental nuance: 'I shall avoid going more closely into the question of whether our linguistic usage means the same thing or something clearly different by "*Angst*", "*Furcht*" and "*Schreck*". I will only say that I think "*Angst*" relates to the state and disregards the object, while "*Furcht*" draws attention precisely to the object. It seems that "*Schreck*", on the other hand, does have a special sense; it lays emphasis, that is, on the

sometimes classified as a form of anxiety. Others do not draw a strong distinction between fear and anxiety, and hold that anxiety can have both a definite and indefinite object. It seems the distinction here is primarily in the cognitive symptoms.

Anxiety, moreover, can be experienced in varying degrees or intensity.[8] It can manifest itself in what therapists call a low level: a generalized, constant low-grade worry with uneasy feelings, self-doubts and may be accompanied by irritable bowel or mild nausea. It can intensify to a medium state of a constant high-grade worry with all the characteristics of the first degree but intensified. Finally the anxiety can become so intense that it mounts into a panic attack which can suddenly appear and is so horribly intense that a person may think he is about to die, and would prefer to die rather than to ever experience another one.[9] A person experiencing an anxiety attack often feels like they are having a heart attack or suffocating to death, that death is imminent, and often precipitates a visit to the emergency room of a hospital.

Anxiety is also classified in psychiatry as normal and abnormal (or disordered). Most individuals have some anxiety in response to danger (normal), whereas some people have so much anxiety that it is considered a disorder (abnormal). Anxiety as a mental disorder is 'the most prevalent psychiatric condition in the United States and in most other populations studied'.[10] Anxiety disorders include Panic Attack Disorder, Agoraphobia, Specific Phobia, Social Phobia, Obsessive–Compulsive Disorder (OCD), Post-traumatic Stress Disorder (PTSD), Generalized Anxiety Disorder and Anxiety disorder due to a general medical condition.[11] Psychiatry describes the phenomenon of anxiety in terms of three often inseparable clusters of symptoms: physiological, cognitive and behavioural.

Physiological symptoms

Physiological symptoms, also called somatic and autonomic symptoms, describe how the human body experiences anxiety. Anxiety creates a physiological response in the body to the perceived threat. It triggers an alert in the

effect produced by a danger which is not met by any preparedness for anxiety. We might say, therefore, that a person protects himself from fright by anxiety' (S. Freud, *The Complete Introductory Lectures on Psychoanalysis* [trans. J. Strachey; New York: W. W. Norton & Co., 1966], p. 395).

8. There is debate in psychiatry as to whether the intensity of anxiety should be classified categorically, that is, as qualitatively different types of anxiety, or dimensionally, that is, as differing only in degree or intensity. The latter view understands anxiety as existing on a continuum, rather than as distinct states with no sharply defined lines between various 'types' of anxiety.

9. Cf. American Psychiatric Association, *Diagnostic and Statistical Manual of Mental Disorders-IV-TR* (Washington D.C.: American Psychiatric Association, 2000), p. 395.

10. Sadock and Sadock (eds), *Kaplan and Sadock's Comprehensive Textbook of Psychiatry* (vol. 1; Philadelphia: Lippincott Williams & Wilkins, 2000), p. 1441.

11. Cf. *DSM-IV-TR*, pp. 393–444.

brain which then turns on the autonomic nervous system.[12] The autonomic nervous system sends out impulses to activate the organs of the body so that the individual experiences a readiness for self-preservation by fighting or fleeing which involves brain processes, neurochemical changes, hormonal release and changes in blood pressure and circulation. Common physiological, and objectively measurable, symptoms include heart palpitations, difficulty in breathing, hyperventilation, dry mouth, sweating, trembling or shaking, nausea, abdominal churning, cold skin, chest pain, dizziness, numbness or tingling, chills or hot flashes, diarrhoea, flatulence, difficulty in swallowing, muscle soreness, weak knees, overactive bladder, dilation of the pupils of the eyes and fatigue.[13] Such somatic phenomena may be isolated or coincide with others. During a panic attack, four or more of these can occur simultaneously. In short, anxiety has a universal impact on the body affecting every organ in the body to some degree.[14]

Cognitive symptoms

Anxiety is also experienced as a phenomenon in the mind. The mental symptoms include anxious anticipation and inner (psychic) terror which can manifest in anxious thoughts: 'Something terrible is going to happen'; 'I cannot handle this'; 'This situation is too much for me'; 'Perhaps I have done something that has inadvertently caused calamity'; 'I am a terrible failure'; 'I want to run away from here'; or 'I want to jump out of my body'. The thoughts can range 'from excessive concern about a specific event such as dying in a plane crash or being contaminated by germs, or about a myriad of everyday events such as family matters, personal finances or personal health'.[15] These anxious cognitions appear as recurring, intrusive and unwanted, and can include a sudden flashback to a traumatic event as in PTSD, a fearful or catastrophic thought connected with a particular object or event as in a Specific Phobia, or recurrent and hard to eliminate thoughts, images or impulses, as in OCD.[16] Anxious cognitions can also be focused on God and can take the form of 'Will I be acceptable?'; 'Am I able to please him even with my weakness, failures and sinfulness?'; 'Will I ever be able to achieve what is being asked of me?'

12. There are two schools of thought in psychiatry on whether the biological triggers the psychological or vice versa. Cf. Sadock and Sadock (eds), *Kaplan and Sadock's Synopsis*, p. 594.

13. Cf. Kazdin (ed.), *Encyclopedia of Psychology*, 212; R. Gregory (ed.), *The Oxford Companion to the Mind* (Oxford: Oxford University Press, 1987), p. 30.

14. Cf. Gregory (ed.), *The Oxford Companion*, p. 30. The biological sciences have contributed greatly to elucidate the physiological mechanisms underlying the somatic symptoms of anxiety, for example, in the role of various neurotransmitters (such as norepinephrine, serotonin, and GABA) play, or the neuroanatomical changes in the limbic system and cerebral cortex due to new techniques of functional brain imaging such as SPECT and PET scans, that mediate the somatic symptoms of anxiety.

15. Kazdin (ed.), *Encyclopedia of Psychology*, p. 212.

16. Ibid., 212.

and, during times of spiritual darkness, 'Will he ever return to me again with consolation?'. Anxious cognitions can be conscious thoughts or unconscious dreams which are called 'anxiety nightmares' which have themes of humiliation, failure or danger and usually take place towards the end of sleep.[17] Psychic symptoms also include irritability, difficulty in concentrating, insomnia and inability to relax.[18] As in the physiological symptoms, the cognitive symptoms can be triggered by the occurrence of a specific event, which can appear spontaneously or be constant.

Listening to the views concerning the genesis of anxiety can help paint a clearer picture of the content of anxious cognitions. Melanie Klein locates it in the fear of death, Rollo May holds that it is caused by the fear of losing essential values, while H. S. Sullivan contends that the cognitions are focused on disapproval in relationships beginning with the foundational relationship of mother and her infant.[19] Existentialist theorists would say that the content of anxious thoughts is comprised of the fear of being alone or being nothing.[20] Aaron Beck, a major theorist and developer of 'cognitive-behavioral' therapy, locates the origin of anxiety in automatic negative thoughts associated with danger, risk, uncontrollability and incapacity.[21] Some locate a cause of disordered anxiety in parents not being consistent or on target in their responses to the infant's or child's signals for help, and classify it as Insecure Attachment Disorder.[22] This may become so ingrained in the child's brain that he will feel insecure and experience anxiety in all subsequent significant relationships. David Barlow suggests that early experiences of helplessness and lack of control produce 'psychological vulnerability' predisposing a person to feel anxious even without an identifiable stressor.[23]

The human brain also learns from its own interior experiences. If, for example, one is anxious about giving a speech, one's brain will be traumatized by the current anxiety and will automatically remember to trigger an anxiety reaction if in the future one is about to give another speech. Some hold that anxious cognitions have their source in some unconscious conflict usually rooted in some unresolved or traumatic event in childhood. Traumatic

17. Cf. Corsini (ed.), *Dictionary of Psychology*, p. 58.

18. Sims, *Symptoms in the Mind*, p. 331.

19. Corsini (ed.), *Encyclopedia of Psychology* (vol. 1; New York: John Wiley & Sons, 2nd ed, 1994), p. 92.

20. Cf. Gregory (ed.), *The Oxford Companion*, p. 31.

21. Cf. A.T. Beck and G. Emery, *Anxiety Disorders and Phobias: A Cognitive Perspective* (New York: Basic Books, 1991).

22. Cf. M. Ainsworth, *Patterns of Attachment: A Psychological Study of the Strange Situation* (Mahwah: Erlbaum, 1978); J. Bowlby, *A Secure Base: Parent-Child Attachment and Healthy Human Development* (New York: Basic Books, 1990); S. Greenspan, *Building Healthy Minds: The Six Experiences That Create Intelligence and Emotional Growth in Babies and Young Children* (Cambridge: Da Capo Press, 2000) and D. Siegel, *The Developing Mind: Toward a Neurobiology of Interpersonal Experience* (New York: Guilford, 1999).

23. Cf. D.H. Barlow, 'The Nature of Anxiety: Anxiety, Depression, and Emotional Disorders', in R.M. Rapee and Barlow (eds), *Chronic anxiety: Generalized Anxiety Disorder and Mixed Anxiety-Depression* (New York: Guilford Press, 1991), pp. 1–28.

experiences in childhood (e.g., death of parents, fires, terrorism, abuse, etc.) or later in life (e.g., abuse, abortion, etc.) may become ingrained in both the central and peripheral autonomic nervous system as anxiety with PTSD.

Behavioural symptoms

The phenomenon of anxiety also has a behavioural component. When experiencing anxiety, a person acts in response to the perceived danger in order to avoid the anticipated pain. The most common behaviour in anxiety is *avoidance* in which the individual avoids situations, events or places in which he feels anxious. Behavioural avoidance can take the special form of rituals or compulsions, which are 'repetitive, specific acts designed to prevent or undo the effects of certain stimuli, events, or situations'.[24] Though the behaviour may be effective in avoiding the pain, it also prevents one from exploring further the dangerous situation. Some examples of behaviour avoidance are repetitive washing or cleaning behaviours, procrastination and indecisiveness.

A Perennial Yet Uniquely Modern Theme

Long before the advent of psychiatry and other psychological sciences, the problem of anxiety occupied the thinking of such diverse figures as Aristotle, the Stoics, St. Augustine (354–430), St. John Chrysostom (c. 347–407), St. Thomas Aquinas (1225–1274), St. Thomas More (1478–1535), Martin Luther (1483–1546), Søren Kierkegaard (1813–1855), Frederick Nietzsche (1844–1900), Sigmund Freud (1856–1939), Martin Heidegger (1889–1976) and Jean-Paul Sartre (1905–1980).

Anxiety was initially classified by Aristotle and the Stoic philosophers as a *passio animae*, that is, a movement of the sensitive appetite of the soul away from the perceived danger. The traditional definition is that anxiety or fear is the apprehension of a threatening future evil from which escape might be possible. This type of suffering, intensified and given a unique quality by the ability to reason, is also closely related to the fundamental philosophical act of wonder (*admiratio*).[25] *Admiratio*, regarded as a positive emotion, is an outward movement of the soul towards the object to be known while fear (*timor*) is the recoil from an object that appears to be threatening. *Admiratio* is indeed an estrangement from what is known but differs from anxiety since *admiratio* pushes *towards* the future to know the existing thing, while anxiety *shrinks* from it to avoid the coming evil. Aquinas classifies wonder as a type of fear since the one who experiences it, shrinks from forming a judgment concerning

24. Kazdin (ed.), *Encyclopedia of Psychology*, p. 212. Although ritual compulsions can have an obvious relationship to anxiety-provoking obsessions, they can also appear totally unrelated to the obsessions.

25. St. Thomas Aquinas classifies *admiratio* as a type of *timor* (fear). Cf. *STh*. I–II, q. 41, a. 4.

the event or thing which causes him to wonder because he fears to fall short of the truth of the matter. Anxiety in the modern sense does not arise in ancient and medieval thought because of its restriction to the senses and sense appetite as a *passio animae*.

It took an age in which the confidence of being was profoundly shaken to shift anxiety from a *passio animae* to what Hans Urs von Balthasar (1905–1988) terms a 'fundamental situation' (*Grundbefindlichkeit*) of the human mind.[26] As confidence in metaphysics eroded in the post-Enlightenment period, *admiratio* was thought more in terms of anxiety by such thinkers as Kierkegaard, Heidegger and Sartre. Instead of emphasizing reason's movement of trust they instead place the emphasis on reason's movement of flight. For Kierkegaard anxiety comes from man's realization of his own contingency. The perceived threat is not so much a beast coming to devour or a calamity like losing one's job, but rather anxiety comes from the very act of thinking: the threat of one's finitude and contingency stretched out over the abyss of infinite possibility. For Heidegger, anxiety arises less from the possibilities inherent in finite freedom vis-à-vis God, as the possibility for one to become one's authentic self in all its unique individuality. Anxiety for Heidegger shakes man out of his tendency to bury himself in a less demanding and more superficial mode of existence that ultimately is not truly his own. Anxiety is a necessary part of the process of having one's 'inauthentic' self disintegrate and opened up to the possibility of who he should be. Sartre, heavily influenced by Heidegger, views anxiety as arising from the responsibility of human freedom. Though the responsibility of embracing this freedom without God is burdensome and causes anguish, it is the apex of human existence. In Sartre's view, other people become a source of anxiety because the 'other' is a direct obstacle to one's own ability to remain absolutely free and actualize oneself. Relationships, therefore, become an arena of suspicion, anxiety and panic. Since the shift from *passio animae* to a *Grundbefindlichkeit*, anxiety as a theme has taken on a uniquely modern hue in which its objectless and existential qualities are emphasized. This modern sense of anxiety is the focus of the present study.

A Timely Theme

The responses to anxiety in the twentieth century have come primarily from the psychological sciences, philosophy and Lutheran theology.[27] Many of the theological responses have focused on defending the Christian faith from the

26. *CA*, 73; Eng., 123. H. U. von Balthasar's term, *Grundbefindlichkeit*, could also be rendered a 'fundamental *condition*' of the human mind.

27. Most notable among the Lutheran theologians are P. Tillich, *The Courage to Be* (New Haven: Yale University Press, 1970) and *Systematic Theology* (vol. 1; Chicago: University of Chicago, 1973); J. Moltmann, *The Crucified God* (trans. R.A. Wilson and J. Bowden; London: SCM Press, 1974) and *Theology of Hope* (trans. J.W. Leitch; New York: Harper & Row, 1967); and W. Pannenberg, *Systematic Theology* (trans. G.W. Bromiley; vol. 1; Grand Rapids: Eerdmans, 1991).

charges of Nietzsche and Freud that Christianity was a religion of anxiety. Although the reality of this suffering has not escaped the attention of the Magisterium,[28] Catholic theologians unfortunately have left this theme largely untouched.[29] With the contemporary situation of the West profoundly marked by anxiety, and the recent silence in Catholic theology on the subject, it is a timely theme for reflection by the Catholic theologian who has the responsibility to speak to the 'other' a reason to believe the saving message of Jesus Christ (1Pt. 3.15).[30]

28. The magisterial usage of the term and the treatment of the theme of anxiety is applied in several ways. The terms *angustia* (a narrow place or disposition, a short time, distress) and the related word *inquietudo* (unrest, disquiet, stormy) appear in several places, most prominently in Vatican II's *Gaudium et Spes*. Anxiety describes the Pope's concern for the well being of all the faithful (Paul VI, *Evangelii Nuntiandi, AAS* 68 [1976], n. 5) and for the world (John XXIII, *Pacem in Terris, AAS* 55 (1963), n. 117; John Paul II, *Dives in Misericordia, AAS* 72 (1980), n. 12). The terms are applied to man most frequently to describe his distress about his current situation and the world's future (Vatican II, *Gaudium et Spes, AAS* 58 [1966], n. 4; John Paul II, *Sollicitudo Rei Socialis, AAS* 80 (1988), n. 27), especially in the face of evil (John-Paul II, *Salvifici Doloris, AAS* 76 [1984], nn. 9–10), from rapid scientific and technical progress without meaning (John Paul II, *Familiaris Consortio, AAS* 74 [1982], n. 30), from man's awareness of his freedom and responsibility for the world being created and its ensuing problems (Vatican II, *Gaudium et Spes*, nn. 12, 56; John Paul II, *Laborem Exercens, AAS* 73 [1981], n. 9), from the nuclear threat (Vatican II, *Gaudium et Spes*, nn. 77, 81), and from living one's vocation (Pius XI, *Casti Connubii, AAS* 22 [1930], n. 90). Anxiety is something from which the Church prays to the Father to be delivered (*Catechism of the Catholic Church* [Vatican City: Libreria Editrice Vaticana, rev. edn, 2000] n. 2854). It arises in the struggle with faith's obscurity, and can be a threat to faith when anxiety nourishes doubt (CCC, n. 2088). It is a mitigating factor in determining culpability in the moral life (John Paul II, *Evangelium Vitae, AAS* 87 [1995], nn. 11, 18). The term *angustia* can also mean 'narrow' and so the term is used at least once in the sense of being narrow minded (Vatican II, *Gaudium et Spes*, n. 75).

29. One is hard pressed to find a systematic treatment of anxiety among Catholic theologians in the twentieth century. Among conceptual Thomists such as R. Garrigou-Lagrange and G. Journet, one finds the theme only indirectly in their spiritual or moral writings. Cf. Garrigou-Lagrange, *God: His Existence and His Nature: A Thomistic Solution of Certain Agnostic Antinomies* (trans. B. Rose, OSB; vol. 2; London: B. Herder, 1936); Journet, *The Meaning of Evil* (trans. M. Barry; London: Geoffrey Chapman, 1963). K. Rahner wrote only one short essay on the topic toward the very end of his life. Cf. Rahner, 'Anxiety and Christian Trust in Theological Perspective' in *Theological Investigations*, vol. XXIII: *Final Writings* (trans. J. Donceel and H. Riley; London: Darton, Longman & Todd, 1992), pp. 3–15. No entry for the theme appears in R. Latourelle and R. Fisichella (eds), *Dizionario di teologia fondamentale* (Assisi: Cittadella, 1990), or in the hefty theological encyclopedia, G. Barbaglio (ed.), *Teologia* (Milano: Edizioni San Paolo, 2002). The contemporary manuals for fundamental theology give passing mention: D. Cassarini, *Elementi di teologia fondamentale* (Assisi: Cittadella, 2003); H. Fries, *Fundamental Theology* (trans. R. Daly; Washington D.C.: Catholic University Press, 1996), and S. Pie-Ninot, *La teologia fondamentale* (Biblioteca di Teologia contemporanea, p.121; Brescia: Queriniana, 2002).

30. I agree with Latourelle that 'these crisis factors (in twentieth-century man) which give rise to protest, rebellion, frustration, restlessness and anxiety, can become points of insertion or stepping-stones for the Gospel and be an unexpected "opportunity" for encounter and dialogue with Christ' (Latourelle, *Man and His Problems in the Light of Jesus Christ* [trans. M. J. O'Connell; New York: Alba House, 1983] pp. 8–9).

The Purpose of the Present Study

The Christian faith claims that anxiety is not only important to God, but that he took this suffering upon himself and thereby redeemed and changed it. One of the most poignant accounts of divine concern for anxiety is St. Thomas More's *De tristitia Christi* which More wrote in his latter days in the Tower while experiencing his own anxiety in the face of probable torture and possible capitulation and apostasy. More's most striking insight is that the Lord Jesus' agony in Gethsemane was so important to the Lord that he went to great lengths after the Resurrection to recount the events that transpired on the Mount of Olives to those who were not present or who were asleep at the time.[31] He wanted to ensure that his apostles knew in detail what happened to him in Gethsemane. Jesus' suffering in anxiety and ultimate victory over it as man in the Garden of Gethsemane makes it possible, in More's view, for man to conquer his in Christ.

As the title of this study suggests, this present work offers a Catholic theological response to the problem of anxiety from the point of view of Hans Urs von Balthasar. The title also suggests that Catholic theology, as represented in Balthasar's work, has something original and profound to contribute on the topic of anxiety. The theme of anxiety became important for Balthasar from his friendship with Albert Béguin (1901–1957), through whom Balthasar became acquainted with the work of Georges Bernanos (1888–1948) and Gertrude von Le Fort (1876–1971),[32] and from the anxious states he observed in Adrienne von Speyr's (1902–1967) mystical experiences of anxiety, who otherwise was a naturally anxiety-free woman.[33]

Balthasar's Methodology in Der Christ und die Angst

The origin of anxiety as a theme in the work of Hans Urs von Balthasar arose in the early 1950s at a time when, during the fervour of Freudian psychoanalysis and existential philosophy, much was being written on the topic. Balthasar saw in the writing of the time, however, a lack of a truly theological treatment of the theme. This lack of a theological perspective among contemporary interpretations of anxiety originates, in his view, in Søren Kierkegaard, although his overall evaluation of Kierkegaard on the theme of anxiety is quite positive. On the one hand, he was the first among Christians, in Balthasar's view, to respond to the rising 'cosmic anxiety of the modern,

31. Cf. T. More, *The Complete Works of St. Thomas More*, vol. XIV: *De Tristitia Christi* (New Haven: Yale University Press, 1976), p. 189. I am grateful to Prof. Seymour House, PhD., for showing me More's insight into Christ's agony in the Garden.

32. Cf. *UA*, pp. 97–98; Eng., pp. 101–2, 161. Balthasar eventually received Béguin into the Church around the same time as A. von Speyr, and von Speyr served as his godmother. Béguin for his part served as von Speyr's confirmation sponsor. Cf. *EB*, p. 27; E. Guerriero, *Hans Urs von Balthasar* (Novocento teologo, 18; Brescia: Morcelliana, 2006) 161n.

33. Guerriero, *Balthasar*, pp. 153–54.

secular era',[34] and convinced subsequent philosophers that the theme should be given a central place in philosophical and religious reflection. On the other hand, as much as Kierkegaard sought to offer a Christian interpretation of anxiety, he, according to Balthasar, never surpassed the philosophical and psychological perspectives he sought to address. As a result, our author observes that the decades after Kierkegaard were characterized by a 'two-fold secularization' in which the focus of reflection was either philosophical or psychological. Theologians, for their part, remained silent on the theme offering no serious theology of anxiety to engage the philosophical and psychological interpretations, even after the growing tide of anxiety, with its phenomena and various interpretations, washed into the lives of Christians and into the Church. The first among Catholic thinkers to respond to the flurry of writing by psychoanalysis and existential philosophy were, in Balthasar's view, the poets rather than the theologians. Thus our author intends to offer in *Der Christ und die Angst* an explicitly theological treatment of the theme in conversation with the major figures and ideas already in circulation from psychology, philosophy and literature.

In order to offer a serious theological treatment of anxiety which also engages the interpretations offered by psychology, philosophy and literature, Balthasar adopts a particular methodology in *Der Christ und die Angst*. He fixes Divine Revelation as his point of departure and constant point of reference. The Word of God, in his view, is the ultimate authority and measure of anxiety. By taking this point of departure, he seeks to avoid Kierkegaard's problem of remaining within the psychological and philosophical perspective while nevertheless building upon the Danish philosopher's insights and developing them more along the lines of dogmatic theology. By taking this point of departure, furthermore, he intends to avoid a 'false decadence' which wallows in the anxiety it wishes to address, and a 'false escapism' which stands aloof from the problem. He seeks rather to bring the power of Divine Revelation to bear on the contemporary situation of human anxiety.

Balthasar's work is divided into three major parts. The first part is devoted to an investigation of anxiety in Divine Revelation, specifically Sacred Scripture,[35] and constitutes the logical centre of the work. He gleans a selection of passages from Sacred Scripture and attempts to give them a rational ordering so that an outline of an interpretation can appear. Balthasar shows in an original way, through the course of the chapter, how anxiety is profoundly transformed between the Old and New Testaments by Christ's redemption.

He then constructs his theological interpretation of anxiety in the second part of the book. He presents the complex and interrelated phenomena of anxiety as described in Sacred Scripture from which he develops three laws or rules with which the theologian must interpret anxiety. Balthasar's theological interpretation of anxiety in this section engages Martin Luther, and

34. *CA*, p. 7; Eng., p. 31.

35. In his estimation Sacred Tradition has contributed little to the theme. Cf. *CA*, p. 11; Eng., p. 37.

Kierkegaard to a certain extent, on the nature of the Christian's anxiety as well as the Catholic literary figures who portray it: Georges Bernanos, Gertrude von Le Fort, Paul Claudel (1868–1955) and Reinhold Schneider (1903–1958). Balthasar's interpretation manifests the great divide between the Catholic and Protestant interpretations of anxiety. Throughout the course of the first two chapters, he sketches in outline form the biblical, Christological, soteriological and Trinitarian dimensions of anxiety.

In the third chapter, Balthasar takes the discussion of anxiety to its essence in which he brings the discoveries of the biblical and theological investigation to bear on the philosophical discussion. This line of thinking reveals not only his methodological intention of truly connecting the theological with the psycho-philosophical without losing the theological, but also his apologetic intention to connect his theology of anxiety with his contemporaries. The figures he engages in the final part of the book are primarily St. Thomas Aquinas and Kierkegaard on the way anxiety is produced from the operation of human rationality. Balthasar's theological conversation integrates the ontological conversation about the origin of anxiety in original sin and Christ's redemption of it. In the final pages of the work, Balthasar indicates that his theology of anxiety, as expressed in *Der Christ und die Angst*, required further development in its ecclesial dimension, and outlines in a brief manner some aspects of such a development.[36]

Balthasar's theology of anxiety as presented in *Der Christ und die Angst* suggests five ways of analyzing anxiety: the biblical, the phenomenological, the anthropological (comprised of the psychological and philosophical), the theological and the ecclesial. However, in *Der Christ und die Angst* the phenomenological seems underdeveloped and the ecclesial is only briefly sketched.

Balthasar's theological treatment of anxiety in this work also brings to the surface some of the major protagonists on anxiety: Aquinas, Luther, Kierkegaard, Freud and Bernanos, with Kierkegaard given pride of place. Freud is briefly mentioned by name in the text, yet Balthasar refers to his ideas at different points, most especially when referring to the contemporary situation. These six have greater presence of thought in Balthasar's interpretation over some of the other figures mentioned such as Léon Bloy (1846–1917), Paul Claudel, Heidegger, Le Fort and Reinhold Schneider. Also the discreet presence of Nietzsche, Henri de Lubac (1896–1991) and Karl Rahner (1904–1984) can be detected. Jean-Paul Sartre is not mentioned by name, though the final chapter of the text could be viewed as an attempt to connect with his thought. The fact that Balthasar's theology of anxiety engages several figures outside of theology reveals a typical style for our author – he thinks and writes in conversation with other intellectual systems.

Balthasar achieves in this little text a serious theology of anxiety, perhaps one of the only serious Catholic theologies of anxiety from the twentieth

36. Balthasar admits, 'On all these pages there has been much talk about the Christian but little about *the Church*. "The Church and anxiety" could be the central theme for a new treatise' (*CA*, pp. 91–2; Eng., p. 149). (Italics Balthasar's)

century. His theology of anxiety takes Divine Revelation as its point of departure and constant point of reference, and engages the contemporary psychological, philosophical and literary currents concerning anxiety. He succeeds in building upon Kierkegaard's insights while avoiding the insufficiencies of his treatment.

The Methodology of the Present Study, its Scope and Limits

The present study is a systematic presentation, analysis and development of Balthasar's original theology of anxiety. His initial theology of anxiety suggests certain lines of possible development. A first line of development is indicated by Balthasar himself in the need for further reflection on the ecclesial dimension of anxiety.

A second aspect of development appears when one considers that he wrote this text early in his writing career. Balthasar authored most of his other works, including his celebrated trilogy, after *Der Christ und die Angst*. He delineates and develops in these subsequent works his theological anthropology, Trinitarian theology, Christology, soteriology and ecclesiology. The theology of anxiety expressed in *Der Christ und die Angst* could benefit from the ideas expressed in these later works.

A third line of development can be found in Balthasar's phenomenology of anxiety. Our author's primary intention in *Der Christ und die Angst* is to offer his interpretation and devotes scant attention to the phenomenon itself. A more ample phenomenology, developed in light of his other writings, could assist his theology of anxiety to connect with the psychological, philosophical and literary treatments which share a similar view of the phenomenon.

A fourth line of development appears when one considers the explosion of writing about anxiety from the psychological sciences in recent decades. Although Balthasar alludes to Freud in the text, most of his attention is devoted to Kierkegaard's ideas. His emphasis thus falls more on the philosophical than the psychiatric side of anxiety's interpretation. A systematic presentation and analysis of his theology of anxiety could develop Balthasar's conversation with these psychological sciences which dominate current discussions about anxiety.

Balthasar's initial theology of anxiety could be developed further by a comparison with another Catholic theology of anxiety. Our author's theology of anxiety in *Der Christ und die Angst* does not explicitly engage other interpretations of anxiety within Catholic theology. He addresses the psycho-philosophical concerns of his time, yet a comparison with another Catholic theology of anxiety can help to clarify and to develop aspects of Balthasar's interpretation as well as help to show its significance in the Catholic theological tradition.

Finally, the biblical dimension of Balthasar's initial theology of anxiety could be developed. He mentions that Sacred Scripture is the primary font of Divine Revelation on this theme, and the Sacred Page is full of passages on fear.[37] Our author, however, bases his treatment of anxiety in Sacred Scripture almost exclusively on *Job*, the Wisdom literature and selected New Testament passages. Moreover, he does not offer an exegesis of Jesus' anxiety in *Der Christ und die Angst*, but presents it later in *Theologie der drei Tage*. It is understandable that Balthasar does not intend to give a comprehensive treatment of Sacred Scripture in such a short work, but rather to glean passages relevant to his purposes in *Der Christ und die Angst*.[38]

The present study intends to develop his theology of anxiety along these lines through a systematic approach. First, this study attempts to offer a more detailed picture of his grasp of the phenomenon of anxiety. Second, it seeks to develop the conversation between Balthasar's theology of anxiety and psychiatry. Third, this study endeavours to develop Balthasar's briefly sketched ideas in *Der Christ und die Angst* within the wider context of the whole of his theology. Fourth, this study places his theology of anxiety in conversation with another theology of anxiety in the Catholic theological tradition in order to clarify his interpretation and show its significance in the theological tradition. Fifth, this study endeavours to construct in an initial way the ecclesial dimension of his theology of anxiety. The development of the biblical dimension of his initial theology of anxiety is not taken up directly in this study. Balthasar's theology of anxiety keeps Sacred Scripture as its centre and norm, and thus the biblical dimension of his theology of anxiety is incorporated within the phenomenological and theological analyses as their foundation.

In order to present, analyse and develop Balthasar's initial theology of anxiety, the present study employs a thematic methodology based upon four types of analysis identified in *Der Christ und die Angst* (phenomenological, anthropological, theological and ecclesial) rather than replicate exactly Balthasar's method in that text. This four-fold thematic methodology is used so that the wider context of Balthasar's whole theological project can be more easily incorporated, and that the underdeveloped phenomenological and ecclesial dimensions of his theology of anxiety can be logically incorporated with the

37. One example is B. Costacurta's study on fear in the Old Testament. Her study lists twenty pages of scriptural citations on fear in the Old Testament with more than half existing outside Job and the Wisdom literature. Cf. Costacurta, *La Vita Minacciata: Il tema della paura nella Bibbia Ebraica* (Analecta Biblica, 119; Roma: Pontificia Universitas Gregoriana, 1997), pp. 322–42.

38. On this point I would slightly modify Francesc Torralba-Roselló's suggestion that Balthasar offers 'una anàlisi exhaustiva' of the Old and New Testaments in *Der Christ und die Angst*. Balthasar's final analysis may exhaustively account for Sacred Scripture's view of anxiety, but the passages from Sacred Scripture upon which he builds his analysis are far from exhaustive. However, I do agree with Torralba-Roselló that Balthasar's use of Sacred Scripture on the theme of anxiety is much more exhaustive and ordered than S. Kierkegaard's in his *Concept of Anxiety*, although Kierkegaard also takes the Bible as his point of reference. Cf. Torralba-Roselló, 'Teologia de l'angoixa: Kierkegaard i Urs von Balthasar', in J. Busquets and M. Martinell (eds), *Fe i teologia en la història: Estudios en honor del Prof. Dr. Evangelista Vilanova* (Barcelona: Publicacions Abadía Montserrat SA, 1997), pp. 449–56 (452n).

anthropological and theological dimensions. These four analyses constitute the four parts of this study which progresses from the phenomenological to the anthropological to the theological and finally to the ecclesial in which the anthropological is inserted into the theological. The entire study is framed by the two Gardens wherein transpire the most significant events concerning anxiety in Balthasar's theology: the Garden of Eden and the Garden of Gethsemane.

The order of this four-fold analysis also follows the logic of approaching anxiety as an illness in its symptoms, its root cause, its cure and its treatment. Anxiety is not simply a theoretical idea, but a real suffering for many people who desire to make sense of it and to have it relieved or transformed. This thematic progression places the four analyses in intrinsic connection with each other, and also follows Balthasar's own methodology in *Der Christ und die Angst* in which he argues that the anthropological analysis needed to be taken into a theological analysis. Each analysis, by being placed in this order, is thus shaped by a particular focus. The phenomenological analysis shows Balthasar's grasp of the symptoms of anxiety. His anthropological analysis searches for the origins of anxiety within the human person in which the philosophical and psychological investigations are led into his theological anthropology. The theological analysis reveals how Jesus Christ redeemed and changed the objective nature of anxiety. Finally the ecclesial analysis shows how human anxiety is transformed by its insertion into Christ's redemption of anxiety. It is admitted that a systematic treatment of a theme in the theology of Balthasar it difficult due to the breadth of his writing and the complexity of his style and vocabulary. I suggest, however, that the aforementioned methodology harmonizes with Balthasar's method in *Der Christ und die Angst*, offers a more systematic presentation of Balthasar's theology of anxiety and renders the dense text of *Der Christ und die Angst* more accessible to the reader.

Phenomenological analysis: East of Eden

The first part of the thesis begins East of Eden by constructing a more complete description of Balthasar's *phenomenology* of anxiety in both the human condition and in Jesus Christ. Chapter 1 presents the phenomenon of human anxiety in his own life, in the life of Adrienne von Speyr – whose anxiety originally brought the theme to Balthasar's attention – and in the people about whom he writes. Chapter 2 describes the phenomenon of anxiety in Jesus Christ in Balthasar's reading of the biblical accounts in both the Synoptic Gospels and in the Gospel of John. By presenting Balthasar's phenomenology of anxiety, I seek to demonstrate that he grasps the phenomenon of anxiety in a way that resonates with the description offered by contemporary psychiatry. This grasp, in turn, helps his theology of anxiety to connect more deeply with the philosophical and psychiatric approaches.

Anthropological analysis: the Garden of Eden

The second, third and fourth parts of the study unpack Balthasar's theological interpretation of anxiety by placing him in critical discussion with the main protagonists identified in *Der Christ und die Angst*. The method used in these critical discussions is to present these interlocutors in their own words, through the help of contemporary and sympathetic commentators, and then to evaluate each position according to Balthasar noting his agreement, critique and proposal to each interpretation of anxiety. This approach takes into account Balthasar's theological style of listening sympathetically to another thinker before responding to his ideas. These primary interlocutors are Aquinas, Luther, Kierkegaard, Freud and Bernanos. Each of these figures enters the study according to their relevance to the particular dimension of anxiety being investigated: Kierkegaard and Freud on anxiety's origins, St. Thomas on anxiety's redemption and Luther on anxiety's transformation. Bernanos is not given his own chapter because I believe that Balthasar's own thinking on anxiety is so profoundly influenced by Bernanos that Bernanos' ideas surface in Balthasar's interpretation in all four parts of the study. Given the limitations of this study, other noteworthy figures from *Der Christ und die Angst*, such as Nietzsche, Bloy, Heidegger, Claudel and Le Fort are excluded from this study since their appearance in Balthasar's initial theology of anxiety is minor.

Part Two of the study moves from the phenomenology gleaned East of Eden and begins to interpret it by taking the conversation towards the Garden of Eden. This first level of interpretation is an *anthropological* analysis in which Balthasar evaluates the philosophical and psychological interpretation of anxiety represented by Kierkegaard and Freud, respectively. Kierkegaard is treated first not only because he first brought the theme to centre stage in philosophical and religious thought in recent times, but also because Balthasar gives him greatest attention. Chapter 3 investigates Kierkegaard's interpretation of anxiety in the rational activity of the human mind itself, which is formulated and developed by Kierkegaard's concept of anxiety. Balthasar is favourable to Kierkegaard's concept despite its limitations.

Chapter 4 investigates Freud's interpretation of anxiety in the anxiety arising from ego consciousness. Balthasar takes the discussion from psychoanalysis to the anthropological presuppositions governing Freud's theory. The reader may wonder why Freud is given his own chapter when his presence in *Der Christ und die Angst* is not as prominent. A chapter is devoted to Freud because he is the one whom Balthasar is primarily addressing when speaking of psychology's interpretation in *Der Christ und die Angst*, because Balthasar does devote explicit attention to him in the first volume of his *Theodramatik*, and because of the predominance of the psychological sciences on the topic of anxiety in recent decades. Therefore, it is important for Balthasar's theology of anxiety to explicitly engage that interpretation. It can be argued that his theology of anxiety presented in *Der Christ und die Angst* does not sufficiently engage the psychiatric interpretation of anxiety.

Notwithstanding Kierkegaard's and Freud's achievements in interpreting anxiety, our author finds both approaches inadequate for interpreting anxiety, and seeks to orient each approach to the theological level. Chapter 5 takes the psycho-philosophical discussion concerning the origins of anxiety into Balthasar's theological anthropology where Balthasar argues that anxiety ultimately originates neither in discursive reasoning nor in ego-consciousness but in original sin from which comes anxiety in discursive reasoning and ego-consciousness. Thus, the anthropological discussion is taken into the theological realm following Balthasar's own method in *Der Christ und die Angst.*

Theological analysis: the garden of Gethsemane

Part Three moves Balthasar's interpretation further into the theological realm by shifting the discussion from the Garden of Eden to the Garden of Gethsemane, that is, from a consideration of anxiety's causes to its theological cure. This section involves a *theological* analysis of anxiety which brings the anthropological discussion to the Word of God. In this way, Balthasar's primary method in *Der Christ und die Angst* is replicated exactly: Divine Revelation is the ultimate authority and measure of human anxiety. In order to clarify Balthasar's position on the redemption of anxiety, his thought is compared to that of Aquinas.

One may wonder why St. Thomas is the chosen interlocutor on this aspect of the topic since Balthasar has no discussion with him in *Der Christ und die Angst* on the issue of Christ's anxiety. The choice for St. Thomas, however, is not arbitrary. Balthasar does make two explicit references to the Angelic doctor in the text, first in his description of anxiety as a *passio animae*, and second, in his explanation of the philosophical act of *admiratio.*[39] Balthasar's primary intention, it seems, in *Der Christ und die Angst* is to give a theology of anxiety that engages the psycho-philosophical interpretations. Yet it is equally important, especially given the current time when Balthasar's entire theology is undergoing evaluation as to its significance in the tradition of Catholic theology, that his theology enter into dialogue with the Angelic doctor who offers a deep treatment of human affectivity and the human affectivity of Christ, and whose theology holds magisterial status in the Church. Moreover, St. Thomas is chosen because this study is a systematic treatment of Balthasar's theology of anxiety, and the theology of St. Thomas is systematic *par excellence.* Other Catholic theologies of anxiety, for example, that of St. Augustine, is not treated since St. Augustine does not figure prominently in Balthasar's initial theology of anxiety.

Since Balthasar does not explicitly engage St. Thomas on the redemption of anxiety, the mode of inquiry is slightly modified. Chapter 6 presents the Angelic doctor's position on fear as present in fallen human nature, how it came to plague human life through original sin, and how it is redeemed in Jesus Christ. Balthasar's interpretation is presented and developed in Chapter 7, beginning with his understanding of Sacred Scripture's evaluation of anxiety

39. Cf. *CA*, pp. 69–80; Eng., pp. 118–33.

up until Christ, followed by an interpretation of Christ's anxiety in its Christological, soteriological and Trinitarian dimensions. It is shown how human anxiety is appropriated by Christ and his anxiety also becomes a revelation, through analogy, of Trinitarian love. Finally, a comparison is made with St. Thomas in which Balthasar's position is analysed. Since anxiety possesses a strongly cognitive and rational component, the controversial topic of Christ's terrestrial beatific vision enters the discussion between Balthasar and St. Thomas on the redemption of anxiety. By bringing the wider context of Balthasar's theology to bear on the Christological, soteriological and Trinitarian dimensions of anxiety, and by comparing his position with St. Thomas', the originality of Balthasar's theology of anxiety, and its place in the tradition of Catholic theology, is shown. The point of this comparison is not to overcome the differences of interpretation, but to show how each are rooted in the tradition and how they may approach each other.

Ecclesiological analysis: the garden of the church

In the fourth part of the study, the investigation moves from a consideration of the Garden of Gethsemane to the 'Garden of the Church' where the anthropological dimension (Part Two) is inserted into the theological dimension (Part Three). Part Four is constituted by an *ecclesial* reflection in order to show how human anxiety is transformed by Christ's redemptive anxiety in the Church to become either freedom from anxiety or the new salvific anxiety. This final part of the thesis first places Balthasar in critical discussion with Luther on the nature and shape of Christian anxiety. Chapter 8 follows the same method of critical discussion observed in Part Two since our author does engage Luther on this point explicitly, though briefly, in *Der Christ und die Angst.* We first present the genesis of Christian anxiety in Luther's doctrine of *simul iustus et peccator*, and show the dialectic structure of Luther's interpretation. This presentation is followed by Balthasar's agreement, critique and proposal on the nature and shape of Christian anxiety as a trajectory rather than a dialectic.

Since Balthasar left his ecclesial reflection on the transformation of human anxiety unfinished in *Der Christ und die Angst*, the final chapter of the thesis develops Balthasar's theology of anxiety to make this aspect more complete. Chapter 9 develops Balthasar's theology of anxiety by applying the various dimensions of his ecclesiology to the theme of anxiety's transformation.

A general conclusion follows with a synthetic overview of Balthasar's theology of anxiety as presented and analysed throughout the thesis, followed by the final conclusions of the study. The study is concluded with a reflection on Balthasar's theology of anxiety and the contemporary situation.

The role of analogy, convergence and experience

Three important aspects of Balthasar's thought bear mentioning at the outset of this study. They are the role that analogy, his method of convergence and experience play in his thinking. Our author bases his theological language on analogy, that is, the noting of a similarity within a greater dissimilarity.[40] In this way, he seeks to attain to intelligible language about God without compromising divine transcendence and freedom. The analogy of being, written into the created order, establishes a relationship between God and the creature which avoids the extremes of dualism or pantheism. For our author, theology's positive affirmations take precedence while the negations serve the affirmations by giving them the necessary qualifications.[41] Balthasar further shapes his understanding of analogy through his encounter with Karl Barth, in which the analogy of being is concretized in the figure of Jesus Christ. Thus analogy can only reach its fullest meaning within a Christological perspective: Jesus Christ, the God-man is the concrete *analogia entis*. The relationship between the finite and infinite, the creature and Creator is synthesized perfectly in him. He is the measure of every creaturely similarity and difference to God.

Balthasar further approaches theological investigation from the point of view of 'approximation' (*Annäherung*) and 'convergence' (*Einfaltung*) in which he seeks to organize pluriform factors around the central theme under consideration.[42] His theological explanations of a theme thus approach the mystery in which truth about the mystery is attained while preserving the freedom of the mystery being explored. This method of convergence appears in this study of Balthasar's theology of anxiety in how the theme of anxiety, and especially Christ's own anxiety, brings together and orients the various theological disciples (protology, Christology, Trinitarian theology, ecclesiology, etc.) as well as lines of thought from philosophy and psychiatry to the central mystery of Christ.

Finally, Balthasar's understanding of experience is important in order to interpret anxiety.[43] After all, anxiety is something that is experienced. How does our author understand experience? Balthasar strives for a more objective understanding to the concept of experience based upon the dialogical nature of being. Human experience, viewed philosophically, is based upon the

40. Cf. DS 806: Inter Creatorem et creaturam non potest similitude notari, quin inter eos maior sit dissimilitudo notanda. R. Pesarchick observes therefore that 'theology has present within a dynamic tension between a positive moment (*similitudo*) and a negative moment (*maior dissimilitudo*)' (Pesarchick, *The Trinitarian Foundation of Human Sexuality as Revealed by Christ According to Hans Urs von Balthasar: The Revelatory Significance of the Male Christ and the Male Ministerial Priesthood* [Tesi Gregoriana Teologia, 63; Roma: Pontificia Universitas Gregoriana, 2000] p. 41).

41. In this way, Pesarchick observes, Balthasar departs from the position of his mentor E. Przywara. Cf. Pesarchick, *The Trinitarian Foundation of Human Sexuality*, pp. 42–4.

42. Cf. the more detailed explanations of this aspect of Balthasar's thought in G. Meiattini, *Sentire cum Christo: La teologia dell'esperienza cristiana nell'opera di Hans Urs von Balthasar* (Tesi Gregoriana Teologia, 36; Roma: Pontificia Universitas Gregoriana, 1998), pp. 26–9 and Pesarchick, *The Trinitarian Foundation of Human Sexuality*, pp. 55–8.

43. The theme of experience in Balthasar's thought is expounded and analysed in Meiattini, *Sentire cum Christo*. The major ideas of Meiattini's study are summarized in Meiattini, 'Esperienza ed esperienza mistica nel pensiero di Hans Urs von Balthasar', *Rivista Teologica di Lugano* 4 (2001), pp. 9–31.

irreducible relationship between subject perceiving and object being perceived. Meiattini calls this structure in Balthasar's thought the 'subject–object ellipse'. The object is perceived by the subject through the object's phenomenological appearance (*Erscheinung*) to the subject in which the object reveals its essence (*Grund*). Being thus manifests itself by giving itself; a being is known in itself by its being-for-others.[44] The object offers itself to the subject through the symbolic mediation, the 'mediated immediacy' to use Meiattini's term, of *Gestalt*.[45] In Balthasar's view, according to Meiattini, each pole of the ellipse has a creative influence on the other. Both subject and object need each other to reach their full measure.[46] The subject's irrepeatable singularity (*Einzigartigkeit*) comes into play in the hermeneutical aspect of experience in that it can allow new aspects of the *Gestalt* to emerge. The dialogical structure of the subject–object relationship in Balthasar's thought expresses the essentially ecstatic nature of being as being-giving-itself. Thus the subject and object give to each other through time, and through this mutual giving their relationship dilates as the subject moves more deeply into the depths of the *Gestalt*. Such movement is foundational to Balthasar's understanding of truth: the perception of truth entails *walking* in the truth. Thus the 'I' and 'Thou', the subject and object, can truly grasp themselves and the other, but only through the irreducible dialogical and mediated structure of their encounter.

Experience for Balthasar also involves the *totality* of the subject in relationship with the *totality* of the object, and thus is a concept encompassing more than the emotions, sensory or empirical perception, and the cognitive process which understands and judges sensory data. Experience is rather a total resonance or 'according' (*Einstimmung*) of all the subject's being with the objective reality involving being as beautiful, good and true.[47] In such an encounter, all the dimensions of the subject converge: intellectual, intuitive, volitional, affective and corporeal. Since experience is structured by *Gestalt*, it is defined

44. Meiattini writes, 'By virtue of the difference between being-in-itself and being-for others, between ground and appearance, interiority and exteriority, experience is in a position to attain to essence, but not to denude it; it can grasp the in-se, but without exhausting it' (Meiattini, 'Esperienza ed esperienza mistica', p. 13) (author's translation).

45. Gestalt, a delicate and nuanced concept for our author, indicates the unity of the subject–object relationship in its essential, phenomenological and hermeneutical aspects. Meiattini writes, experience is 'the perception of an essence (ontological aspect), through the symbolic mediation of its appearance (phenomenological aspect) to which the subject concurs as interpreter (hermeneutic aspect). Therefore, *the interpretation that the subject makes of the essential depth of the figure coincides with the process of the phenomenological appearance of this essential depth*. In order to avoid any possible subjectivist results of this hermeneutic, von Balthasar conceives it as *the self-interpretation that the figure makes of itself through the singularity of the subject*' (Meiattini, 'Esperienza ed esperienza mistica', p. 13) (Meiattini's italics; author's translation).

46. Meiattini emphasizes in Balthasar's thought the creative role of the subject urging his reader not to overreact to Balthasar's anti-Idealism. The creative role of the subject is understood by Balthasar as serving the object in order to expand its objectivity.

47. Meiattini writes, 'It is perception (beautiful) in a praxis (dramatic) which is internalized as knowledge (logical)' (Meiattini, 'Esperienza ed esperienza mistica', p. 16) (author's translation).

by the symphonic whole of the dimensions united by the transcendental of the Beautiful. Therefore, 'feeling' (*sentire*) is not simply a superficial emotional state or one faculty alongside others (*Einzelakt*) for Balthasar. Rather it is, in Meiattini's view, a total act (*Gesamtakt*) integrating all of one's personal life, and a *Gesamtgefühl*, a total resonance of the subject in all its components to the totality of the object.[48] In Balthasar's thought, experience is the totality of the subject in relationship with the totality of the object which unites practice and knowledge in perception.

This fundamental and dialogical structure in Balthasar's concept of experience is an image and the work of the divine and Trinitarian archetype. The intramundane relationship between phenomenon and essence, subject and object, is an analogy of the relationship between creature and Creator. Through analogy, Balthasar is in a position to speak about the experience of Christ and the unique character of Christian experience, which is a participation in Christ's experience. In other words, the greater dissimilarity of the analogy does not take away the great similarity.

Christian experience possesses the same structure of the subject–object ellipse yet its coordinates are transposed to revelation and faith. Christian experience is the total 'according' of the subject, the Christian, with the objective and archetypical experience of the Incarnate Son. Through obediential conforming to Christ, a Christian does not simply have an experience of the Father, but rather is brought into participation of the *Incarnate Son's experience* of the Father. All Christian experience lies within his. Christian experience then is configured in a Trinitarian manner: the experience of the Father in the Son by virtue of the Holy Spirit.

Christ's archetypical experience is mediated to the Christian's experience through the dependent archetypes constituting the Church: Mary, Peter, John (Paul and James to a lesser extent), along with the Church's Sacraments, Scripture and ministry.[49] Just as in natural experience, the creaturely creativity of each dependent archetype forms part of the mediation of the object to the subject. The Church, as Meiattini explains Balthasar's position, stands not between Christ and the believer, but rather *is* Christ in his act of expressing and impressing his form upon the world in general and upon the Christian in particular. Therefore, no *sentire cum Christo* exists without also *sentire cum* and *in Ecclesia*. Because of the ecclesial reality of Christian experience, when Christ impresses his own experience upon the Christian's experience, he opens it to share with all the other persons bearing his form. Meiattini explains Balthasar's concept in a way important for the theme of the present study, 'on one hand, the experiences of desolation and anxiety can be shouldered in a vicarious manner so that others may be pardoned or consoled'.[50]

Therefore, Christian experience involves more than obediential configurement because this configurement brings an active and creative element. The subject has its own contribution in the structure of experience. In Christian

48. Cf. Meiattini, 'Esperienza ed esperienza mistica', p. 17.
49. Ibid., p. 20.
50. Ibid., p. 20 (author's translation).

experience, the one who recognizes and grasps revelation contributes shapes the figure of revelation, giving human form to the Son of God. The creative newness is Christ's experience taking shape in the utter uniqueness of the individual person. Balthasar's concept of experience shows the intimate connection between theology and the existential reality of the human condition. By this concept, he does not attempt to offer a psychology of anxiety, but rather a theology that necessarily appropriates the existential concerns of contemporary man. These three aspects of analogy, convergence and experience are necessary to interpret Balthasar's theology of anxiety adequately.

The Sources of the Present Study

The primary source of this thesis is the work of Hans Urs von Balthasar himself. This study is intended to be a presentation, analysis and development of his theology of anxiety, and so the bulk of the material in this study belongs to our author. He is the sole primary source.[51] Since his initial theology of anxiety is sketched in *Der Christ und die Angst*, this text remains the centre and constant point of reference in this study. The thesis also seeks to proceed in a way that formally respects and harmonizes with the method used in it. However, the intention of the thesis is to develop that initial theology of anxiety in the context of his entire theological project. Although the theme does not appear in every work to my knowledge, texts spanning his entire career are consulted, from his treatment of Kierkegaard in *Apokalypse der deutschen Seele* to his posthumously published *Wenn ihr nicht werdet wie dieses Kind*. The text within his corpus that figures most prominently for our theme after *Der Christ und die Angst* is his study on Bernanos, *Gelebte Kirche. Bernanos*. Very little secondary literature currently exists on Balthasar's theology of anxiety. At the time of this study's publication, I am aware of the articles by J. Servais, J. Splett, F. Torralba-Roselló and Y. Tourenne, and these have been incorporated into the thesis.[52] For other aspects of Balthasar's theology I have employed the work of scholars as their work on Balthasar pertains to the theme.

Much material forming Balthasar's phenomenology of human anxiety in Chapter 1 is taken from his study of Bernanos. Other material is found, in order of frequency, in *Nochmals. Reinhold Schneider, Schwestern im Geist, Herrlichkeit III/2,1, Der Christ und die Angst, Das Herz der Welt*, and *Unser Auftrag*. The major secondary sources used in Chapter 1 are P. Henrici's article on Balthasar's life and E. Guerriero's biography. The primary source for Chapter 2 on Balthasar's phenomenology of anxiety in Jesus Christ is

51. Although von Speyr's experience of anxiety is behind much of Balthasar's thought, this study will not treat the theme at it appears in her writings but only as her experience of anxiety appears in his.

52. One of the articles by Torralba-Roselló and the article by Y. Tourenne exist as forwards to the translation of *Der Christ und die Angst* into Spanish and French/English, respectively. J. Servais' article appeared subsequent to my doctoral thesis.

Theologie der drei Tage and *Der Christ und die Angst*. The secondary sources utilized are exegetical sources to explicate further Balthasar's biblical description, as well as the studies on Balthasar by W. Becker and G. Meiattini.

The primary source on Kierkegaard in Chapter 3 is his *Concept of Anxiety* and to a lesser extent *Stages on Life's Way*. To better understand Kierkegaard's anthropology, I rely upon J. Cole's study and the article by S. Dunning. The primary source in Balthasar for his discussion with Kierkegaard on anxiety is *Der Christ und die Angst*. The secondary sources on Balthasar's interpretation of Kierkegaard on anxiety are those by P. Henrici, J. Splett, F. Torralba-Roselló and Y. Tourenne. For the chapter on Freud, the primary source is his *Introductory Lectures on Psychoanalysis*. To better understand Freud's theory, the work of E. Jones is used. In order to connect Balthasar's interpretation to the psychiatric approach, readings in the area of contemporary psychiatry serve as background. The primary source for Balthasar's treatment of Freud is the first volume of his *Theodramatik*. I found further material in *Wenn ihr nicht werdet wie dieses Kind, Gelebte Kirche. Bernanos, Theodramatik IV, Theodramatik II/2* and *Spiritus Creator*. I did not use secondary literature on Balthasar for this chapter since little has been done on Balthasar's relationship to psychiatry besides T. Dalzell's article. However, the studies of G. Marchesi and G. Meiattini were consulted for understanding Balthasar's position on the dialogical nature of man in general. The source of Chapter 5 is almost exclusively *Christlicher Stand* in which our author's theological anthropology is found. References are made also to *Der Christ und die Angst*. The secondary sources on Balthasar employed for this chapter are the article by A. Scola and the studies by D. Yeago and R. Pesarchick. I consulted L. Ladaria's study on theological anthropology to familiarize myself with the nature-grace problematic in general.

Chapter 6 is devoted exclusively to Aquinas and his treatment of *timor* as found in human nature and *timor's* redemption by Christ. The preeminent source used in this chapter is his *Summa Theologiae*. His *Commentary on the Gospels* and his *Compendium theologiae* are also employed to a lesser extent. Although the presentation of Christ's *timor* in Gethsemane is my own, I rely heavily on the scholarship of two Thomists who have worked in the area of human affectivity in St. Thomas: S. Loughlin and P. Gondreau. These two scholars greatly shape my presentation of St. Thomas' position on *timor* in general and Christ's *timor* in particular. In the area of Christ's terrestrial beatific vision I rely on articles by J. Galot, T. White, and J. Servais. The primary sources for Chapter 7 are *Der Christ und die Angst* and the relevant volumes of the *Theodramatik* (II/2, III and IV), *Theologie die drei Tage, Sponsa Verbi* and to a lesser extent *Kosmische Liturgie, Herrlichkeit III/2/2*, 'Crucifixus etiam pro nobis' and 'Das Selbstbewußtsein Jesu'. Most prominent among the secondary sources in this chapter are the studies by G. Marchesi and G. Meiattini followed by those of P. Martinelli, J. O'Donnell, A. Nichols, W. Becker and J. Servais.

The primary sources for Chapter 8 are the works of M. Luther. But since his corpus is so vast, I employed the scholarship of J. Wicks to introduce me to Luther's work regarding his *simul* doctrine. From Wick's two articles I read the indicated passages in Luther's work, and discovered new ones relevant to the theme. The presentation of Luther's *simul* doctrine, therefore, is strongly influenced by Wicks. The presentation on Luther's position of Christian anxiety is my own taken directly from Luther's work. The primary sources for Balthasar's treatment of Luther are *Karl Barth* and *Der Christ und die Angst.* On the unity of faith and anxiety, I found material in the study on Bernanos and *Herrlichkeit I.* Other primary sources on Balthasar for this chapter are *Die Wahrheit ist symphonisch* and *Christlicher Stand.* By way of secondary sources on Balthasar for this chapter the studies by R. Howsare and P. Martinelli are used. The final chapter employs as primary sources *Der Christ und die Angst* and those works which present Balthasar's ecclesiology, namely, *Sponsa Verbi, Spiritus Creator, Herrlichkeit I* and *Theodramatik II/2.* To a lesser extent, *Christlicher Stand* and *Der antirömische Affekt* are utilized. The general presentation of Balthasar's ecclesiology is heavily influenced by B. Leahy's study and articles by S. Ackermann, L. Chapp, A. Sicari and J. Servais. I use his works of *Christlicher Stand, Gelebte Kirche* and *Wenn ihr nicht werdet wie dieses Kind* in my own presentation of anxiety's transformation in and by the Church.

Part One

East of Eden: Anxiety Lived

Chapter 1

The Appearance of Anxiety in the Human Condition

The human race expresses itself through its cry of pain, through the wail wrenched from its sides by a supreme effort.

(Georges Bernanos)

Before analysing Balthasar's interpretation of anxiety, it is important first to establish his grasp of the phenomenon of anxiety. How does anxiety manifest itself? What does it look like? How does he describe it? This is a crucial methodological point since this study seeks to connect Balthasar's theology of anxiety both to philosophical and psychiatric perspectives and all three sciences hold the phenomenon in common.

Yet most of the explicit attention which Balthasar gives to anxiety focuses on an interpretation of it and not so much on its appearance. Consequently, one finds few phenomenological observations in his *Der Christ und die Angst*. It is possible, however, to glean a more complete picture of Balthasar's description of anxiety from his other works, especially those from the early 1950s.[1] This chapter presents Balthasar's description of anxiety as it appears in the people that appear in his writings rather than the writings themselves. After all, people are anxious, not ideas. Indeed it is a well-known feature of his theological style to draw inspiration from people and characters – constellations of figures – as much as the ideas they expressed or embodied. Out of respect for this dimension of his style, his description of anxiety's appearance in the human condition is presented through a constellation of figures. This presentation does not claim to be exhaustive, but to demonstrate adequately Balthasar's grasp of the phenomenon of anxiety.

The Appearance of Anxiety in the Life of Balthasar

Those who knew Balthasar say that he rarely, if ever, manifested symptoms of anxiety. He came from a strong and 'straightforwardly Catholic' (*selbstverständlich katholische*) family[2]; he was a man of deep human integration and

1. The two texts where the phenomenon seems more present are his studies on Schneider and Bernanos which were first published in 1953 and 1954, respectively.

2. *UA*, p. 37; Eng., p. 35.

strong character. He comments that he 'grew up with a faith that was equally straightforward, untroubled by doubt',[3] which, as Peter Henrici observes, 'remained childlike in the best sense' throughout his life.[4] His mother stated, on the other hand, that her son had a nervous temperament as a child.[5] He experienced the normal family worries during World War I for those members living in Vienna and Hungary, as well as the 'early and painful death' of his mother just before he entered the Jesuits.[6] Ill physical health which began as a young man and persisted the rest of his life also gave him reason to be anxious.[7] During his time as chaplain in Basel, Balthasar also underwent 'personal tragedies, bitterness and much gossip' in the *Schulungsgemeinschaft* as people reacted to his demanding and, according to some, arrogant style.[8]

Perhaps the strongest pressures for anxiety came in his middle age with his close friendships with Henri de Lubac and Adrienne von Speyr. The emergence of the call to found the Community of St. John brought anguish to both Balthasar and von Speyr.[9] Henrici summarizes this period of his life:

> All his human ties were placed in question. . . . His father had been gravely ill for quite some time and eventually died in June 1946. His godmother [Jeanne Pietzcker], the person to whom he most easily related in the family, who had always understood him, suffered her first stroke, was left paralyzed, and was given the last rites by him. On May 16, 1946 Robert Rast died in Leysin. Shortly before, von Balthasar had received news that his friend and mentor Przywara was suffering from a serious nervous disorder. . . . In August von Balthasar was due in the normal way to make his solemn religious profession. However, at the same time, he was informed that the Society of Jesus could not take responsibility for Frau Professor Kaegi and the Community of St. John. von Balthasar asked for the genuineness her visions to be investigated, and for the postponement until then of his vows.[10]

His superiors, for their part, forbade him to visit von Speyr's home and to even speak with her or the new members of the community.[11] Moreover, his place in the theological world also became constrained.[12] His close friend, de Lubac, was suspended from teaching and the encyclical, *Humani generis*,

3. *UA*, p. 37; Eng., p. 35. He makes another reference to his 'untroubled faith' on p. 38; Eng., p. 36.

4. P. Henrici, 'Hans Urs von Balthasar: A Sketch of his Life', in D. L. Schindler (ed.), *Hans Urs von Balthasar: His Life and Work*. (San Francisco: Communio Books/Ignatius Press, 1991), pp. 7–43 (10).

5. Guerriero, *Hans Urs von Balthasar*, p. 20.

6. *UA*, p. 37; Eng., p. 35. Cf. Guerriero, *Hans Urs von Balthasar*, p. 21; Henrici, 'Balthasar: A Sketch', p. 12.

7. Cf. Henrici, 'Balthasar: A Sketch', p. 14.

8. Ibid., p. 16. The *Schulungsgemeinschaft* was a student group 'primarily aimed at giving students a training in the philosophy of life'.

9. Cf. Guerriero, *Balthasar*, p. 133. His biographer writes that she declared her willingness to pray for her own death so as not to become a burden to his religious profession, which he forbade her to do. See also, p. 134.

10. Henrici, 'Balthasar: A Sketch', p. 20.

11. Cf. Guerriero, *Balthasar*, p. 139.

12. Henrici, 'Balthasar: A Sketch', p. 21.

was published placing Balthasar under theological suspicion. Certainly such a storm of events could bring anxiety even to a strong character as Balthasar.

When Balthasar finally made the painful decision to leave the Jesuits, it became a period of 'real crisis' as a series of losses and troubles descended upon his life in rapid succession. The choice to leave the Society of Jesus for the sake of the Community of St. John, which officially occurred in 11 February 1950, made him an ecclesiastical pariah which culminated in his exclusion as a *peritus* from the proceedings of Vatican II. Worst of all, he was a priest without faculties and without a place to live as he spent 18 months to find a bishop who would take him. Meanwhile his brother Jesuits continued to try to convince him to change his mind about leaving. He went six years without a bishop.[13] In addition to the difficulties of his irregular ecclesiastical situation and lack of stable residence, he also experienced financial difficulties. He now had to provide for himself, and having taken on the burden of a publishing house, set out on lecture tours of Germany which, in Henrici's view, soon became 'a terribly fragmented existence'.[14]

Balthasar also underwent trials from his relationship with von Speyr. Not only was there the inevitable gossip of peers and the suspicion of his superiors, he also had the burden of being spiritual director to a woman who seemed to be the recipient of tremendous mystical graces. As her physical health diminished, Balthasar looked after her. She had been suffering from heart trouble since 1940, and more sufferings were continually added. From 1954 until her death in 1967 she was homebound. During the last three years of her life she was almost totally blind, and her last months were a slow and painful agony as bowel cancer took its course. Her death brought a 'deep caesura in his life'.[15]

Balthasar also had to contend with the anxieties from his own ill health. Under the demands of his lecture and retreat tours he was frequently ill, and in the fall of 1957 had to rest for six months from over exhaustion. Balthasar himself admitted, 'I really thought I was cracking up'.[16] Later he battled with phlebitis in the summer of 1958, and six months later he nearly died from an illness which was later diagnosed as a form of leukaemia. He recovered, but lived with the after-effects of poor motor functioning in his hands and legs. From this brief sketch, our author had many situations of uncertainty, danger and actual threat which gave him reason to grapple with anxiety. Even if he did not manifest symptoms of anxiety, it does not mean that he did not suffer interiorly or necessarily exclude him from being able to describe it.

13. *UA*, pp. 77–8; Eng., p. 80. Eventually the bishop of Chur, Switzerland, gave him permission to say Mass and later on to hear confessions. Cf. Henrici, 'Balthasar: A Sketch', p. 23.

14. Henrici, 'Balthasar: A Sketch', p. 24.

15. Ibid., p. 27.

16. Ibid., p. 26.

The Appearance of Anxiety in the Life of Adrienne von Speyr in His Writings

The true impetus for Balthasar's theology of anxiety, however, came not from his own life but from what he observed in the life of his spiritual directee and close friend, Adrienne von Speyr. How does he describe her anxiety? Up until her conversion to the Catholic Church she reports that she possessed a 'very stable temperament' and 'had never been afraid of anything'.[17] Yet after her conversion she came to understand she could expect suffering 'in which a God-given anxiety would play a key role'.[18]

As she progressed in her mystical prayer, she began to experience strange states of intense anxiety in which she no longer recognized herself.[19] Balthasar describes her bouts with anxiety as 'extreme' and 'reached the very edge of insanity'.[20] He describes an intensification of one of her states of anxiety in January 1943 in which she experienced '"loneliness on the edge of hell", God's love experienced only as "an iron law, as hard as diamond", in fact "the possibility of leading an utterly meaningless life, just to obey God", the experience of final damnation'.[21] She experienced the anxiety that others were undergoing – 'the psychological state of the tortured and starving of people burned to death and of the torturers' as well as scenes of the Passion.[22] She was so overwhelmed by what she saw that she practiced excessive penance. At one point it seems that she was given the choice to be free from this anxiety, but 'no sooner has she uttered her assent than a cloud of anxiety, shame and despair descends upon her'.[23] She had innumerable experiences of abandonment in which she could not find any meaning.[24] What appears strange in these bouts with anxiety is that outside of these episodes her natural, anxiety-free temperament would return, and perhaps even more strange, she still could pray in joy even during these bouts of anxiety.[25]

The Appearance of Anxiety in His Writings

In addition to the lives of Balthasar and von Speyr, anxiety can be found in the figures about which Balthasar writes. What follows are the major figures exhibiting anxiety beginning with Sacred Scripture, since this is the

17. *UA*, p. 98; Eng., pp. 101–2. Balthasar here is citing von Speyr's own words.
18. *UA*, p. 47; Eng., p. 47.
19. Cf. *UA*, pp. 97–8; Eng., pp. 101–2. Balthasar's biographer makes the same point about von Speyr's supernatural anxiety and its inspiration for the writing of *CA*. Cf. Guerriero, *Balthasar*, p. 154.
20. *UA*, p. 98; Eng., p. 102.
21. *UA*, p. 51; Eng., p. 51. Balthasar here is citing von Speyr's words.
22. *UA*, p. 51; Eng., p. 52.
23. *UA*, pp. 52–3; Eng., p. 53.
24. Cf. *UA*, p. 62; Eng., p. 63.
25. Cf. *UA*, p. 50; Eng., p. 50.

constant point of reference in Balthasar's theology of anxiety, and then in the chronological order in which they appear in Balthasar's corpus. This presentation follows Balthasar's own description and prescinds from how the figures may be understood by their original authors or viewed by literary critics or historians.

A glance at sacred scripture

In his biblical evaluation of anxiety in *Der Christ und die Angst*, Balthasar describes the phenomenon of anxiety primarily in the experience of three groups of people – the people of Psalm 107, Job and the disciples of Jesus. The people described in Psalm 107 find themselves in four successive situations of natural danger where the good man is brought to the edge of abandonment 'hanging by a thread': being lost and thirsty in the wilderness, being imprisoned in darkness and in the 'shadow of death', undergoing a sickness unto death which involved a 'loathing and disgust for every sort of food', enduring a storm at sea and the ensuing feelings of powerlessness in being tossed about by the waves. In all these situations of helplessness in the face of danger and death, they give an 'anxious cry' (*Angstschrei*) to God for deliverance.[26]

Job undergoes the experience of being abandoned and terrified by God, and being isolated from his friends. He laments, 'Behold, I go eastwards, but he [God] is not there; and westwards, but I cannot perceive him; in the north I seek him, but I cannot behold him; I turn to the south, but I cannot see him' (23.8–9).[27] But even God's presence becomes a threat to Job; his dreams are troubled and anxious. He cries out 'thou dost scare me with dreams and terrify me with visions, so that I would [rather] choose strangling' (7.14–15).[28] Balthasar continues to describe God's threatening presence to Job:

> He [Job] is 'encircled' by him [God] (3.23), just as those who lamented in Jerusalem were 'walled about with hewn stones' (Lam. 3.9), he is put in a prison (12.14), besieged (19.12) by the God who shows himself to be his enemy. . . . God hunts him down (10.16) and covers him with war (10.17); but such a war it is clear from the outset that God has the 'upper hand' (9.2–3; 9.19; 12.13–25) and therefore 'ravishes' the frail creature and 'despises the work of his hands' (10.3). . . . Even then, this humiliated creature would still stand under God's gaze, but God's act of noticing, observing, indeed of staring relentlessly (7.16–20; 10.20; 14.3) from an invisible ambush (9.11) would then be only the terrible parody of the feeling of security in the wings and in the embracing gaze of God, of which the pious in Israel sing.[29]

The terrifying presence of God even elicits a physiological response in Job: 'When he thinks of God, *the hairs rise on his flesh*'.[30]

26. *CA*, p. 29; Eng., p. 63.
27. *HIII/2,1*, p. 262; Eng., p. 283.
28. *CA*, p. 30; Eng., p. 64.
29. *HIII/2,1*, p. 263; Eng., p. 284.
30. *HIII/2,1*, p. 265; Eng., p. 286 (author's italics).

Job's anxiety also comes from the apparent meaninglessness of his faith. It no longer speaks to his situation. This inadequacy of his religious language is revealed in the conversations with his friends.[31] Job's difficult situation with God puts all the meaning of his life into question. Everything he believed no longer seems to have power in his life.

His friends, for their part, recognize him neither physically nor spiritually. They see in his anxious situation a sign of secret guilt, and 'their charges drive Job away from all communication with others, deeper into the loneliness of his fear in God's presence'.[32] He declares to his friends, 'Your maxims are proverbs of ashes'.[33] Balthasar writes that Job 'has come into absolute isolation, which has the bitterness of abandonment for him: he is "avoided", "evaded", "forgotten", he becomes "a stranger and an alien" for those who live in his house; indeed, he becomes one whose "evil stench" is repulsive to them' (19.13–19).[34]

Interiorly Job can no longer distinguish between his own guilt and the Lord's testing and is both abandoned and terrified by God, while exteriorly he is isolated from his friends. His anxious situation is intensified because this extreme situation is brought about by God, the one who promises freedom from anxiety.

Finally, the phenomenon of anxiety is found in the disciples of Jesus. They are terrified in the midst of the storm on the Sea of Galilee which seems to extend beyond the description found in Psalm 107 because in the midst of the storm the one they call Lord seems like a ghost to them.[35] Balthasar also observes the many prominent figures in the New Testament who experience anxiety from situations of helplessness and confusion such as Zechariah, Mary, Joseph, Peter, the disciples on Mount Tabor, Paul and the seer of Patmos.[36] The disciples' flight on the night of Jesus' passion is the fear of torture and death, while Peter's anxiety perhaps stems from the coinciding awareness of God's presence and his sinfulness.

Balthasar also notices a change in the phenomenon of anxiety in the disciples during Jesus' earthly ministry, for example, in Martha and Mary. These holy women experience anxiety not only from the sickness and tragic death of their brother, but also from the anxiety arising from Jesus' absence and his too-late arrival upon the scene. He who had previously raised the dead did not come to rescue his friend. Balthasar comments, however, that the anxiety of these women is 'anxiety without rigidity or rebellion . . . without pathos'.[37] This newness to the phenomenon of anxiety is also alluded to in Balthasar's meditations on the Stations of the Cross in the Blessed Virgin Mary.[38] After

31. Cf. *HIII/2,1*, p. 261; Eng., p. 282.
32. *HIII/2,1*, p. 265; Eng., pp. 286–7.
33. *HIII/2,1*, p. 263; Eng., p. 284.
34. *HIII/2,1*, p. 262; Eng., pp. 283–4.
35. Cf. *CA*, p. 36; Eng., p. 72.
36. Cf. *CA*, p. 36; Eng., pp. 72–3.
37. *CA*, pp. 49–50; Eng., p. 91.
38. Cf. *Kw*, p. 10; Eng., p. 10.

the Resurrection the disciples of Jesus also manifest a remarkable freedom from anxiety about the world, death and their sins.[39] The manifestation of anxiety in the disciples of Jesus seems to manifest something new.

Saint Thérèse of Lisieux

Another place in the Balthasarian corpus where one can find the phenomenon of anxiety is his study on St. Thérèse of Lisieux. During childhood the thought of her faults was unbearable to her resulting in her struggle with scrupulosity for a time.[40] At the age of ten she grappled with the mysterious illness 'that brought her to the verge of madness'.[41] She also had a disturbing vision of her father's future death, which seemed fulfilled to her when his mental illness emerged. The actions of her sister, Leonie, who struggled in religious life, were a 'veritable agony' for St. Thérèse.[42] Nevertheless, Balthasar also describes the Little Flower as 'fearless and aggressive', and quotes her, 'I regard it as a real *grace* that I have been accustomed since my childhood to overcome fear'.[43]

Her greatest bouts of anxiety came at the end of her life as she faced death from tuberculosis and most, especially a deep spiritual darkness which coincided with it. She expresses her fear 'of not being ready to face death',[44] and even being 'afraid of being afraid of death'.[45] At the end of her life, Balthasar writes, 'How moving and shaking it is to watch her trembling the day before her death: Mother, is this the death agony? How shall I manage to die? I shall never know how to die'[46]. He quotes the Little Flower's agony in his study on Bernanos: ' "Oh, Mother! Is this the end? How am I going to manage to die? I'm never going to know how to die!. . . . If this is the death agony, what will death itself be like? . . . I can't breathe, I can't die. . . . Isn't it over yet, then? Am I not to die?" '.[47] When she first began to spit up blood after Good Friday in 1896, she began to experience her soul 'to be darkened by the thickest gloom, so that the thought of heaven, so sweet to me up until then, becomes an occasion of torment and agony'.[48] She continues to describe her anxious struggle:

> When I want to rest my heart, weary of the surrounding darkness, by the memory of the luminous country after which I aspire, my anguish only increases. It seems as if the darkness, echoing the voices of sinners is mocking me, saying, 'You dream of light, a

39. Cf. *CA*, pp. 43–4; Eng., pp. 83–4; *HW*, pp. 121–3; Eng., pp. 163–5.
40. Cf. *SwG*, pp. 98–9; Eng., pp. 106–7.
41. *SwG*, p. 91; Eng., p. 98.
42. *SwG*, p. 122; Eng., p. 130.
43. *SwG*, p. 124; Eng., p. 132.
44. B, p. 297; Eng., p. 329.
45. *SwG*, p. 345; Eng., p. 357.
46. *SwG*, p. 105; Eng., p. 112.
47. *B*, p. 422; Eng., pp. 471–2.
48. *SwG*, p. 327; Eng., p. 339.

> fragrant homeland, you dream that you will possess the Creator of these works for all eternity, you believe that you will one day emerge from this gloom. . . . Go on! Look forward to death, which will give you – not what you hope – but a still darker night, the night of nothingness'.[49]

She is plagued by 'horrid thoughts' that call into doubt God's existence and his love for her.[50] Such thoughts make her afraid that she is losing her mind and is not surprised that 'so many unbelievers commit suicide'.[51] She is tormented by ' "evil snakes" that "hiss in her ear" ', and declares that 'The devil is slithering around me, I do not see him, but I feel him, he torments me, holds me in an iron grip and prevents me from feeling the slightest alleviation. He increases my torments to tempt me to despair'.[52] She goes so far as to make her 'most extreme statement' according to Balthasar: 'I no longer believe in eternal life; it seems to me there's nothing beyond this mortal life. Everything is brought to an end. Love alone remains'.[53] He observes, however, that while her anxiety increases, so does her joy. She writes, 'in spite of this trial, which deprives me of all my joy, I can still cry, "You have given me, O Lord, a delight in all your doings, for is there any greater joy than to suffer for love of you?" '[54]

Georges Bernanos

The author

The greatest amount of material in the Balthasarian corpus on the phenomenon of anxiety is found in his study of the French novelist, Georges Bernanos. It perhaps is not surprising that he wrote this study during one of the most difficult parts of his own life. He writes, 'Few books have I written with more interior involvement than this one [*Bernanos*], which I worked on immediately after leaving the Jesuits'.[55] Yet before examining the anxiety of Bernanos' characters, an initial pass should be made through Bernanos' own life. Balthasar notes, 'From his childhood on, Bernanos himself knew anxiety, for it dogged his footsteps and never let him go as long as he lived'.[56] He suffered from anxiety for which he sought medical help, which nevertheless served him well as a writer. These frequent bouts of anxiety even 'shook him awake at night and gave him the sensation he was experiencing death's agony in advance'.[57]

49. *SwG*, p. 328; Eng., p. 340.
50. *SwG*, p. 329; Eng., p. 341.
51. *SwG*, p. 345; Eng., p. 357.
52. *SwG*, p. 345; Eng., p. 357.
53. *SwG*, p. 330; Eng., p. 342.
54. *SwG*, p. 329; Eng., pp. 340–1.
55. *UA*, p. 100; Eng., p. 104.
56. *CA*, p. 62; Eng., p. 108.
57. *B*, p. 56; Eng., p. 67. Cf. *B*, p. 61; Eng., p. 73.

Bernanos who always was a man of deep faith expresses his anxiety, according to Balthasar, often in anxious *thoughts* such as the fear of death and the overwhelming reality of eternity.[58] Bernanos comments later in life, 'I fear death and, unfortunately (although perhaps my guardian angel would say fortunately), I'm always thinking about it', and he makes reference to a physiological reaction reminiscent of Job: 'I'm so afraid of death and of the inevitable decomposition it entails, which almost makes the hair on my head stand on end'.[59] His fear of eternity went beyond his fear of death. He suffered 'the anguish of sensing the abyss gaping wide behind the appearance of the ephemeral and the intimation of the enormous power of eternity to destroy existence as if by suction'.[60] From this awareness of eternity beginning with his first Holy Communion, it seems that faith and anxiety would always be closely related in Bernanos' life.

Bernanos' years in boarding school indicate some behavioural characteristics in his anxiety from his deep sensitivity by being withdrawn, deliberately going unkempt and compensating through arrogance.[61] His time with *Action Française*, in Balthasar's view, was an attempt to protect himself against this deep sensitivity which rendered him so vulnerable. Later on Bernanos was to experience the anxiety of disillusionment with the movement and its hero, Charles Maurras, when after leaving the movement Bernanos endured the rejection and criticism of his former friend. In Balthasar's words, the young Bernanos endeavoured 'to create a counterweight to the claim the Absolute was making upon him'.[62] The life of the young Bernanos 'reveals a stormy and most animated and dramatic wrestling with God. Seasons of deep darkness and despair alternate with lightning strike certitudes and encounters'.[63]

Bernanos also experienced the anxiety as a soldier in World War I. One example is mentioned in a letter: 'My anguish is full and continual. Some days are horrendous'.[64] Bernanos continued to struggle with 'the fragility and exposure of Christian life in the face of eternity, particularly of the life that of those entrusted with the highest Christian missions'.[65] In a letter dated 26 August 1919, which Balthasar terms 'an important letter on anguish', Bernanos writes, 'I write this at the anguish of hope, shaken with sobs of the foot of the cross. The only thing we have left by way of strength – and this one thing we have in abundance, lavished, squandered and thrown up with full hands – goes by the name of agony'.[66] The physiological description he gives to this anxiety is 'shuddering' and 'shivering'.[67]

58. *B*, p. 49; Eng., p. 59. A similar comment is made again on pp. 414–15; Eng., p. 463.
59. *B*, p. 415; Eng., p. 463.
60. *B*, p. 37; Eng., p. 47.
61. Cf. *B*, p. 50; Eng., p. 60.
62. *B*, p. 38; Eng., p. 47.
63. *B*, p. 37; Eng., p. 46.
64. *B*, p. 430; Eng., p. 480.
65. *B*, p. 430; Eng., p. 481. Balthasar makes the same comment earlier in his study, p. 180; Eng., p. 199.
66. *B*, p. 430; Eng., p. 481.
67. *B*, p. 431; Eng., p. 482.

Bernanos' vocation as a husband and a writer gave ample fuel to his anxiety. The life of a writer cannot support easily a growing family, especially since he was thirty-eight before his first novel was published. After a few years of financial uncertainty and increased bouts of anxiety, Bernanos became an insurance salesman.[68] This new job meant much travelling, mixed success and continual financial difficulties. Bernanos expresses his anxiety about his life in his mid-twenties: 'With all my forces I've striven for greatness, the greatness God himself desires we should seek – I mean, out of the dark abyss of my nakedness, to the point of being disgusted with myself. . . . I have truly become a humiliated being. And so, if greatness should ever really touch me, I have no right to count on anything except being incinerated on the spot'.[69]

Another difficulty for his family life, which seems to indicate the behavioural dimension of his anxiety, was the constant change of residence in which valuable work was often lost. In 1938, he moved with his family to South America and even there changed residences from Paraguay to Brazil. Although Bernanos had many friends, it is at this time the troubles within his family were at their greatest. Balthasar writes, 'Less than ever was he spared painful and dramatic experiences in his own home and these contributed to keeping alive the tragic undertones of his life. He commented: "It seems that the Bernanos house is an unsolvable problem". The strongest crises of anguish occur during these years'.[70] Balthasar writes 'Bernanos was a loyal and devoted husband and father to his wife and children', yet there were 'frequent clashes between the writer's temperament and the reprehensible behaviour of his children, some of whom caused him sorrow beyond words'.[71]

Our author perhaps expends the most energy describing Bernanos' anxiety vis-à-vis his vocation as a Christian writer. Bernanos seemed acutely aware of being charged with a mission from God and struggled with feelings of inadequacy and even self-hatred.[72] Balthasar draws out Bernanos' experiences of inner anguish in failing to express adequately his inner thoughts and feelings. In fact, Balthasar states that Bernanos worked in 'continual despair'.[73] An example of such thoughts emerges from his work in composition: 'Another possesses the secret of the world that creates. . . . Only, he doesn't speak. . . . Will I forever, forever, remain a useless servant?'[74] Bernanos' anxiety is further revealed in the incredible slowness with which he wrote, the slightest piece undergoing ten or eleven drafts.[75] Bernanos lived in the anxiety of self-doubt as a Christian writer, remaining 'distrustful – to the point of self defeat – of

68. Cf. *B*, p. 54; Eng., p. 65.
69. *B*, p. 60; Eng., p. 71.
70. *B*, p. 67; Eng., p. 79.
71. *B*, p. 51; Eng., pp. 61–2.
72. Cf. *B*, p. 138; Eng., pp. 154–5; *B*, p. 140; Eng., p. 156.
73. *B*, p. 118; Eng., p. 133; *B*, p. 40; Eng., p. 50.
74. *B*, p. 40; Eng., pp. 49–50. Balthasar makes reference to this line of Bernanos again. Cf. *B*, p. 431; Eng., p. 482.
75. Bernanos admits, 'I have learned to endure a whole day in despair before a blank sheet of paper, just in order not to lose one true thought' (*B*, p. 52; Eng., p. 62).

everything he could attain in his literary endeavours. . . . He would nurture a lifelong insecurity concerning his own creative powers'.[76] Even when Bernanos is able to give expression to his inner vision, he also contends with anxiety about the characters he has created.[77] The result of Bernanos' anxious sufferings is that his 'work had for him the value of something he had paid for with his heart's blood: "It appears unbearable to me that one could derive profit from what I have created in one uninterrupted state of anguish and enduring so many agonies" '.[78] He continues, 'Everything is giving way under me. I seem to be walking in slime. If I go forward I'll surely sink, if I don't move I'll sink just the same'.[79]

After Bernanos' initial success began waning and before his next successes had begun he struggled with the pressure to write 'books that keep you well fed'.[80] Such anxious thoughts would be typical of a writer and family man. He was experiencing anxiety from pressure of his readership, his publishers, and his family, and saw no success in the near future. Balthasar comments, 'Was he not a writer? Should he not submit to the laws of his profession? Was he not writing for his readers? And, beyond this, did he not have to provide for his wife and six children? But the price to pay was "the prostitution of our poor talents", and Bernanos refused to pay it'.[81]

Bernanos also experienced the anxiety from the decline of western culture and modern man and the feeling of helplessness before this event. He observes, 'We continually repeat, with tears of helplessness, laziness, and pride, the world is becoming de-Christianized'.[82] He continues, 'Mankind is afraid of itself. ... It is sacrificing its liberty to the fear it has of itself', and, 'Modern man is man in anguish. Anguish has taken the place of faith'.[83] He continues about the insecurity of the world, 'This world no longer protects anyone or offers anyone security. It no longer defends anyone; rather, it is a world that needs defending, it is we who must save the world'.[84] At the same time Bernanos was troubled by the prevailing attitude among many within the Church who, in his mind, had distanced the Church from the world and whose lack of personal holiness lessened the Church's credibility. Bernanos also saw modern man's fascination with the development of systems and pressure for cultural conformism on a societal level as a way of avoiding the anxiety inherent in thinking and choosing as a human person. These pressures

76. *B*, p. 53; Eng., p. 63. Balthasar quotes Bernanos' lifelong friend, Vallery–Radot, 'He showed them [the manuscripts] to me, anxiously awaiting my judgment, . . . always full of doubt about his own talent and yet with the feeling of an inner world pressing to be born – something heavy, dark, threatening, and secret, like a silent pressure by storm' (*B*, p. 55; Eng., p. 66).

77. Cf. *B*, p. 119; Eng., p. 134.

78. *B*, p. 61; Eng., p. 72.

79. *B*, p. 438; Eng., p. 490.

80. *B*, p. 187; Eng., p. 207.

81. *B*, p. 187; Eng., p. 207.

82. *B*, p. 89; Eng., p. 102.

83. *B*, p. 445; Eng., p. 499.

84. *B*, p. 224; Eng., p. 246.

push man to abdicate his freedom and to dispense him from the daily risk of judging so that the 'system' may decide for him. Here it could be said that Bernanos puts his finger on the pulse of a societal anxiety and a consequent behaviour which seeks to avoid it. Bernanos saw this anxiety having its source in a human reason that had grown cowardly. His outspoken manner on this issue meant that he was often alone in academic and literary circles.

When describing the phenomenon of anxiety in Bernanos, Balthasar nevertheless avoids exaggerating it. Balthasar makes sure to point out that 'Bernanos loved to laugh, and his great guffaws more than qualify him for a role as "Catholic rascal"', and he 'rejected as boring and false the earnest, pathetic image of him that his friends tended to fashion'.[85] Bernanos himself would urge his friends not to take him or his work too seriously, and criticized other authors for what he saw was an over-indulgence of anxiety.[86] Thus, in Balthasar's description of Bernanos' anxiety one finds a full range of the phenomenon in its physiological, cognitive and behavioural dimensions.

Characters in Bernanos' novels

Blanche de la Force, Carmelite nun and martyr of the Robespierre Terror, appears first and foremost among Bernanos' characters in Balthasar's description of anxiety. She is the fictional heroine of Bernanos' *Dialogues of the Carmelites* which was written in his final days for a film scenario.[87] Balthasar observes that Blanche is a woman who perhaps was even born with an anxious disposition. The dimension of her anxiety mentioned most often by Balthasar is her avoidant behaviour. Balthasar notes that she is susceptible to 'continual panic' and her behaviour is characterized by 'avoidance of all situations that call for steadfastness – an attitude that cannot be interpreted other than as cowardice'.[88] To avoid the feelings of helplessness she tries to avoid situations that trigger the anxiety. She would invent different reasons why she could not face something that frightened her: fatigue, illness, forgetfulness and engaging in another activity. Blanche's anxiety is so great that she feels that she cannot protect herself against their outbreaks and even her entry into Carmel is an attempt to avoid the fears of living in the world.[89]

Nevertheless her anxiety continues within the cloister. Balthasar observes that her hands tremble in fear and she drops and shatters the statue on

85. *B*, p. 162; Eng., p. 180.

86. Cf. *B*, p. 269; Eng., p. 295.

87. G. Bernanos used Gertrude von Le Fort's *Die Letzte am Schafot* as his source, and his story eventually became the libretto for Poulenc's opera by the same name. The fictional character of Blanche originated with Le Fort. For a historical reconstruction of the actual people involved and the events of the martyrdom of the Carmelites of Compiègne see W. Bush, *To Quell the Terror* (Washington D.C.: ICS Publications, 1999).

88. *B*, p. 440; Eng., p. 492.

89. Cf. *B*, p. 441; Eng., p. 493.

Christmas Eve.[90] Even her religious name is indicative of her anxiety.[91] Blanche's anxiety is intensified by her witnessing the anxiety of her prioress, her anchor of support, who undergoes 'a frightfully anguished death'.[92] Added to Blanche's anxiety is also a sense of shame. She is ashamed that she is so anxious. Her cowardly behaviour surfaces again when she becomes the only sister to vote against the community's intention to take the vow of martyrdom, but later with the help of Constance is able to utter the vow, 'using up her last reserve of strength'.[93] However, Balthasar observes, 'The moment she has "offered up her life to God for the salvation of Carmel and of France", Blanche flees definitively into the world'.[94] In the face of potential martyrdom, Blanche leaves Carmel to avoid the fear of possibly suffering a violent death.[95] When she leaves to take care of her sick father, however, the anxieties only intensify and indicate perhaps some depression in her inability to come to terms with her fears.[96] The fact that she is able in the end to climb the scaffold free from anxiety is for Balthasar a miracle of grace. In the character of Blanche, we find Balthasar giving a more ample description of the behavioural dimension of anxiety.

Abbé Donissan is the priest hero from Bernanos' first novel, *Under Satan's Sun*. Father Donissan's anxiety stems primarily from his mission as a priest and in the relationship with his spiritual director, the Abbé Menou-Segrais. Balthasar writes that Donissan 'believes that his mission must be interpreted in the sense that God is demanding of him that he should "pursue Satan even into the very souls of people", in such a way that he "cannot avoid endangering his own peace of soul, his priestly honor and even his eternal salvation"'.[97] Donissan's anxiety from looking in the face of evil is characterized by a vertigo which seems to posses physiological and cognitive elements. Granted Bernanos writes about this situation in a mythic sort of way, but his portrayal seems nevertheless helpful for the purposes of the present inquiry. Balthasar describes Donissan's anxiety in the following manner:

> When Donissan peers for the first time into Satan's eyes, he sees there the vertigo of the abyss: 'A man tied by both hands to the peak of the mast and suddenly losing the balance of gravity would see the rending and swelling beneath him no longer now of the sea but of the cosmic abyss of the stars – and, seeing trillions of leagues away, he would see the foam of nebulas in gestation through the gaping void that nothing can measure and that his everlasting fall is about to traverse. Such a man would not feel in the hollow of his chest a more absolute vertigo [then Donissan now felt]. . . . The daring man, in some sense bending forward and sucked from the earth by the immense

90. *B*, p. 442; Eng., p. 495.

91. The English translator notes the ironic inversion of her original name, *Force*, when she takes her religious name, *Faiblesse* (cf. *B*, Eng., 495n).

92. *B*, p. 440; Eng., p. 492.

93. *B*, p. 458; Eng., p. 514.

94. *B*, pp. 458–9; Eng., p. 514.

95. Cf. *B*, p. 280; Eng., p. 308.

96. Cf. *B*, p. 442; Eng., p. 494.

97. *B*, p. 248; Eng., p. 271.

> call of nothingness, saw himself this time irretrievably lost. And yet, at this very instant, his final thought was still a confused act of defiance'.[98]

In his confrontation with the demon, Donissan seems to manifest anxious thoughts from his felt helplessness and vulnerability before evil which his priestly calling seems to demand: 'What's this, my Lord? Are we then so transparent to the enemy lying in ambush for us? Are we then released wholly unarmed for his calculating hatred?'[99] This priest has doubts and anxiety about loss. Balthasar writes, 'But this poor priest, when he doubts, has doubts not only about himself but about his one and only hope'.[100] Moreover, Donissan has ' "the unbearable feeling of having been caught in a trap", until all hope has eclipsed his heart and his one need will be "to die, just as you long to pour out tears", a yearning for eternal night, for "something more secret than solitude: the vertigo of an everlasting fall into all engulfing darkness" '.[101]

His failures, his work as a confessor and his reading of souls are moments which fill him with anxiety. He allows the demands on him to pile up to such an extent that he cannot accomplish them, and as a confessor he feels devoid of the graces others receive through him.[102] Though he is achieving great things in his ministry the priest is awash with feelings of helpless and failure. At one point Donissan says, 'What priest has never wept out of helplessness before the mystery of human suffering?'[103] Donissan has the feeling of 'being used' by souls and 'feeling the "futility" of it all, the wasteful squandering of one's "efforts" '.[104] Donissan is plagued by self-doubt and self-hatred, and puts himself through strong mortification which perhaps connects with the behavioural dimension of anxiety.

His gift for reading souls is nothing less than an overwhelming experience of anguish. Balthasar observes that 'it is at least a kind of atonement and compensation when Donissan must in the future pay with expressed mortal anguish for the gift of reading into the hearts of sinners in the confessional'.[105] Donissan expresses those anxious thoughts about being in the confessional: 'Could it be that they've never been face-to-face with the human countenance in the throes of anguish? Have they never felt pierced by one of those unforgettable glances, already full of hatred for God, the longing to people to whom one has nothing left to give – nothing?'[106]

The anxiety of Father Donissan extends into his spiritual director, Abbé Menou-Segrais. The spiritual director of a saint feels anxiety from the weight of responsibility for the holy soul: 'With prayerful anxiety he accompanies,

98. *B*, pp. 336–7; Eng., p. 372.
99. *B*, p. 379; Eng., p. 423.
100. *B*, pp. 434–5; Eng., p. 486.
101. *B*, p. 461; Eng., pp. 518–19.
102. Cf. *B*, p. 391; Eng., p. 436.
103. *B*, p. 462; Eng., p. 519.
104. *B*, p. 462; Eng., p. 520.
105. *B*, p. 383; Eng., pp. 426–7.
106. *B*, p. 387; Eng., p. 432.

unseen, the one whom he has launched on the ways of sanctity'.[107] In response to Donissan's conception of his mission whereby he must risk all, even his own soul, for souls, Abbé Menou-Segrais intervenes. At one point he exclaims in his anxiety: '*And you have been entrusted to me! You belong to me! How my hands tremble as I offer you up to God! I am not allowed a single mistake. How brutal the thing it is for me not to be able to fall on my knees alongside you and join you in a profound thanksgiving!*'[108] The director must cast Donissan not only into the arena of the battle between sanctity and the demonic, but also into 'the huge machinery of the Church's administration, between the wheels of which we can foresee that the young priest is about to be crushed'.[109]

Donissan also manifests anxiety 'with a curiosity full of fright' in ecclesial obedience with his spiritual director whom he struggles to admire.[110] Donissan struggles much in his death revealing even a somatic manifestation of the anxiety in his face which is described as 'a frightful face, as if struck by lightning'.[111] Balthasar seems to highlight in this character primarily anxious thoughts but also physiological and behavioural examples, all surrounding Donissan's mission as a priest.

Chantal, Abbé Cénabre and Monsieur Ouine comprise another set of characters from Bernanos' work. Balthasar observes that Chantal, who is modelled on the traits of St. Thérèse, does not as such manifest moments of anxiety but rather an anxious condition that slowly unfolds.[112] She gropes to find the proper object of her anxiety, and eventually enters a spiritual darkness in which she 'can no longer understand her own fear'.[113] She expresses the symptoms of feeling 'weary, weary, weary unto death', 'an immense fatigue', being 'reduced to utter powerlessness', and feeling that all her struggles and efforts were hopeless.[114] As a holy Christian she experiences anxiety in dealing with her apparent spiritual mediocrity.[115] Her anxiety is not exempt from a somatic manifestation in that even in joy Chantal had a 'tragic face, made taught by distress'. Chantal's anxiety appears to become despair just before her director dies. In the midst of her own storm, she witnesses him struggle and even push her away. Abbé Chevance cries out to Chantal who is shocked and frightened, 'I don't want to . . . I don't want to . . . I don't want to die. . . . You cannot save me from this situation, neither you nor the others. It's hard to die, my daughter. . . . It's not good for you to watch me die. It's a worthless site, a worthless site to tell you. Go away!'[116] Added to his death is the shame of it. Balthasar

107. *B*, p. 247; Eng., p. 270.
108. *B*, p. 249; Eng., p. 273 (Balthasar's italics).
109. *B*, p. 250; Eng., pp. 273–4.
110. *B*, p. 246; Eng., p. 269.
111. *B*, p. 422; Eng., p. 471.
112. *B*, p. 435; Eng., p. 487.
113. Cf. *B*, pp. 435–6; Eng., p. 487.
114. *B*, p. 436; Eng., p. 487; cf. *B*, p. 437; Eng., p. 488.
115. *B*, p. 395; Eng., pp. 440–1.
116. *B*, p. 423; Eng., p. 472.

writes, 'The dedicated, humble, and merry man dies the atrocious and smothering death of a sinner. This horror forever deprives her of a part of her ability to understand'.[117] Chantal faces the death of a loved one and must watch him die without understanding the situation. In this situation, 'God becomes for her "invisible and mute", and the dark cloud of the supernatural sadness overshadows her soul'.[118]

Abbé Cénebre, the evil character in *Imposture*, manifests the anxiety that arises from wickedness. Even his own laughter becomes 'something that frightens him to the core',[119] and he becomes isolated from himself and suicidal.[120] Like his characters Donissan and Chantal, Bernanos also gives Cénabre a physiological manifestation of his anxiety. In his death agony, Cénabre has 'the petrified face of agony'.[121]

The character of Monsieur Ouine also expresses the anxiety of one caught in evil. He suffers from insomnia and finds the morning hours to be an anxious and an unbearable time of day.[122] In his death agony, Ouine experiences intensely the unbearable nature of the nothingness that his life has become.[123] Descriptions of anxiety from involvement with evil can also be found in some of the less prominent characters in Balthasar's treatment of Bernanos' novels.[124]

The Curé de Ambricourt is Bernanos' priest hero from *Diary of a Country Priest*. He is, in Balthasar's view, a more mature version of the priest heroes in Bernanos' novels. He, like Donissan, manifests anxiety having its source in his priesthood. The Curé of Ambricourt, like Donissan, feels isolation and the apparent futility of his priestly ministry. The priest manifests anxious thoughts as he writes in his diary, 'My life and all the energies of my life are running out of me and becoming lost in the sand'.[125] When he faces death he reveals a somatic manifestation of his anxiety when he says 'I cried with wide-open eyes, I cried as I've seen the dying cry. And still it was my life flowing out of me'.[126] He expresses the anxiety from the felt absence of God's presence, the inability to pray, feeling broken and covered in a thick spiritual darkness.

117. *B*, p. 251; Eng., p. 275.
118. *B*, p. 252; Eng., p. 276.
119. *B*, p. 340; Eng., p. 376.
120. Cf. *B*, p. 340; Eng., p. 377.
121. *B*, p. 447; Eng., p. 501.
122. Cf. *B*, p. 295; Eng., pp. 325–6.
123. Cf. *B*, p. 345; Eng., p. 382.
124. Bernanos' character Simone Alfieri, the murderess in *An Evil Dream*, experiences isolation, even from herself, and nightmares from her evil, especially lying (cf. *B*, pp. 131, 262; Eng., pp. 147, 288). Dr Lipotte, in Bernanos' *An Evil Dream*, takes morphine to avoid thinking about death (cf. *B*, p. 356; Eng., p. 395). Mouchette's anxiety from her wickedness 'makes her jovial and talkative', a behavioural defence against anxiety (*B*, p. 446; Eng., p. 500). Mouchette, the mayor of Fenouille and Simone all manifest self-hating behaviour as an attempt to cope with their anxiety (*B*, pp. 468–69; Eng., p. 527). Bernanos' portrayal of sexual sin, according to our author, is rife with the phenomenon of anxiety (cf. *B*, pp. 209, 351–2; Eng., pp. 229, 390).
125. *B*, p. 461; Eng., p. 518.
126. *B*, p. 461; Eng., p. 518; cf. *B*, p. 463; Eng., pp. 520–1.

The Curé, in a manner similar to St. Thérèse, expresses fear of feeling unprepared to face death.[127] And before his death he announces, 'More than once I've felt the dread of not knowing how to die once the moment arrives'.[128] When he begins to realize his terminal condition he expresses anxious thoughts: 'By what frightful wonder was I able to forget the very Name of God? I was alone, unutterably alone in the face of my death. . . . The truth is that I've always been in the Garden of Olives . . . our Lord has done me the grace of revealing to me that nothing would ever snatch me from the place chosen me for me from all eternity, my position as *prisoner of the Holy Agony*?'[129] The anxiety is expressed physically, comments Balthasar, when the ex-priest Dufréty remarks that 'after his death his face "seemed to express a great anguish"'.[130]

Madame de Croissy, the prioress of Carmel in *Dialogues of the Carmelites*, receives passing, but nevertheless helpful, mention from Balthasar on the phenomenon of anxiety. A woman with a long history of freedom from anxiety experiences profound and shameful anxiety in her death. She declares:

> [B]ut nothing can help me anymore. . . . I am alone, my good mother, absolutely alone, without any consolation. My mind remains quite capable of forming reassuring ideas, but these too are only phantoms. They cannot comfort me anymore than the shadow on the wall of a leg of mutton can satisfy one's hunger. . . . I've meditated on death every hour of my life, yet now that's no good to me at all.[131]

Her anxiety is felt bodily as she says 'anguish clings to my skin like a wax mask'.[132] Balthasar emphasizes her vulnerability and helplessness in this situation: 'Here, both as things have become one namely, absolute, *open* vision ... and an absolute *helplessness* that is so great that it can be only understood as unconscious participation in Christ's anguish in the face of death'.[133] He notes that in her anguish she also experiences shame in 'the incapacity to accomplish well precisely the thing for which one has prepared oneself through a whole lifetime'.[134]

Reinhold Schneider

The author

Another author who enters into Balthasar's portrayal of the phenomenon of anxiety is the German playwright Reinhold Schneider. A description of

127. Cf. *B*, p. 297; Eng., p. 329.
128. *B*, pp. 422–3; Eng., p. 472.
129. *B*, pp. 433–4; Eng., pp. 484–5.
130. *B*, p. 424; Eng., p. 473.
131. *B*, p. 419; Eng., p. 468.
132. *B*, p. 447; Eng., p. 501.
133. *B*, p. 419; Eng., p. 468.
134. *B*, p. 424; Eng., p. 473.

Schneider's anxiety is focused in two places, as a young man and in his final years. The most prominent feature of anxiety's phenomenology to emerge in Balthasar's description of Schneider's life is its depressive aspect.[135]

He describes the young Schneider in terms of the landscape of Portugal in which he 'absorbs into all his pores the oozing away of the West'.[136] It is in Portugal where Schneider grapples with 'the collapse of culture, of the transience of life, an unsurpassable measure of melancholy and the hopeless flight from the sinking ship'.[137] Balthasar continues:

> No nihilism can be more profound than that of the twenty-three-year-old for whom all faith had disintegrated, every firm outline had become fluid, every sheltering wall had been shattered, so that he emerged from the crumbling house of history into an existence with nothingness as its most certain mark.[138]

The young Schneider grappled with the felt nothingness in human existence in tremendous vulnerability through his reading of the Spanish poet Miguel de Unamuno and the discovery of his concept of *Saudade*.[139] Life is a struggle not only without victory but without hope for victory. Balthasar writes that Schneider 'experiences reality as something that is already decaying and broken open',[140] and quotes him: 'That which is beautiful is surrounded in a special way by the terror of death, by a yearning for eternity that is contradicted by all experience'.[141] Portugal depicts for Schneider the anxiety that comes from a life without God, the anxiety of the non-believer, of living in a decaying and dying civilization hurling towards death with only the burning passion that yearns but never obtains.

Like Bernanos, Schneider also struggled with his mission as a writer. Schneider's mission as a writer, comments Balthasar, is like the prophet Jeremiah who ' "suffered the Word" and was driven by this Word into an impossible situation, when he "had to shatter the pitcher in the presence of the men of his age" and was instructed not to pray for the people'.[142] Schneider's

135. It is unclear in Balthasar's work as to whether Schneider's depressive symptoms were anxiety or depression. The psychiatric description given in the Introduction indicates that depression can be a form of anxiety. In any case, a close relationship exists between both.

136. *RS*, p. 32; Eng., p. 35.

137. *RS*, p. 31; Eng., p. 33.

138. *RS*, p. 31; Eng., p. 33.

139. *Saudade* is 'the word for the innermost contradiction between this yearning that consumes itself and yet wants itself to live in this very act of consuming' (*RS*, p. 33; Eng., p. 35). Balthasar calls it an 'existential feeling' which denotes the fundamental contradiction between the human spirit and life (*RS*, p. 33; Eng., p. 35). It would seem that the 'existential feeling' of *saudade* would give rise to anxious thoughts for one who is conscious in the face of death, but has no meaning or certainty before the inevitability of death. Anxiety also arises from a life being lived in alienation to oneself. Life is seen as agonic, a yearning yet never attaining.

140. *RS*, p. 42; Eng., p. 43.

141. *RS*, pp. 48–9; Eng., p. 50.

142. *RS*, p. 17; Eng., p. 19.

mission as a writer carries anxiety with it since his message demands facing 'a dying existence'.[143]

The landscape of decay appears again as a central symbol of Schneider's last years, not in Portugal but at the demolition of his family's home. While watching it, Schneider comments, 'You are there in order to see how a whole age is cleared away, so to speak. . . . How rotten everything is'.[144] Balthasar notes that Schneider had to endure 'expressions of hostility, calumnies of all kinds, the boycott of all Catholic newspapers and periodicals'.[145] He makes the observation that this passing away of things in his life brings Schneider into a situation of unfamiliarity, vulnerability, loss of security, helplessness and interior trembling, all of which appear to be manifestations of anxiety.[146] Late in life Schneider also struggled in his faith and prayer; Balthasar wonders whether it was a 'critical night of faith',[147] and assesses this final period of anxious struggle in Schneider's life as primarily cognitive and depressive in nature.[148]

Characters in Schneider's plays

Schneider focuses his work on the tragedy inherent in the exercise of power by free yet fallen creatures, especially Christians. The tragic nature of fallen existence gives rise to anxiety in his characters since it seems to place them in situations of suffering, evil, death and even damnation. It would seem that anxiety is what a person undergoes as the tragedy unfolds; it is woven into the very fabric of tragedy.

It seems that most of the anxiety experienced by Schneider's characters comes from the impossible situation of administering power as a fallen human being and Christian. They seem to be aware that they must act and yet cannot act without bringing about some harm. These indicate two points of contact with anxiety: internal conflict as source of anxiety, and anxiety as a defence against guilt. It is the combination of that element of personal freedom exercised within an impossible situation that gives rise to their anxiety. Time and history bring with them the necessity to act and to make choices that cannot be reversed. The decision made in such an hour by a fallen creature will inevitably entail anxiety. Although mention could be made of other figures,[149] we will focus on Saint Joan of Arc and the three papal figures of

143. *RS*, p. 19; Eng., p. 21.
144. *RS*, p. 287; Eng., p. 269.
145. *RS*, p. 287; Eng., p. 269.
146. Cf. *RS*, p. 288; Eng., p. 270.
147. *RS*, p. 11; Eng., p. 13.
148. Cf. *RS*, p. 297; Eng., p. 278.
149. For example, Philip II's anxiety from the burden of kingship (cf. *RS*, pp. 51–8; Eng., pp. 52–8; Otto IV's anxiety from his excommunication (cf. *RS*, pp. 247–8; Eng., pp. 232–3; *SC*, pp. 428–30; Eng., pp. 484–6); and Saint Elizabeth of Hungary's anxiety over the choice to renounce her crown and family for religious life (cf. *RS*, pp. 254–5; Eng., pp. 238–9).

Celestine V and Boniface VIII (in *Der grosse Verzicht*), and Innocent III (in *Innozenz III*) which seem to manifest the phenomenon of anxiety more clearly.

Saint Joan of Arc, as seen in Balthasar's studies on Schneider and Bernanos, reveals the anxiety of the believer who suffers at the hands of those within the Church. Whereas the characters of Chantal, Donissan and the Curé of Ambricourt experienced priests who were excellent examples of ecclesial love, Saint Joan of Arc's experience of those representing the Church is markedly different. In her trial and execution, she experiences loneliness, isolation and abandonment. She must also face the intrigue of her inquisitors and a horrible execution. Her anxiety stems not only from these harsh outside forces but also her interior vulnerability. 'In the midst of the official church', writes Balthasar, 'sanctity agonizes'.[150] Her life, and the ones called like her, becomes 'a struggling, suffering, perishing existence'.[151]

Balthasar provides his reader a sense of the anxious thoughts regarding her situation. He writes, 'But what if sin lives in the Church herself, if sin anchors itself most securely precisely where the Church is most vulnerable – in her hierarchical structure? What if the horror occurs that the face of Satan should begin to glimmer in the very heart of that Trinitarian image, which is the relationship of ecclesial obedience?'[152] He quotes Bernanos' comments on the physiological dimension of Saint Joan's anxiety: 'They saw your pale cheeks ravaged by fever. They saw the beads of sweat under your small stubborn forehead, and the quivering of your mouth, when, in the stuffy courtroom, you suddenly refused to resist them any longer after so many days of harassment'.[153] Bernanos writes about her agony: 'We must consider this agony face-to-face, or better still, we must enter into it. How deep and dark it is! All the fire of the stake cannot melt its chill'.[154]

Popes Celestine V, Boniface VIII and Innocent III comprise another group of characters from Schneider's plays. Peter of Morrone, the aged hermit, is elected Pope in the midst of turmoil: the papal see has been unoccupied for two years, Christian kings are at war with each other and heresy rages.[155] Unfortunately, as Pope Celestine V, he is ill equipped to deal with the political and ecclesial intrigue of the time, and suffers anxiety from these weaknesses and his inept management of the Church. Balthasar's description of Celestine's state is comparable to Bernanos' exasperation as a writer, 'Peter, who becomes Celestine, is a contemplative who receives his certainties only in prayer (109), but this prayer has and needs its own times – it cannot be summoned on demand'[156]. He is asked by Charles of Anjou to bless his weapons for a campaign against Sicily which he refuses

150. *B*, p. 255; Eng., p. 279.
151. *RS*, p. 201; Eng., p. 191.
152. *B*, p. 254; Eng., p. 279.
153. *B*, p. 255; Eng., pp. 279–80.
154. *B*, p. 447; Eng., p. 501.
155. Cf. *SC*, p. 421; Eng., p. 477.
156. *SC*, p. 421; Eng., p. 477.

to do and consequently is imprisoned in Naples by Charles. Celestine also must face intrigue from those within the Church culminating in Benedetto Gaetani's 'superhuman temptation' of Celestine which results in his renunciation of the papal throne, thus enabling Gaetani's ascent as Pope Boniface VIII.[157]

The scene of Celestine's temptation is rife with anxious thoughts. Balthasar describes Schneider's portrayal of it in the following way:

> In a stormy night he [Gaetani] stands adjacent to the pope's bedroom with Jacopone, who is devoted to him, and through a hatch he whispers – with Jacopone's mouth – words into the pope's prayer that Celestine understands in the storm to be a voice from heaven: 'Peter, are you chosen? You do not want to bless any weapons. You refuse to utter the sentence of excommunication. You have proposed to do something that no pope has ever yet dared to do: Do you intend to challenge the world face to face?. . . . This is not truly you, Peter! It was the tempter who offered you the crown, and your rule, Papa Angelicus, is in reality a feast of hell, Satan's triumph over the Church, the form of an angel in the power of the devil!. . . . What, are you fleeing after all? But from whom are you fleeing? From your own self, perhaps? (*quietly:*) Peter Celestine, take from your head the crown that is destroying your soul. . . . You will be able to pray again, you can expiate and do penance!'[158]

In this temptation Pope Celestine experiences a loss of security and an increase in self-doubt and isolation. In the next act of the play, Celestine abdicates before all the cardinals 'confessing his "great guilt" in having offered himself to God for an office for which he had not been chosen'.[159] Before his death, Celestine declares, 'It is true, I have sunk in the waves, because my faith was weak. The Lord did not come to meet me'.[160]

The anxiety of Pope Boniface begins where Pope Celestine's left off. Schneider portrays Pope Boniface constantly haunted by the figure of Celestine. His conniving for power finds culmination in the anxiety and misfortunes he has during his reign. He attributes the attack on his security and confidence to his own sinfulness.[161] He eventually descends into madness when he, seeking to compensate for his own insecurity, seems driven by anxiety: 'Quick! Gather the cardinals together. I am summoning the great Council that requires the kings of the earth to appear before its judgment seat. I am holding the Last Day. Here, this is the throne of the judge of the world'.[162] He is tormented in his thoughts by the figure of Celestine, and exclaims, 'Lamb! Lamb! Who made you so powerful? Where are you? Where are you hiding yourself? But you were always there. That is the terrible thing, that you were always there, and yet I do not know where you are'.[163] When news of Celestine's murder arrives Boniface says to himself: ' "Benedetto Gatani, are you so foolish as to

157. *SC*, p. 420; Eng., p. 476.
158. *RS*, p. 236; Eng., p. 222; cf. *SC*, p. 422; Eng., p. 478.
159. *RS*, p. 236; Eng., p. 222; cf. *SC*, pp. 422–3; Eng., p. 479.
160. *SC*, p. 425; Eng., p. 481.
161. Cf. *RS*, pp. 237–8; Eng., p. 223.
162. *SC*, pp. 423–4; Eng., p. 480.
163. *SC*, p. 423; Eng., p. 479.

say that you did not wish it?". … His last word is: "The holy Peter is dead, and I am his murderer"'.[164]

Innocent III is the third example whereby Schneider portrays the excruciating tension of the papacy and its anxiety.[165] Balthasar draws greatest attention to the physiological and cognitive dimensions of Pope Innocent's anxiety. In the opening lines of the play, Schneider writes: 'He is feverish. He is always feverish'.[166] The play is framed by two intensely anxious dreams where he 'sleeps feverishly'.[167] Three aspects of Innocent's reign fuel the cognitive dimension of his anxiety. First is his struggle with self-doubt about the way he wields his power, having authored the work, *On Contempt for the World*. Second is his anxiety from his position between Emperors and he is haunted by guilt in the death of Philip of Swabia.[168] The third, and probably most intense anxiety, stems from his decision to use the secular sword against the Cathar heretics which results in the burning of women and children inside a church. Balthasar portrays the dramatic scene:

> When the young Raymond brings the pope a cross that he picked out of the great embers of the church of Lavaur, from between the charred bodies of the women and children, and gives it to him with the iron words: 'The one who began the war, who summoned to arms for the war, must have desired this, the death of the innocent in the fire' (209), the Pope says in a toneless voice, 'Why did not my thoughts go as far as this – to this cross and to the One to whom it bears witness?. … I will bear it on my heart: it will be like a burn on my body'.[169]

On his deathbed, Innocent is again tormented in an anxious dream by the heretic. Balthasar writes, 'the contemptuous apparition of the burned heretic, who calls himself "the word branded in letters of fire", will terrify the dying Pope: "You have demonstrated in the literal manner that the Church is hell"'.[170]

Conclusion

The strongest theme to emerge from the above survey is that our author understands anxiety as a universal phenomenon in human existence. He

164. *SC*, p. 424; Eng., p. 480.

165. Balthasar asks, 'How can one who rules in the name of the glorified Christ at the same time follow the poor, humiliated Christ – something that he is obliged to do? How can the one who is installed in office "to build and to plant, to uproot and to destroy", as Innocent says of himself (in the words of the prophet), at the same time be the one who does not break the bruised reed? Are not contradictory demands made of a man here?' (*RS*, pp. 246–7; Eng., pp. 231–2).

166. *SC*, p. 433; Eng., p. 490.

167. *SC*, p. 426; Eng., p. 483.

168. *SC*, p. 428; Eng., p. 484.

169. *SC*, p. 431; Eng., p. 488.

170. *SC*, p. 431; Eng., p. 488.

portrays this universality of anxiety both in the human condition and within the human person. Balthasar suggests that the phenomenon is universal in the human condition regardless of one's faith (or lack thereof), goodness, education or socio-economic status. Anxiety overtakes all people: the rich and the poor, the saint and the sinner, the believer and the non-believer, the noble and the ignoble and the sophisticated and the childlike.

Anxiety, according to Balthasar, invades the life of one facing danger and death, or leading a sinful life. The people of Psalm 107 face the dangers of being lost and thirsty in the wilderness, the loss of freedom of prison, facing a possibly fatal sickness, being tossed about on the sea by a storm. Blanche is faced with the danger of possibility being caught by the authorities and guillotined. Monsieur Ouine and Abbé Cènabre have anxious thoughts about the growing darkness, meaninglessness and isolation of their lives because of their evil deeds.

Anxiety is present in the life of one attempting to fulfil one's calling in the life of the believer and even the saint. Bernanos is anxious about his mission as a Christian writer, and the growing abdication of freedom among many because of their anxiety. Even the one who attempts such an abdication, whom Bernanos calls the *imbecile*, is still caught in anxiety.[171] The Christian is anxious, in Schneider's view, from his responsibility for the world, or in Bernanos' view, 'the impending threat of their own brethren's damnation'.[172] Moreover, the believer is anxious about his own salvation and being summoned to a life that overtaxes his capabilities.[173] Even the saint experiences anxiety from the vulnerability that holiness demands.[174] This path is a difficult one, and Balthasar shows Bernanos' characters struggling with their own weakness and inability to embrace it. The saint is not spared from the anguishing experience of being abandoned and handed over to evil. Perhaps the greatest anxiety of the saint comes from suffering at the hands of those in the Church. Balthasar also indicates that phenomenologically speaking no difference can be detected within the experience of the phenomenon save one: the growing joy that is found in the anxiety of the saints. Joy can be found in

171. Cf. *B*, pp. 330–1; Eng., p. 364. The minor characters of Pernichon or Jérome in the novels of Bernanos seem to illustrate both physiological and behavioural dimensions of anxiety in the *imbecile*. Such a person finds in his own reactions 'a very physical anguish, a feeling of suffocation induced by "certain cynical manifestations the world normally looks upon with indulgence"' (*B*, p. 328; Eng., p. 362). Bernanos argues, however, that this is precisely the sign that the person is 'shrinking back into' himself, and in a manner which would resonate with the behavioural dimension he writes, 'such repeated trials strengthen and harden him, increasing the thickness of his hide' (*B*, p. 328; Eng., p. 362). Further on Balthasar notes that the *imbecile's* behaviour is a type of defence mechanism for self-preservation, reducing himself to avoid suffering (cf. *B*, p. 330; Eng., p. 363).

172. Cf. *RS*, pp. 241–2; Eng., p. 227; *B*, p. 307; Eng., p. 340.

173. Cf. *Kw*, p. 20; Eng., p. 20.

174. Balthasar quotes Bernanos, 'For sanctity is an adventure, we might even say the only adventure. Once you have understood this, you have reached the very heart of Catholic faith, you have felt the thrill in your mortal flesh of a terror different from that of death – the terror of a superhuman hope' (*B*, p. 238; Eng., p. 261).

the midst of the deepest anxiety, such as in Saint Thérèse and in the Curé of Ambricourt.

Balthasar portrays anxiety in its universality also within the human person in its physiological, cognitive and behavioural components. His descriptions include anxious thoughts and dreams in the mind, for example, Pope Celestine's temptation, Pope Innocent's tormented sleep, and Father Donissan's recurring thoughts that he is a failure. His descriptions include anxious behaviours such as Blanche's flight from the world and then from the convent, as well as physiological manifestations, most, especially Bernanos' panic attacks. Yet Balthasar's greatest emphasis falls on the cognitive dimension of anxiety.

Chapter 2

The Appearance of Anxiety in Jesus Christ

Now [Jesus] begins to experience, to feel, at what a price he must do this.
(Adrienne von Speyr)[1]

Having examined Balthasar's grasp of the phenomenon of anxiety in human persons, we now direct our attention to his description of anxiety in the God-man, Jesus Christ. How does Balthasar describe the phenomenon of anxiety in the Incarnate Son in both its similarity and uniqueness to the portrayal in Chapter 1? The following presentation describes the appearance of anxiety in Jesus Christ in Balthasar's writings in a straightforward, even naive manner, prescinding as far as possible from interpretation, which is taken up in Chapter 7. His description is not only based upon his reading of Divine Revelation as found in the Gospels, but also through the lens of Adrienne von Speyr's mystical experience.

The First Stages of Christ's Anxiety

Our Lord's anxiety, according to Balthasar, begins with the exposed and vulnerable heart he assumed in his Incarnation. The 'first direct echo' of Balthasar's involvement with Adrienne's mystical experiences is *Das Herz der Welt* where one can find the beginnings of a description of Jesus' anxiety.[2] Jesus' heart, writes Balthasar, 'was experienced in all the windings and wanderings, changes of weather and drives – in a word, experienced in all the bitter joy and joyful bitterness which any human heart has ever savoured'.[3] He enters his human life in utter vulnerability. Balthasar writes, 'For in the heart's interior all mystery lies open and displayed, and the waves of the blood carry it, defenceless and wholly unmasked, from one man's heart to another's. It was in this circulation that he shared'.[4] Such vulnerability allows the incarnate Son to experience anxiety, and allows our author to observe that 'God could not become man in any other way than by

1. Von Speyr, *Johannes*, vol. II: *Streitreden* (Einsiedeln: Johannes Verlag, 1949), p. 517; Eng., p. 426.
2. *UA*, p. 93; Eng., p. 96.
3. *HW*, p. 28; Eng., p. 45.
4. *HW*, p. 29; Eng., p. 45.

coming to know human fear [*menschliche Angst*] and by taking it upon himself', and that anxiety 'was granted and entrusted to him to the utmost degree'.[5]

Balthasar is not afraid to place words in the mouth of Jesus during his earthly ministry anxious thoughts of abandonment and failure:

> Hope: but then what? In myself? In the power of my love? But will it hold onto the end? What if it should fail? If on the Cross I must acknowledge that all has been in vain? And the Kingdom is swallowed up in the night and my Heart breaks in two with a great cry because it cannot go on, because the power of God by which it beat – beat in hope – was withdrawn from it? And when the last drop of water and blood has escaped from my heart and his gaping void stares up to heaven, what if then the imperious command of the angry Judge should blaze against me with terrible threats? Hard the task, but harder still the failure. Harder the experience of impotence and the certitude of the end.[6]

Jesus manifests anxiety in his dealings with the blind hypocrisy of the Pharisees. Our author quotes Bernanos, 'The curses he hurled at the Pharisees convey a unique tone of wrath and anguish and express a kind of unbearable amazement'.[7] In the face of Lazarus' tomb, Jesus 'shudders' as he 'brushes against the world of the dead, against the soon-to-be-unsealed abyss of smoke and darkness', and he 'shudders' again in disclosing the inevitability of the hour of his own suffering and death.[8]

Christ's Anxiety in Gethsemane

The fear and terror which isolates

Jesus' growing anxiety reaches its most intense level in the Garden of Gethsemane and his cry of abandonment on the Cross. 'Gethsemane' in Aramaic means 'oil press', a fitting image to describe the interior squeezing of Jesus in anxiety.[9] 'On the Mount of Olives', writes Balthasar, 'it is a final, precipitous plunge into the abyss of anxiety [*Abgrund der Angst*] that immediately breaks over him. . . . All that the Old and New Covenants know of anxiety is here gathered together and infinitely surpassed, because the person who in this human nature is frightened [*sich ängstigt*] is the infinite God himself'.[10]

Our author gleans his description of Christ's anxiety from the Gospel accounts, especially those found in Mark and John. Jesus' distress in the

5. *CA*, p. 37; Eng., pp. 73–4.
6. *HW*, p. 48; Eng., pp. 70–1.
7. *B*, p. 326; Eng., p. 360.
8. *CA*, p. 37; Eng., p.74.
9. Cf. G. Buttrick (ed.), *The Interpreter's Bible*, vol. VII: *General Articles on the New Testament, Matthew and Mark* (New York: Abingdon Press, 1951), p. 578.
10. *CA*, p. 37; Eng., p. 74.

Garden is so intense that he is 'dashed to the ground'.[11] His anxiety breaks out from within him as 'fear' (ἐκθαμβειθαι)[12] and 'the horror which isolates' (ἀδημονειν).[13] Εκθαμβέω means 'to be moved to a relatively intense emotional state because of something causing great surprise or perplexity'.[14] The word can also convey the physiological sense of trembling. The Greek word ἀδημονέω connotes 'to be in anxiety', 'to be distressed' or 'troubled'.[15] Balthasar also describes Jesus' anxiety according to the account in John when Jesus expresses 'being troubled' (τετάραται).[16] It takes on a special meaning in John as the 'inner agitation, emotion, distress on the part of Jesus'.[17]

Balthasar emphasizes in his description the isolating effect ἀδημονειν has on Jesus. He feels isolated from both the Father and his disciples, the ones with whom he is most intimate. He pleads using the tender name, Abba, yet no response is given except the angel mentioned in Luke, and the voice that is heard in John, which 'affirms the glorification of the Father (not of Jesus!) through the suffering'.[18] He experiences isolation from the disciples first in their physical distance when he commands them to remain while he moves further away (Matthew) and when the chosen three 'may come within earshot but no nearer' (Mark, Matthew), and second in their spiritual distance in their 'incapacity . . . (excused by Luke as "sadness") to sustain Jesus in his solitary struggle in prayer'.[19] Jesus cries out to the Father and his cry is met with silence. His apostles cannot stay awake, cannot continue to pray and, reminiscent of Job's friends, cannot understand his situation.

11. *TDT*, p. 96; Eng., p. 100. Balthasar prefers the description in Mark stating that the phrase is 'weakened by Matthew who presents this moment as an act of adoration by Jesus who prostrates himself, his face touching the earth, as by Luke who reduces it to the action of kneeling' (*TDT*, p. 96; Eng., p. 100).

12. Balthasar translates the Greek word as 'Grauen' which carries the stronger sense of 'shuddering', 'dread' and 'horror' than simple 'fear'. Meiattini translates the word in Italian as 'il brivido' which connotes 'shiver' or 'shudder' (Meiattini, *Sentire cum Christo*, p. 145).

13. *TDT*, p. 96; Eng., p. 100; cf. Mk 14.33. The word also connotes 'fright', 'fear', or 'terror'.

14. BDAG, p. 303. The root word, Θάμβος is 'a state of astonishment brought on by exposure to an unusual event' (BDAG, p. 442). Θάμβος connotes 'astonishment', 'fear' and 'terror', and describes Jesus' 'emotional duress' in Gethsemane. Cf. Mk 14.33. It is 'an expression of deep perplexity: direct experience of the divine will in what is now happening' (EDNT, pp. 128–9).

15. BDAG, p. 19.

16. Cf. Jn. 12.27; 13.21. This Greek word has the sense of 'agitation', 'disturbance', 'tumult' or 'inward disturbance' (BDAG, p. 991).

17. EDNT, p. 336. The same word is used by Jesus in Jn. 14.27: 'Do not let your hearts be troubled'.

18. *TDT*, p. 96; Eng., p. 100.

19. *TDT*, p. 96; Eng., pp. 100–1. Luke uses the same Greek word (λυπεισθαι) to describe the disciples' sorrow (Lk. 22.45) as Matthew does to describe Jesus' sorrow (Mt. 26.37). Balthasar continues, 'This dialectic of an absent presence of the Church at the side of the suffering Head is irresoluble' (*TDT*, pp. 96–7; Eng., p. 101).

On the brink of the hour, the cup of wrath and the baptism

But what is the cause of his 'anxious prayer agony'?[20] Why the shuddering, terror and sadness? If anxiety is the emotional response to a future evil that is imminent, what future evil presses upon Jesus? His Passion would be the obvious answer. Yet Balthasar emphasizes three aspects to describe the content of Jesus' anxious thoughts when considering his impending Passion: the arrival of the 'hour', drinking from the 'cup' and receiving his 'baptism'. In the Garden of Gethsemane, Jesus is led to the brink of his hour, of drinking to the dregs the cup of divine wrath, and of receiving the baptism, all of which he has been anticipating, preparing for and moving towards his entire earthly life. These comprise the port of entry of the world's sin 'into the personal existence, body and soul' of Jesus.[21]

His hour arrives, according to Balthasar, at the end of his time in Gethsemane in the Synoptics, while in John it arrives at the scene in the Temple and the washing of the feet (cf. Jn. 12.23, 27; 13.1).[22] The arrival of the hour, writes Balthasar, 'leaves him "deeply moved", "troubled" in spirit . . ., but this change in him is less a psychological detail than the signal that a new phase of his existence has begun'.[23] Jesus' consciousness of the content of his hour would have an impact on the intensity of his anxiety. According to Becker, Jesus was at all times 'aware that his mission relentlessly directed him towards a decisive and climatic "hour", whose exact content or future date were hidden from him; these details were obediently left to the Father's will'.[24] Becker also argues that Balthasar thinks at the very least that Jesus was aware that his hour would ultimately include his death.[25] For the purposes of this chapter, two ways of viewing his consciousness of the content of his hour present themselves. One is that the more he knew the more material he had for his cognitive consideration, and thus the possibility for cognitive symptoms. The other is that by placing the content of that hour in the hands of the Father without knowing the specific details other than his ultimate death made his anxiety increase in intensity by virtue of the lack of a specific object. The thorny debate concerning Jesus' consciousness will be treated in greater depth in Chapter 7.

The chalice from which Jesus must drink and the baptism which he must receive signify the laying bare the sin of the world in its absolute fullness, and

20. *TDT*, p. 97; Eng., p. 101.

21. *TDT*, p. 97; Eng., p. 101.

22. Cf. *TDIII*, p. 216; Eng., p. 236.

23. *TDIII*, p. 217; Eng., p. 236. He continues, 'Thus the last prayer of Jesus [in John] is not really a prayer *before* and *with regard to* the Passion, is a prayer that expresses the total content of the "hour"; both disaster [*Untergang*] and the new Dawn [*Aufgang*], that is, it is the transition, the passing over [*Übergang*]' (*TDIII*, p. 217; Eng., pp. 236–7). (translator's italics).

24. W. M. Becker, *The Historical Jesus in the Face of his Death: His Comprehension of its Salvific Meaning in the Writings of Edward Schillebeeckx and Hans Urs von Balthasar (internal, historical and systematic perspectives)* (Roma: self-published, 1994), p. 263.

25. Cf. Becker, *Historical Jesus*, pp. 264, 296–7.

the revelation of God's judgment upon this world.[26] Balthasar writes that Jesus' drinking of the cup 'is not a matter of just any suffering, but the Old Testament, and also apocalyptic cup of the divine anger which the sinner must drain'.[27] His baptism 'corresponds to the Old Testament sinking beneath the destroying flood'.[28] The judgment that Jesus accepts by draining the cup and receiving the baptism 'is a judgment which unveils, convicts, condemns. It is not only a sentence passed on the state of the world, but a judgement which chastises, which ends, which destroys. Through it, "this world", the old aion, really ceases to exist, it comes to its end, and – this is the quite decisive point – to Jesus Christ himself'.[29] Jesus places himself before such a judgement on behalf of sinners to stand in their place.

These three aspects of the hour, the cup and the baptism all indicate the cognitive content for Jesus' consideration in Gethsemane. Yet the divine judgement of sin which Jesus accepts upon himself, according to Balthasar, is a mystery extending beyond the psychological.[30] He comments, 'What we are dealing with here is one of those "pointed" Johannine expressions, which contain more than the customary use of language allows, and which aim to mark out a unique Christological event in an analogical manner. "A spiritual motion takes possession of Jesus, having such strength that it would throw other men into utter confusion" '.[31]

The deepest kind of anxiety: Timor gehennalis

Balthasar's description of Christ's anxiety from standing on the brink of the hour, drinking the cup of God's wrath, and receiving his baptism can go further because he insists that the subject who suffers this anxiety is the divine Person of the Son. Meiattini elaborates on Balthasar's point, 'Pure and absolute is the experience of anxiety, because absolute is the abandonment of

26. The cup of wrath is an expression in Sacred Scripture of the consequences of divine wrath. It is 'a symbol of godlessness which brings down the wrath of God', and 'God's chastisement reserved for the godless' (X. Léon-Dufour [ed.], *Dictionary of Biblical Theology* [trans. J. Cahill, S. J. and E. M. Stewart; Boston: St. Paul Books & Media, rev. edn, 1988], p. 104); cf. Isa. 51.17; Ps. 11.6; Rev. 14.10; 15.7–16.19.

27. *TDT*, p. 118; Eng., p. 123. He makes reference to Isa. 51.17,22; Jer. 25.15; Ezek. 23.31ff; and Ps. 75.9.

28. *TDT*, p. 118; Eng., p. 123. He makes reference to Isa. 43.2; Ps 42.8; and 68.2ff.

29. *TDT*, pp. 118–19; Eng., p. 124.

30. He writes, 'The expressions "to be troubled" and "to be deeply moved" (*enebrimesato*, 11,33; cf. Matthew 9, 30; Mark 1, 43) are closely related. Jesus must "suffer to the end" the counter-godly power, and that "in the Spirit" – which is "not a magnitude of the psychological order" but the selfsame reality in which, in 4, 23, "the Father is worshipped". By the additional remark that Jesus "bears testimony", this "trouble" is "still more stoutly fortified than the figure of speech in 11, 33 against misinterpretation a simple feeling impulse. . . . As *tarache* the suffering comes ultimately from the Father and is something accepted" ' (*TDT*, p. 118; Eng., p. 123).

31. *TDT*, p. 118; Eng., p. 123.

the Father and divine is the subject who suffers'.[32] By virtue of him being the divine Son, Jesus' anxiety runs deeper than is possible for any human being. For this reason Meiattini terms Christ's anxiety 'archetypical' for all human anxiety.[33] His hour, the cup and the baptism all express his entering into Godforsakenness [*Gottesverlassenheit*], a Godforsakenness into which only the Divine Son could go. Meiattini continues quoting Balthasar, 'Since he as the Son has a perfect and unspeakable knowledge of the Father (cf. Mt 11, 27), none other than he "can experience such an abandonment on the part of God. . . . This is the deepest suffering possible: knowing, through experience, who is God and having lost (apparently forever) this God" '.[34]

This deeper cognitive anxiety of Jesus in Gethsemane can be understood, according to our author, in a threefold manner. Jesus' anxiety is heightened by his infinite purity and righteousness which is then invaded by that which is most abhorrent to God.[35] Because he is God, Jesus has a unique experience of the horror of sin. Our author offers a more poetic and vivid description of Christ's anxious thoughts as sin makes its entry into his personal existence:

> But shame itself, shame-in-itself, that shame which none of us wants to taste or has ever tasted: what is it? You will find out. You will be shamed before all the world, before the dead stones of the Mount of Olives, before every creature, and, most of all, before your Father. . . . You cannot be rid of the disgust you feel. For now you are disgust itself. Everything base has entered you, and you are an aversion not only to yourself, but to all of us.[36]

Secondly, Jesus suffers the anxiety that each and every sinner would undergo before divine judgement, not only the anxiety of being judged but also of being rejected by God because of one's sins. Balthasar calls it 'the vicarious suffering [*stellvertretende Leiden*] of this Pure One for all the impure'.[37] This vicarious anxiety for sinners extends far beyond that of any other individual even to the point of the *timor gehennalis*, that is, the anxiety of being damned. Jesus appropriates to himself 'the weight of the second death'.[38] Balthasar reasons, 'if Jesus undergoes the "experience" of sin [*Sünde "Erfahrung"*] on our behalf, he also endures "genuine fear of death and hell" [*wirkliche Todes- und Höllenfurcht*]'.[39] He writes, 'on the Mount of Olives, Christ's anguish was a co-suffering with sinners, of such a kind that the real loss of

32. Meiattini, *Sentire cum Christo*, p. 146 (author's translation).

33. Cf. Meiattini, *Sentire cum Christo*, p. 146. Meiattini reasons, 'Every anguish and pain both of the new and of the Old Testament are overcome and in a way embraced by those that are Christological. In fact the distance from the Father that Christ measures is the infinite intra-trinitarian distance that now assume the form of abandonment and of dereliction' (author's translation). See also, p. 146.

34. Meiattini, *Sentire cum Christo*, p. 146 (author's translation).

35. Cf. *CA*, p. 37; Eng., pp. 74–5.

36. *HW*, p. 78; Eng., p. 108.

37. *CA*, p. 37–8; Eng., p. 75.

38. Meiattini, *Sentire cum Christo*, p. 145 (author's translation); cf. *CA*, p. 37.

39. *TDIII*, p. 266; Eng., p. 287.

God which threatened them (the *poena damni*) was assumed by the incarnate Love of God in the form of a *timor gehennalis*'.[40] Balthasar sees the *timor gehennalis* as a definite part of Jesus' anxiety suffered vicariously for sinners. Whether or not Christ did or even could experience the *timor gehennalis* is a controverted topic and will be taken up in Chapter 7 of this study.[41] Jesus experiences in Gethsemane the anxiety and horror of every sinner which by right they should have in God's judgement of sin for Jesus 'no longer distinguishes himself and his fate from those of sinners'.[42] Jesus allows all the blame for the entirety of sin to be laid upon himself, and because he is the Divine Son, he paradoxically can plunge most deeply into the sinner's position of Godforsakeness.

Our author describes of Jesus' apparently objectless *timor gehennalis* in his meditations on the Sacred Heart:

> Is fear finally coming over you – a fear men know nothing about? I don't mean fear of some impending, some definite catastrophe. For such fear is limited: it has its object and man's consciousness is directed to that object. And, with us men, hope always remains as an inseparable companion of fear. Maybe I can still escape from the burning house; perhaps we can still succeed in reaching the caved-in-mine-shaft in time; perhaps I will still be pardoned even at the last minute? What you suffer is a shapeless fear. It is a sea of fear without shores, fear-in-itself. The fear which is the core of sin. The fear of God and his inescapable judgment. The fear of hell. The fear of never again seeing the face of the Father for all eternity. The fear that love itself and every creature with it is have dropped you irretrievably into the abyss. You fall into the bottomless; you are lost. Not the faintest shimmer of hope to limit this fear. For in what could you still have hope? That the Father might still pardon you? He will not, cannot, does not want to do it. Only for the price of your sacrifice does he intend to pardon the world: the world, not you. Nothing at all is said about anything beyond your fear. Mercy? But you are yourself God's mercy, and it consists in your own ruination. Someone has to be the scapegoat, and you are it. Indeed, you yourself wanted it this way.[43]

His thoughts continue, according to Balthasar's meditation, to consider the apparent futility of his mission and the future sinfulness of his Church.[44]

40. *TDT*, p. 100; Eng., p. 104.

41. Balthasar poses the question aptly quoting R. Pullus: 'How, then, did the anguish dominate? Did he, for example, experience the anguish which is ours when we face some prospect that we know by reason will not eventualize? At night, we fear to encounter a dead man, but we know that that will not happen. Or again, when we find ourselves on an exposed height, a feeling of vertigo takes us over completely, so that we are anxious lest we fall over a precipice, even though our reason tells us that we are quite safe, and our anxiety is baseless. Now if it is superstitious in such a state of anxiety to pray that what we fear may not happen, while we know, however, that it will not happen, how could the prayer of Christ be rational (admitting that the feeling of being damned did seize him) if it was a persistent request to escape damnation but if too Christ remained, despite that, convinced that he was saved?' (*TDT*, p. 98; Eng., pp. 102–3).

42. *TDT*, p. 100; Eng., p. 104.

43. *HW*, pp. 78–9; Eng., pp. 108–9.

44. Cf. *HW*, pp. 80–2; Eng., pp. 111–13.

Balthasar also describes this vicariously suffered anxiety in his work on Bernanos. He quotes Bernanos, 'Fear of death is a universal feeling that necessarily comes in all sorts of forms. Some of these are surely beyond the reach of human language. There is only one man who has known them all and this is Christ in his agony'.[45] He quotes Bernanos again:

> From the Garden of Olives to Calvary, our Lord has in advance experienced and expressed all agonies – even the most humble, even the most desolate. . . . Many theologians believe that, in Jesus Christ at the moment of his Passion, human nature was abandoned to the experience of every feeling a man is capable of. . . . Christ does indeed want to blaze for martyrs the glorious highway of a death without fear, but he also wants to precede each one of us through the darkness of mortal anguish.[46]

A third aspect of the deepest kind of anxiety for Jesus is that it not only expresses the anxiety of sinners in the *timor gehennalis*, but also reveals 'God's own anguish' for the world.[47] Balthasar describes it as 'the anguish [*Angst*] that God (in human form) suffers on account of his world, which is in danger of being lost to him – which, indeed, at that moment *is* an utterly lost world'.[48] By suffering anxiety, Jesus reveals in a human way how much the world matters to God, and how concerned he is for it. These three dimensions which help describe the cognitive dimension of Jesus' anxiety, according to Balthasar, combine to describe 'an anguish [*Angst*] he wanted to have without any consolation or relief, since from it was to come every consolation and relief for the world. Therefore, it is, in the proper and strict sense of the word, the absolute anxiety, which undergirds and surpasses every other anxiety and thus becomes the standard and tribunal for all'.[49]

The ultimate trial

Jesus' anxiety in Gethsemane from awareness of the imminent hour, cup and baptism, and suffering the *timor gehennalis* in a unique and vicarious manner, places him within the situation of the most profound testing (πειρασμός). In a general sense, πειρασμός is an expressly human experience meaning to put to some sort of test, which is accompanied by risk, uncertainty, burdening and danger and is rarely found in secular Greek.[50] Within such testing, some danger threatens 'to cause a person to depart from the correct path'.[51] This testing in Gethsemane evokes the memory of his temptations before embarking on his public ministry as well as God's testing of the righteous in the Old Testament. The context of his prayer in Gethsemane suggests that this πειρασμός is

45. *B*, p. 420; Eng., p. 469.
46. *B*, p. 420; Eng., p. 469.
47. *CA*, p. 37; Eng., p. 73.
48. *CA*, p. 38; Eng., p. 75 (Balthasar's italics).
49. *CA*, p. 38; Eng., p. 75
50. Cf. EDNT, pp. 64–5.
51. EDNT, p. 65.

eschatological and apocalyptic in nature.[52] Our author observes, 'Jesus prays *in* the peirasmos, whereas the disciples pray to be preserved *from* it'.[53] The situation of Gethsemane places Jesus in this greatest of trials in which his mission hangs in the balance of his choice. Anxiety is present because the possibility to avoid the suffering still exists.

Notably absent from the testing in Gethsemane is the devil. Jesus' agony in the Garden is played out entirely between him and Father. Balthasar writes, 'What matters in it is the bearing away of the sins of the world (John 1, 29). By that event, the enemy power is "disarmed" (Colossians 2, 15) without the appearance of struggle against it'.[54]

Declared useless

A final dimension to Christ's anxiety in Gethsemane is his being declared useless, that his mission is meaningless. Balthasar writes that this aspect 'already appears in the earliest stratum of the passion predictions (*apodokimasthenai*: "to be declared useless", Mark 8, 31; Luke 9, 22; 17, 25)'.[55] The Greek word, ἀποδοκιμάζω, means to reject after scrutiny and deem unworthy and unfit, even to be rejected by God.[56] Jesus' experience of shame and suffering falls beyond the reach of the righteous of the Old Testament who would not be abandoned by God. Balthasar notes, 'John sets down in conscious opposition the contrary affirmation – Jesus has continued his own "right to the end", *eis telos*, 13, 1) [*sic*], namely, without looking to anything beyond the death in abuse that was his'.[57] Our author describes the walling off of meaning from Jesus' consciousness in the culmination of all his obedience in Gethsemane: 'If the first Passion predictions explicitly mention Resurrection on the third day, and so exaltation after abasement, on the Mount of Olives all such peep-holes into future glorification are walled off'.[58] The Old Testament schema of the suffering servant subsequently exalted and rewarded dissolves into the one thing necessary.[59] At this point the only meaning left for Jesus is doing the Father's will.

Jesus is then handed over (*tradere*, παραδίδωμι) to Judas which inaugurates the arrival of the hour. His anxiety finishes as the threatening (and destructive) evil which was imminent on the horizon now crashes upon him. The significance of Jesus' being handed over for our theme is that the word indicates that

52. Cf. EDNT, p. 65; BDAG, p. 793.

53. *TDT*, p. 96; Eng., p. 100 (Balthasar's italics).

54. *TDT*, p. 102; Eng., p. 107.

55. *TDT*, p. 101; Eng., p. 106. He continues that it is further developed in 1 Cor. 4.10ff, 1 Pt. 2.19ff. and Heb. 12.2; 13.13, cf. 10.33.

56. Cf. BDAG, p. 110; Jer. 6.30; 7.29; 14.19.

57. *TDT*, p. 102; Eng., p. 106. The hanging parenthetical mark is a typographical error in the English translation.

58. *TDT*, p. 101; Eng., p. 106.

59. Cf. *TDT*, p. 101; Eng., p. 106.

Jesus is marked as the abandoned one.[60] In commenting on the *Dialogues of the Carmelites*, Balthasar indicates Jesus' abandonment in quoting a conversation between two of the Carmelites:

> Sister Martha: In the Garden of Olives Christ was no longer master of anything. Human anguish had never risen to that pitch of intensity, nor will it ever reach that level again. Anguish had submerged everything in him, except for the uppermost tip of the soul where his divine acceptance was realized. . . .
>
> Sister Claire: The martyrs were upheld by Christ, but Christ himself was aided by no one because all help and all mercy come from him. No living being ever went into death more alone and more unarmed than he.[61]

Some aspects of Christ's anxiety in Gethsemane are not treated by Balthasar. He does not include in his description the other Greek words like περίλυπός ('deeply grieved') found in Mk. 14.34 and Mt. 26.38, and that this grief is ἕως Θανάτου ('unto death') in Mk. 14.34 and Mt. 26.38. Our author also does not dwell upon the αγωνία and the physiological dimension of the ambiguous ὁ ἱδρὼς ἀυτοῦ ὡσεὶ θρόμβοι αἵματος ('the sweat of him as drops of blood') found uniquely in Lk. 22.44. He also does not dwell on Jesus' petition that the cup pass from him. These other aspects could provide a fuller picture of the phenomenon of Jesus' anxiety.

Christ's Anxiety on the Cross

The anxiety of Gethsemane culminates in 'absolute anxiety' [*absolute Angst*] in the Son's abandonment in the 'hour of darkness' and manifested in his anguished cry on the Cross.[62] Balthasar writes that the anxiety of Jesus crucified surpasses the experience of the prophets: 'My loins are filled with anguish; pangs have seized me, like the pangs of a woman in travail; I am bowed down so that I cannot hear, I am dismayed so that I cannot see. My mind reels, horror has appalled me; the twilight that I longed for has been turned for me into trembling' (Is 21.3–4).[63] The hour of darkness which engulfs Jesus on the Cross heightens his anxiety beyond all previous revelation since 'the Light of

60. Balthasar writes, 'Though Jesus' being handed over has its deepest roots in the Father handing over the Son to the world, the term can also mean God delivering his people into the hands of its enemies. Thus 'He who is thus handed over is, in the truest sense of the word, abandoned by God'. God ceases to dispose of him, and his enemy does so instead' (*TDT*, p. 103; Eng., p. 108). Balthasar holds that the theology of the *traditur* 'can only be maintained in a Trinitarian fashion'. He writes, 'The Christ was deliberately given over by the Father to a deadly destiny. God rejected him and delivered him to the death-dealing powers, whether these be called "man" or "death" . . . "God made him to be sin" (II Corinthians 5, 21), the Christ is the accursed of God. . . . Here the *theologia crucis* comes to expression in a way than which none more radical can be conceived' (*TDT*, p. 107; Eng., pp. 111–12).

61. *B*, p. 420; Eng., p. 469.

62. *CA*, p. 38; Eng., p. 75.

63. *HIII/2/2*, p. 194; Eng., pp. 209–10.

the world itself has been obscured'.[64] The cosmic darkening of the light corresponds to the inner darkness of Jesus in his abandonment. This absolute anxiety that Balthasar observes in Jesus on the Cross is predicated on the fact that the subject who dies is the Divine Son. Balthasar describes this absolute anxiety:

> This anxiety is drained to the dregs upon the Cross in the actual abandonment of the Son by the Father. Since the subject who endures this abandonment in his human nature is divine, it is an absolute forsakenness [*absolute Verlassenheit*] and therefore the absolute measure of the abyss (ἄβυσσος) and of every other abysmal experience. Only the Son knows exhaustively what it means to be forsaken by the Father, for he alone knows who the Father is and what the Father's intimacy and love are.[65]

Our author gives poetic voice to this anxiety in *Das Herz der Welt*:

> At that time, when I hung in torment and dread rushed into my soul because of the forsakenness, rejectedness, uselessness of my suffering, and all was gloomy, and only the seething rage of that mass of teeth hissed up mockingly at me, while heaven kept silence, shut tight as the mouth of the scoffer (but through the open gates of my hands and feet my blood bubbled out in spurts, and with each throb my Heart became more desolate, strength poured out from me in streams and there remained only faintness, death's fatigue, infinite failure), and at last I neared that mysterious and final spot on the very edge of being, and then – the fall into the void, the capsizing into the bottomless abyss, the vertigo, the finale, the un-becoming: that colossal death which only I have died.[66]

The Uniqueness of Christ's Anxiety

Balthasar's description shows Christ's anxiety as completely human, yet at the same time radically unique.[67] The uniqueness of Christ's anxiety vis-à-vis all other human anxiety is based upon the hypostatic union of his two natures, and that the subject of his sufferings, the 'I' of Jesus who suffers is the 'I' of the divine Person of the Son. Thus he is able to suffer anxiety in a manner a human person could not. His anxiety, furthermore, is not only

64. *CA*, p. 39; Eng., p. 76. 'Darkness came over the whole land' – 'Eli, Eli, lama sabachthani?' (Mt. 27.45–46, 51–52). The external darkness of the crucifixion expresses for our author 'the objectivity and cosmic significance of the inner "hour of darkness"' of Jesus. The darkness in the Matthean view also 'coincides with the end of the world, with – to be more precise – the "Day of Yahweh". The darkness over the whole earth is not primarily, in the light of Amos 8, 9–10, a sympathetic mourning of the cosmos for the death of the Jesus, but a mourning of God himself [as in Zech. 12, 10]' (*TDT*, p. 123; Eng., p. 127).

65. *CA*, p. 38; Eng., p. 75.

66. *HW*, pp. 129–30; Eng., p. 175.

67. As mentioned in the Introduction, Christ's experience is the archetype for human experience. Thus the relationship that Balthasar establishes between Christ's experience and ours is through analogy and 'approximation'. Cf. Meiattini, *Sentire cum Christo*, pp. 27–8.

his appropriation of all human anxiety, but also the revelation of God's own 'anxiety'.

In bringing Christ's anxiety in such close proximity to that of the sinner, Balthasar also sees the necessity to distinguish Christ's anxiety from that of the sinner. Our author seeks to safeguard both the full solidarity of Christ with sinners and his utter holiness as the sinless One. Meiattini comments, 'Balthasar searches for a way that allows one to attribute to Jesus a more profound (archetypical) suffering of the separation from God, but at the same time the substantial difference from that of the sinner'.[68] In appropriating the anxiety of the sinner, Jesus experiences 'not their sin, but the hopelessness of their resistance to God and the graceless No of divine grace to this resistance'.[69] Jesus is brought into intimate knowledge of the interior effects (divine wrath) and of the nature of sin without ever having committed it. The uniqueness of Christ's anxiety from that of the sinner also means that Christ's anxiety is *greater* than that of the sinner since his anxiety expresses the distinction between the divine Son and the Father, a distinction which subsumes within itself the distance created by the 'No' of the sinner towards God. Christ's anxiety is an expression of Trinitarian love.

Conclusion

Balthasar's description of Christ's anxiety, gleaned from the Gospels, focuses on Christ's fear and terror which isolates, his realization of standing on the brink of his hour, of drinking from the cup of divine wrath and of receiving his baptism all the way to experiencing the *timor gehennalis*. Gethsemane also involves the anxiety of being put to the ultimate test and being declared useless and a failure in his mission. Finally, Jesus' anxiety culminates on the Cross with his cry of abandonment in Godforsakenness.

Balthasar's presentation of the phenomenon of Jesus' anxiety does not draw attention to the physiological aspect, but rather emphasizes above all the cognitive dimension in facing a shameful death, the apparent failure of his mission, and his appropriation of the entire sin of the world. There is no indication of any behavioural avoidance in Jesus' anxiety. According to Balthasar, Jesus' is the deepest and most unique anxiety, far surpassing any level of anxiety in the human realm, because he is the Incarnate Son, most intimate with the Father and totally innocent. His anxiety not only appropriates all human anxiety, but also reveals God's 'anxiety' for the world as a manifestation of Trinitarian love. He writes, 'if the suffering of man points only to that Son of Man behind him, then the Son through his suffering points to *the wounded Heart of Father*'.[70]

68. Meiattini, *Sentire cum Christo*, p. 147 (author's translation).
69. *TDIII*, p. 325; Eng., p. 349; cf. Meiattini, *Sentire cum Christo*, p. 147.
70. *B*, p. 172; Eng., p. 191.

Part One Conclusion

The first part of this study was framed by the question: Did Hans Urs von Balthasar understand the phenomenon of anxiety? We can answer that he offers a phenomenology of anxiety that resonates with the psychiatric description offered in the Introduction and, therefore, did indeed have an adequate grasp of the phenomenon both in the human condition and in Jesus Christ. He experienced difficult situations in his own life as well as his intimate acquaintance of von Speyr's anxiety. Besides living through the anxious situations of his life, Balthasar most often employs his attentive, sympathetic listening – especially in literature – to show that he understood the phenomenon. Moreover, he argues that the Lord Jesus himself suffered anxiety in his human life, and Jesus' anxiety not only brings the phenomenon of anxiety into the Triune God, it also reveals God's love for the world.

Part Two

The Garden of Eden: Anxiety's Origins

Chapter 3

Anxiety from Discursive Reasoning

This is the profound secret of innocence, that at the same time it is anxiety.
(Søren Kierkegaard)[1]

After establishing Balthasar's grasp of the phenomenon of anxiety, we are now in a position to begin to unpack his interpretation of it. Part Two of this study moves from the description of anxiety gleaned 'East of Eden' and begins to interpret it by taking the conversation towards the 'Garden of Eden'. The phenomenon of anxiety provokes the thinking person to seek an explanation. From where does anxiety come? Where does it reside within a person? The first level of interpretation in this study is an *anthropological* analysis in which Balthasar evaluates the philosophical and psychological interpretations of anxiety concerning its operation and origin in the human person, represented by Kierkegaard and Freud, respectively. In this investigation, we seek to locate the various *loci* of anxiety as well as its deepest origin according to Balthasar.

Kierkegaard is treated first not only because he was the first in recent times to bring the theme to centre stage in philosophical and religious thought, but also because Balthasar gives him greatest attention. The present chapter investigates Kierkegaard's interpretation of anxiety in the rational activity of the human mind according to his concept of anxiety. Balthasar recognizes that Kierkegaard's treatment of anxiety is 'lucid and equally profound', and was 'the first and last attempt to come to terms theologically with his subject . . . even if only in an introductory manner'.[2] Before entering into the 'very subtle'[3] debate between the two authors, we first offer a basic sketch of Kierkegaard's concept of anxiety and its origin.

1. Kierkegaard, *The Concept of Anxiety* (trans. R. Thomte; Kierkegaard's Writings, vol. 8; Princeton: Princeton University Press, 1980), p. 41.

2. *CA*, 7; Eng., pp. 31–2. Balthasar's dialogue with Kierkegaard on the origin of anxiety takes place mostly if not entirely in *CA*, and only briefly mentions the theme in relation to Kierkegaard in *Apokalypse der deutschen Seele*. Jörg Splett observes that Balthasar gives a brief mention of Kierkegaard's notion of anxiety in the first volume of this work, yet does not develop it (cf. Splett, 'Der Christ und seine Angst erwogen mit Hans Urs von Balthasar', in P. Reifenberg and A. van Hooff (eds.), *Gott für die Welt: Henri de Lubac, Gustav Siewerth und Hans Urs von Balthasar in ihren Grundanliegen* [Festschrift W. Seidel; Mainz: Matthias Grünewald Verlag, 2001] pp. 315–31 [315]).

3. Tourenne, 'Un théologien et son temps', in von Balthasar, *Le Chrétien et l'angoisse* (repr. 2, Paris: Desclée de Brouwer, 1994), pp. 7–31 (25; Eng., 23).

Kierkegaard's Concept of Anxiety

Man as body–soul and spirit

Kierkegaard presents his concept of anxiety and its origin in *Sickness unto Death* and especially *The Concept of Anxiety*.[4] He posits that man is compound of body and soul – body denoting the physical aspect of his being and soul the psychological aspect. Yet for Kierkegaard, the body–soul composite does not yet constitute man as a self, an 'I'. One becomes an 'I' when the third aspect of his being comes into play, his 'spirit'. Kierkegaard writes, 'Man is a synthesis of the psychical and the physical; however, a synthesis is unthinkable if the two are not united in a third. This third is spirit'.[5] Spirit is the power of being within the body–soul unity which allows this unity to relate to itself. Man's spirit brings a dialectical aspect to man's being. Spirit is 'the power of possibility', a 'restless possibility for man', yet 'independent of the self'.[6] It is 'the instinct of the self to take responsibility for itself'.[7] At the beginning of man's individual development, according to Kierkegaard, his 'primal state' consists of the body–soul unity existing in an immediate and passive way with spirit latent within in a 'dreamlike' state.

Spirit, however, does not remain latent. It emerges from within man and provokes the passive unity of body and soul. Spirit pushes man to open himself up, and to move outside himself into the realm of possibility in order to actualize himself. Kierkegaard's view will differ from Freud's, as we will see in the next chapter, in that man is not brought out of himself by an external force, namely, the frustration of desire, but rather is provoked from within himself by his spirit. It is only in this outward movement to actualize his potentiality that man becomes an 'I', a true self. In this way, Kierkegaard's position will be closer to Balthasar's relational-I. Spirit mediates the relationship of the immediate unity of body and soul with itself forming it into a synthesis which is both rational and responsible. If in spirit he remains engaged with Being in taking responsibility for himself in moving into the realm of possibility, man is a self. To the degree that he does not engage Being, either through weakness or defiance, his selfhood is diminished. The synthesis of body–soul and spirit is not necessary but is done in freedom, a self-determinate rather than indeterminate freedom.

Man, therefore, is constituted by body, soul and spirit, with his spirit grounding his selfhood in a dialectic of the body–soul unity in relation to itself. He oscillates within himself in his body–soul unity being in relation to

4. Cf. Kierkegaard, *The Sickness Unto Death* (trans. W. Lowrie; Garden City: Doubleday, 1954).

5. Kierkegaard, *The Concept of Anxiety*, p. 43.

6. J. P. Cole, *The Problematic Self in Kierkegaard and Freud* (New Haven: Yale University Press, 1971), p. 15. 'Spirit' in the Kierkegaardian sense resembles man's rationality (his ability to reflect and engage Being), and possesses characteristics reminiscent of St. Augustine's restless heart or the scholastic *desiderium naturale*.

7. Ibid., p. 57.

itself through spirit. This micro-dialectic also indicates the macro-dialectic of philosophical inquiry between the finite and infinite, the necessary and the possible, and the temporal and eternal. In the expanding movement of the dialectic, the body–soul unity moves outward 'infinitizing' itself amid the possibilities, then it returns back to itself in a 'finitizing' movement. Cole writes, 'the self is a dialectical relation between the finite, immediate self one is, and the infinite image of the self which Spirit projects before it'.[8] Kierkegaard nevertheless holds that one cannot move outward to engage Being and 'infinitize' itself unless in relation to God.[9]

The origin of anxiety in the realization of possibility

From Kierkegaard's point of view, man's spirit is an ambiguous, ambivalent reality. He calls it 'a sympathetic antipathy and an antipathetic sympathy'.[10] Spirit is both attractive and threatening. On the one hand, writes Kierkegaard, it is a 'hostile power, for it constantly disturbs the relation between soul and body, a relation that indeed has persistence and yet does not have endurance, inasmuch as it first receives the latter by the spirit. On the other hand, spirit is a friendly power, since it is precisely that which constitutes the relation'.[11] Man's spirit disturbs the passive unity of his body and soul, yet only through spirit can man's body–soul unity develop into an 'I'.

What then is man's relationship to spirit? Kierkegaard's answer is that the relationship is constituted by anxiety. The ambivalent presence of spirit, that is, man's engagement with Being, both threatens and helps man's body–soul unity develop into an 'I'. He states, 'Do away with itself, the spirit cannot; lay hold of itself, it cannot, as long as it has itself outside of itself. Nor can man sink down into the vegetative, for he is qualified as spirit; flee away from anxiety, he cannot, for he loves it; really love it, he cannot, for he flees from it'.[12] It is in this freedom that man understands his contingency, that is, his being can be threatened with non-being. For when a man projects himself into possibility in order to actualize himself and achieve selfhood, the possibility of losing himself also appears on the horizon and along with it anxiety. Thus anxiety arises in the exercise of spirit as man engages Being in the process of becoming a rational and responsible individual.

The goal to which man strives in his freedom, according to Kierkegaard, is to become a self. However, this goal is only attained by the spirit's disturbance or alienation of man's body–soul from itself. Kierkegaard characterizes this development into a self through alienation as threefold: first, from one's immediate sensate being, second, from taking ethical responsibility for one's relations, and third, acknowledging one's ultimate dependence on God. This

8. Ibid., p. 27.
9. Cf. Kierkegaard, *Sickness unto Death*, p. 162.
10. Kierkegaard, *The Concept of Anxiety*, p. 42.
11. Ibid., pp. 43–4.
12. Ibid., p. 44.

threefold development, which Kierkegaard presents in *Stages on Life's Way*, is the passage from the 'aesthetical' to the 'ethical' and finally to the 'religious' man. Each of these stages of development entails risk and threat, and therefore anxiety.

In other words, anxiety stems from the simultaneity of the delight of possibility and the dread of responsibility in one's existential choices to actualize himself in freedom. Anxiety is a shuddering before one's freedom in the dialectic and ambivalence of spirit. Kierkegaard describes the individual's position before the ontological difference: the fascination of apprehension (*admiratio*) and a strange, shrinking dread (anxiety). Man is simultaneously fascinated and fearful of the abyss of possibility. Thus, Kierkegaard concludes that anxiety is the natural reaction of man when faced with the enormous possibilities of his freedom, even before the choice for sin. This anxiety is natural, morally neutral and inherent in man's rational activity. The anxiety of freedom in the choice for the first sin then becomes anxiety over sin.

The origin of anxiety in discursive reason

Kierkegaard's theory on the origin of anxiety hinges on the position he takes towards Adam and his relation to the rest of the fallen human race. Before Adam's fall, Kierkegaard locates anxiety emerging in Adam's 'dreaming spirit':

> In this state there is peace and repose, but there is simultaneously something else that is not contention and strife, for there is indeed nothing against which to strive. What, then, is it? Nothing. But what effect does nothing have? It begets anxiety. This is the profound secret of innocence, that it is at the same time anxiety. Dreamingly the spirit projects its own actuality, but this actuality is nothing, and innocence always sees this nothing outside itself.[13]

In the state of innocence, the spirit is present in Adam but in an immediate or dreaming state[14] which elicits anxiety in Adam because of its simultaneously hostile and friendly character. The anxiety of innocence is 'freedom's reflection within itself in its possibility'.[15]

In his innocence and ignorance of sin, Adam receives a prohibition from God which, according to Kierkegaard, 'induces in him anxiety, for the prohibition awakens in him freedom's possibility'.[16] Anxiety is the psychological state of man before sin for the Danish philosopher. Adam lives in the ambiguity of anxiety from God's prohibition and its consequences which Adam cannot understand. Kierkegaard holds that this initial anxiety for Adam in the passage from possibility to actuality is the presupposition for his original sin. Kierkegaard describes this state of anxiety as dizziness or vertigo. He writes,

13. Ibid., p. 41.
14. Cf. Kierkegaard, *The Concept of Anxiety*, p. 43.
15. Kierkegaard, *The Concept of Anxiety*, p. 56.
16. Ibid., p. 44.

> He whose eye happens to look down into the yawning abyss becomes dizzy. But what is the reason for this? It is just as much in his own eye as in the abyss, for suppose he had not looked down. Hence anxiety is the dizziness of freedom, which emerges when the spirit wants to posit the synthesis and freedom looks down into its own possibility, laying hold of finiteness to support itself. Freedom succumbs in this dizziness.[17]

Out of the vertigo inherent in finite freedom, Adam makes the qualitative, unexplainable leap into original sin. The primary difference for Kierkegaard between the anxiety of pre- and post-lapsarian man is that it is *quantitatively* more because of his increased reflection on it and the additional anxiety that sin brings to his life. Kierkegaard writes, 'Sin enters in anxiety, but sin in turn brought anxiety along with it'.[18] Stephen Dunning summarizes the difference in the following way: 'Whereas sin enters the world identically in each individual, so that Adam is not be blamed for any other person's sin, sinfulness entered the world with Adam's sin, and therefore cannot be said to have "entered" again'.[19]

Kierkegaard thus places Adam in continuity with the fallen human race. He writes, 'Adam is the first man. He is at once himself and the race.... Therefore that which explains Adam also explains the race and vice versa'.[20] Although he affirms that Adam's sin differs from everyone else who follows him, his description of Adam's pre-lapsarian state does not seem *qualitatively* different from man after the Fall. He writes,

> The consequence of hereditary sin or the presence of hereditary sin in the single individual is anxiety, which differs only *quantitatively* from that of Adam. In the state of innocence – and of such a state one might also speak in the case of subsequent man – inherited him must also have the same dialectical ambiguity out of which guilt breaks forth by a qualitative leap. On the other hand, anxiety will be more reflective in a subsequent individual than in Adam, because the quantitative accumulation left behind by the race now makes itself felt in the individual.[21]

Since Adam possesses what might be termed an 'anxious predisposition' before the Fall, and his state after the Fall is one of compounded anxiety, one may draw the conclusion that Kierkegaard understands anxiety as originating in the exercise of human reason before possibility in man even before the Fall. Anxiety is thus constitutive of human nature, a fundamental condition of the finite human mind. Kierkegaard's theory, in other words, does not exclude placing the origin of anxiety in God's own creative action of man's nature. God made Adam this way by making him finite. Adam just made the anxiety worse through original sin. Kierkegaard's concept of anxiety suggests that a

17. Ibid., p. 61.
18. Ibid., p. 53.
19. S. N. Dunning, 'Kierkegaard's Systematic Analysis of Anxiety', in Perkins, R. (ed.), *The Concept of Anxiety* (International Kierkegaard Commentary, vol. 8; Macon: Mercer University Press, 1985), p. 13.
20. Kierkegaard, *The Concept of Anxiety*, p. 29.
21. Ibid., p. 52 (author's italics).

transformation of man's anxiety is doubtful if not impossible because anxiety is built into his very creaturality.

Kierkegaard's Concept Presented by Balthasar

When Balthasar turns to a philosophical inquiry with Kierkegaard about anxiety in the third part of *Der Christ und die Angst*, it is important to note that he does so from within his theological interpretation in which he seeks to connect Christian revelation to man's anxious condition. Our author begins his philosophical discussion with Kierkegaard indirectly by first describing the fundamental philosophical act of *admiratio* as traditionally understood in philosophy. *Admiratio*, or 'wonder', is the fundamental philosophical act whereby one glimpses an existing thing as such through the estrangement of the mind from what is familiar. The 'distance' of the known thing is created by its suddenly being made unfamiliar through philosophical inquiry. The unfamiliarity makes the thing ultimately more recognizable, and arouses *admiratio* in the individual.

Anxiety arises in the human mind, according to Balthasar, from the 'ontological difference', that is, from the relationship between contingency and transcendence, or, in Kierkegaardian terms, from the realization of possibility. In order to recognize an existing thing (*ein Seiendes*) as an existing thing, the mind must transcend all existing things and glimpse Being itself (*das Sein*). A difficulty immediately presents itself, however, because Being is neither an existing thing, nor all existing things together, nor finite, but rather that which holds an existing thing in existence. Being is not an 'object' that the mind can grasp; rather it is that by which the mind is able to grasp. The human mind realizes whenever it thinks that it both *is* and *functions* by virtue of something beyond itself which it cannot grasp. Therefore, Balthasar observes, the finite mind which desires to know must take a stance of indifference towards existing things, widening itself 'so that from such a perspective it can get the measure of every difference'.[22]

But what is this 'emptiness', this condition of possibility, this transcendent view of existing things? Our author reasons that it cannot be 'nothing' because it is not a complete negation of Being but only a negation as 'not this or that being'.[23] 'Nothing' cannot be a place from which existing things are apprehended in themselves. On the other hand, it cannot be 'something' in the sense of one existing thing alongside others. It also cannot be, he reasons, the sum of all existing things because existing things never exhaust Being, and Being as such transcends all existing things in holding them all in existence. In other words, the mind abstracts the form of a particular thing (*abstractio*) and thus uproots itself from its familiar environment and touches upon Being itself. Then the mind returns to the particular thing which now is recognized

22. *CA*, p. 74; Eng., p. 125.
23. *CA*, p. 74; Eng., p. 125.

as an appearance (*phantasma*). In both movements the mind is taken into the constant unfamiliar 'territory' of the ontological difference.

This activity of the mind makes the world abstract in two directions. The first movement makes the particular thing decrease in importance because it is seen as contingent in the light of Being, and Being gains no greater importance since it 'depends' on the existing thing in order to make an appearance in the world. This relationship between contingency and transcendence, the abyss between Being and existence, is precisely where Balthasar locates anxiety in the mind. He concludes, 'The ontological difference gives to worldly being an abstract-ghostly outline which the mind, insofar as it stands in the middle of the difference during the cognitive act, can register in no other way than as anxiety'.[24]

The exercise of discursive reason, which reveals the ontological difference to the finite mind, simultaneously exposes this mind's contingency to itself. Balthasar writes, 'In every act of cognition, the mind must relinquish and lose its footing in existing things and align itself with Being – in which one can never become firmly established [*Boden fassen*], because it is incomprehensible [*unfassbar*] – so as to be referred then back from Being to the existing thing'.[25] The finite mind, in other words, must let go of itself in order to know, and oscillate between the two poles of the ontological difference (the pole of Being itself and the pole of a particular being), neither of which it can know in itself. It cannot know Being in itself since Being cannot be objectified in the mind, and it cannot know the individual existing thing because, according to Balthasar, 'it would really be known only if it could be placed in an intelligible relationship with Being, by which it is the way it is in all its parts – only, I say, if it could be derived from Being and proven to stand in a necessary relationship to it'.[26]

Therefore, our author reasons, the cognition of the finite mind must be suspended over the yawning chasm *between* the two poles of existence and Being. The problem that the human mind stumbles upon is the impossibility for Being to be represented in an existing thing and an existing thing 'to offer a full and complete image of Being'.[27] He writes,

> All the woven artifacts of meaning that experience and science establish and trace between facticity [*Faktizität*] and the norm . . . are actually hanging unsupported, with no way to connect either end, within the void of the ontological difference. It is a void because thinking not only sees that it is not filled but understands that it cannot be filled.[28]

Therefore, every act of cognition means that the existent as such becomes a cause for anxiety because the act always considers the existent in relation to Being. Balthasar continues,

24. *CA*, pp. 78–9; Eng., p. 131.
25. *CA*, p. 75; Eng., p. 126.
26. *CA*, p. 75; Eng., p. 126.
27. *CA*, p. 77; Eng., p. 129.
28. *CA*, pp. 76–7; Eng., p. 128.

> The mind that stands outside in transcendence in order to know what exists cannot help wondering whether it is *worth* the effort expended – indifference with respect to all that exists – if it thereby gains real knowledge neither of Being (which never becomes objectified) nor of the existent (which can never be deduced from Being), and this because the gulf yawns in the very structure of objectivity.[29]

The realization of the ontological difference brings one's childhood to an end. The child understands the particular as absolute. Childhood is ended when 'I' and 'thou' are no longer co-extensive with Being, but recognized as contingent existents. The first act of transcendence in the exercise of reason results in a profound disappointment because the particular loses its absolute character since it is understood to be no longer necessary. Knowing gains an abstract quality. Balthasar explains this disappointment:

> The transcendence opening up to him appears at first to be something enticing, an invitation to all sorts of adventures like the awesome 'descent to the [archetypical] mothers' in the second part of Goethe's *Faust*. Eventually, though, he realizes that the path does not lead *toward* any place, but rather leads *back* unexpectedly to the particular again, and that this path was intended as a cognitive method of knowing better the particular in the world. And yet from this point onward, because the vista of transcendence has opened up, the particular can no longer have the weight of an absolute, as it did for the child; somewhere along the route the particular has become indifferent.[30]

The beginnings of anxiety lie in thought's ecstasy beyond sensation. The reason for this is that the 'space' in which the conceptualization was made possible 'is still inadequate to offer a satisfactory interpretation of the objective world, indeed, precisely because this yawning ontological difference rules out such an interpretation'.[31] He continues, 'The same structure that reveals the truth of Being also veils it; the same structure that causes the light of Being and of the agent intellect (*intellectus agens*) to dawn also spreads to the same extent the night of meaninglessness and incomprehensibility'.[32]

The anxious situation of the finite mind intensifies when considered not simply from the point of the view of the intellect but also that of the will. The aforementioned explanation shows how the intellect arrives at a place of 'indifference' in its abstraction and dilation towards Being in coming to know a particular thing as such. This indifference also appears in the will as the prerequisite for freely choosing the good. Being itself cannot be chosen by the will just as it cannot be known by the intellect, yet openness to Being is necessary for the will to freely choose any particular good. Balthasar writes, 'The same thing that removes (sensual) necessity from the will and transforms it from a blind drive into a superior intellectual faculty of choosing is also what forces upon it an indifference that includes a certain lack of concern with

29. *CA*, p. 77; Eng., p. 129 (Balthasar's italics).
30. *CA*, pp. 77–8; Eng., pp. 129–30.
31. *CA*, p. 78; Eng., p. 130.
32. *CA*, p. 78; Eng., pp. 130–1.

respect to all worldly goods'.[33] It takes a position not immediately oriented towards this or that particular good. The will is free because no particular choice presents itself with serious finality, and this position of the will is both positive and negative. The positive aspect is that the will attains a distance that is free from compulsion; the negative aspect is that it finds itself having to arbitrate between viewpoints, none of which appears *a priori* as 'right in an absolute, totally compelling sense'.[34] The will, therefore, finds itself in a situation like the intellect: having to choose something contingent. Balthasar concludes

> Herein lies the real 'vertigo of freedom' [*Schwindel der Freiheit*] faced with its own infinite, indeterminate and unfathomable character, which can become vertiginous [*Schwindelgefühl*] only because this 'possibility' is counterbalanced by no actuality, that is, no necessary character in the object-to-be-chosen. Once more, it is not our purpose in making this point to undermine true ethics and advocate relativism. But the best moral calculus and abstract hierarchy of values with the surest formulas for choosing cannot relieve the will of its fundamental anxiety of being elevated in the first place to the dizzying level of arbiter and judge (*liber arbiter*).[35]

Anxiety, therefore, arises in the very process of discursive reasoning. Both intellect and will reveal the location of anxiety in the human mind (*Geist*) from the philosophical perspective, although Balthasar gives greater attention to the intellect in his presentation.[36]

Balthasar's Agreement: Anxiety is Fundamental to Human Reason

Balthasar's summary of the ontological difference places him in a position to respond to Kierkegaard's concept of anxiety and its origin in the rational activity of the human mind. It is not difficult to observe the high degree of agreement Balthasar has with Kierkegaard about the fundamental philosophical act and how it inevitably produces anxiety. Just as Balthasar's sympathetic and attentive listening to the phenomenon of anxiety is demonstrated earlier, his sympathetic and attentive listening to the philosophers shows here as well. *Admiratio* stretches forth to know the object; anxiety recoils from it. Yet their close connection helps to explain the choice of a philosopher like Kierkegaard to make anxiety 'the fundamental act of philosophy' not so far-fetched.[37] Instead of the movement of trust Kierkegaard places greatest emphasis on the movement of flight. Balthasar characterizes this movement of flight as a philosophical *via negativa*. Its contracting movement gives the object more 'space' to emerge in its objectivity, and thus is arguably a higher

33. *CA*, p. 79; Eng., p. 132.
34. *CA*, p. 79; Eng., p. 132.
35. *CA*, p. 79–80; Eng., pp. 132–3. The word *Schwindel* in German also connotes the sense of staggering or dizziness and even of being deceived.
36. Cf. *CA*, pp. 74–80; Eng., pp. 124–33.
37. *CA*, p. 70; Eng., p. 119.

way of knowing since the knowing comes not from 'what is good for me' but from the thing itself.[38]

Balthasar admits that Kierkegaard makes some noteworthy achievements in his analysis of anxiety. First, Kierkegaard succeeds in drawing out anxiety as a fundamentally important theme for philosophy and psychology.[39] Second, Kierkegaard correctly identifies the place of anxiety within the very process of discursive reasoning. The finite, human mind as it exists today necessarily produces anxiety from its relationship to the ontological difference.[40] Our author further agrees with Kierkegaard that an explanation of original sin cannot begin with the *liberum arbitrium* because that position presupposes the knowledge of good and evil which 'cannot legitimately be presupposed with certainty'.[41]

He also agrees with Kierkegaard that the transition from innocence to sin requires an 'intermediate term' (*Zwischenbestimmung*) of anxiety, 'which is latent at the basis of innocence and ignorance, insofar as the slumbering mind dimly senses in its depths the endlessness and possibility that are awakened in it by the boundary of the prohibition'.[42]

Balthasar even agrees with Kierkegaard that the activity of discursive thought in post-lapsarian man necessarily produces anxiety. Our author does not deny that the activity of discursive reasoning in the human mind is a primary locus of anxiety. The question becomes whether Adam's anxiety is from his original nature or a consequence of the Fall. Kierkegaard's position is correct, according to Balthasar, on the psychological or philosophical level.

Balthasar's Critique: Anxiety is not Original to Human Reason

While Kierkegaard correctly identifies the human cognition as a source of anxiety, his theory about the ultimate origin of anxiety, according to Balthasar, is inadequate for two reasons: the undue influence of German Idealism and the limitations imposed on his reflection by Lutheran dogmatics. Although Kierkegaard criticizes aspects of both of these currents of thought, they nevertheless exert a strong influence on his thinking about anxiety. Considering these influences Balthasar constructs his critique.

Balthasar's first disagreement lies at the level of Kierkegaard's anthropology. Kierkegaard, in Balthasar's view, overemphasizes the individuality of man's spirit, and does not sufficiently emphasize its relationship to God. Even in his criticism of German Idealism and attempt to sever the 'demonic knot' of its 'Christian-anti-Christian amalgam', Kierkegaard does not succeed in

38. Cf. *CA*, p. 70; Eng., p. 119. On this point, Balthasar shifts the emphasis on the analogy of being, mentioned in the Introduction, from the great similarity to the greater dissimilarity.

39. Cf. Tourenne, 'Un théologien et son temps', p. 25; Eng., p. 24.

40. Cf. Torralba-Roselló, 'Prefacio', p. 17.

41. *CA*, p. 81; Eng., p. 134.

42. *CA*, p. 82; Eng., p. 136.

freeing himself entirely from its 'entanglement'.[43] Man's spirit in itself is not sufficiently related to God, but somewhat constrained by the body–soul and spirit dialectic. Balthasar writes, 'Although his intention is Christian, he so emphasizes the relation of the spirit to itself that he runs the risk of forgetting the main point: the relation to God'.[44]

The second influence on Kierkegaard which invites Balthasar's criticism are the Lutheran dogmatics underlying his theory. These restrict Kierkegaard from granting a state of original justice to Adam.[45] Kierkegaard therefore concludes that the anxiety of pre-lapsarian Adam is only quantitatively, not qualitatively, different after the Fall. Before the Fall, Adam's rational consideration of the divine prohibition makes him anxious, and this anxiety precipitates his fall into original sin. Balthasar comments on Kierkegaard's view of pre-lapsarian Adam:

> Kierkegaard does not admit that Adam is qualitatively different from the rest of mankind. Vehemently rejecting the 'state of original justice', he banishes it to the realm of myth, which ruins theology. Consequently, Adam's state before sin is not qualitatively different (although it is quantitatively different) from that of every man in the ignorance and innocence of unawakened consciousness.[46]

In response, our author poses the crucial question to Kierkegaard's theory taken as theology: 'What is this human nature we are describing [in Adam]'?[47] Where is the starting point for considering the origin of anxiety in human nature, the original state or original sin? Pre- or post-lapsarian Adam? Is this structure within the human mind, which Kierkegaard describes so well according to Balthasar, God's original creation, or a consequence of the Fall? Kierkegaard suggests that no qualitative difference exists between the two states. In denying an original state to Adam, Kierkegaard makes anxiety part of the original creation, that is, God's work. Tourenne comments on Balthasar's criticism of the Kierkegaardian origin of anxiety:

> Kierkegaard's analysis, while showing clearly the genesis of man's anxiety in the face of the void that the mind discovers in itself, fails to evidence the mind's openness to divine transcendence. Balthasar agrees that anxiety is immanent in the mind, but he sees the ultimate root of this immanence, not in man's finitude, but in a disorder caused by original sin. . . . For Balthasar, original sin enables us to understand that the void structuring man's acts of knowledge and freedom is not neutral but is a deficiency, indeed, an estrangement from God.[48]

43. Balthasar, 'On the Tasks of Catholic Philosophy in Our Time', trans. B. McNeil CRV, *Communio: International Catholic Review* 20 (1993), pp. 147–87 (167).

44. *CA*, p. 83; Eng., p. 138.

45. Torralba-Roselló states it even more forcefully: Kierkegaard rejects the Catholic doctrine of the original state (cf. Torralba-Roselló, 'Teologia de l'Angoixa', p. 453).

46. *CA*, pp. 83–84; Eng., p. 138.

47. *CA*, p. 80; Eng., p. 133.

48. Tourenne OFM, 'Un théologien et son temps', p. 26; Eng., pp. 24–5.

The over-emphasis on the relation of man's spirit to itself, combined with his rejection of Adam's original state, 'precludes the idea that man's relation to God affects the structure of the human spirit'.[49]

Kierkegaard's concept of anxiety, according to Balthasar, is based on Luther's dialectic in the mutual causation of sin and anxiety which 'inevitably led to . . . the vertigo of the finite mind when faced with itself, with the rupture between the finite and infinite that it finds within itself, with its own unfathomable freedom'.[50] In our author's view, Kierkegaard deepens this dialectic to tremendous depths. Balthasar continues, 'It is characteristic of Kierkegaard's Lutheranism to the nth degree [*unendlich*] that the fundamental anxiety [*Grundangst*] for him is not (as in Calvin's scheme) an anxiety before the judgments of divine predestination, but rather the anxiety of one faced with the abyss of his own mind'.[51]

Balthasar instead argues that anxiety neither caused Adam to fall nor was it a prerequisite for his fall. Anxiety first entered him through original sin. It was not his finite reason that brought him to take the impossible stance of arbitrating between being for God or against God. Rather the cause of the Fall was the evil serpent tempting Adam to sin. Balthasar writes, 'What brought man from a state of neutrality and indifference to such a position vis-à-vis God that man presumes to arbitrate between God and anti-God? This is ascribed to the influence of the serpent, that is, of evil plain and simple, and therefore belongs to the sphere of ungodliness'.[52] It is not Adam's nature itself that produced anxiety, but rather an evil, preternatural influence which harmed his nature to the point that now the rational activity of his mind produces anxiety. The 'pernicious neutrality' of indifference between good and evil is not God's fault for creating Adam as a finite and rational creature. God did not place Adam in this anxiety producing situation. In fact, Balthasar writes, 'the whole point of the prohibition in paradise was to preserve his creature from it'.[53] Anxiety entering the structure of discursive thought was a consequence of eating of the fruit of the Tree. Man's lukewarm neutrality before good and evil is from eating of the tree, not from the original creation. In attempting to take the knowledge of good and evil unto himself, Adam necessarily opened up his nature to anxiety because he takes upon himself something a finite creature by nature cannot do.

Once Adam falls, Balthasar agrees with Kierkegaard that 'anxiety is the order of the day'.[54] Anxiety is then intrinsic to the mind, but not so much as a natural vertigo before possibility but as a distance and alienation from God. Balthasar writes, 'The mind is made anxious, not by the void of nothingness in

49. Ibid., Eng., p. 25; cf. Splett, 'Der Christ und seine Angst', p. 327.

50. *CA*, p. 58; Eng., p. 102.

51. *CA*, p. 58; Eng., p. 103.

52. *CA*, p. 86; Eng., p. 141. Splett adds, 'Seen in this way, anxiety does not arise simply from the internal emptiness of spirit, but that which could be transferred from the "Serpent" ' (Splett, 'Der Christ und seine Angst', p. 327) (author's translation).

53. *CA*, p. 81; Eng., p. 134.

54. *CA*, p. 86; Eng., p. 141.

its own interior dimension, but by the void that yawns wherever the nearness and concreteness of God have withdrawn into a distant estrangement and have yielded their place to "someone over there", to an abstract relation to an "other" '.[55] The nothingness that makes the finite mind anxious is not simply living in the midst of the ontological difference, for the ontological distance was present to Adam's mind in the original state, but 'the awareness of a fundamental falsehood, displacement, guilt – an awareness called forth by the absence of the One who ought to be present in this "Nothing" '.[56] In the original state, God was present to Adam in his mind so that he experienced no void, and thus no anxiety, when Adam's rational activity came across the ontological difference.

The limitations imposed by Lutheran dogmatics to Kierkegaard's theory, according to Balthasar, do not allow Kierkegaard's analysis of anxiety to attain to an adequately theological level. For Balthasar, Kierkegaard correctly identifies the psychological and philosophical origin of anxiety – within the activity of discursive reasoning. So long as Kierkegaard's interpretation is taken as a psychological and philosophical analysis, Balthasar thinks it correct. Balthasar observes that while Kierkegaard intentionally raises his questions in a psychological manner in order to engage the psychological and philosophical challenges of his time, his interpretation never rises to a truly theological treatment, and 'as a result, anxiety remains for him a matter of the finite mind horrified by its own limitlessness, and God and Christ are rarely mentioned explicitly in this work'.[57] Balthasar does not believe that Kierkegaard sufficiently describes *how* the human mind became intrinsically anxious. The answer to that question lies in the theological realm.

Balthasar's Proposal to Kierkegaard: The Theological Analysis

If anxiety is the result of the Fall and not of God's original creation, does the ontological difference have anything to do with the Fall and the ultimate origin of anxiety? Balthasar reasons that if anxiety is located in original sin and not in God's creative act, then 'God did not create anxiety as a component of nature, and all of the distance or remoteness within nature (as it became evident in the description of the ontological difference and its reflection in intellect and will) would be *partially determined*, in its concrete reality, by the distance of the sinner from God'.[58] Thus, anxiety is not natural to human nature, and Balthasar purports that original sin partially determines the distance between man and God. What does our author mean by 'partially determined'? He suggests that the 'distance' between man and God is also related to the ontological difference, which is expressive of man's status as a rational creature, and is established through God's creative act of a finite, rational creature.

55. *CA*, p. 85; Eng., p. 141.
56. *CA*, p. 86; Eng., p. 142.
57. *CA*, p. 7; Eng., p. 32.
58. *CA*, p. 80; Eng., p. 133 (author's italics).

Balthasar reasons that the ontological difference in Adam's original state did not produce anxiety, but rather anxiety was present to Adam's finite, unfallen mind only as a *condition of possibility*. We could say that the ontological difference in the original state indicated a *distinction* between God and Adam, but not a separation or distance. The fact that anxiety *has* entered this structure is due to his falling away from God in original sin. Our author writes, 'The void that opens up in the mind, the cause of its anxiety, could then be traced back to an *absence* – and whose absence, if not that of its Creator and grace-giver, the "sweet guest of the soul" who had chosen it as his dwelling place'?[59] The ontological difference existed in Adam's state of original justice, but it had a different character than now. In Adam's mind before the Fall no empty chasm yawns between universal and the particular because he sees both as 'transparent towards God, who, standing beyond both of them, grants that he may be known in both'.[60]

What keeps the void from appearing in Adam's mind? Balthasar's answer is the 'natural faith', the trusting adherence that Adam possessed in the state of original justice. The state of original justice and how it precluded anxiety will be discussed at greater length in Chapter 5. God's presence in Adam's mind, writes Balthasar, 'was a presence in faith, naturally', in an 'obedience and love that possessed and embraced God immediately and with childlike certainty'.[61] Our author further describes Adam's natural faith in the original state as a 'faith for which God, though not seen face to face, is the most present, *most concrete* reality, whence all that is substantial in the world receives its equally certain and unquestionable rightness, obviousness, and nameability'.[62] This natural faith is Adam's 'invisible, yet tangible and all-pervasive' relationship with God as they walk and talk together in the evening breeze of Eden.[63] Adam's natural faith prevents the ontological difference from producing anxiety in his unfallen, finite mind. God is not absent from Adam's finite thinking and willing.

But Adam's situation in the original state begs the question: did Adam's finite constitution serve as a kind of 'set up' for the Fall? Balthasar argues that the original state in which Adam was vulnerable to temptation was not characterized by 'creaturely anxiety'[64] (*kreatürliche Angst*) at the possibility of falling. Moreover, God did not withdraw from Adam deliberately in order to open the void so that Adam was in a position to be tempted. In other words, God did not withdraw his presence from Adam's mind so that the ontological difference made Adam mentally 'dizzy', as in Kierkegaard's position. Rather Balthasar reasons that God allowed for the possibility of Adam being tempted. Balthasar writes, 'God had to leave open to man the space that made it

59. *CA*, p. 80; Eng., pp. 133–4; cf. J. Splett, 'Der Christ und seine Angst', pp. 327–8 (author's italics).

60. *CA*, p. 82; Eng., p. 136.

61. *CA*, p. 81; Eng., p. 135.

62. *CA*, pp. 81–2; Eng., p. 135 (Balthasar's italics).

63. *CA*, p. 82; Eng., p. 135.

64. *CA*, p. 86; Eng., p. 141.

possible for man to move away. And God could not spare man the experience of being tempted by what God had excluded and forbidden'.[65] How then was Adam tempted? Splett argues for a distinction between the 'anxiety' of the temptation and what it became after the Fall:

> Instead it would be differentiated within anxiety itself: between the anxiety of the temptation (i.e., that which it accompanied and to a certain extent *is*) and what it became by the fact that the creature gave in. In the anxiety of tempted innocence love at the same time invites, to hold onto it, to which – like his Son – it says: Do not cling to me. Not only, therefore, does *anxiety* and its vertigo prevail here. *Freedom* leaves itself against the invitation for *mistrust* to occupy ('*The faith of little ones*' it is called in Scripture).[66]

Thus, it seems that Kierkegaard's position touches upon a truth about Adam's situation in the original state. However, that which precipitated the Fall into original sin was not due to anxiety from the ontological difference, but rather in Adam's freedom being tempted by evil in which lies the possibility to distrust God's goodness when the divine prohibition and all its ramifications were not completely evident to Adam's finite intellect. His free choice to distrust God in the midst of temptation began to move him away from God, and to take a stand as his own arbiter between good and evil, a stance that is away from God.

Balthasar indicates two paths in Catholic thought that can affirm the truth of Kierkegaard's position while still acknowledging Adam's original state. The first is to make the original state of nature converge as much as possible with nature as such by minimizing Adam's privileges in original justice and maximizing his proclivity to sin. In this line of thinking, which is 'the oldest and best-documented tradition of the Church', Adam cannot attain his fulfilment without 'passing through a choice and a temptation'.[67] The second path begins with a dialectic view of the original state in terms of ideal and reality. In this line of thinking, the reality of the original state can be understood as the only possible (and complete) good of the beginning while the ideal of the original state intended by God 'can only be regarded as an initial prerequisite for the subsequent history and drama of the decision'.[68]

Our author does not offer an explanation in *Der Christ und die Angst* of Adam's leap into sin, but rather investigates it further in his *Christlicher Stand*. He merely asserts in his critical discussion with Kierkegaard about anxiety's origins that 'the space within Adam that became a place of emptiness and indifferent freedom through the withdrawal of the divine presence was a space that God had originally created for himself and had filled with his mysterious and, on the other hand unquestionable presence'.[69] Seen from this perspective, the anxiety producing void within Adam's mind in the act of

65. *CA*, p. 86; Eng., p. 141.
66. Splett, 'Der Christ und seine Angst', p. 330 (Splett's italics, author's translation).
67. *CA*, p. 84; Eng., p. 139.
68. *CA*, p. 85; Eng., p. 140.
69. *CA*, p. 81; Eng., p. 135.

cognition is not a neutral (or even good) void put there by God in the act of creation, but an evil void, namely, the *absence* of what originally was present. The ontological difference was not a problem for Adam in the Garden of Eden. It did not cause him anxiety because of God's immediacy to his mind in their intimate relationship. Anxiety enters the finite mind through the expulsion of God's presence in the choice for original sin, and henceforth invades the intellectual and volitional structure of every fallen human nature. After the Fall, the ontological difference is a never ending source of anxiety for man. Without that intimacy with God in the human mind, anxiety is found in every rational apprehension, in every act of discursive reasoning. If Adam did in fact have a state of original justice with God in Eden, then a deeper origin for anxiety is possible than the operation of discursive reason. Balthasar indicates that anxiety's ultimate origin lies in original sin which brought anxiety into the structure of man's finite mind. Thus does he affirm Kierkegaard's achievement without accepting his conclusion, and instead indicates a deeper origin of anxiety accessible only in the theological realm. Divine revelation discloses the anxiety-free original state and how original sin left man anxiety-ridden.

Conclusion

Balthasar gives a response to Kierkegaard and to all philosophers in the modern period, such as Heidegger and Sartre, who maintain that anxiety is fundamental to man's existence. The short answer that Balthasar gives is that it may be fundamental but it is not original. Our author's philosophical discussion with Kierkegaard brings the theme of anxiety to the threshold of the theological, and even indicates a line of argument into the theological realm. Taking into account Adam's original state and the effects of original sin would help to clarify the deepest origins and character of Kierkegaard's positions about the 'inbetween' in the human mind which causes anxiety. Balthasar is not satisfied with Kierkegaard's attempt at a theological interpretation of anxiety, and neither is he content to remain on the philosophical level. Yet philosophy's ability to grope down to the origin of anxiety in discursive reasoning brings it to the very threshold of revelation, and therefore can be illuminated by divine revelation.

The connection that Balthasar makes with the philosophical inquiry about anxiety opens a door towards his theological analysis. The experience of anxiety opens up for the finite creature the ontological difference between Being and beings, and although that experience brings anxiety, it can also bring wonder and, by grasping the radical discontinuity between Being and beings, come the bedrock of philosophical inquiry which brings philosophical and theological inquiry into close proximity: why there are beings rather than nothing? David C. Schindler makes an astute observation about Balthasar's philosophical treatment of anxiety: 'Balthasar shows how a refusal to allow philosophy to open up to theology cannot avoid identifying that aspect of Angst that is due to fallenness with the Angst in general that is an essential expression of finitude: in other words, when philosophy closes to (the possibility of) theology, sin and creatureliness as such get conflated'.[70] According to philosophy, seen through the eyes of Kierkegaard, anxiety is constitutive of the human mind and its origin lies therein. Balthasar's theological treatment seeks to engage 'the philosophical–theological efforts at interpretation by Kierkegaard and his successors' to see if 'the biblical approach can be more instructive and more profound than the great Danish thinker's "psychological" approach'.[71] The deepest origin of anxiety, contends Balthasar, lies not in man's original nature but as a consequence of original sin in the events that transpired in the Garden of Eden.

70. D.C. Schindler, *The Dramatic Structure of Truth: A Philosophical Investigation* (Perspectives in Continental Philosophy, 34; New York: Fordham University Press, 2004) 45n.

71. *CA*, p. 12; Eng., p. 38.

Chapter 4

Anxiety from Ego-Consciousness

The act of birth is the source and prototype of the affect of anxiety.
(Sigmund Freud)[1]

We continue Balthasar's anthropological approach to anxiety and its origins by moving from philosophy to psychiatry. If the origin of anxiety lies elsewhere than discursive reason, where does it lie? The present chapter investigates Freud's theory of anxiety arising from ego-consciousness in a critical discussion with Balthasar.

Freud's Theory of Anxiety

Why Freud?

Our author treats the thought of Freud in the latter part of the first volume of his *Theodramatik* in which he begins to explore the question of role. Freud is a logical choice representing psychiatry. The most obvious reason is that of the three major psychoanalysts that our author treats – Freud, Jung and Adler – Balthasar devotes the most attention on anxiety to Freud.[2] Some in the psychiatry, however, may dispute the choice of Freud to represent psychiatry in a contemporary discussion about the origin of anxiety. Such an objection is not without grounds for psychiatry itself is in disagreement about Freud's ultimate significance. Freudian techniques in psychoanalysis have been greatly modified over the past few decades, and some aspects of his approach have been abandoned altogether. The choice of Freud, however, is not only warranted but in fact vital to the present discussion for two reasons. First, as a physician specialized in neurology and the father of the new medical specialty of psychiatry, Freud has exerted tremendous influence on the theory and practice of psychiatry and its non-medical offspring, psychology. Second, even if his approaches have been modified or abandoned, it may be argued that his anthropological presuppositions about the human person still carry enormous weight among the contemporary theorists and

1. Freud, *The Complete Introductory Lectures*, p. 397.
2. Cf. *TDI*, pp. 474–99. Moreover, Adler and Jung as disciples of Freud are marked in their presuppositions by Freud even if they eventually broke away from his 'school'.

practitioners of psychiatry.[3] As will be shown below, this second reason will become crucial in discovering the deepest origin of anxiety.

The ego as the seat of anxiety

The bulk of Freud's presentation of his theory on the origin of anxiety can be found in his *Introductory Lectures on Psychoanalysis* which he gave in two series.[4] He reasons in his first lecture that anxiety comes from recognizing a danger and is a signal to flee such danger. He calls this type of reaction 'realistic' anxiety. In a situation that is perceived to be dangerous, the person either responds with fight-flight, or is unable to cope with the anxiety. This second response he calls 'neurotic' anxiety, which he then classifies into three categories: free floating ('expectant anxiety'), phobic ('a relation to external danger can be noted, but the reaction is disproportionate') and hysterical (a reaction without any perceivable external danger).[5]

His initial theory on the origin of neurotic anxiety was based upon his understanding of the opposition between the ego (the conscious self), and the id (the unconscious instinctual drives). Anxiety is produced as the ego's reaction to an accumulation of undischarged or inadequately employed libido which the ego transforms into anxiety. The excited libidinal energy, created by unfulfilled, and primarily sexual, desires, cannot find adequate expression and makes the person feel endangered and, therefore, anxious. The ego then represses the energy in order to avoid feeling anxious. However, the repressed libidinal energy manifests itself unconsciously in anxious symptoms.

The connection Freud notes between realistic and neurotic anxiety is that both have an object of danger, but that the neurotically anxious person's feared object is within himself and is not consciously recognized.[6] Repression, therefore, is the ego's attempt to flee from the libido.[7] The fear of the libido

3. Cf. P. Rieff, *The Triumph of the Therapeutic: Uses of Faith after Freud* (Chicago: University of Chicago Press, 1987); *Freud: The Mind of the Moralist* (Chicago: University of Chicago Press, 1979). Even Freud's most trenchant critics agree on his influence. Cf. R. Allers, *The Successful Error: A Critical Study of Freudian Psychoanalysis* (New York: Sheed & Ward, 1940); F. Crews, 'The Making of a Freud Skeptic', *Skeptic* 7 (1999), pp. 42–9; Crews, 'The Verdict on Freud', *Psychological Science* 7 (1996), pp. 63–8; Crews (ed.), *Unauthorized Freud: Doubters Confront a Legend* (New York: Viking, 1998). Balthasar was a close friend of Allers and the significance of their friendship for Balthasar's view of Freud is discussed below.

4. The first series was given in 1916–1917 (Lecture XXV: 'Anxiety') and the second in 1933 (Lecture XXXII: 'Anxiety and the Instinctual Life') in which he greatly modifies his first theory.

5. Cf. Freud, *Introductory Lectures*, p. 546. The page reference is Freud's own summary of the first lecture at the beginning of the second.

6. Ibid., p. 405.

7. He writes, 'We have received a strong impression of the way in which the generation of anxiety is linked to the vicissitudes of the libido and the system of the unconscious' (Freud, *Introductory Lectures*, p. 411).

is externalized, according to Freud, as a phobia, but this outward projection is never entirely successful. Thus he initially locates anxiety's origin in the ego's repression of libidinal energy, although he admits that he cannot connect this position with his other position that anxiety signifies the ego's flight from libido.[8]

Freud reverses his position by the time he presents his second theory of anxiety in 1933 based upon his newly developed interpretive tool of the pleasure-unpleasure principle (*Lust-Unlustprinzip*) which in turn is founded upon his more explicit theory of the instincts (*Trieb*). Repression does not cause anxiety; anxiety causes repression. In his revised theory, the ego registers an emerging demand being made by the id, and then thinks through the implications of satisfying the demand in a type of reality-testing within the mind. As the ego considers the demand at the beginning of the dangerous situation, it registers the feelings of 'unpleasure' (*Unlust*). The ego, fearing the suffering from the dangerous situation, represses the id's demand. The 'pleasure principle' is the overriding motive force of this compromise between the demands of the id, and the demands of the 'reality principle'. The ego calculates that this compromise will maximize pleasure and minimize the 'unpleasure'. Freud admits that this repression takes place neither in the conscious or preconscious but 'between quotas of energy in some unimaginable substratum'.[9]

The result of the repression can be varied. It is possible for the ego to withdraw entirely from the objectionable arousal producing an anxiety attack, to respond with an 'anticathexis'[10] of its own against the excitation which fuses with the repressed impulse to form a symptom, or the ego itself is altered by the anticathexis. In other words, the ego is able either to divert, destroy or absorb the libidinal energy. The three main aspects of the ego's anxiety – realistic, neurotic and moral – correspond to the ego's dependent relationships with the external world, the id and the super-ego, respectively.[11] The source of the anxiety, Freud conjectures, is ultimately traceable to an external situation of danger whose deepest root lies in the act of birth. Freud is more cautious in his second than in his first theory in describing the id's functioning in the anxious situation due to his pleasure-unpleasure principle.

This modified theory of anxiety affects his view of the ego. Initially he supposed a weak ego when compared to the id, a position he basically retains in the second theory. However, he adds that the ego is capable of exerting its own influence over the id.[12] Nevertheless, the weakness of the ego before the id is revealed in its need to repress. The ego must withdraw to cope with the anxiety. From these two theories, it becomes clear that Freud locates anxiety in the ego, a person's self-awareness.

8. Cf. E. Jones, *The Life and Work of Sigmund Freud*, vol. II: *Years of Maturity 1901–1919* (New York: Basic Books, 1955), pp. 223–4.

9. Freud, *Introductory Lectures*, p. 554.

10. 'Cathexis' (*Besetzung*) basically means a 'change of energy' (Jones, *Sigmund Freud*, p. 323).

11. Cf. Freud, *Introductory Lectures*, p. 549.

12. Ibid., p. 557.

The origin of anxiety in the act of birth

The aforementioned summary helps to clarify Freud's position about the origins of anxiety in a person's ego-consciousness. The ego must contend with the super-ego and the id, both of which continually threaten the ego. If the ego is the locus of anxiety, then how does anxiety enter it? Freud believes in his first lecture, following the etymology of *Angst* (*angustiae, Enge* – a constriction), that the origin of all of the ego's anxiety is physiologically traceable to the trauma of one's birth: 'the act of birth is the source and prototype of the affect of anxiety'.[13] He explains the advent of this primordial ego-anxiety in the following manner:

> We believe that it [the early impression of the affect of anxiety] is in the *act of birth* that there comes about the combination of unpleasurable feelings, impulses of discharge and bodily sensations which has become the prototype of the effects of a mortal danger and has ever since been repeated by us as the state of anxiety. The immense increase of stimulation owing to the interruption of the renovation of the blood (internal respiration) was at the time the cause of the experience of anxiety; the first anxiety was thus a toxic one.[14]

Freud suggests that the location of all anxiety lies in that initial moment of physiological separation from one's mother at birth. The disappointment and longing from being separated from the mother is transmuted into anxiety.

In the second theory, he continues to hold the earlier position stating that birth is 'our model for an anxiety state' and posits that all subsequent experiences of anxiety flow from the threat of the repetition of that moment.[15]

The origin of anxiety in ego-consciousness

Freud's interpretation of the origins of anxiety does not end with the act of birth. For a complete picture of his theory, we must dig more deeply into what he calls his 'metapsychology' (*Metapsychologie*),[16] that is, the anthropological and metaphysical presuppositions which underlie his theories of anxiety. His metapsychology is based upon his theory on instinct which he terms 'our

13. Freud, *Introductory Lectures*, p. 397; cf., p. 407. He writes in a letter to Oskar Pfister in 1909, 'In the matter of anxiety one has to remember that children begin their experience of it in the act of birth itself' (Jones, *Sigmund Freud*, p. 445). Freud's location of the primal event of anxiety in the act of birth was opposed by Adler who nevertheless thought that the primordial event of anxiety was traceable to childhood.

14. Ibid., p. 396.

15. Cf. Freud, *Introductory Lectures*, pp. 557–9.

16. Jones thinks that Freud invented the term himself, and that 'metapsychology' occupied a central place in Freud's thinking by which 'he wished to designate a comprehensive description of any mental process' (Jones, *Sigmund Freud*, p. 185). The term is quoted also by Balthasar (*TDI*, p. 480; Eng., p. 511) and by Servais as Freud's own. Cf. Servais, 'Il dualismo Freudiano di vita e morte', *Civiltá Cattolica* (1989), pp. 240–52 (240).

mythology'[17] yet nevertheless contends that this foundation has a biological foundation.[18] In the second lecture on anxiety, he alludes to this metapsychology in noting the opposition of the instincts of 'hunger and love'.[19] These instincts arise, according to Freud, within the biological processes of the person from which the person cannot escape by way of some external stimulus.

The opposition of these two basic instincts, hunger and love, is the bedrock upon which Freud builds the edifice of his theories on anxiety. The ego, in this view, is 'the restricting and repressing power' towards self-preservation, and the id, represented by 'sexual trends as the restricted and repressed', is the power towards propagation.[20] The ego 'is always the main reservoir of libido, from which libidinal cathexes of objects go out and into which they return again, while the major part of this libido remains permanently in the ego'.[21] At this point Freud broadens his hypothesis on libido from sexual energy to eros (creative) and opposes it to the aggressive instincts which he calls *thanatos* (destructive).[22] The primal instincts of *eros* and *thanatos*, of love and death, contend within the human person.

Jacques Servais comments further on what Freud alludes to in this second lecture about the two contradictory instincts of *eros* and *thanatos*. The life instinct of *eros*, formulated from Freud's own attentiveness to the emerging science of cellular biology in which he observed the constant effort in organisms towards development, is the drive towards development.[23] The death instinct of *thanatos* is a regressive drive towards the past repose of one's original 'inorganic' state as a self-enclosed, primal monad, which was rudely and irrevocably fissured through ego-consciousness and involves a disintegration of one's identity.[24] In this view, the subject is only apparently alive, and basically forced to come out of itself by the external action of other beings. These two instinctual urges create a struggling and compromising dualism within man between the drive which seeks to combine living substances into a larger unity, and the drive which opposes such a movement and seeks rather to dissolve the connection.[25] Freud mentions the similarity of his theory with

17. Freud, *Introductory Lectures*, p. 559. This metapsychology is only sketched in the second lecture and receives further development in his other works. Freud's metapsychology is described in greater detail in Balthasar's presentation below.

18. Cf. Freud, *Introductory Lectures*, pp. 559–60. He makes another reference to the biological foundation of his instinct theory on p. 567.

19. Freud, *Introductory Lectures*, p. 559.

20. Ibid., p. 560.

21. Ibid., p. 567.

22. Cf. Freud, *Introductory Lectures*, p. 571. Freud's position in this lecture is derived from his *Beyond the Pleasure Principle*. See also, p. 572, translator's footnote.

23. Cf. Servais, 'Il dualismo Freudiano', p. 245.

24. Ibid., p. 241.

25. Ibid., p. 250. Freud's theory on *eros*, reasons Servais, pushed him to modify the preceding, more extreme, concept of the primacy of the death instinct, but only slightly. Thus the dualism between *eros* and *thanatos* is disproportionate with *thanatos* in ascendancy, although Freud admits his difficulty in providing evidence for the death instinct. See also, p. 248.

Schopenhauer yet disagrees with what he sees as Schopenhauer's pre-eminence of the death-instinct.

Freud thus theorizes that anxiety originates in the ego through the biological process of birth and in the ego coming to consciousness in the mother–child relationship. This theory rests upon his metapsychology which characterizes the human person as a self-enclosed monad irrevocably fissured and driven by the two basic instinctual drives of *eros* and *thanatos*. In order to reduce his anxiety, man's only option is to reduce his ego – his conscious self.

Freud's Theory Presented by Balthasar

It is admittedly difficult to construct Balthasar's analysis of Freud's theory on the origins of anxiety. When Balthasar comes to treat Freud's ideas in the first volume of the *Theodramatik*, his primary concern is to evaluate Freud's anthropology as it relates to his own theodramatic theory, specifically the relationship between person and role, and not to investigate directly Freud's theory of anxiety or its origin. In fact, our author offers no direct treatment of Freud in *Der Christ und Die Angst*. What follows is an attempt to construct in a reasonable fashion Balthasar's thought on the theme. Balthasar presumes his reader is already familiar with Freud's theories and offers a careful reading in his short presentation of Freud's position which is dense with footnotes.[26]

From 'metapsychology' to anxiety

Instead of proceeding *downwards* from clinical observations and theories of anxiety to their ultimate origin in a foundational metapsychology, as Freud does, Balthasar proceeds *upwards* beginning from Freud's metapsychology to a consideration of Freud's second, more developed, theory of anxiety. The fundamental assumption for Freud's metapsychology, according to Balthasar, is that man is fundamentally a 'narcissistic primal monad' (*narzißtische Urmonade*).[27] Man's first condition is 'an original pregential state in which the developing human being, like a monad, is a closed-in, worldless, "autoerotic" system governed by the "pleasure principle"'.[28] This original state, as Balthasar understands Freud, is an 'eternally (timelessly) self-contained and

26. His eight page treatment contains over 75 citations of Freud's works. Cf. *TDI*, pp. 474–82; Eng., pp. 506–13.

27. *TDI*, p. 478; Eng., p. 509.

28. *TDI*, p. 477; Eng., p. 508. In the footnote, Balthasar quotes three passages of Freud which further describe his initial stance toward the ego: 'The ego, insofar as it is autoerotic, does not need the external world'; 'Love arises from the ability of the ego to satisfy a part of its instinctual desires autoerotically, through sensual pleasure. In origin it is narcissistic, and then projects onto the objects which are incorporated in the expanded ego'; 'the social instinct is not primitive and proof against dissection'.

complacent bliss' and an 'absolute, self-satisfied narcissism'.[29] This primal state is comprised of contradictory instincts, ultimately rooted in the opposition of *eros* and *thanatos*, which exist side by side and are malleable into their opposite.[30] Freud's anthropological starting point, as Balthasar views it, is man as a self-enclosed monad with the dual urges of life and death contending within him. This fundamental anthropological assumption is essential for the development of Freud's theory about anxiety. With such a point of departure, the person's encounter with the world can only be characterized as an anxiety-producing clash.

Anxiety in ego-consciousness

Balthasar then moves from the foundation of Freud's metapsychology to Freud's theory of anxiety. Anxiety originates in the violent and irrevocable fissuring of the self-enclosed, narcissistic monad into the ego, id and super-ego. Balthasar draws attention to the moment of this fissuring not so much in the act of birth, but rather a subsequent act of separation of child from mother also described by Freud: the withdrawal of the nipple during nursing. Balthasar explains Freud's position in the following manner. Initially the infant (monad) views the mother's nipple (source of survival) as part of his own system, and the 'child's pleasure-"I"' is content in 'the bliss of sucking'. At some point, however, the nipple is removed by the mother thereby frustrating the infant's pleasure-'I', and breaks the monad out of isolation because it is made to realize that the nipple is not part of him. Thus the infant's first coming to consciousness as a self is in a threatening situation: 'My desire is not being fulfilled. The nipple is not a part of me'. The clash forces the infant's pleasure-'I' (*Lust-Ich*) to recognize the real-'I' (*Real-Ich*), which represents, for its part, the 'integration of the behaviour patterns acquired through concrete experience'.[31]

The initial clash of having the nipple withdrawn awakens the baby to his own dependence on something outside himself. This experience of dependency (hunger, self-preservation), argues Freud, is how the ego begins to fix the objects of the external world, and thus distinguish itself from them. The infant comes to consciousness as a self in the midst of, and because of, a threatening situation: a mother who frustrates her infant's desire. Balthasar impresses upon his reader that in Freud's system the mother is no interpersonal 'thou', but is perceived by the infant as an 'object' of its own drive.[32] The child's awareness of himself and the outside world, therefore, comes about not

29. *TDI*, p. 477; Eng., p. 508. Freud's monadic starting point is reinforced by his assertion that the human person is 'fundamentally bisexual' (*TDI*, p. 480; Eng., pp. 510–11). His view that male and female are contained within a single human person reinforces the presupposed anthropology that man is not completed outside himself in a 'thou', and understandably therapeutic 'healing' comes not from relationship but from a return to the self.

30. *TDI*, p. 479; Eng., p. 510; cf. the instincts of *eros* and *thanatos* explained above.

31. *TDI*, p. 478; Eng., p. 508.

32. Cf. *TDI*, p. 478; Eng., p. 508.

through the love indicated by the mother's smile, but in the frustration of the child's desire to be self-satisfied. The monadic infant is initiated into the external world amid threat and frustration, not wonder and love.

The primal clash with the mother produces a fissure within Freud's monad. The drive for self-preservation and the drive for pleasure clash within the monad making the fulfilment of its desire unattainable in 'reality', and 'the ego gradually organizes itself as the conscious part of the psyche'.[33] The 'I' thus becomes only a fragment of the whole person, while the remainder (the monad's 'unacceptable' desires) is repressed into the unconscious (id).[34] The 'I' can only partially represent the person, while underneath the ego lies an ocean of libidinal energy in the unconscious. Balthasar observes Freud's eventual broadening of the primal desire of the id from sexual desire to *eros* while nevertheless maintaining a heavy emphasis on the sexual drive.[35]

The fissuring of the monad continues with the emergence of what Freud terms the 'superego' (*Über-Ich*), understood as 'conscience' or socially acquired control mechanisms which have been internalized. The super-ego is outside authority internalized in the person, yet it also represents the unconscious id which opposes the ego, and 'sadistically and aggressively tyrannizes it'.[36] The ego's projection beyond itself towards the super-ego is the vain attempt to recover 'the lost narcissism of its childhood, in which it was its own ideal'.[37] The super-ego does violence to the ego by employing the unconscious energy of the id for its own purposes. Outside authority combined with the libidinal energy of the unconscious combine to form a powerful, anxiety-inducing threat to the ego.

Thus the autoerotic primal phase is fractured and differentiated into the various aspects of ego, id and super-ego through the individual's separation from the mother and in subsequent encounters with the outside world. The totality of the primal phase, which is the totality of man, can never be regained after the encounter with the world. The primal phase exists after that first clash only as the id latent in the ego. The ego, moreover, is not the 'primary phenomenon' but is only the 'conscious part, it is the exposed upper and outer surface of the id which faces the world' while the largely unconscious super-ego representing the id lies underneath.[38] The human person in Freud's system, according to Balthasar, is less the 'I' of the ego and more the id of the irrational and contradictory unconscious, that is, not so much a person but a drive. In this world, for the rationalist Freud, 'there are only "objects", there is no "thou" that could form a bridge leading out of the lonely isolation'.[39]

33. *TDI*, p. 478; Eng., p. 509.
34. Cf. *TDI*, p. 479; Eng., p. 509.
35. Cf. *TDI*, p. 479; Eng., p. 509.
36. *TDI*, p. 479; Eng., p. 510.
37. *TDI*, p. 479; Eng., p. 510.
38. Cf. *TDI*, p. 481; Eng., p. 512.
39. *TDI*, p. 482; Eng., p. 513. This conclusion is developed by adherents to Melanie Klein's 'object relations theory' in which people are referred to as 'objects' (cf. E. Bott-Spillius (ed.), *Melanie Klein Today*, vol. 1: *Mainly Theory* [New Library of Psychoanalysis, 7; New York: Routledge, 1988]).

By working upwards through Freud's theory, Balthasar is then in a position to comment on Freud's theory of anxiety. Balthasar notes the two stage change in Freud's theory of anxiety's origin, first in the repressed libido, than as the cause of repression as a defence mechanism. The threatened ego feels overwhelmed with a possible loss of identity and the threat is compounded by the threat of loss or separation from the mother or punishment from the father in the super-ego. Balthasar comments quoting Freud:

> Freud portrays the situation of the ego, full of pathos: 'Helpless in both directions, the ego vainly defends itself against the suggestions of the murderous id on the one hand and the reproaches of punishing conscience on the other'. It is a 'poor thing', under a threefold subjection and consequently threatened by dangers of three kinds, from the external world, from the libido of the id and from the severity of the super-ego. The three kinds of anxiety correspond to these three dangers.[40]

It would seem then that anxiety is the constant state of man living the conscious life of his 'I', helpless as 'the plaything of higher powers'.[41] A person's arrival at self-awareness, in Balthasar's reading of Freud can be nothing other than self-awareness-in-anxiety. The ego's anxiety lies in being in the crossfire between the id and the external world, and within in the struggle between *eros* and *thanatos*. Freud has *eros* and *thanatos* battling within the person 'in which ultimately eros . . . appears to be only a complicated, circuitous path to death'.[42] Balthasar points out that Freud himself acknowledges that his psychological path has 'inadvertently made landfall in the harbour of the philosophy of *Schopenhauer*', but does not mention Freud's objection to a simple identification of his metapsychology with Schopenhauer[43]. Because of this, Balthasar observes, 'the root out of which we "live" our ego' is amid 'the uncanny, the dangerous and the menacing'.[44] Freud's metapsychology leads to his ego-id-super-ego structure which in turn produces an ego which is necessarily anxiety-ridden.

Four observations can be made by way of conclusion from Balthasar's presentation of Freud's position about the origin of anxiety. The first is his analysis of Freud's anthropology. Man is originally a self-enclosed monad which is irreversibly fissured. Freud's anthropological starting point encloses man within himself. Second, Freud's theory of the origin of anxiety of the ego coming to consciousness through the separation and even threat of the mother is built upon his metapsychology of the instincts. Anxiety is the fate of every human person coming to consciousness because one only comes to consciousness through the threat of the outside world. Third, Freud holds that the ego, therefore, is the seat of anxiety in the human person. Fourth, the ego must

40. *TDI*, p. 481; Eng., p. 512. Balthasar's mention of the three kinds of anxiety refers to Freud's classification of realistic-neurotic-moral anxiety mentioned above.
41. *TDI*, p. 481; Eng., p. 512.
42. *TDI*, pp. 481–2; Eng., p. 512.
43. *TDI*, p. 482; Eng., p. 513.
44. *TDI*, p. 481; Eng., p. 511.

reduce itself through repression in order to cope with anxiety and live in the threatening external world. The conscious 'I' is a mere fragment of his original narcissistic unity.

Freud's approach to therapy for the anxious ego, according to Balthasar, is, therefore, one of negotiating between the id and external world.[45] The encounter with the world always involves a compromise in which something is always sacrificed, for example, the direct satisfaction of a drive by way of repression or another defence mechanism. Balthasar's analysis of Freud's theory draws attention to a type of subtle despair about man's situation. Man cannot be whole again once the differentiation happens within him through his experience with the outside world. No regression can ever regain it. For Freud, the completion for self lies in the self but is impossible to attain. Finally, Freud's view of *thanatos'* ultimate ascendancy over *eros* in his metapsychology solidifies that despair of ever recovering what was lost in man's original fissuring leaving anxiety as the order of the day.

Balthasar's Agreement: The Ego is a Primary Seat of Anxiety

For all his criticism of Freud's anthropology, our author would agree with Freud that the ego is a primary *locus* of anxiety, and even agrees that anxiety is part of the fabric of conscious life for a human being in the world. In his study on Bernanos, Balthasar quotes a passage from *Diary of a Country Priest* that seems to connect with Freud on the anxious nature of conscious human existence:

> More and more I have come to believe that what we call sadness, anguish, despair – as if to convince ourselves that we're dealing with certain movements of the soul – is actually the soul itself. Ever since the fall, man's condition is such that *he is incapable any longer of perceiving anything within or outside himself except in the form of anguish*. Even the person most indifferent to the supernatural nonetheless retains, even in his pleasures, the dark awareness of the frightening miracle that is the burgeoning of a single joy *in a being capable of conceiving his own annihilation. . . . It seems to me that, but for God's ever-watchful mercy, man would crumble again into dust the very first instant he became aware of himself.*[46]

To be self-aware in this world is to be in anxiety, although Balthasar understands this self-awareness far differently than Freud. 'Human self-awareness', writes Balthasar, 'is thus conceived as anguish, but enveloped, shielded, and essentially made possible by the sweet mercy of God'.[47]

45. Cf. *TDI*, p. 482; Eng., p. 513. Cf. Rieff's Freudian description of the 'psychological man' in *The Triumph of the Therapeutic*.
46. *B*, p. 433; Eng., p. 484 (Balthasar's italics).
47. *B*, p. 433; Eng., p. 484.

Elsewhere in his writings, Balthasar indicates four ways in which the ego is a primary locus of anxiety.[48] First, anxiety can surface in the ego through the damaging of the relationship between mother and child. Second, it emerges in the relationship between one's 'I' and his role both in knowing and executing it. Third, anxiety comes about in the ego through the relationship between one's 'I' and the horizon of meaning which measures its action from which can come a sense of guilt. Fourth, anxiety can surface in the relationship between one's 'I' and the future. We now turn to an examination of these points.

Within the relationship between mother and child

Balthasar shares with Freud the importance of the primordial relationship between mother and child. While noting the positive and relational structure of this primary relationship, which our author calls the 'archetypical model' of love, Balthasar is not naive about the precariousness of a child's initial encounter with the world for a child comes to consciousness amid the danger of fallen human existence. The child eventually comes to the realization of the precariousness of his very existence; for example, he did not have to exist. The child's relationship with the world, and even God, furthermore, is dependent on the mother's love. If parents do what they are supposed to do, then the archetypical identity will be confirmed in a more expanded form. If this occurs the child can experience that love comes from being in relationship with another.[49] That initial relationship, however, can easily become a source of anxiety in the moments of separation. He writes:

> The mother is not always there, often even in moments when the child thinks it cannot do without her. The feeling of being sheltered, which can span wide distances, is nonetheless threatened from within by a fear that a life of love could die: this is a fear that can penetrate to the very bottom of the heart, as with a child who, in the middle of the whirlwind of urban traffic, suddenly feels helplessly abandoned.[50]

Any deficiency in the relationship can produce anxiety in the child. The archetypical model can be 'shot through with an anguishing intimation of a deeper, more dangerous separation: the mother can be absent when needed; the child can experience what it would be like to be left alone'.[51]

The anxiety of separation is intensified through the failure of the parents. Their fallen nature reveals how interiorly threatened the seemingly protected world of the child. Balthasar observes:

> Any disturbance the child begins to sense – whether between the parents or one parent and the child – confuses and clouds over the horizon of absolute being and, therefore,

48. These four ways are my own construction from Balthasar's writing. The first way is found in *Wenn ihr nicht werdet wie dieses Kind* and the other three can be gleaned from *Theodramatik I*.

49. Cf. *WdK*, p. 21; Eng., p. 18.

50. *WdK*, pp. 23–4; Eng., p. 20.

51. *WdK*, pp. 38–9; Eng., p. 31.

also its bestowal of all creaturely being as a gift of God. Such a vision becomes troubled, too, because the child can grasp the gift of all existence only within the concreteness of its relationship of love with its parents within the peaceful realm of the familiar space it inhabits. Any violence in this realm of wholeness inflicts wounds in the child's heart which for the most part will never heal.[52]

The relationship between mother and child is precarious in a world where evil exists. Balthasar acknowledges, therefore, that anxiety can exist in the emergence of self-consciousness of the ego, but he does not fix the origin of anxiety there since the anxiety is caused by a failure by one of the parties on the relationship and not by the relationship itself. Therefore, our author will look beyond the relationship to locate the origin of anxiety.

In the relationship between the 'I' and its role

A second locus of anxiety in one's 'I', identified by Balthasar, lies in the relationship it has towards one's role. Being is discovered through action, or, in Aidan Nichols' words, 'it is a feature of human *essence* that it cannot be seized except in the midst of dramatic *existence*'.[53] Therefore, one's role is indispensable in Balthasar's anthropology for the discovery, development and possible fulfilment of one's 'I'.

The 'I' and its role, however, are not identical. Both psychology and sociology, he notes, seize upon this same dualism 'between what I represent and what I am in reality',[54] of who I am and who I am supposed to become. The ego's possible identification with its role is based upon their non-identity. The role, however, conceived is something normative given to the ego to which he is asked to conform.[55]

An occasion for anxiety arises, therefore, from the non-identity of ego and role. Anxiety can arise from the search for its role, the free acceptance of it, and it's execution of the role. The apportioning of roles then becomes crucially important in the process of role identification, and necessarily involves one's relationship towards an Absolute.[56] How are the roles assigned? By fate (Greeks)? By the super-ego (Freud)? By the archetypes (Jung)? By society (Adler)? By God?

Anxiety can then surface in the difficult negotiation of the ego's identification with the role. The world of drama helps to illustrate the ego's position for the actor ('I') to act well makes himself transparent and vulnerable to his role.[57] In human life, this identification is attempted, in Balthasar's view,

52. *WdK*, pp. 22–3; Eng., p. 19.

53. A. Nichols, *No Bloodless Myth: A Guide through Balthasar's Dramatics* (Washington D.C.: Catholic University Press, 2000), p. 81 (Nichols' italics).

54. TDI, p. 454; Eng., p. 481.

55. Cf. *TDI*, pp. 388–9; Eng., p. 415.

56. *TDI*, p. 244; Eng., p. 264 (Balthasar's italics).

57. Cf. *TDI*, p. 273; Eng., p. 295.

'within or above the empirical world', 'by the subject's own efforts', or 'received as a gift in the process of striving for it'.[58]

Balthasar contends that both psychology and sociology propose that the assigned role involves a reduction or a constraint on the 'I'. The solution he develops through the second and third volumes of his *Theodramatik* conceives role in terms of 'mission', a concept which will be explored in greater depth in the Chapter 9 of this study. This relationship between 'I' and its role does not exhaust the possible entry of anxiety into the ego, for it can experience anxiety in the failed execution of the role. For Balthasar, the ego's struggle with role identification, however conceived, produces anxiety.

In the execution of its role before the horizon of meaning

A third *locus* of anxiety in the ego in Balthasar's thought lies in the ego's relationship to a horizon of meaning which measures its action and, therefore, opens the possibility of guilt. The ego, having accepted its role, is now measured by this horizon as to whether it executes the role well or not. In the dramatic context, the actor has responsibility vis-à-vis his role, the director, the playwright and his performance. He must render an account to the playwright for his performance which requires his being faithful to the playwright as well as his own creative action in the role. The 'I' must make its decisions within all the complexity of heredity, and the dimensions of objective and subjective guilt.

The ego's failure towards its role gives rise to anxiety because the wrong action affects one's relationship towards the Absolute. In the Christian context, the anxiety experienced by the guilty ego is called by our author 'sin-anxiety' (*Sündenangst*).[59] Guilt, however, presupposes two realities: an absolute horizon of meaning which serves as a measure of action, and a free and responsible individual.[60] For Freud, guilt arises only from not living up to the ego ideal of the super-ego, which ultimately is derived from 'society'. But whence do these social norms arise? Guilt arises from the failure of the 'I' in its performance of the role when judged by the Absolute horizon whether it is the playwright, the director, fate, the super-ego, society or God.

The relationship between the 'I' and the horizon of meaning culminates and receives its definitive shape in one's death agony. Balthasar observes that death, as in Bernanos' character of Madame Dargent, can become 'a moment

58. *TDI*, p. 454; Eng., p. 482.

59. Cf. *CA*, pp. 48, 53, 55, 57, 59, 61, 65.

60. Throughout the first volume of *Theodramatik*, Balthasar argues that only with the backdrop of an absolute horizon and a free individual, is a meaningful execution of roles possible. With the loss of the Absolute, man loses the ability to measure action (*TDI*, p. 167; Eng., pp. 183–4). But not just any Absolute horizon will do, for it must allow for free action on the part of the individual. Balthasar uses the example of Brecht and his Marxist horizon to show how the Marxist horizon of materialistic determinism eviscerates meaningful measurement of action (cf. *TDI*, p. 304; Eng., p. 327).

of supreme self-recognition, of insight into the nature of things, and an expression of her whole life'.[61] In the dying process, a person's life is revealed as exactly as it is before God, and this death agony 'that closes a life so emphatically becomes that life's measure and judgement'.[62]

In the relationship between the 'I' and the future

A fourth *locus* of anxiety in the ego for our author is its relationship to the future. Anxiety has everything to do with the future since it arises from the awareness of a threat-not-yet-arrived. The predicament of time and death places man in an anxious situation. The individual awakens to life within a finite time over which he has no control and thus which is a gift. Though possibly gentle at the beginning, life's end is abrupt. Time in the world is time-running-out. The 'I' is fast becoming an 'I-that-is-no-longer' (*Nichtmehr-Ich*).[63] The awareness of the future's advent, which inevitably means death, gives the 'I' a sense of urgency and anxiety: What am I to do with the time I have? The 'I' must make decisions in the narrow space of this life.

Balthasar's Critique: Anxiety is not Original to the Ego

Although our author agrees with Freud that the ego is a primary *locus* of anxiety, he nevertheless rejects Freud's position that the origin of anxiety lies in the biological event of birth and in the ego-consciousness. Balthasar's disagreement is not explicitly given and so we attempt to construct his critique. His critique of Freud's position lies in the essentially philosophical, and not biological, foundation of Freud's metapsychology, the construal of the mother–child relationship as essentially threatening, and the treatment of anxiety by reducing the ego either through the normal process of repression or through psychotherapy.

Balthasar's presentation of Freud exposes the mythical and philosophical underpinnings of Freud's theory on anxiety.[64] Freud's theory rests on the two crucial presuppositions. The first is that man is a primal, narcissistic, genderless and self-enclosed monad. In this view, man is essentially non-relational, a 'monadic-I' who lacks an open horizon outside himself. The second presupposition is that contending within man are the two primal instincts of *eros* and *thanatos* which basically constitutes a twentieth century

61. *B*, p. 417; Eng., p. 466.

62. *B*, p. 427; Eng., p. 477.

63. *TDIII*, p. 112; Eng., p. 122. Balthasar connects this point with Kierkegaard, 'Man's being is bound for death.... That is why, as in Kierkegaard, it is unavoidably permeated by *Angst*' (*TDIII*, p. 113; Eng., p. 122).

64. The term 'mythic' not used in a pejorative sense, but in its positive meaning of an attempt to give an overall explanation of the world.

re-proposal of the cosmology of Love and Strife proposed by the philosopher Empedocles (c. 492–432 BC).[65]

These two presuppositions of the primal monad and primal instincts are formulated by Freud in his sincere attempt to interpret his clinical experience, yet Freud himself admits that these presuppositions are not proven. Freud appeals to a mythology for the ultimate justification of his theory, an unusual causative hypothesis for a neurologist. To be fair he thought his mythological causation would be justified through further scientific research. Nevertheless, it is a fair question to ask, if Freud is proposing his theory based upon anthropological assumptions, then what is his ultimate justification for them? Is his proposal just one mythology alongside all the others in human history? Balthasar's supposed objection, thus, is aimed not at the level of the science of psychiatry, but in the unexamined presuppositions which shape Freud's interpretation of anxiety. Balthasar argues that Freud's psychoanalytical theory is not essentially 'hard science', but instead is more philosophical and mythical in origin. Balthasar calls into question these humanistic underpinnings of his theory.[66] Freud's presupposed monadic anthropology leads him to locate anxiety's origin in the ego itself, and this anthropological starting point prevents him from seeing beyond the ego to a deeper point of origin for both the ego and anxiety.

This monadic anthropology in turn affects his construal of all of one's relationships, especially the relationship with one's mother, as essentially threatening. But is the mother–child relationship essentially threatening? Freud thinks so, but what if man is not essentially monadic? What if he is in fact, as Balthasar argues, essentially relational? This would affect how anxiety enters the ego through that relationship and that the ego may not be the point of origin for anxiety.

Finally Balthasar criticizes Freud's proposal for coping with anxiety through repression and defence mechanisms. Freud's theory brings the ego to reduce itself, withdraw into itself, in order to deal with anxiety. But this proposal is again based on his assumption of the 'monadic-I'. If the 'I' is essentially relational, then the way in which the 'I' copes with anxiety is not withdrawal from relationships and the outside world, but to go in the opposite direction: to expand outward, away from oneself, towards relationships and the outside world.

65. Cf. Servais, 'Il dualismo Freudiano', p. 251.

66. This approach of Balthasar seems the most effective among the various theological responses to the critique of religion by Freud and Freudian psychoanalysts. Some theologians engage Freud on the level of his critique, for example, ritual practices as a manifestation of neurosis. Cf. Moltmann, *The Crucified God*, especially the section entitled, 'Ways Towards the Psychological Liberation of Man', pp. 291–310. But it is Balthasar who takes the discussion to its foundation and center – the anthropological presuppositions governing the Freudian critique of Christianity.

Balthasar's Proposal to Freud

The 'Relational-I' and the gift of the mother

Balthasar's writings propose a view of the mother–child relationship in sharp contrast to Freud's.[67] Balthasar understands man as created in the image of the Triune God, three Divine Persons sharing one divine nature. The archetypical relationship of the Divine Persons within the Godhead is characterized by absolute, total, self-giving love. The Divine Persons are constituted by relationship, and thus man who is made in this image is essentially relational. The structure of the mother–child relationship is based upon the archetypical relationship of the unity-in-difference of the Divine Persons. The relationship of mother and child is founded upon identity and non-identity. The archetypical identity of mother and child begins with conception and child's life *in utero* where mother and child exist together almost as one. Balthasar's concept, however, is radically different from Freud's view in which the child perceives the mother as an extension of himself. The child is completely dependent on the mother yet nevertheless is distinct from her since the child exists through the indispensable action of the father and of God. Thus the archetypical identity of mother and child is based on their non-identity insofar as the child is distinct from her. The identity-in-difference of the mother and child, for Balthasar, reveals an image of the Trinity in the human person. The newly created life of the child surpasses both spouses and indicates a deeper divine-human archetype which founds that of the mother and child.

Balthasar's starting point in turn affects his position of how the 'I' comes to consciousness. The unity-in-distinction of mother and infant continue from the womb to the breast and then the miraculous moment when for the first time, in contrast to Freud, 'the child will recognize in its mother's face her protective love and will reciprocate this love with a first smile'.[68] For our author, the mother is no object of the child's drive, but a 'thou', a person. The child becomes aware that he is a unique subject, not through the frustration of his desire, but by being drawn out of himself through the smile of his mother. In that primal encounter of love between mother and child, the child 'awakens to self-consciousness through being addressed by the love of his mother'.[69] Her 'loving "thou" summons forth the "I" ',[70] and awakens him to the transcendental of Being.[71] It is precisely through being addressed by the

67. Balthasar's anthropological view uncovers the crucial question of presuppositions in a theory of anxiety and its origin. Freud is but one example that every psychological theory and psychotherapy implies a certain view of the human person.

68. *WdK*, p. 19; Eng., p. 17. The child's awareness of the mother's love is not the result of a discursive process, but an immediate intuition since the love is recognized as it appears.

69. *SC*, p. 13; Eng., p. 15.

70. *SC*, p. 13; Eng., p. 15.

71. Balthasar writes, 'The infant is brought to consciousness of himself only by love, by the smile of his mother. In that encounter, the horizon of all unlimited being opens itself for him, revealing four things to him: (1) that he is one in love with the mother, even in being other than his mother, therefore, all Being is one; (2) that that love is good, therefore, all

'thou' of the mother that the child becomes conscious that he is 'I' – not the mother but the one-loved-by-the-mother.[72] The awakening of the child's 'I' by the mother's 'thou' establishes an ellipse of love circulating between the two. When the 'I' moves towards the 'thou', it becomes aware of itself. Balthasar writes, 'By giving itself [the child], it experiences: *I give myself*. By crossing over from itself into what is other than itself, into the open world that offers it space, it experiences its freedom, its knowledge and its being as spirit'.[73]

The ellipse of love indicates the inherent relationality of the 'I'. The mother's smile gives the child 'the awareness of a permission to exist that can never be mastered, never taken into one's own possession, an awareness of the gracious favour that grants access to the realm of Being as a whole'.[74] Thus being itself is at its foundation gift, love and, therefore, gratitude. The very process of biological generation of a child through the spouses, moreover, indicates for our author that 'Being in-the-flesh always means receiving from others'.[75] In Balthasar's anthropology, the mother is essentially a gift, not a threat, through whom the child's 'I' becomes aware of itself. Balthasar is clear that the ellipse is never reducible to a circle, which would be another way of characterizing Freud's self-enclosed monad. The child realizes, in this elliptical relationship, that he is somehow singular and exclusive, and possesses the capacity to encounter other human subjects.

From the mother's love and the beginning of the child's self-awareness, the child is initiated further into the external world. The archetypical model of love between mother and child possesses absolute importance for the child because that love is the key not only for the child to become aware of itself but more importantly to open the child beyond the mother's love to God's.[76] The foundational relationship between mother and child establishes the child's relationship with the rest of reality, including God. At first the child cannot distinguish the rest of reality from his mother. She is everything and only later does the child begin to distinguish the mother from God and the rest of the world. This initial moment of self-awareness is understood as love, and this love as the source of all being, both the child and his outside world. If all goes well, he writes, 'The child will see clearly that love is realized only in reciprocity, in an oppositeness that is encounter and not opposition, a

Being is good; (3) that that love is true, therefore, all Being is true; (4) that that love evokes joy, therefore, all Being is beautiful' (*ZSW*, p. 98; Eng., p. 114).

72. Balthasar observes, 'The interpretation of the mother's smiling and of her whole gift of self is the answer, awakened by her, of love to love, when the "I" is addressed by the "thou"; and precisely because it is understood in the very origin that the "thou" of the mother is not the "I" of the child' (*SC*, p. 13; Eng., p. 15).

73. *SC*, pp. 13–4: Eng., p. 16 (Balthasar's italics).

74. *SC*, p. 15; Eng., p. 18.

75. *TDII/2*, p. 162; Eng., p. 177.

76. Cf. *WdK*, pp. 20–1: Eng., p. 18. Certainly the father's love is important as well, for not only does he contribute to confirming the Trinitarian archetype of love through his own love but also his love reminds the child that the child is distinct from the mother.

relationship that is held together in its very difference by the spirit of love and that, far from being endangered by mutuality, is rather strengthened by it'.[77]

This initial instance of self-awareness, according to our author, is both positive and indicates the essentially dialogical nature of Balthasar's theological anthropology.[78] The emergence of self-consciousness is, therefore, not through the frustration of desire and its subsequent anxiety, but rather the perception of love from the other. In Balthasar's thought the 'thou' brings one to a sense of his 'I' as a person. Self-identity comes not from within the self but as a gift from the other. Love enables the child to experience his inferiority and dependence not as a threat but as a way to be loved.

Balthasar's proposal certainly challenges Freud's theory on a fundamental level. However, is Balthasar's position, attractive as it is, just another mythology based in the human sciences alongside Freud's? Freud thought that the biological sciences would lend support to his anthropological foundation. Does any evidence from the 'hard sciences' support one position over the other? Developments within the psychological sciences themselves in recent years seem to lend greater support to Balthasar's 'relational-I' rather than to Freud's 'monadic-I'. Although Freud's concepts of the unconscious, transference and counter-transference, the importance of dream analysis and talking therapy are still respected, his theory on motivation has been seriously challenged in recent years by neurobiological and relational studies.[79] These newer studies show that infants are not motivated by oral, anal and sexual needs as in Freud's theory, but rather are motivated *to be in relationship*, to have reciprocal contingent exchange of communication, and to become competent. The Freudian practice of having the patient lie down and freely associate with little comment by the analyst is considered now to be counter intuitive. The human person learns through direct eye-to-eye and contingent and collaborative communication. The patient-psychiatrist relationship, although asymmetrical, that is, focused on the patient's interior life and not on the doctor's, is a corrective and healing *relationship*. It is precisely through the relationship to the therapist, through talking therapy, that neurosis can be healed. It seems as though Freud did not pay close enough attention to his own insight on the value of talking therapy. However, Freud's underlying anthropology, and even his structural theory of the mind

77. *WdK*, p. 21; Eng., p. 18.

78. Cf. G. Marchesi, *La Cristologia Trinitaria di Hans Urs von Balthasar: Gesù Cristo pienezza della rivelazione e della salvezza* (Biblioteca di Teologia contemporanea, 94; Brecia: Queriniana, 2003), pp. 131–2; Meiattini, *Sentire cum Cristo*, pp. 255–63, for a summary of Balthasar's thought on this topic.

79. Cf. Ainsworth, *Patterns of Attachment: A Psychological Study of the Strange Situation* (Mahwah: Erlbaum, 1978); Bowlby, *A Secure Base: Parent–Child Attachment and Healthy Human Development* (New York: Basic Books, 1990); Greenspan, *The Growth of the Mind: And the Endangered Origins of Intelligence* (Cambridge: Da Capo Press, 1998); Siegel, *The Developing Mind: Toward a Neurobiology of Interpersonal Experience* (New York: Guilford, 1999); and D.N. Stern, *The Interpersonal World of the Child: A View from Psychoanalysis and Developmental Psychology* (New York: Basic Books, 1985).

(id, ego, super-ego), remain influential among psychologists, psychiatrists and the wider culture. It is for this reason that this present chapter remains relevant.

A second development is that psychotherapy has modified its own self-understanding more in terms of philosophy and the humanities rather than the hard sciences. Paul Vitz states that while two of the branches of psychology (experimental and test-and-measurement) have developed into hard sciences, psychotherapy on the other hand has 'grasped that its founding inspiration is humanistic, and that its founders made a serious category mistake in declaring it to be a [hard] science'.[80] The founders of psychotherapy, Vitz observes, used literary, mythical or religious models, for example Freud's Oedipus theory or Jung's archetypes, for understanding the mind as much as scientific ones, and psychotherapists in the current day have grasped that psychotherapy works best by making use of concepts and approaches traditionally found in the human sciences.

'Transpsychological' anthropology

Balthasar's relational anthropology takes a further step. Freud's error springs from the incarceration of man within a self-enclosed system. The father of psychoanalysis seeks to help man overcome anxiety in the ego, but his solution leads him to reduce the self since it has no other measure than the self. Balthasar's relational anthropology remains open to a reality greater than the self, and because of its openness towards God that, while psychological, is also *transpsychological*. By this term our author means a psychological approach to man which understands man as a 'relational-I' not only with other human persons but in his relation to God. In other words, our author appeals to a measure of man that is beyond (*trans*) the psychological.[81] Our author illustrates this transpsychological openness when commenting in his study on Bernanos about the priest and penitent within the Sacrament of Confession:

> The 'experiences' lived by each in this process are the wholly particular kind. On the one hand, they cannot be reduced to the categories of psychology, because the sacramental event at its center is not a psychic but a christological and ecclesial reality, and the psyche merely participates in it by association, although really and necessarily so. And, on the other hand, neither can they be reduced to the categories of mysticism in the narrow sense of the word, because it would be an abuse of the words involved if

80. P. Vitz, 'Psychology in Recovery', *First Things* 151 (2005), pp. 17–21 (18).

81. Balthasar writes, 'A subject's penetration through knowledge into the openness of another's spiritual being can be defined as an act of truth, in the strict sense, only by being grounded in love – the love of God, which God makes available to his creatures. In the absence of such love, the medium of knowledge can only be love's opposite: the concupiscence of hell. Here there can be no neutral middle ground. The knowledge of another's spirit must either be creative through love or destructive through greed: for the other's spirit, as spirit, necessarily stands before God and is, therefore, inaccessible without God' (*B*, p. 385; Eng., p. 429).

> we were to equate the normal, *transpsychological*, sacramental experience of a living faith with mysticism. . . . Since they are genuine *experiences*, they have a psychological side and are therefore accessible to the novelist. And, as genuinely *sacramental* experiences, their meaning and our understanding of it gravitate toward reality that is greater than the soul, but also a reality toward which the soul gapes open and is intensely inclined.[82]

Balthasar's transpsychological anthropology has an effect on how to cope with anxiety. Instead of restricting the ego to cope with anxiety, he proposes that the ego must go actually in the opposite direction: outwards. The unity of the person which the psychoanalyst strives to restore is not found within the person's self but in that person's relationship with God. Balthasar would argue that the unity of man himself is found in the 'Thou' of God. The direction of the ego's movement then consists not in its reduction, but casting itself forward towards God.

Balthasar, Psychiatry and the Measure of Man

This anthropological critique of Freud by Balthasar helps to shed light on some of his critical, if not seemingly outrageous, comments about the psychological sciences. Some of the more poignant examples are psychotherapy is a 'poisonous antidote' (*giftigen Gegengift*) for anxiety.[83] Psychologists, understood as 'the self-appointed scientific "experts of the soul" with all their theories and analyses', are to be cast off.[84] Psychology attacks 'the power of judgement and conscience of a free man' through the 'technicalization of the spirit'.[85] He goes so far as to call psychoanalysis in one place as a 'suspicious caricature of sacramental confession',[86] and in another place 'a pseudoscience that is often nothing more than a truly satanic caricature of sacramental confession'.[87]

Yet it would not be fair to consider our author uncritically dismissive of the science. During his time as a doctoral student in Vienna, Balthasar himself mentions his 'inevitable encounter with depth-psychology and the Freudian circles'.[88] Certainly a bright and inquisitive scholar studying in Vienna during the 1920s would have had substantial contact with psychoanalysis. In fact,

82. *B*, p. 263; Eng., p. 289 (Balthasar's italics).
83. *CA*, p. 10; Eng., p. 36.
84. *B*, p. 198, Eng., p. 218; cf. *B*, Eng., 218n.
85. *B*, p. 22; Eng., pp. 30–1.
86. *B*, p. 368; Eng., p. 410.
87. H. U. von Balthasar, *Gottbereites Leben: Der Laie und der Rätestand: Nachfolge Christi in der heutigen Welt* (repr. 2, Einsiedeln-Freiburg: Verlag, 1993), p. 100; Eng., p. 117. Balthasar leaves this comment unexplained in the text. The general context is the discussion of the various occupations that a layman living the evangelical counsels might undertake.
88. H. U. von Balthasar, *Prüfet alles das Gutet behaltet* (Ostfildern: Schwabenverlag AG, 1986), p. 8; Eng., p. 10.

according to our author, a primary influence on him during his studies in Vienna was the psychoanalyst and student, and eventual critic, of both Freud and Adler, Rudolf Allers (1883–1963).

The friendship with Rudolf Allers

Balthasar's critical openness to psychiatry came through his friendship with Allers, a friendship which would profoundly shape Balthasar's own positions on anthropology. Surprisingly little has been written concerning their friendship, yet our author mentions him first in thanking his friends in his *Rechenschaft 1965*.[89] In Balthasar's view, Allers 'played a part in interesting me [Balthasar] in genuine theology',[90] and made a lasting impression. Yet what is the content of such an impression? John Bonnici and Peter Henrici rightly point towards the importance of the relationship, but do not describe further their relationship or more precisely the nature of Allers' influence.[91] Giovanni Marchesi offers some direction towards the content of such influence suggesting that Allers' thought impressed upon Balthasar the essentially dialogical nature of man and his relationship with God, which in turn influenced his entire approach to theology.[92] Francesc Torralba-Roselló proposes that Allers also inspired the topic of Balthasar's doctoral thesis.[93] Moreover, his Balthasar's friendship with Adrienne von Speyr, herself a physician, brought him in contact with those with psychiatric struggles. Henrici describes her as 'devoted to her patients, especially the poor ones and those with psychological problems', and her uncle was also the director of the Waldau psychiatric clinic in Berne.[94] Such indications suggest that the influence of this psychoanalyst was a central guiding force informing Balthasar's entire theological project and, therefore, makes it unlikely that Balthasar's critical comments about psychiatry are simply uncritically dismissive of the science.

89. This text was later incorporated into *ZSW*, pp. 75–8; Eng., pp. 88–9. He writes, 'To the student in Vienna, the friendship with Rudolf Allers, doctor, psychiatrist, philosopher and theologian . . . was an almost inexhaustible source of stimulation. An opponent of Freud and a free disciple of Alfred Adler, he possessed and imparted the feeling for interhuman love as the objective medium of human existence; it was in this turning from the "I" to the reality full of a "thou" that he saw philosophical truth and psychotherapeutic method' (*ZSW*, pp. 75–6; Eng., pp. 88–9).

90. *UA*, p. 38; Eng., p. 36.

91. J. Bonnici, *Person to Person: Friendship and Love in the Life and Theology of Hans Urs von Balthasar* (New York: Alba House, 1999), pp. 9–10; Henrici, 'Hans Urs von Balthasar: A Sketch of His Life', p. 10.

92. Cf. Marchesi, *La Cristologia Trinitaria di Hans Urs von Balthasar*, pp. 25–6.

93. Cf. Torralba-Roselló, 'Prefacio', in H.U. von Balthasar, *El Cristiano y la Angustía* (Madrid: Caparrós Editores, 1998), pp. 11–23 (11).

94. Henrici, 'Balthasar: A Sketch', p. 19; cf. *UA*, p. 30; Eng., p. 28.

The measure of man

Balthasar's criticism of psychiatry lies in his opposition to Freud's self-enclosed anthropology which leaves man closed in upon himself and not open to the horizon of God. Not only is this anthropology inadequate for the reasons mentioned earlier, but also such anthropology reduces psychiatry's ability to dialogue with major currents of philosophy and theology. Balthasar argues, furthermore, that the science of psychiatry is incapable of adequately measuring man by itself and, therefore, needs to be in dialogue with philosophy and theology. Balthasar's sharp words such as psychoanalysis being 'satanic caricature of sacramental confession' arise from a conviction that psychiatry cannot claim to possess the full measure of man, and in his view, it sometimes claims that it does thereby overstepping its scientific competence and substituting the psychoanalyst for the priest.[95]

Freud's self-enclosed anthropology, and the influence it has exerted in psychiatry, measures man from the perspective of the self. Man has no other measure than himself. Balthasar argues that without recourse to the horizon of the divine, or even its possibility, man ends up being reduced. Our author offers three examples from Bernanos' characters, Drs La Pérouse, Lipotte and Malépine, as analysts who demonstrate the limitation of the psychological sciences in measuring man. La Pérouse's cannot understand Chantal's holiness and finds its scandalous, so he thinks she must undergo treatment.[96] Dr Lipotte, in an *Evil Dream*, finds himself in a situation similar to La Pérouse, but instead of being unable to understand holiness he is unable to understand and properly diagnose the evil manifested in demonic possession.[97] A third example is Dr Malépine in his fight with the priest about the condition of the mayor. Balthasar writes,

> As far as Malépine is concerned, the mayor suffers from nothing but a banal sexual obsession. But what the priest discovers in the mayor instead are the final causes of a process that, even though it could be dressed up in medical categories, nevertheless in reality is nothing less than a self-consuming longing for purity, the nostalgia for 'what we call, by its true name, the primeval paradise on earth, the yearning for lost joy', for God. The doctor is right in a superficial sort of way – in the foreground, as it were; but, because he cannot see the background, which is the all-decisive factor, he is in reality totally wrong.[98]

The inadequacy of such an approach is the attempt to measure man in terms of the self, that is, through self-knowledge. Psychotherapy's goal, at

95. Von Speyr also offers a brief critique of psychiatry similar to that of Balthasar at the beginning of her work on the Sacrament of Confession (cf. A. von Speyr, *Confession* [trans. D.W. Stott; San Francisco: Ignatius Press, 1985], pp. 14–15). Psychotherapy and confession, she clarifies, are not opposed but if done authentically the former will necessarily lead to the latter.

96. *B*, p. 363; Eng., p. 404.

97. Cf. *B*, p. 364; Eng., p. 404.

98. *B*, p. 365; Eng., p. 406.

least as it was initially conceived, is self-knowledge, while Balthasar's goal lies in the opposite direction: knowledge in God, which involves a fundamental turning away from self. The person's fractured unity cannot be healed by throwing him back upon himself, but by moving him outward towards God.[99] This self-limiting first step of a psychiatric approach based upon a Freudian anthropology creates the second inadequacy. It is unable to measure the phenomenon of both evil and sanctity, and thus cannot measure man in his highest human development (maturity) as a saint.[100] Without a horizon beyond man himself, evil remains an enigma.[101] Balthasar writes, 'Eden – Cross – grace and rebirth: this remains the line of the horizon against which alone the catastrophe of evil may be measured. Only the person with a sense for the fullness of truth can know what parts of it have been lost'.[102] Without recourse to the whole of the truth and the tools of the Church, evil remains a step ahead of psychoanalysis or worse, it makes psychoanalysis its plaything.[103] Yet perhaps the greatest reason is that psychoanalysis operating from a closed anthropology that denies the horizon of God fundamentally cannot understand or adequately treat that which it denies.

99. He writes, 'The only true self-knowledge occurs in God, and there man does not see himself but, through faith, God. This vision of God is the truth of what man is. To look back upon himself is already untruth, impurity' (*B*, p. 210; Eng., p. 230). He continues, ' "Personality development" as an ideal is not only a lie; it is also an enslavement, for freedom is to be found in God alone, in the Infinite One, who delivers us through love from the chains and dungeons of our finitude and hence gives us the only possibility of moving, not toward a permanent end, but toward a new beginning' (*B*, p. 211; Eng., p. 231).

100. Clearly the proper object of psychiatry is not divine revelation or its effect on man in the life of grace. However, a psychiatrist operating from an anthropology open to transcendence would be in a position to engage in fruitful dialogue with theology on adequately measuring man the saint. On the other hand, Balthasar writes that it would be 'a fundamental mistake to think that . . . the kingdom of evil . . . can be adequately confronted with "psychology" in the usual sense of the term' (*B*, p. 341; Eng., p. 377).

101. Balthasar comments on the literary attempts to plumb evil by means of psychology: 'Proust, Gide, and all those who have tried to plumb the abyss of evil in man by means of psychology or by a process of uninhibited "stripping-down" have experienced the shipwreck of absolute boredom, of the void with nothing to say. To reconnoiter hell by means of "analysis" results in the kind of disintegration that in the end leads precisely to hell. Such "analysis" will never produce the desired "synthesis" of hell, which can be achieved only from the standpoint of its opposite, namely, God' (*B*, p. 177; Eng., pp. 196–7).

102. *B*, p. 177; Eng., p. 197.

103. Cf. *B*, p. 341; Eng., pp. 377–8. Balthasar writes: 'Despite its intrinsic powerlessness, evil possesses a definite ascendancy over man: it has the power to "seduce" and to lure man into the bottomless abyss, so that the man who would set out to "fathom the depths of Satan" (Rev 2:24) would necessarily be lost in them. The question may be solved only by reference to Church and sacrament: this is where a man can be outfitted with the required armament as with a diver's suit, and the armament is not drawn from the arsenal of human psychology but from the supernatural storehouse of the sacraments. Thus equipped, he can penetrate into the house of the Evil One dispassionately, as one fulfilling his mission, to emerge from it unscathed after having robbed the devil of his goods (Mt 12:29)' (*B*, p. 334; Eng., p. 369).

Balthasar illustrates the point by referring to *Under Satan's Sun*, 'Gallet has no inkling about the depths of Germaine's demonic immersion, any more than La Pérouse understands the sublimity of Chantal's mystical experiences'.[104] Mouchette is 'released from a medical clinic "fully cured", and yet she is still in full possession of her demon'.[105] The priest character, Chevance, in *Imposture*, exorcises a possessed woman 'who had three times spent long periods in insane asylums and had come out of them only more frantic. The doctor had diagnosed her imminent death, but the exorcism cured her'.[106] Balthasar comments, 'If the moralists were right with the image of man they had constructed, then the psychologists' methods would suffice and vice versa. But the dimensions of evil as found by Bernanos in Christianity are beyond the reach of both moralists and psychologists'.[107]

Just as evil remains an enigma to psychoanalysis, so too is holiness. The saint too eludes analysis by the psychological sciences. Balthasar writes, 'The nature of sanctity is not psychological: holiness is rooted in the depths of the sacramental mystery. Precisely for this reason, sanctity has a compact unity that shatters all attempts by sinful reason to analyse it'.[108] Later Balthasar comments, 'The definitive judgement that psychology pretends to pass on genuine mysticism, the very feasibility of approaching the mystical dimension with the categories of analysis: these things are part and parcel of the form of the crucified servant assumed by the experience of God in Christianity'.[109] Balthasar holds that the man finds his fullest measure only in Christ, the new Adam.

Conclusion

The father of psychoanalysis arrived at his theories of anxiety from a sincere effort to interpret his clinical experience. We observed how ego-consciousness is a primary *locus* of anxiety in the human person, which Freud develops in great detail. Freud suggests that the origin of anxiety lies in the biological event of birth and the ego coming to consciousness. Balthasar's presentation of Freud's theory of anxiety, which is not immediately evident, leads from Freud's theory of anxiety to the 'metapsychological' and anthropological presuppositions of Freud's entire system. Balthasar agrees with Freud on the importance of the mother–child relationship, the relationship between the 'I' and its role as well as its relationship to the horizon of meaning and to the future. However, our author disagrees with Freud locating anxiety's origin in ego-consciousness, his construal of the mother–child relationship, and the mythic foundation of his metapsychology.

104. *B*, p. 367; Eng., p. 409.
105. *B*, p. 368; Eng., p. 409.
106. *B*, p. 368; Eng., p. 410.
107. *B*, p. 369; Eng., p. 411.
108. *B*, p. 284; Eng., p. 313.
109. *B*, p. 368; Eng., p. 410.

Balthasar's proposed relational anthropology, supported by current findings within neurobiology, alters the approach to anxiety and its origin. Anxiety is not produced by the structure of the mother–child relationship itself, but arises from the failure to love. Therefore, this view leaves open the possibility that anxiety does not ultimately originate in the ego. This critical discussion discloses the importance of philosophy and theology collaboration with psychiatry, indeed a collaboration that is beginning to occur with its increasing openness towards religion[110] and philosophy.[111] Balthasar's contribution can help orient psychiatry towards a relational anthropology which grants man an open horizon towards God and can open it towards a consideration of philosophy's and theology's position on the deepest origin of anxiety. Balthasar's solution lies not in reducing man by his role to help him cope with anxiety, but rather to open him in vulnerability to the divine 'Thou'. In other words, to quote Bernanos, 'We must all "overcome" life. But the only way of overcoming life is to love it'.[112]

110. Cf. Vitz, 'Psychology in Recovery', p. 20; C.C.H. Cook, 'Psychiatry and Mysticism', *Mental Health, Religion & Culture* 7 (2004), pp. 149–63 (152); Larson, D.B., J.P. Swyers and M.E. McCullough (eds), *Scientific Research on Spirituality and Health: a Report based on the Scientific Progress in Spirituality* (Rockville: National Institute for Healthcare Research, 1998). A closer connection with religion might have modified Freud's theory. For example, Servais suggests that part of the inadequacy of Freud's theory of the love-death dualism is that he views them only in opposition to each other. Christianity offers psychiatry the perspective that does not view love and death solely in terms of opposition. Freud grasped very well the ego's desperate crisis 'derived from a death that does not reach death', yet – Servais writes – 'does not love reveal itself precisely in its movement of free self-giving as the *unity* of love and death? In its deepest sense, in fact, love consists in "giving one's life" (cfr. *Jn* 15, 13; *1Jn* 3, 16) and, in its free death, "bears fruit" (*Jn* 15, 16), "produces much fruit" (*Jn* 12, 24)' (Servais, 'Il dualismo Freudiano', p. 252). (author's translation)

111. Noteworthy in regard to this shift is the emergence of 'positive psychology', intimated by Adler and Maslow and developed by M. Seligman, in which human strengths function as the therapeutic point of departure rather than the heretofore, nearly exclusive 'negative psychology' whose therapeutic point of departure is illness (cf. C. Peterson and Seligman, *Character Strengths and Virtues: A Handbook and Classification* [Oxford: Oxford University Press, 2004]). Seligman, who is not a believer, argues that empirical research on character strengths seems to reduce all character strengths to seven, which not-surprisingly line up remarkably well with the seven which come to us from Greek and Christian tradition.

112. *B*, p. 203; Eng., p. 224.

Chapter 5

Anxiety from Original Sin

> *[Adam] was to entrust his life to God and receive from God's hand, and in God's good time, the fruit of life.*
>
> (Hans Urs von Balthasar)[1]

Since neither Freud nor Kierkegaard indicate the possibility of man being free from anxiety, was his life ever anxiety-free? If it was, how then did anxiety enter? Balthasar agreed with Kierkegaard that anxiety is produced by man's cognitive activity of thinking and choosing in his fallen state. Kierkegaard held that Adam in the original state thought discursively, and that this was the cause of Adam's anxiety which precipitated the Fall. Balthasar contested this position arguing that anxiety was absent from life in Eden. Balthasar's conclusion was that the discussion regarding anxiety needed to be taken into the theological realm, specifically, the original state and the Fall. The present chapter continues the anthropological portion of this study by exploring the origin of anxiety from a Catholic theological perspective. This investigation can be done through a more dogmatic reflection on the anxiety-free original state of man in order to examine how human nature became anxiety ridden. Balthasar's theological anthropology, as it is primarily explained in *Christlicher Stand*, brings the philosophical and psychological discussion to a theological interpretation concerning the origins of anxiety.[2] Such an examination will begin to indicate the meaning of anxiety in man's present state, and how it might be transformed.

Man's Anxiety-Free Original State According to Balthasar

Man as imago trinitatis and the unity of creation and mission

In the original creation, Adam and Eve had a primal stance (*Ur-stand*) in God. Their *Ur-stand* in original creation can be viewed through the double lens of

1. *CS*, p. 71; Eng., pp. 89–90
2. The following exposition of Balthasar's theological anthropology as it relates to our theme is taken from *Christlicher Stand*. It is noted that our author summarizes many points of his theological anthropology in the section entitled 'Das Paradies und das Kreuz' in *Die Grossen Ordensregeln* (repr. 3, Einsiedeln: Verlag, 1974), pp. 11–14; Ital. pp. 22–25.

their being made in the image of God, and the inseparability of their creation and mission predicated on their status as *imago Trinitatis*. Balthasar construes this original *Ur-stand* in a similar manner to his view of the mother–child relationship discussed in Chapter 4. Man's identity as an image of the Trinity is based upon his non-identity with the Trinity. His *Ur-stand* is thus shaped by his two-fold *Abstand* (remove): he is both not God and not merely dust. His creation in the image of God and that he was formed from the dust of the earth placed man in a paradoxical stance towards God. Balthasar reasons, 'On the basis of this mystery (that the state of being-at-a-remove from God is precisely the state in which the creature can come closest to God), man's calling to love is seen from a new perspective. Man is indeed called to love, but only in a manner that permits him to live to the full his condition as creature'.[3]

Our author's intention in using image and archetype to explain the relationship between God and man is to think with a sufficiently *theological* understanding of man's original nature.[4] Balthasar avoids the language of *natura pura*, preferring to speak of human nature in terms of its supernatural end. Thus he interprets man's nature (body and soul) according to its end which is God who is love: 'All beings are, in the last analysis, interpreted according to their goal and calling, which, in man's case, is always love'.[5]

Man's original *Ur-stand* is also based on the unity of creation and mission, or better, that his graced nature has the inner form of mission. His nature was created for mission whereby his image would develop into an ever greater likeness to the Blessed Trinity, specifically to that of the Son. Thus a fundamental principle of the original state for Balthasar is that man 'has been incorporated into and established in the service of love',[6] and this original mission is 'to till [the garden] and keep it' (Gen. 2.15).[7] Vital to Balthasar's understanding in the anxiety-free original state is man's living according to the *mission* given to him by God. Balthasar continues, 'Man's final goal has always been a supernatural one. He has always been called to achieve his

3. *CS*, p. 52; Eng., p. 68.

4. The theme of nature and grace in Balthasar has been treated at length in other studies. We will only refer to them as they pertain to our present theme of anxiety (cf. A. Scola, 'Nature and Grace in Hans Urs von Balthasar', *Communio: International Catholic Review* 18 [1991], pp. 207–26 [208], and D. Yeago, *Theology and Drama: A Study in the Work of Hans Urs von Balthasar* [New Haven: Yale University Press, 1992]). Cf. L. Ladaria, *Antropologia teologica* (Casale Monferrato: Piemme, 1995), pp. 190–202, for a summary of the nature-grace problematic.

5. *CS*, p. 55; Eng., p. 71. Ladaria comments on this view, 'The only original and primary theological "definition" of man is that which begins from God's plan above him. Any other definition will be, from the theological point of view, secondary and cannot be taken as the point of departure for our reflection on the problem of the supernatural' (Ladaria, *Antropologia teologica*, p. 195). (author's translation).

6. *CS*, p. 53; Eng., p. 70.

7. Balthasar writes, 'this first transposition and change of status, this first distinction between man's (natural) being and his (graced) calling, is at once superseded, for, simultaneously with this calling, there is breathed into man a living soul, the final meaning of his existence' (*CS*, pp. 53–4; Eng., p. 70).

intended development in this "beyond" of his nature'.[8] Adam is given the necessary means of grace to perform his loving service towards God and thereby grow in his likeness. God gives the grace as if it were Adam's own, and he accepts it as it truly is – a grace. Otherwise he would fall into the 'psychologically untenable', and anxiety producing, position of oscillating between the naturalness expected of him and the constraint of his nature. This cruel, resentment-producing dialectic is avoided if we understand grace 'as the inner form of man's personal mission rather than as a beautiful garment that clothes him without removing the underlying poverty of his nature and origin'.[9] Grace instead brings a task, opens up a field of activity, and helps him to carry it out. It is through the execution of his mission that man becomes a person.[10] Balthasar's idea indicates an interesting point of connection with Freud's simple definition of mental health: the ability to love and to work. Of course their understandings of love and work would differ, yet the connection is nevertheless noteworthy. Thus, man's mission, his graced calling by which he is to become truly a person, is to offer God-loving service by keeping and tilling the Garden.

In the original state, man's two-fold *Abstand* as not God and not simply dust does not create anxiety for him because, paradoxically, he maintains the centre of himself *outside* himself. Balthasar writes, 'Thus every life contains a center that is eccentric – that is, outside itself'.[11] Man's eccentric centre constitutes the fundamental paradox of his nature. The relationship between mother and child in which one comes to consciousness of 'I' only in relationship to a loving 'thou', explored in Chapter 4 of this study, finds its ultimate foundation in man's creation as *imago Trinitatis*. If man keeps God as his centre, and not himself, his graced mission holds him in this unifying centre so that no tension exists between who he is and who he is supposed to become by virtue of his mission. Adam and Eve in their original state are constituted this fundamental paradox of being both godlike and creature-like, that is, creatures with an eccentric centre to themselves.

The divine archetype to which man's paradoxical image points is the divine Son. The loving service, which at first seems to indicate man's creaturality, is revealed in divine revelation as the inner form of divine love of the Son's loving service to the Father. Man's relationship to God as image and archetype is predicated from the relationship between the Son and the Father. Thus the relationship is image to archetype, and archetypical love within the Blessed Trinity has the form of service – the Son who eternally is utterly attuned and does the Father's will.[12] The Son lives his existence with an eccentric centre – the Father. The Son, in turn, establishes the pattern of mission for all who are made in his image and are to grow in his likeness. Our author reasons, 'The Son finds his *raison d'etre* in cooperating with, approving and giving thanks to

8. CS, 8; Eng., p. 75.
9. CS, p. 57; Eng., p. 74.
10. Cf. CS, p. 58; Eng., p. 74.
11. CS, p. 58; Eng., p. 75.
12. Cf. CS, p. 59; Eng., p. 77.

the will of the Father by which he has been sent and established in his mission. He knows himself only as that by which he is able to glorify his origin'.[13] The Son reveals the pattern of the creature's existence:

> It is only in contemplating the love of the Son that man comes to understand his own calling: to perceive and understand himself from no other standpoint than that of mission and, accordingly, to find in perfect service his perfect self-fulfillment, his eternal bliss, because there is for him no happiness outside of love, which has for him the form of service, because there is for him no other happiness than the accomplishment of the service to which he is called and which – O wonder of wonders! – consists for him exclusively in the calling to love.[14]

Balthasar goes at length to describe man's nature as made in the pattern of the Divine Son because it is a necessary precondition for understanding the original state. If man takes his creaturely stand in his God-given mission, then he would have much less about which to be anxious. Problems arise when one begins to consider himself or the world de-centred from God and his will. Mission united all the aspects of man's creaturality in the reciprocal union of love and service in his initial *Ur-stand.* Mission is the measure of an individual's life since it is God's will concretized in one's life.

The 'foundation stones' of man's spiritual being

A second aspect of the wider context of the anxiety-free original state is what our author calls the 'foundation stones' (*Grundsäulen*) of man's spiritual being, which further describe the absence of anxiety from human nature in Eden.[15] He posits three foundation stones in the original state. Adam's and Eve's spiritual being in the original state was without shame (Gen. 2.25), without death (Gen. 2.7,16), and without knowledge of the difference between good and evil (Gen. 2.16). These he calls, in a language evocative of Kierkegaard's vocabulary, 'the three foundation stones of our spiritual being, of our ethical and religious conduct' before the Fall, and these three characteristics of life in paradise are vastly different to man's life after the Fall.[16] Thus it is difficult to imagine human life without these characteristics. Each of these dimensions play an essential role in man's anxiety now, and although these dimensions can form a positive force in human life after the Fall, they are nevertheless a consequence of original sin.

Shame has to do with our embodied life, and, in Balthasar's view, is unique to man among all the embodied creatures. Our author locates it as a consequence of sin in the rebellion of man's lower nature against his higher nature, and the severing of the sexual drive from love. Shame involves a type of anxiety about our embodiment and the lack of control of our sexual drive

13. *CS*, p. 60; Eng., p. 78.
14. *CS*, p. 62; Eng., pp. 79–80.
15. *CS*, p. 67; Eng., p. 85.
16. *CS*, p. 67; Eng., p. 85.

and its bodily expression. The scholastic tradition calls it disordered passions in their rebellion against reason. Shame suggests anxiety about being vulnerable to, or being seen by, another, both by God and the other spouse, hence after the Fall Adam and Eve hid themselves from God and from each other.

The presence of death creates anxiety in human nature now because it is the ultimate and total future threat of a destructive evil. Death appears as the complete undoing of man's existence, and man is helpless against its inevitability. The presence of death in post-fall man, however, gives sense to his moral activity and procreation, two other decisive factors in man's anxiety after the Fall.

Finally, the original state did not require that man know the difference between good and evil. Having to choose between good and evil, as seen previously in Chapter 3, is a primary source of anxiety for man. Man's freedom to choose is the reason why Kierkegaard understood anxiety as man's natural condition. Thus the anxieties from shame, death and ethical choosing from a position over and above good and evil were not present in the Garden of Eden.

To these three foundation stones identified by Balthasar in *Christlicher Stand*, we may also add a fourth foundation stone in man's spiritual being: the coherence between his 'I' and his mission. Adam and Eve experienced no anxiety between who they were and who they were supposed to become. Balthasar does not make this connection explicitly; however, his discussion about mission in the original state in *Christlicher Stand*, and his position that full personhood is only achieved in mission, argued especially in the third volume of his *Theodramatik*, makes evident this characteristic of man's original state. A perfect, albeit not complete, correspondence existed between man's 'I' and his mission in the original state. He experienced no tension within himself between who he was as image and dust and who he was supposed to become by mission. His trust in God, moreover, eliminated any anxiety over the future – all would unfold in due time according to God's good will. These four foundation stones of Adam's and Eve's life in Eden indicate that they were not anxious in the Garden of Eden.

The lack of anxiety in the functioning of human reason

Adam's and Eve's intuitive knowledge

Balthasar holds that Adam and Eve did not possess the beatific vision in their original state, otherwise it would not have been possible for them to turn away by sin. At the same time their reasoning ability was far above our own.[17] Adam and Eve possessed, in our author's view, both the *cognitio matutina* and the *cognitio vespertina*, a way of superior knowing shared in common with

17. *CS*, 72-3n; Eng., 92n. Compare with *STh*. I, q. 94, a. 1.

the angels.[18] On this point, he follows the line of scholastic theology. The *cognitio matutina* of an angel, according to St. Thomas, is that 'knowledge of things in their absolute beginning, namely as they are in the Word'.[19] On the other hand, an angel's *cognitio vespertina* is his 'knowledge of created reality as existing in its own nature'.[20] Aquinas reasons that the being of something is derived ultimately from the Word. Yet the flow of being from the Word to the thing means that the thing has existence in itself, though its existence is both derived and dependent. Therefore, the distinction of the two terms does not imply a division between the two types of knowledge.[21] The distinction simply is a logical one to preserve the integrity of an existing thing as distinct yet nevertheless derived from its ultimate cause.

In the proper functioning of such an intellect, the *cognitio vespertina* is constantly referred back to its origin in the Word. It does not 'cling' (*figuntur*) to created being but refers this knowledge back to God.[22] Although the *cognitio vespertina* is less perfect than the *cognitio matutina* they are not opposed for 'to know a thing in itself is not opposed to knowing it in its cause'.[23] Original sin can be described in these terms as the attempt to separate *cognitio vespertina* from the *cognitio matutina* and take it for oneself, which then becomes 'night knowledge' (*cognitio nocturna*) in Aquinas' terminology.[24]

The important point for our theme of anxiety is that the *cognitio matutina* and the *cognitio vespertina* indicate a way of knowing that is not discursive, that is, does not reason from one thing to another as, for example, in a syllogism. Discursive reasoning, whether inductive or deductive, whether analytic or synthetic, requires a movement advancing from one thing to another. It requires that the intellect actively abstract the form from the matter of a thing so that the form can enter the intellect, quite literally to 'in-form' the intellect. An angel's thinking does not reason from one thing to another, does not need to follow a syllogism to see the conclusion of an argument, and does not need to analyse or synthesize. An angel knows a thing and its causes and consequences of it in an instant, immediately and intuitively.[25] The angelic

18. Cf. *STh.* I, q. 94, a. 1. The *cognitio matutina* and the *cognitio vespertina* describe the operation of an angelic intellect. The origin of the terms lie in St. Augustine's commentary on Genesis in viewing the angels' knowledge in terms of a day during the days of Creation.

19. *STh.* I, q. 58, a. 6 *c*; Eng., IX, p. 163.

20. *STh.* I, 58, 6 *c*; Eng., IX, p. 163.

21. St. Thomas writes 'that evening knowledge is that which angels have of things as they are in their own natures: not however as though the angels drew their knowledge from those natures and the preposition "in" expressed a causal relation; for, as we have seen, the angel's knowledge in no way depends on external things. The phrase "in their own natures" merely points to the object known and the fact that it is known; in other words, that with their "evening knowledge" angels apprehend the being that things have as existing in their own natures" ' (*STh.* I, q. 58, a. 7 *c*; Eng., IX, p. 165).

22. Cf. *STh.* I, q. 58, a. 6 *ad* 2; Eng., IX, p. 163.

23. *STh.* I, q. 58, a. 7 *ad* 3; Eng., IX, p. 167.

24. Cf. *STh.* I, q. 64, a. 1 *ad* 3; Eng., IX, p. 284.

25. The Dominican master further clarifies discursive knowledge in *STh.* I, q. 58, a. 3 *ad* 1–2.

intellect knows what a syllogism is, and can reason from cause to effect, but does not need to in order to know something. Thinking discursively would be an *inferior* way of knowing to an angel's intuitive and immediate knowing. Aquinas continues, 'If our souls were endowed with an angelic abundance of intellectual light, then in the very act of intuiting first principles we would understand all their consequences; we would know by intuition all that reasoning can deduce from them'.[26] The fact that we must induct, deduct, analyse and synthesize in order to know something is due to our *fallen* intellect, that our intellect has been dimmed by original sin.[27]

Aquinas applies this way of knowing to Adam in his original state stating that Adam knew God 'with a loftier sort of knowledge than we do now' located *between* our fallen state and the beatific vision of the final state.[28] In other words, Adam's intellect functioned more akin to that of an angel's than to ours. Adam's intellect in the original state was not dimmed and distracted by sensible things from the rebellion of his lower nature against his higher nature.[29] Adam did not know God through a discursive process, but knew God simultaneously with his apprehension of the reflection of God's being in his intelligible effects.[30] The Dominican master reasons further: 'the first man was so established by God that he understood everything which it is natural for man to be instructed in. This means all things that exist virtually in self-evident principles, namely whatever men can get to know naturally'.[31] Adam also received knowledge of supernatural things to the degree that he needed it in order to direct his life in the state of innocence, and his entire knowing was free from any sort of falsehood since falsehood is a kind of intellectual evil and no evil had yet touched him.[32]

Balthasar agrees with St. Bonaventure on Adam's pre-lapsarian knowledge, and states that it was a way of knowing which understood the material through the spiritual. He writes, 'But it was because he possessed the *cognitio matutina* that he was able, by reason of the *cognitio vespertina*, to see all material things directly and clearly in terms of the spiritual'.[33] This way of knowing is exactly the opposite way man knows in his fallen state where he must laboriously abstract the formal from the material via discursive

26. *STh.* I, q. 58, a. 3 *c*; Eng., IX, p. 153.
27. Cf. *STh.* I, q. 58, a. 4 *c*.
28. Cf. *STh.* I, q. 94, a. 1 *c*; Eng., XIII, p. 89.
29. St. Thomas writes, 'And so the first man used not to be hampered by external things from the clear and steady contemplation of God's intelligible effects, which he would observe, whether by natural or gratuitous knowledge, under the illumination of the first truth. And thus Augustine says: *Perhaps God used of old to speak to the first man as he now speaks with angels, illuminating their minds with unchangeable truth itself; . . . even though they did not have such a grasp of the divine essence as the angels do.* So therefore by such intelligible effects of God he used to know God more luminously than we could do now' (*STh.* I, q. 94, a. 1 *c*; Eng., XIII, pp. 89–90). (editor's italics)
30. Cf. *STh.* I, q. 94, a. 1 *ad* 3; Eng., XIII, pp. 89–90.
31. *STh.* I, q. 94, a. 3 *c*; Eng., XIII, p. 99.
32. Cf. *STh.* I, q. 94, a. 3 *c; STh.* I, q. 94, a. 4 *c*.
33. *CS*, 73n; Eng., 92n.

reasoning. The functioning of Adam's intellect in the original state did not produce an intellectual vertigo from the intellect's suspension between the particular thing and Being itself. The intellect of innocent Adam instead swam in the harmonious, transparent milieu of both particular things and Being itself. Adam's intellect operated effortlessly in this milieu of reciprocal transparency; no discursive activity was necessary. Recognition of the ontological difference produced no anxiety in his intellect.

However, Balthasar is adamant in emphasizing the discontinuity of the two states of Adam before and after the Fall.[34] Although Kierkegaard's Lutheran standpoint did not admit access to the original state, Balthasar's Catholic perspective nevertheless is cautious in ascribing too strong a likeness between pre- and post-lapsarian Adam. Balthasar seems to emphasize the devastating effect original sin had on human nature, and admits the difficulty of reflecting on man's original state: 'Yet anyone who would venture to express an opinion about man as he was in paradise must first consider how far – not in the temporal order, but in the order of grace – this first man differed from man as he is today'.[35] He continues, 'we are unable to imagine, to reconstruct for ourselves in any concrete fashion, the inner form of his life, his fate, his awareness of self'.[36]

Our author exercises caution in considering this question so as not to view Adam's original state through his fallen state. For Balthasar, the theologian must be careful not to proceed from a too philosophical starting point beginning from the world as it is – a fallen world, and instead must proceed from the starting point of revelation. This starting point avoids falling into the same trap as he saw in Kierkegaard's position. Balthasar's sensitivity to proceed always from an adequately theological starting point offers a warning to philosophy: any philosophy that considers only man's fallen state 'as the starting-point of a valid anthropology is doomed to go astray'.[37] Our author would seem to deem as inadequate not only Kierkegaard's and Freud's interpretations, but every other attempt to explain human nature in its totality by means of a theory that excludes theological realities.

Consequently, Balthasar makes two minor criticisms, one structural and the other material, of the Angelic Doctor's approach to the original state in his *Summa*. Balthasar's structural critique is based upon what he sees as an undue influence of Aristotle.[38] The material critique follows upon the structural in

34. Cf. *CS*, 72n; Eng., 91n.
35. *CS*, p. 66; Eng., p. 84.
36. *CS*, p. 66; Eng., p. 84.
37. *CS*, 73n; Eng., 92n.
38. Aquinas inserts his philosophical anthropology (man as he is now) between the six days of creation and Adam in paradise, that is, before treating Adam's original state. Balthasar comments: 'Only *after* he has completely worked out this philosophical anthropology does he depict man's original state – and here we learn, to our astonishment, that Adam, the first man, "had knowledge of all things by divinely infused species" (ST 1a 94, 3 ad 1). In other words, Adam does not resemble the nature just depicted. On the contrary, he belongs to the company of those beings, like the angels, who learn intuitively and abstractly' (*CS*, 73n; Eng., 92n). (Balthasar's italics)

that Adam's uniqueness in the original state could have had a much greater impact on Aquinas' anthropology.[39] Nevertheless, Balthasar stands in substantial agreement with St. Thomas about the operation of Adam's intellect in the original state.[40] Adam did not have to think discursively and so the ontological difference did not make him anxious. Balthasar's treatment on the operation of Adam's intellect in the original state suggests a difference of emphasis with St. Thomas. The Angelic doctor seems to emphasize the continuity between the original and fallen state, while Balthasar places greater emphasis on their discontinuity. Perhaps the difference of emphasis lies in the intention of each author. Aquinas is interested in the *Summa* to provide a systematic presentation of the original state, and therefore emphasizes the continuity in order to preserve man's rationality and ability to know truth after the Fall. Balthasar's interest in *Christlicher Stand*, on the other hand, is an investigation into a Christian's choice of a state of life in the Church, and emphasizes the discontinuity after the Fall to preserve the uniqueness and necessity of Christ's redemption in making that choice. The discontinuity emphasized by Balthasar, however, depends upon the continuity emphasized by St. Thomas, that is, that rational discourse is a necessary prerequisite for observing any discontinuity.

Intuitive knowledge within their natural faith

Balthasar contextualizes the operation of man's intellect in the original state within his natural faith. He delineates man's natural faith in both its volitional and intellectual dimensions. He characterizes Adam's and Eve's natural faith

39. Balthasar writes, 'Did Thomas realize what consequences the construction of such a first man had – and still has – for his whole system?' (*CS*, 73n; Eng., 92n). Why, Balthasar seems to ask, did St. Thomas not have the uniqueness of Adam's original state inform not only his anthropology but his entire system? Perhaps we would have seen differently framed or entirely new *quaestiones* in his *Summa*. Our author continues: 'In his teaching about Adam he depends on earlier theology when he speaks, for instance, of the possibility of a twofold knowledge (ST 1a 94, p. 3) and explicitly labels it *cognitio naturalis* (*De ver* q. 18 a. 4). But whereas theologians regard this original constitution of man's nature as actually intended by God and therefore as foreseen for Adam's descendants, Thomas draws the line of division straight through the centre of man's original state by ascribing this nature only to Adam, since he was the origin and source of the whole race, but not to the children who might have been born to him in his original state (*De ver* q. 18 a. 7)' (*CS*, 73n; Eng., 92n). In other words, Balthasar suggests that Aquinas was aware of the uniqueness of Adam original state from the fallen state of man, but that uniqueness was not given sufficient voice in his work.

40. J. Buckley, O.P. argues that the vast majority of Balthasar's use of Aquinas is positive rather than critical, and delineates in a nuanced and cautious manner, a possible evaluation of Balthasar's use and criticism of Aquinas. Cf. Buckley, 'Balthasar's use of the Theology of Aquinas', *The Thomist* 59 (1995), pp. 517–45. The theme of anxiety in pre- and post-lapsarian Adam supports Buckley's position. Balthasar does not differ significantly from Aquinas on this issue beyond these two minor criticisms in a footnote concerning the original state.

first as 'the movement by which they accepted their being from God and returned it to him again and again in love'.[41] Natural faith relieved Adam and Eve of knowing the difference between good and evil latent in the original state. Instead Adam and Eve 'lived in the fire of goodness – not yet in the lukewarmness of indifference to good and evil, not yet at the point where the choice between good and evil first becomes possible. They lived not below, but above this "ethical" situation in a condition of which their already having chosen in favor of good was constitutive'.[42]

Their natural faith involved not only trusting adherence of their will to God's but also intellectual knowledge signified in his naming of the animals (Gen. 2.20) and in keeping and tilling the garden. Their knowledge was thus both entirely positive and situated within their divinely mandated vocation.[43] A symphony of critical intellect and free will thus played harmoniously within natural faith: 'They [critical intellect and freedom of will] had originally been intended to function as internal organs within faith, which is the form of obedient love'.[44] Balthasar indicates in pre-lapsarian man a childlike, intuitive knowing based on his immediate and concrete relationship with God. Anxiety enters into man when he loses that childlike living in the Lord's presence. The cruel irony of the serpent's twisted words is that by taking the fruit of the tree of knowledge of good and evil for themselves, Adam and Eve would actually *lessen* their knowledge of the good, and instead substitute knowledge of evil. Moreover, gaining knowledge of the good after the Fall becomes much more elusive and arduous while gaining knowledge of evil requires little effort.

Balthasar further describes the natural faith of the original state was expressed in a life of obedience, purity – in a mysterious union of virginity and fecundity – and poverty. In other words, Balthasar characterizes this natural faith in terms of the evangelical counsels. First, man's faith was expressed by his free obedience to God. Man's obedience meant concretely that he would not grasp after life by seeking it in the knowledge of good and evil, but rather patiently wait to receive it from God at the proper time.[45] Man's obedience kept him from a loveless curiosity, from seeking any knowledge outside of love. Knowledge without love, that is, knowledge independent of God, could only bring evil and death.

Man's task in obedience 'was to *entrust* his life to God and receive from God's hand, and in God's good time, the fruit of life. . . . Man was unable to

41. *CS*, p. 72; Eng., p. 91.

42. *CS*, p. 72; Eng., pp. 90–1. In other words, their wills operated above 'freedom of choice' or 'gnomic willing' in the 'freedom of love'. Only when love decreases does the will fall into the zone of standing in between the choice for good or evil.

43. Cf. *CS*, p. 72; Eng., p. 91.

44. *CS*, p. 74; Eng., p. 93.

45. *CS*, p. 70; Eng., p. 89. Our author sides with the current of the tradition which holds to the one tree theory of Eden. He writes, 'Gregory of Nyssa and others comment that, since there could not have been two trees in the center of the garden, there must have been a mysterious identity between the tree of life and the tree of knowledge of good and evil. The tree was forbidden insofar as it gave knowledge of good and evil, for this was the only fruit that man could take for himself' (*CS*, p. 70; Eng., p. 89).

pluck this fruit, this eternal life, for himself because it is the free gift of God's grace'.[46] Their 'lack' of the knowledge of good and evil, in other words, was not really a lack, and the divine prohibition not a restriction. Adam and Eve did not view their obedience to God as contrary to their freedom until the serpent's temptation. Therefore obedience to God's will in the original state did not require Adam and Eve to renounce their own. Balthasar reasons, 'Their wills were simply and unquestioningly identical with this obedience, which was but the instrument by which they accepted the will of God'.[47] Thus we can see that their obedience to God's will, in fact, protected their freedom.[48]

The serpent was the first to introduce the idea that their knowledge of the good was a lack and a restriction on their freedom. The serpent's temptation assailed the essential unity of man's freedom and obedience by insinuating that God's prohibition limited man's sovereignty, that sovereignty was found in self will rather than God's will. The serpent was the one who suggested that they compare their wills with God's. The anxious position in which man finds himself after the Fall is anxious precisely because it is a place he cannot, and therefore should not, occupy – taking that knowledge for himself thereby establishing himself as arbiter between good and evil. Fallen man is anxious for good reason for how can a finite creature know and then arbitrate between good and evil independently from God?

The lack of anxiety from the evangelical counsels

The lack of anxiety in the original state, according to Balthasar, also stems from the evangelical counsels constituting Adam's and Eve's life before the Fall. Obedience was explained in the previous section. This inner harmony of natural faith expressed in free obedience extended also to Adam's and Eve's embodiment. Their natural faith was not merely the assent to intellectual truth but the assent of their entire selves to God who walked with them 'in the cool of the day' (Gen. 3.8). Their original chastity can be described as the embodied expression of their inner faith. Man's innocent soul irradiated his body; it 'enclosed and enveloped the body', which in turn operated in harmonious obedience with his faith.[49] Balthasar writes in a manner that connects the scholastic idea of man's ordered passions in the original state: 'The irradiation of the body by the soul's purity is, in fact, absolute chastity. . . . Drives existed in man even in paradise, but only to serve and be helpful to him. Just as intellect and will exercised their sovereign functions in man only within the circumference of obedience in faith, so the bodily drives and functions exercised their role only within the circumference of a love that was proper to both soul and body'.[50] In other words, Adam and Eve always and immediately

46. *CS*, p. 71; Eng., pp. 89–90 (author's italics).
47. *CS*, p. 72; Eng., p. 90.
48. Cf. *CS*, pp. 72–3; Eng., p. 91.
49. *CS*, p. 74; Eng., p. 93.
50. *CS*, p. 74; Eng., pp. 93–4.

understood their eros with agape.[51] Adam and Eve received the command to 'be fruitful and multiply; fill the earth' (Gen. 1.28) even before Adam 'knew' Eve (Gen. 4.1), and so our author reasons with the tradition that in the original state there was no division between virginity and fecundity.[52]

Finally man's natural faith was expressed in his poverty. So long as his will reposed in the will of God, creation was obedient to man. There was no need to procure, no need to distinguish 'mine' and 'thine'. The inexhaustible riches of Eden surrounded Adam and Eve, and so the anxiety of having to procure the necessities of life, of providing for one's family, the anxiety of whether there would be enough in the future, was unknown to them.

The original state, according to Balthasar, was thus 'the perfect, seamless and unassailable unity of obedient faith as insight and freedom; of virginal purity as fecundity; and of poverty as fullness and riches without distinction of mine and thine'.[53] He then suggests that 'the three counsels express the highest perfection of love to which man can attain by grace'.[54] The presence of the evangelical counsels in the original state helps us make sense as to why Jesus' life was characterized by the counsels, and also why the life of the evangelical counsels are upheld as the most perfect form of the Christian life since man's life is characterized by them in both his original state and final state.

The Origin of Anxiety in Original Sin

Having observed how Balthasar acknowledges the various *loci* of anxiety in ego-consciousness and in discursive reason, he identifies the ultimate origin of anxiety in original sin. Our author describes the devastating effects of original sin in terms of a four-fold rupture which damages the inner harmony of man's nature. To this four-fold rupture we may add a fifth from our discussion thus far. The four-fold rupture, described in *Christlicher Stand*, is the rupture of intellect and will from natural faith, of the sexual drive from love, of earthly life from eternal life and of mine from thine. The fifth that we could add is the rupture of man's 'I' from his mission. These five effects indicate, according to Balthasar, how man's fallen nature became riddled with anxiety.

The destructive nature of the choice to commit original sin is 'curiosity about the light – about the naked reason – concealed within it, about a reason without faith'.[55] This quote is reminiscent of Balthasar's work on Bernanos who characterized the epitome of evil as knowledge without love, that is, seeking knowledge simply to know and to know independently from God

51. Cf. Balthasar, *Die Grossen Ordensregeln*, p. 11.

52. However, the manner in which that unity is understood is a controverted point among the Fathers. Cf. *CS*, pp. 75–81; Eng., pp. 95–103, for Balthasar's summary of this controversy.

53. *CS*, p. 92; Eng., p. 121.

54. *CS*, p. 93; Eng., p. 121.

55. *CS*, pp. 72–3; Eng., pp. 91–2.

without seeking to love in the knowing. This curiosity of knowing without love and seeking a measure of reality outside of God also formed the basis for our author's critique of certain approaches in psychotherapy. Natural faith gave Adam and Eve the ability to measure reality not in terms of themselves or from the thing being measured, but in terms of God. In their choice for original sin, Adam and Eve turn away from their free obedience and wrest their intellect and will away from their natural faith. The first 'knowledge' that their fall into sin produces is that of their nakedness and the ensuing feeling of shame. The symphony of intellect and will operating within natural faith deteriorates into a cacophony as their intellects fall into a discursive process (producing inherently anxious thinking), and their wills enter the lukewarm place of indifference between good and evil, the impossible position to know and arbitrate good and evil independently from God.

Our author further explicates this rupture of the intellect from natural faith in *Der Christ und die Angst* where he notes that reason's activity continues after the Fall, but it cannot attain what it had in the original state. Balthasar holds that man's reason is darkened by the Fall. He writes, 'In paradise God was the *primum notum* (in faith, not in sight), both *quoad nos* and *in se*. . . . Today he is the *primum notum* only *in se*, no longer *quoad nos*'.[56] God, in other words, is not the first thing known with respect to fallen man but only in himself. Man's fallen reason is still able to operate, but in the modes of intellectual abstraction and volitional indifference which open up the anxiety producing void in his mind. Christ's redemption and Christian faith can transform man's fallen nature by 'surrendering one's own void together with its anxiety into the unfelt fullness . . . of God's Totality', but they do not eliminate the void in this life.[57]

Adam's and Eve's disobedience in grasping for life in the knowledge of good and evil sets off a similar rupture in their bodies as their drives are wrested from love. This description is similar to Aquinas' description of the disordering of the passions and, if taken to an extreme, has analogies to Freud's idea of the id. Their first knowledge is the loss of bodily purity in their sense of shame as 'the drives of the body issue naked from the protection of the spiritual' and become disordered.[58] This rupture also tears virginity away from fecundity. Although neither the drives nor the sense of shame are evil, their disordered state is. The rupturing of man's sexual drives from the spiritual which characterizes man's fallen state gives credence to psychiatry's attentiveness to the disordered drives in fallen human nature.

Man's choice for sin also brought about a rupture of earthly life from eternal life which introduced him to death. In scholastic terms, Adam's nature becomes passable and corruptible. Balthasar writes indicating the anxiety producing effects related to death:

56. *CA*, p. 87; Eng., p. 143. The English translators add an explanation of *quoad nos* and *in se* which is the reason for the elision in the quote above (translator's italics).

57. *CA*, p. 87; Eng., p. 143.

58. *CS*, p. 75; Eng., pp. 94–5.

> Through sin death came into the world (Rom 5:12), and through death, anxiety about the flame of life in this world, imperiled as it is from within and without. For death is not just the sudden ending of life. It is also the corroding illness, the aging, the blunting of one's powers, the weariness, the disgust with boredom and barrenness, with the transitoriness and hopelessness of earthly life. Because of man, all nature is affected by this decay (Rom 8:20).[59]

Original sin also produced the anxious situation of having to procure the necessities of life amid sweat and toil. The original state was perfect wealth in union with perfect poverty of spirit. Because of the abundance of Eden, Adam and Eve had no need to procure anything for themselves because all was given by God and earth responded with its own generosity. All was given, received and given back since 'love knows only how to give; it keeps nothing for itself'.[60] There existed no need to conceal or withhold anything in this free exchange of love between God and man and between Adam and Eve. Only after the Fall, and the shame it produced, do we see the beginning of private property in the feeble attempt to make clothing from leaves – the first act of delineating mine from thine. In the loss of his original poverty, the richness of Eden is lost and replaced by the scarcity of a fallen earth, thereby beginning 'the painful necessity of private ownership'.[61] East of Eden, Adam and Eve live amid anxiety producing pressures from this rupture. Balthasar describes these pressures:

> [P]ressure in the family, where the wife – instead of the unconstrained relationship that had existed between Adam and the helpmate given him by God (Gen. 2:18) and with whom he formed one flesh (Gen. 2:24) – was placed under the dominion of her husband (Gen. 3:16); pressure in procuring the necessities of life, since Adam, by the terms of the curse, had to accumulate, save, worry and plan; pressure, finally, in the political community, where the close association of so many individuals engaged in procuring for themselves the staples of existence inevitably resulted in those conflicts between *mine* and *thine* that can be resolved only by new pressures of authority and power.[62]

These ruptures within fallen human nature are all interconnected and henceforth inseparable. Sexuality is linked to death and the signs of death (Gen. 3.16) as well as the will to acquire possessions and thus becomes 'the arena of man's most deadly struggles for power'.[63] The moral autonomy from the knowledge of good and evil is now inseparably linked to the use of man's drives and property. 'The *will to ownership*', from the rupture of mine from thine, 'is basically identical with the will to know good and evil and to be responsible for one's own bodily fecundity'.[64] The Fall corrupts his freedom from obedience to God 'into a hateful obedience to the laws of this world, into

59. *CS*, pp. 81–2; Eng., p. 103.
60. *CS*, p. 91; Eng., p. 119.
61. *CS*, p. 82; Eng., p. 104.
62. *CS*, pp. 82–3; Eng., pp. 104–5 (Balthasar's italics).
63. *CS*, p. 92; Eng., p. 120.
64. *CS*, p. 92; Eng., p. 120 (Balthasar's italics).

the bitter drudgery of painful obligation, to whose yoke he is now harnessed'.[65] In the same way, his purity is corrupted so that fecundity 'is linked by the drives of his lower nature to his loss of virginity and of the humility of spiritual love'.[66] Finally, the ownership of the knowledge between good and evil which man took for himself in the Fall now 'compels him to be solicitous about the property he cannot acquire without struggle or defend without struggle and that, in the end, will be wrenched from him by death if he has not already consumed or lost it'.[67] The fifth rupture that may be added to those explicitly mentioned by our author is the rupture of who man is as image from who he is supposed to become through mission, thus producing anxiety in the dissonance between his 'I' and his mission.

Original sin places man under a curse which constricts him, causing him anxiety in his intellect, will, body and relationships. Through the trickery of the serpent, Adam and Eve grasped for life and freedom and found themselves riddled with anxiety and clapped in the irons of a constricting slavery they could not escape on their own. The origin of all anxiety, according to our author, lies in this first sin.

Conclusion

This chapter considered the origin of anxiety according to Balthasar's theological anthropology. The ultimate origin of anxiety lies in original sin. Man is created in the image of the Blessed Trinity and given the mission to cultivate the earth. Nothing in the original state of man gave him reason to be anxious. Balthasar shows that in the original state, the ontological difference did not register as anxiety in man's reason since his reason functioned in a higher way than discursive reasoning. Man was not anxious about who he was or what his mission was in Eden. His life was characterized as free from shame, death or the knowledge of good and evil. His life was also characterized by the evangelical counsels of loving obedience, chastity in the unity of virginity and procreation and freedom from possessions. Anxiety is spawned by the choice for sin in the Garden of Eden. Original sin ushered in a five-fold rupture in man: the rupture of intellect and will from natural faith, the sexual drive from love, earthly life from eternal life, mine from thine, man's 'I' from his mission. Out of original sin and this rupture comes all the negative anxiety in the human condition.

65. *CS*, p. 93; Eng., p. 122.
66. *CS*, p. 93; Eng., p. 122.
67. *CS*, p. 93; Eng., p. 122.

Part Two Conclusion

The chapters on Freud and Kierkegaard in this study show Balthasar's attentive listening and critical discussion with two thinkers outside of Catholic theology on the origins of anxiety. Balthasar recognizes how both Freud and Kierkegaard discover primary *loci* of anxiety within the human person in discursive reason, the process of birth and ego-consciousness. Thinking rationally and being conscious of oneself create anxiety for human beings. Our author emphasizes the importance of identifying the implicit anthropology of a given position, and of interpreting anxiety with an adequate anthropology. Balthasar agrees with Kierkegaard and Freud that anxiety is part of the fabric of human nature. Yet he remains unconvinced of their conclusions concerning anxiety's ultimate origin. These two writers fall short in explaining the deepest origin of anxiety because of the limitations of their interpretive tools. The critical discussion with philosophy and psychiatry demonstrate the necessity for both of those sciences to engage the science of theology in the search for a more adequate interpretation of anxiety's origins.

Balthasar instead locates the ultimate origin of anxiety in original sin. His treatment connects with both Kierkegaard's and Freud's positions: Kierkegaard's in the explanation of the operation of man's reason in the original state, and Freud's in the explanation of the relationship between man's 'I' and mission and the important role that the evangelical counsels play in the original state. In other words, anxiety is not natural to man but was a result of the choice for sin. Anxiety is not rooted in God's creative action but in man's destructive choice. Only with an adequately theological perspective, which allows access to the original state, are we able to distinguish between creatureliness and sin in evaluating human anxiety. The search for the origin of anxiety is crucial in that by locating the deepest origin of this troublesome emotion, which is often so destructive to human life, we may discover how it might be transformed. If anxiety was not original to human nature, then man's anxious situation can perhaps change.

Part Three

The Garden of Gethsemane: Anxiety Redeemed

Chapter 6

Aquinas' Interpretation of *Timor* and its Redemption

> *Christ was captured in a Garden, he suffered his agony in a garden. . . . The virtue of his Passion frees us from the sin Adam committed in the garden of Eden.*
>
> (St. Thomas Aquinas)[1]

Part Three of this study moves Balthasar's interpretation of anxiety further into the theological realm by shifting the discussion from the Garden of Eden to the Garden of Gethsemane, from anxiety's causes to its cure. The following *theological* analysis of anxiety brings the anthropological discussion to the Word of God in how anxiety is redeemed by Jesus Christ, for Divine Revelation in Balthasar's view is the ultimate authority and measure of human anxiety. To what extent did Jesus experience anxiety, and how did he redeem it? We frame such questions within Catholic theology by placing our author in critical discussion with St. Thomas Aquinas. He is the chosen interlocutor with Balthasar for three basic reasons. First, this study is a systematic treatment of anxiety in Balthasar's work, and the Dominican master's work is systematic *par excellence*. Second, Balthasar's entire theology is currently undergoing evaluation by scholars as to its significance in the tradition of Catholic theology. Thus it is important that his theology of anxiety dialogue with that of St. Thomas who offers a deep treatment of human affectivity and the human affectivity of Christ, and whose theology holds magisterial status in the Church. Third, a dialogue with St. Thomas is important for the purposes of mutual clarification and stimulus for further thought for scholars of Balthasar as well as Aquinas. The comparison between these two thinkers on Christ's anxiety focuses not so much on anxiety itself as on each one's view of how it is redeemed.

The present chapter, therefore, is an exposition and analysis of St. Thomas' interpretation of the redemption of anxiety, which is subsequently compared to Balthasar's interpretation at the conclusion of Chapter 7. We first examine St. Thomas' view of fear, *timor*,[2] as it appears in fallen human nature,

1. Aquinas, *Super Evangelium S. Ioannis Lectura* (http//:www.corpusthomisticum.org), pp. 19, 6; Eng., *Theological Texts* (trans. T. Gilby; London: Oxford University Press, 1955), p. 331.

2. Aquinas' use of *timor* ('fear') substantially resembles *Angst* as it is used by Freud, Kierkegaard and Balthasar. In fact, Balthasar translates St. Thomas' term as *Angst* (cf. *CA*, p. 69; Eng., p. 118). The Angelic doctor's classifies *anxietas* as a type of *timor*. Therefore, we present the Angelic doctor's treatment of *timor* rather than simply *anxietas*. A primary

followed by a consideration of his position on the anxiety-free original state and how anxiety originates in original sin. Next we investigate the human nature that was assumed by the Son in the Incarnation, and how he understands Christ's human perfection. We will then be in a position to analyse which *timor* Christ could and did experience as man and which he could not. Finally we will examine how Jesus' uninterrupted beatific vision during his earthly life conditions his experience of anxiety.

Aquinas on Timor

Timor *within the unity of human nature*

St. Thomas Aquinas treats our theme from within his philosophical anthropology delineated in the *Summa*. He understands the passion of *timor* within a rich and complex vision of man's emotional life. He defines passions in general as various manifestations of the sensitive appetite but which are nevertheless experienced and developed within the unity of the human person.[3] As a passion, *timor* is a complex human experience which involves not only the sensitive appetite, but also the body's physiology and the operations of intellect and will.[4] Thus fear as an event of the sensitive appetite is more than an instinctual drive, shared in common with other animals.[5]

St. Thomas' view of the unity of reason and affectivity places the emotions as an integral part of attaining human happiness, and therefore the emotions pertain directly and intimately to the moral life.[6] In St. Thomas' theory, the

difference between Aquinas and contemporary writers on anxiety lies in that objectless fear and repression do not enter into his theory. For St. Thomas *timor* always has an object. His presentation on fear can be constructed from *STh.* I–II, qq. 41–4 (on *timor* itself); II–II, qq. 123, 125 (on its relation to fortitude) and II–II, q. 19 (as a gift of the Holy Spirit). Cf. P. Gondreau, *The Passions of Christ's Soul in the Theology of St. Thomas Aquinas* (Münster: Aschendorff, 2002), pp. 101–135, pp. 404–8; S. Loughlin, 'The Complexity of *timor* in Aquinas's *Summa Theologiae*' in A. Scott and C. Kosso (eds), *Fear and Its Representations in the Middle Ages and Renaissance* (Belgium: Brepols, 2002), pp. 1–16; K. White, 'The Passions of the Soul (Ia IIae, qq. 22–48)', in S. Pope (ed.), *The Ethics of Aquinas* (Washington D.C.: Georgetown University Press, 2002), pp. 103–15. In presenting Aquinas on fear I follow closely the interpretations of Loughlin and Gondreau.

3. Cf. *STh.* I–II, qq. 22–5. The unitive view of the human person is called 'hylomorphic' or 'hylemorphic', among scholars on St. Thomas. The term expresses man's psychophysical unity based upon the unity of matter and form. Loughlin describes St. Thomas' hylomorphic view as 'a psychological theory of the human person which does *not* consider man as a composite of two distinct things, body and soul', but 'as "one substance, in which two component factors can be distinguished"' (Loughlin, 'Complexity of *timor*', p. 2).

4. Gondreau adds, 'the passions are necessarily a psychosomatic affair, as they involve the entirety of human nature, including body and soul' (Gondreau, *The Passions of Christ's Soul*, p. 207).

5. Cf. Loughlin, 'Complexity of *timor*', 3; cf. *STh*, I–II, qq. 22, 23 and 25, especially 22.

6. Cf. Gondreau, *The Passions of Christ's Soul*, pp. 107–9; G. Busiello, 'Le passioni in Tommaso d'Aquino tra etica, antropologia e metafisica', *Angelicum* 83 (2006), pp. 95–120.

emotions are identified so that they may be properly related to, and perfected by, the virtues. Because fear is experienced by a unified rational creature, it is a uniquely human experience, and one that is 'intimately tied to man's nature, destiny, and happiness'.[7] Man's appetitive directedness is distinguished from his apprehensive powers, yet these apprehensive powers play a large role in the generation of emotion because one must judge the thing itself as good or bad for the one perceiving it in order for an emotion to be generated.[8]

Timor arises, according to St. Thomas, in the irascible aspect of the sensitive appetite as a reaction to a future evil that is overwhelmingly and imminently threatening, yet also difficult to oppose or avoid.[9] Before such a threat, the person makes the judgment that the evil is unavoidable and shrinks from it instead of overcoming it by daring (*audacia*). The uniqueness of *timor* among the other emotions is the object's futurity. Since fear's object lies in the future and thus is perceived through reason, human rationality plays a great part in shaping one's perception of the future threatening object. *Anxietas* is classified by St. Thomas as a specific kind of fear due to the feared object's unforseeability and unexpected appearance.[10] Aquinas also locates anxiety (*anxietas*) and perplexity (*angustiae*) under the third type of sorrow (*tristitia*), that is, the 'sorrow we experience that prevents our natural flight from an evil that afflicts us. . . . This sorrow is one that weighs upon the mind (*animus*) so as to make escape or flight seem impossible'.[11] In this way *timor* is related to *tristitia*, with the specific difference that in *tristitia* the evil is already present afflicting us while in *timor* the evil is still in the future and present cognitively.[12] In the reaction of fear, the object is present to the person cognitively via the intellect which thinks about the pain that is coming. We might say that every fear results in a cognitively induced sorrow. Because of the object's futurity, the emotion of fear is less passive than the other emotions. The sensitive appetite, therefore, is aroused through the object's presence in the intellect and not directly through the senses.[13]

7. Loughlin, '*Tristitia et Dolor*: Does Aquinas Have a Robust Understanding of Depression?', *Nova et vetera (English edition)* 3 (2005), pp. 761–84 (762).

8. The strong moral thrust of St. Thomas' theory on *timor* connects with the importance Balthasar gives to mission which helps preserve Adam from anxiety in the original state. Mission for Balthasar propels man toward his supernatural end.

9. Cf. *STh*. I–II, q. 41, a. 1.2; q. 42, a. 3 *ad* 2. St. Thomas writes that fear is not primarily from the concupiscent appetite (I–II, q. 41, a. 2 *ad* 3). Fear has as its object, according to Aquinas, something disagreeable, overwhelmingly threatening, imminent and in the future (*STh*. I–II, q. 41, a. 1 *c*). On the object's futurity and imminentability, cf. *STh*. I–II, q. 42, a. 2 *c*. Aquinas does not share the same perspective as Freud on the unconscious sources of fear. For St. Thomas fear is from an external object; for Freud fear is primarily from within the subject, namely, unwanted impulses, wishes or fantasies threatening from one's unconscious.

10. Cf. *STh*. I–II, q. 41, a. 4.

11. Loughlin, '*Tristitia et Dolor*', pp. 766–7.

12. Cf. *STh*. I–II, q. 41, a. 1, *c*. The closeness of *timor* and *tristitia* in St. Thomas' view is also held in psychiatry which hold that depression can be a symptom of anxiety.

13. Cf. *STh*. I–II, q. 41, a. 1 *ob* 2, *ad* 2.

Man can experience natural or sensitive fear, by virtue of his embodiment, in which a bodily suffering occurs, and can also experience intellectual fear, by virtue of his rationality, which does not require bodily suffering to occur.[14] Loughlin concludes, therefore, that although Aquinas prefers to locate fear in the sensitive appetite, he does not interpret fear simply in terms of the common understanding of *passio*, but emphasizes the important role played by the apprehensive powers.[15] Because of man's sensitive and intellectual comprehension his concern extends beyond the present to include matters regarding past and future.[16] For *timor* to be generated, therefore, there must first be the judgment that some evil person, thing, or situation is immanently approaching from the future which is unsuitable to one's well-being. This evaluation brings about the sensitive appetitive movement Aquinas calls *timor* along with a physiological reaction of the body. Man's rationality, therefore, enables him to experience fear in a far deeper way than an animal.

Timor *as an appetitive, intellectual, volitional and physiological event*

Timor is structured according to form and matter: the formal aspect is the appetitive reaction and the material aspect is the physiological reaction which 'reproduces the characteristics of the appetitive reaction'.[17] In the appetitive reaction, man can experience the most basic type of fear, 'natural fear', which can be described as the instinctive withdrawal from whatever threatens one's nature based upon the natural drive to exist.[18] Following Aristotle's classification, the object of fear is either a corruptive or constrictive evil with death as the ultimate.[19] This level is the summit of *timor* for animals, the Dominican master reasons, since they possess a sensitive appetite but not reason. Man, however, can undergo a much deeper experience of fear since his reason allows him to consider an object freely, a fear which Aquinas calls 'non-natural' to distinguish it from the fear he shares with animals. Non-natural fear can be manifested in three ways: a 'reduplication' of natural fear in the intellect, its ability to consider of a far greater range of fearful objects, and the consideration of the object as good or bad in themselves and not merely in terms of the individual.[20]

St. Thomas maintains St. John Damascence's classification of non-natural fear into six types divided into two groups.[21] The first group are fears towards

14. Cf. *STh*. I–II, q. 22, a. 1; I–II, q. 22, a. 3; I–II, q. 41, a. 1 with the above, and *STh*. I–II, q. 31, a. 4.
15. Cf. Loughlin, 'Complexity of *timor*', pp. 5–6.
16. Cf. *STh*. I–II, q. 35, a. 2 *ob* 2, *ad* 2.
17. *STh*. I–II, q. 44, a. 1 *c*; Eng., XXI, 61. Cf. Loughlin, '*Tristitia et Dolor*', p. 769; *STh*. I, q. 20, a. 1 *ad* 2; I, q. 75, a. 3 *ad* 3; I–II, q. 22, a. 2 *ad* 3; I–II, q. 37, a. 4; I–II, q. 44, a. 1.
18. *STh*. I–II, q. 41, a. 3.
19. Cf. *STh*. I–II, q. 42, a. 2 *sed contra*.
20. Cf. Loughlin, 'Complexity of *timor*', pp. 8–9; cf. *STh*. I–II, q. 80, a. 1, qq. 82–83, and *De Veritate* q. 22, a. pp. 4–6.
21. Cf. *STh*. I–II, q. 41, a. 4.

the evil in men's actions: laziness (fear of too much toil), shamefacedness (fear of damaging one's reputation through disgraceful actions about to be done), and shame (fear of damaging one's reputation through disgraceful actions having been done). The second group contains the types of fear towards the evil with respect to external things that exceed a person's power of opposition: *admiratio* (by the object's magnitude), *stupor* (by the object's unusual or unaccustomed appearance) and *anxietas* (by the object's unforeseen or unexpected appearance).[22]

According to the Aquinas, the intensity of fear is conditioned in two ways, either by the magnitude of the object or by the weakness of the subject perceiving the object.[23] The subjective element plays an important role in the generation and intensification of fear because the emotion affects one's perception of reality.[24] St. Thomas understands that the object of fear can be external to anything that threatens man's bodily integrity, but can also extend to objects that threaten his mental and spiritual integrity. The fear having to do with one's mental and spiritual integrity has much to do with the weakness of the subject. One may fear experiencing certain negative and unsettling passions. Disordered desire, especially sexual desire, can be a primary source of fear. Concupiscence, which strongly resists the governance of reason and the shaping force of the virtues, possesses fear-inducing qualities such as 'suddenness, uncontrolled vehemence, and the clouding of rational judgment'.[25] He also recognizes that one may be afraid of fear itself, that is, of being afraid of the reaction against a certain threatening object now and of having that same reaction in the future.[26]

Fear also possesses a positive dimension for St. Thomas when experienced in a moderate way. It can make one alert, ready for action, and willing to take counsel in order to avoid or overcome the imminent danger.[27] Although primarily understood as a withdrawal from something judged bad for oneself, fear also concerns the good indirectly since it considers that which is to be protected against harm or loss. Fear is good insofar as it protects one from evil. All the emotions, including fear, have their foundation in love.[28]

22. Cf. *STh*. I–II, q. 41, a. 4.

23. Cf. *STh*. I–II, q. 43, a. 2 *c*.

24. Cf. *STh*. I–II, q. 42, a. 4, *c*. On this point, Aquinas connects with Freud's distinction between realistic and neurotic fear.

25. J.P. Reid, 'Emotional Psychopathology', in Aquinas, *Summa Theologiae*, vol. XXI: *Fear and Anger* (London: Blackfriars, 1965), pp. 156–63 (161). St. Thomas sees repression, to use Freud's terminology, as the cutting off of these passions from rational control yet they remain dynamically present and results in the fragmentation of mental energies. Although one is hard pressed to find a theory of unconscious motivation in St. Thomas, his treatment of the passions does not rule out the possibility for the movement of unconscious emotionality.

26. *STh*. I–II, q. 42, a. 4.

27. Since fear can make one deliberate, it is distinguished from the concupiscent appetite.

28. Loughlin writes, 'it is a central feature of Aquinas's doctrine concerning the emotions that each of them finds its root in love. For love establishes the context out of which the

However, excessive fear hinders the proper operation of reason making deliberation difficult if not impossible, and can immobilize the subject in taking action against the threat.[29] If left unchecked, fear can morph into despair.[30]

Fear also includes a physiological dimension, bodily changes which mirror the shifts happening in the sensitive appetite. The basic movement of fear is *contraction*. Just as the sensitive appetite shrinks from the feared object, the body also contracts and turns inward. The physiological reaction in fear moves in the opposite direction of anger. Instead of bodily energies moving to the extremities, the energies withdraw towards the inside. One's limbs experience chill, and motor coordination, the body's natural functions (heart, bowel) and the higher faculties, such as speech, can all be impeded.[31] The withdrawal of bodily heat also causes 'trembling, chattering of teeth, and blanching'.[32] Because it can demand so much of one's attention and energy, fear can hamper physical and mental vitality, and lessen one's capacity to engage in activities proper to our humanity like learning, following a conversation, or holding a job. Aquinas considers fear second only to sorrow has having the most harmful effect upon the body.[33]

Servile and filial timor

Timor, for Aquinas, also involves an individual's relationship with God. The Angelic doctor treats this aspect of *timor* through considering fear as regards the good, and identifies four types of fear: worldly, servile, filial and initial.[34] Worldly fear arises from a love of the world and its goods and the threat of their possible loss. This type of fear is good insofar as it moves one to act against losing his life, to respect legitimate authority and to marvel at the natural world. This fear becomes reprehensible for the Christian if it is not subordinated completely to his love of Christ and the world that is to come. The other three fears in this category are built upon the love of God, and are actually required for an integral life in Christ. Servile fear is the fear of God's punishment, filial fear is the fear of offending God and initial fear considers both the fear of punishment and of giving offence together.

emotions might arise. And so, with respect to fear, love binds a person to a good, which then allows him to desire it. The context has now been established wherein fear can possibly arise, namely when something prevents or endangers the fulfillment of one's desire for this good. Without love, no fear would arise. Indeed, as Aquinas states, fear is born of love' (Loughlin, 'Complexity of *timor*', p. 10; cf. *STh*. I–II, q. 42, a. 1 and q. 43, a. 1).

29. Cf. *STh*. I–II, q. 44, a. 2 (especially *ad* 2) and a. 4.

30. Cf. *STh*. I–II, q. 45, a. 2.

31. Cf. *STh*. I–II, q. 44, a. 1.3.

32. Reid, 'Somatic Reactions', in Aquinas, *Summa Theologiae*, vol. XXI: *Fear and Anger* (London: Blackfriars, 1965), pp. 172–77 (176).

33. Sorrow does greater harm to the body, according to St. Thomas, because the evil has already arrived and is presently harming the person. With fear, the evil is still in the future.

34. Cf. *STh*. I–II, q. 67, a. 4 *ad* 2; II–II, q. 7, a. 1, and especially II–II, q. 19.

Servile fear while initially helpful is an imperfect love shaped more by a love of self than by a love of God. Fear of punishment is good insofar as it deters one from committing sin, but it must mature towards filial fear. Otherwise one's love of self would be greater than his love of God. St. Thomas suggests that servile fear can also include other loves besides self love, but one is withdrawing from punishment in the fear and thus falls short of filial love. Filial love fears to lose the ultimate object of his love, God, and gives rise to reverence and the avoidance of whatever would offend him. This fear is a righteous fear and listed by St. Thomas as one of the gifts of the Holy Spirit given to combat the deadly sin of pride as well as presumption. The one with filial fear understands rightly that separation from God (the supreme good) as the absolutely worst possible evil, and therefore something which must be avoided at all cost, even one's life. Initial fear, the fourth type of fear classified by St. Thomas, relates imperfect (servile) and perfect (filial) fear in the movement from servile to filial fear. As one exercises the virtue of charity, his fear is transformed progressively from servile to filial. The more man loves the more he fears to be separated from his beloved. Thus, the more man loves God, the less he fears punishment (servile fear) because he loves the good more its own sake and the more confident he becomes of his reward in God.[35]

Aquinas also reasons that a type of *timor* perdures even in the life of Heaven. This *timor* will not be a servile fear since Heaven once gained can never be lost but rather a perfect filial fear of the Lord.[36] Fear plays an important role in man's redemption insofar as it brings him in proper relationship with God as his servile fear is transformed progressively into filial fear. Filial fear brings about a living faith, reminds man of his creaturality, liberates him from the capital sins of pride as well as presumption, and is revealed in its fullest sense in the life of Christ. Fear, therefore, is not an emotion to avoid at all cost. The Dominican master also understands poverty of spirit as the beatitude corresponding to the gift of fear since poverty of spirit involves reverence and submission to God.[37] Perfect filial fear attains to perfect poverty of spirit in which one no longer seeks his own greatness and renounces worldly goods in some way. This connection between fear and poverty figures prominently in

35. Cf. Loughlin, 'Complexity of *timor*', p. 13; cf. *STh*. II–II, q. 19, a. 8; II–II, q. 19, a. 10.

36. Cf. *STh*. II–II, q. 19, a. 11. Loughlin observes that although St. Thomas has difficulty in describing perfect filial fear in Heaven, it will certainly manifest a reverence rarely seen in the world and that it will involve a pure act of wonder which will never cease given man's finitude and God's infinity (cf. Loughlin, 'Complexity of *timor*', p. 14; *STh*. I–II, q. 67, a. 4 *ad* 2). Loughlin argues at this point on perfected filial love that fear in St. Thomas ceases to be analogical and becomes an equivocal notion. He writes, 'For the somatic characteristics central to fear are, for the most part, missing from its higher species, especially in its perfected form. The reverence characteristic of fear's perfected form bears little resemblance to the disruption of one's being caused by the lesser forms of fear. Better, therefore, to call the intellectual and perfected forms of "fear" by some other name since the analogy has clearly broken down' (See also, 16n).

37. *STh*. II–II, q. 19, a. 12.

Balthasar's thinking on anxiety regarding not only the original state but also the transformation of anxiety considered in Chapter 9.

Overcoming negative timor

How is fear overcome in the fallen state according to the Angelic doctor? For Freud, the ego reduced itself, for Kierkegaard the fear is faced with the courage of spirit. Aquinas takes a different approach. Since he understands emotions as greater than a bodily experience and intimately bound up in human cognition, will and love, he proposes that the negative emotions are shaped and overcome through an approach that is rational, volitional and bodily. Aquinas' holistic approach would connect somewhat with contemporary psychiatry's approach of talking therapy and medication. He avoids, however, the dualism and materialism that so often plagues the implicit assumptions of certain psychological approaches to healing anxiety. Aquinas focuses instead upon the human person which unites soul and body, and situates the emotional life within the moral life aimed towards happiness. They can be considered the 'matter' of the moral virtues through which human nature is perfected.[38] In other words, fear cannot be treated adequately outside of the context of man's transcendence.

Sensitive and servile fears are perfected by the virtue of fortitude and filial fear is perfected by the virtue of charity.[39] Aquinas does acknowledge the physiological dimension of fear, and thus leaves room for the use of medications in helping to deal with its somatic aspect. However, he does not view man's emotional life as primarily somatic. Pharmacological intervention would be considered treating the symptom, not the problem. St. Thomas goes further than Freud and Kierkegaard in pushing the person experiencing the negative emotion towards the practice of the virtues in the moral dimension of his nature. Finally, fear is transformed by holy fear as a gift of the Holy Spirit.

St. Thomas understands that fallen human nature is a *locus* of anxiety, understood in his broader term of *timor*. His description, more holistic and moral in character than Freud or Kierkegaard, nevertheless shows the deep and debilitating effects fear can have on man's well being not only in his body but also in his soul. In *Der Christ und die Angst*, Balthasar explicitly summarizes aspects of St. Thomas' treatment of fear in general and agrees with him, including the close relationship and distinction between *admiratio* and *timor*, the futurity of fear's object and the difference between natural and non-natural fear given the unique shape that rationality gives to the passion of

38. Cf. Gondreau, *The Passions of Christ's Soul*, pp. 264–71, especially 267; J.L.A. West, Review of *The Passions of Christ's Soul in the Theology of St. Thomas Aquinas*, *Theological Studies* 64 (2003), pp. 626–7.

39. Loughlin, 'Complexity of *timor*', 11n; cf. *STh*. II–II, q. 123; I–II, q. 60, a. 4. St. Thomas' attention to the develop habits of virtue connect with the behavioural dimension of anxiety described in the Introduction of this study.

fear.[40] Balthasar also observes that St. Thomas' classification of fear as a *passio animae* distinguishes it from the anxiety described by Kierkegaard and those who came after him.[41] Anxiety in the modern sense does not arise for St. Thomas, in Balthasar's view, because of fear's restriction to the senses as a *passio animae*. The lack of metaphysical confidence of the post-Enlightenment age created a situation unfamiliar to scholastic thinking. While we can recognize the profound loss of confidence in metaphysics in more recent centuries, Loughlin's interpretation of *timor* within the unity of the human person suggests that Balthasar perhaps overly restricts his understanding of *passio animae* in St. Thomas and overly distinguishes the *passio animae* of fear from *geistigen Angst*.[42] Balthasar would also be favourable to St. Thomas' perspective of viewing man's emotional life within the unity of his whole nature and its transcendence towards God, to the debilitating effects of *timor*, and to his emphasis on the moral dimension of overcoming *timor*.

The origin of negative timor *in original sin*

If the aforementioned summary describes man's fear in his present fallen state, what was man's condition vis-à-vis *timor* in the original state? This section investigates St. Thomas' view of the anxiety free life of the Garden of Eden.

Adam's freedom from negative *timor* in the original state

As was presented in the previous chapter, St. Thomas holds that Adam had the *cognitio matutina* and *cognitio verpertina* in the original state. Adam's intellect in the original state, though he did not see God in his essence, nevertheless possessed a knowledge superior to our own. In contrast to Kierkegaard, Aquinas holds that Adam's intellect did not function discursively in the original state, and therefore the ontological difference did not register as anxiety in the unfallen human mind. Yet he also emphasizes the continuity of human nature between the original and fallen state. Adam's soul in the original state

40. Cf. *CA*, pp. 69–72; Eng., pp. 118–22.

41. Cf. *CA*, pp. 72–4; Eng., pp. 122–4; *STh*. I–II, q. 22, a. 1, *c*. Balthasar does point out that ancient philosophy did correctly view anxiety as not merely intellectual but also psychosomatic.

42. Cf. *STh*. I–II, q. 22, a. 1; I–II, q. 22, a. 3; I–II, q. 31, a. 4; I–II, q. 41, a. 1. Balthasar is correct that the anxiety of the present age has a quality that would appear strange to a medieval scholastic because of the soul's consciousness of its immortality and the scholastic's great confidence in being. It appears, therefore, that St. Thomas' understanding of human *timor* falls between *Angst des Tieres* and *geistigen Angst* sharing characteristics of both. Although Balthasar sees the distinction between human and animal fear in St. Thomas' treatment, it is not clear that Balthasar's treatment of Aquinas on *timor* sufficiently expresses the hylomorphic dimension of Aquinas' theory and how this human fear is developed by this hylomorphic dimension.

is of the same nature as ours today.[43] The relationship between Adam's soul in the original and fallen states is not one of changing from one nature to another, but changing from integrity to corruption. In St. Thomas' view, therefore, the original state precluded any sort of intellectual anxiety in human nature. The ontological difference, which Adam recognized in his original state, did not cause him to be anxious.

If the original state precluded anxiety in Adam's intellective operations, what about the anxiety from relationships, external objects, bodily integrity and the passions? Adam lived in right relationship with God and the world in his original state. Both Adam's body and soul although perfectible were not corruptible.[44] Aquinas posits that man's body was preserved from the possibility of injury in the original state either through the use of his reason or through Divine Providence which would prevent hard objects from hurting his body.[45] Thus in the original state no object yet existed to make him afraid. His only fear would be his good filial fear of the Lord.

Adam's nature in the original state was also characterized by integrity. St. Thomas reasons that although Adam had emotions in the original state, he had no negative emotions since no evil was in the Garden of Eden.[46] Adam, therefore, desired without deficiency or excess. He had emotions like joy and love in terms of possession and as hoping without being cast down.[47] Adam and Eve, furthermore, had no unruly sexual desires even though Aquinas holds that procreation occurred through the conjugal act in the original state.[48] Moreover, their emotions were all being shaped and perfected by their virtues.[49] All their emotions were perfectly ordered and subject to reason, which in turn was completely subject to God.[50] Adam and Eve, although they were not yet perfect, were whole and integral within themselves in the original state. Their nature possessed no weakness by which objects became fearful to them, nor did their passions produce anxiety in the original state.[51]

The spawn of negative *timor* in original sin

The *timor* that is not the good filial *timor* invaded Adam's life consequent to original sin. He then experiences the fear of shame as his emotions, especially the concupiscent appetite, rebel against his reason and are no longer

43. Cf. *STh.* I, q. 94, a. 2 *sed contra.*
44. Cf. *STh.* I, q. 95, a. 2 *ad* 2.
45. Cf. *STh.* I, q. 97, a. 2 *ad* 4.
46. Cf. *STh.* I, q. 95, a. 2 *c.*
47. Cf. *STh.* I, q. 95, a. 2 *c.*
48. Cf. *STh.* I, q. 98, aa. 1–2.
49. Cf. *STh.* I, q. 95, a. 3 *c.*
50. *STh.* I, q. 95, a. 2 *c.*
51. Balthasar's description of the role that chastity played in the original state in the previous chapter connects with St. Thomas' position on this point.

completely subject to it.[52] He alienates himself from God and experiences sin-anxiety for the first time, expressed in his hiding in the Garden.[53] All the powers of his soul become disordered.[54] His intellect is darkened with ignorance, and his will is no longer ordered towards the good. His irascible faculty becomes weak in acting, and his concupiscent faculty is now characterized by disordered desires. These wounds are exacerbated by actual sin so that the intellect is further darkened in practical matters, the will further hardened against the good, which in turn further weakens good action and makes desires less manageable.[55] His body also becomes subject to sickness and death.[56]

The world, for its part, becomes a dangerous place. In his disobedience to God, Adam loses creation's obedience to him.[57] As a consequence of original sin, objects become fearful to man both by reason of the objects themselves and by reason of man's wounded and weak nature. Adam's reason and Divine Providence no longer completely protects man from the threat of objects moving about in the world which could damage or destroy his bodily integrity. Man is at odds with God, himself and others, all of which make him anxious. Aquinas locates the origin of negative *timor* not in fallen human nature itself but in original sin in which human nature was harmed.

It is evident that Balthasar is in wide agreement with Aquinas about the origin of anxiety in original sin, Adam's anxiety-free original state and the anxiety producing effects of the Fall. Balthasar takes a slightly different approach, for example, in casting his presentation on the original state in terms of the evangelical counsels, and expresses his wariness of any anthropology that does not take sufficient account of the Fall. He also emphasizes the importance of mission which pulls out of anxiety the all important tension between one's 'I' and his role.

Aquinas on Christ's Timor *and its Redemption*

The human nature assumed by the incarnate Son

Having sketched St. Thomas' treatment of *timor* in fallen human nature and the genesis of negative *timor* in original sin, we are in a position to examine how he understands redemption of negative *timor* in Christ. According to the Angelic doctor, the human nature the divine Son assumed in the Incarnation

52. Cf. *STh.* I–II, q. 82, a. 1 *ad* 3. Aquinas notes that the greatest effect of original sin is felt in man's generative power and the concupiscent appetite.

53. Aquinas views negative *timor* as a punishment for sin. Cf. *STh.* I–II, q. 87, a. 1 *sed contra*.

54. Cf. *STh.* I–II, q. 85, a. 3 *c*. He writes that original sin wounds man's nature in the four powers of his soul.

55. Cf. *STh.* I–II, q. 85, a. 3 *c*.

56. Cf. *STh.* I–II, q. 85, a. 5.

57. Cf. *STh.* I, q. 96, aa. 1–2.

was 'without sin, in the purity which it had in the state of innocence' yet possessed certain defects of body and soul which enabled him to suffer.[58] His passibility belongs to his *voluntary* assumption of the 'punishment of sin' (*poena peccati*) or 'condition of punishment wrought by original sin' rather than the 'guilt of sin' (*reatus peccati*).[59] If Christ, Gondreau writes, 'pulls his humanity from the stock of a corrupt and weakened nature, it in no sense comes at the expense of his perfect sinlessness, or of his consummate moral integrity, nor certainly of his perfection in grace'.[60] In this way his human nature differed somewhat from the original state of Adam. Jesus as man possessed Adam's pre-lapsarian innocence but not his impassability.

Unlike Adam in the original state, Christ was able to suffer in his body due to his divine will which suspended the natural relationship between soul and body so that the beatitude of his higher soul did not redound (*redudancia*) in his lower soul and body.[61] The Lord Jesus, however, did not assume every bodily defect but only those common to all people and not in conflict with his perfect knowledge and grace.[62] Christ also did not assume all defects of soul, but only in its relationship to the body and in its sensitive appetite. He did not assume the defects of sin, concupiscence or ignorance in his human soul. The Lord Jesus' purity of the state of innocence as man means that his human nature was free from concupiscence and any disharmony between his sense appetite and reason. Jesus' passions, therefore, functioned more like Adam's did in the original state and not like ours do in the fallen state.[63] Every movement of his sensitive appetite was simultaneously governed by reason and ordered to virtue. Jesus' human reason determines the mode of his human affections.[64] By virtue of his divine and human perfection, he also possessed all the gifts of the Holy Spirit which in Aquinas' system perfects the virtues.[65] Thus St. Thomas excludes any defect from the body and soul of Jesus that would compromise or destroy the soteriological aim of the Incarnation and Passion.

58. *STh.* III, q. 14, a. 3 *c*; Eng., XLIX, p. 181.

59. Gondreau, *The Passions of Christ's Soul*, pp. 243–244. In this section I follow closely Gondreau's treatment recognizing that his study was influenced heavily by Jean-Pierre Torrell, O. P., whose positions on Aquinas are respected though not universally shared by scholars on St. Thomas.

60. Ibid., p. 244; cf. *STh.* III, q. 14, a. 1 and q. 15, a. 5 *ad* 2.

61. Cf. *STh.* III, q. 14, a. 1 *ad* 2. The main reason for Christ's bodily suffering is that bodily suffering is one of the punishments for original sin, thus it is fitting that in making satisfaction for us, he also suffered bodily. Since part of the bodily punishment due to sin is 'death, hunger, thirst, and the like', then Christ would have been subjected himself to those punishments in his body (*STh.* III, q. 14, a. 1 *c*).

62. Cf. *STh.* III, q. 14, a. 4 *c*.

63. Cf. Gondreau, *The Passions of Christ's Soul*, pp. 301–2. Our passions, according to St. Thomas, move *ex necessitate* whereas Christ's move *ex imperio rationis* (cf. Aquinas, *Super Evangelium S. Ioannis Lectura*, pp. 12, 5).

64. Aquinas comments that Jesus' turbulence of soul in the Gospel of John is not against reason but according to it (cf. Aquinas, *Super Evangelium S. Ioannis Lectura*, 12, 5).

65. Cf. *STh.* III, q. 7, a. 5.

In line with the Council of Constantinople III (AD 680–681), St. Thomas argues for the complete human soul of Christ consisting of human intellect, will, appetites and passions.[66] Thus Christ has a single existence or hypostasis with two complete natures, each operating according to its proper nature. Yet Christ's human activity takes on a divine character in that his human nature operates instrumentally according to his divinity.[67] This gives Jesus' human nature unparalleled uniqueness that is entirely, supremely and perfectly *human*. The uniqueness of the Lord's human affectivity leads Aquinas to attribute, in Gondreau's view, a more restricted understanding of 'defect' to Christ's passions. Gondreau observes, 'whereas Thomas' reflections on general human affectivity employ a broader and more inclusive sense of *passibilitas*, his treatise on Christ's passions opts for a narrower and more restrictive use of *passibilitas*'.[68] With this overall view from St. Thomas on the perfect human nature assumed by the divine Son in his Incarnation, we are now in a position to asses the types and degree of *timor* Christ was able to experience.

The exclusion of sin-anxiety and intellectual anxiety

Christ's perfect, sinless human nature, and thus the perfect ordering of his passions by reason and virtue, excludes certain kinds of *timor* from his experience. He could not experience sin-anxiety for himself since he in no way assumed the defect of sin or concupiscence for such defects would have impeded, even eviscerated redemption.[69] He could not have the fear of sin for himself since he never sinned nor could sin. One cannot be afraid of the impossible.[70] St. Thomas writes that Jesus 'did not fear the evil of being separated from God by sin; nor did he fear the evil of being punished for guilt. What he did fear was all that is overwhelming in God'.[71] Our Lord did not experience anxiety from disordered desires either in excess or defect, and therefore could not experience internal temptation due to concupiscence. He possessed every virtue in its perfection.[72] However, he could and did experience external temptation on the part of the world and the devil.[73] The perfect ordering of his

66. For example, *STh*. III, q. 18, aa. 1–2.

67. Cf. Aquinas, *Compendium Theologiae* (Opera omnia; vol. 42; Romae: Editio Leonina, 1979) I, 212; *Summa contra Gentiles* (Opera Omnia; vols. 14–15; Romae: Editio Leonina, 1926–1930) IV, p. 27.

68. Gondreau, *The Passions of Christ's Soul*, p. 204. The uniqueness of the passibility of Christ's human soul is the combination of 'certain non-culpable ontological weaknesses' and perfect moral integrity. In other words, Christ's human soul is ontologically passible out of compassionate love, but morally it is incomparably strong. Cf. Id., *The Passions of Christ's Soul*, p. 304; *STh*. III, q. 14, a. 2 *sed contra*.

69. Cf. *STh*. III, q. 15, a. 1 *c* and III, q. 15, a. 2.

70. Cf. *STh*. III, q. 7, a. 6 *ob* 2.

71. *STh*. III, q. 7, a. 6 *c*; Eng., XLIX, p. 23.

72. Cf. *STh*. III, q. 15, a. 2.

73. Cf. *STh*. III, q. 15, a. 2 *ad* 3.

passions would also exclude the anxiety from ego-consciousness presented in Chapter 4. He was never confused about who he was or what he was supposed to do. Jesus has no interior struggle and frustration from contending with unfulfilled or excessive emotions or confusion about his identity.

But did Christ's experience intellectual anxiety as delineated in Chapter 3 of this study? How did Christ's human intellect function, and did he experience the intellectual vertigo described by Kierkegaard? Aquinas thinks not for he excludes any ignorance from Christ.[74] Although the Angelic doctor argues that Christ's human intellect did function discursively, he also holds that the discursive functioning of Christ's human intellect was in relationship with his beatific and infused knowledge. From the moment of his conception in the womb of his Blessed Mother, Jesus possessed the beatific vision in his human soul. This vision gave rise to the beatific knowledge (*scientia beatorum*) in his human soul. He possessed, therefore, beatific knowledge as man by virtue of his divine nature which communicated this knowledge to his human intellect.[75] Jesus as man in his earthly life, therefore, had a vision greater than Adam in the original state since Jesus as man had essential, direct knowledge of God. His human soul beholds the divine essence as perfectly and fully possible for a finite human soul.

In addition to Christ's beatific knowledge, St. Thomas posits that he also had the *cognitio matutina* and *vespertina* in his human intellect.[76] Christ as man knew things intuitively and did not need discursive reasoning to come to know things, although St. Thomas affirms the place for discursive reasoning in order to preserve Christ's full and integral humanity.[77] Christ's human intellect, therefore, possessed both passive and active operations by which he could acquire knowledge as man. The passive operation of his human intellect received his beatific and infused knowledge, and his active intellect abstracted forms from material things via his senses. Yet this discursive operation of his active intellect did not add anything to his knowledge, but rather reproduced his knowledge in his active intellect so that man's active intellect could be perfected.[78] St. Thomas in the *Summa* reasons that it would be unfitting that anything pertaining properly to human nature should be lacking in Christ, and thus admits a habit of knowledge which could increase by this abstraction of species. Thus one can speak of Christ increasing in not in beatific or infused knowledge but in acquired and empirical knowledge. Aquinas admits, therefore, a qualified discursive knowledge in Christ.[79]

We can deduce that Christ did not experience anxiety from ignorance, or intellectual vertigo from the discursive functioning of his human intellect in St. Thomas' view. The void in the intellect created by original sin in which fallen man reasons is not present in Jesus' mind. The discursive functioning of

74. Cf. *STh*. III, q. 15, a. 3 *c* and III, q. 11, a. 1 *ad* 3.
75. Cf. *STh*. III, q. 9, a. 2; *STh*. III, q. 34, a. 4.
76. Cf. *STh*. III, q. 9, a. 3 *c*.
77. Cf. *STh*. III, q. 9, a. 4 *c*; q. 11, a. 1–2.
78. Cf. *STh*. III, q. 9, a. 4 *ad* 2.
79. Cf. *STh*. III, q. 11, a. 3 *c*; q. 12, a. 2 *ad* 1.

Christ's human intellect does not render the world abstract since it constantly adheres to his divine knowledge. St. Thomas gives a place for the full human knowing of Jesus which was perfect and lacking in nothing,[80] for human perfection must be in Christ before it can be in any of us. Given Christ's full and perfect human knowledge a further conclusion may be drawn in relation to the anxiety springing from – using Freudian terms – his ego-consciousness. Christ would have experienced no anxiety from his 'I' (which is always the 'I' of his divine Person) and his mission. He would have no anxiety arising from ignorance or confusion about who he was and what he was supposed to do.

Aquinas' position on Christ's knowledge has an impact on the relationship to the virtues of faith and hope, which play an important role in the shaping of anxiety in fallen humanity. The Lord did not possess the virtue of faith according to the Angelic doctor since he understands faith as assent to that which is not seen but attested to by an authority. In Christian faith this authority is God himself. But Jesus as man in his earthly life *saw*, in his beatific vision, from the moment of his conception, and thus it would be inappropriate to attribute faith to him.[81] It does seem, however, that St. Thomas leaves room for Christ to have the moral value of faith through his utter obedience to the Father. For the same reason, Aquinas holds that Christ also did not possess the virtue of hope.[82] Hope has as its ultimate object, God and the enjoyment of him. But since Jesus is God and in his human nature has the vision of God, he already possesses the object and does not expect it to come. Thus it would be inappropriate to attribute hope to Christ. But he does leave room for a type of hope in Christ in that during his earthly life he had not yet attained everything that would make him perfect, for example, his Resurrection and glorification.

Christ's timor *as a natural propassion and perfect filial fear*

With sin-anxiety and intellectual anxiety excluded from Christ, in what way does St. Thomas say that Christ experienced *timor*? Suffering cannot be attributed to Jesus' divinity in Aquinas' thought because the Godhead is impassible.[83] But Jesus in his human nature could and did suffer both in actual bodily suffering and more importantly for our theme in the *apprehension* of bodily suffering.[84] Christ's soul could experience some form of negative *timor* since the soul is the form of the body and his body was passible, and Christ's soul could also experience *timor* as an animal passion, that is, as a movement in his sensitive appetite. Aquinas reasons, 'Since the soul is the form of the body it follows that the soul and body have but one existence. So, when the body is upset by some physical suffering, the soul has to be indirectly upset'.[85]

80. Cf. *STh*. III, q. 12, a. 2 *ad* 1.
81. Cf. *STh*. III, q. 7, a. 3 *c*.
82. Cf. *STh*. III, q. 7, a. 4 *c*.
83. Cf. *STh*. III, q. 46, a. 12.
84. Cf. Gondreau, *The Passions of Christ's Soul*, p. 408.
85. *STh*. III, q. 15, a. 4 *c*; Eng., XLIX, p. 203.

He certainly could experience natural fear in his sensitive appetite such as bodily injury since his body, as a human body, naturally shrinks from anything which endangers its existence or welfare. St. Thomas thus allows for a limited experience of fear in Christ because of his full human nature which possesses a sensitive appetite and certain defects of soul and body.[86]

Yet his natural fear would have been perfectly ordered to the rule of reason and perfected by his perfect fortitude; thus any fear would have never hampered his intellect and will in their operations.[87] Christ's strength of virtue prevented any increase in magnitude of any threatening object to his understanding since any lack of virtue is not part of the defects that the Son assumed in his Incarnation. Aquinas, moreover, excludes from this natural fear the fear stemming from the uncertainty of an event since Jesus had perfect knowledge of all things. Because of Christ's perfect knowledge and perfect virtue, fear could not be in Christ as a full-blown passion but only as what the Angelic doctor calls a 'propassion', that is, he could voluntarily *begin* to experience fear as an instinctive feeling but the fear would go no further.[88]

In addition to Jesus' natural *timor*, St. Thomas holds that he also experienced wonder (*admiratio*). However, wonder has two senses according to the Dominican master. On one hand, *admiratio* is a species of fear, the fear from encountering an object that is new and unwonted and considering a threatening evil.[89] On the other hand, Aquinas also classifies wonder as a desire for knowledge and so not all wonder is a species of fear but only the wonder which results in a great evil.[90] When attributing *admiratio* to Christ, St. Thomas emphasizes the second, more positive view of *admiratio*, yet also grants that he expressed *admiratio* as a type of fear not with respect to himself but with respect to others.[91]

By emphasizing the second meaning of *admiratio*, St. Thomas identifies the Lord's *admiratio* as a movement more of the intellective rather than the sensitive soul.[92] Jesus' *admiratio* did not reside in his beatific or infused knowledge, but in his human empirical knowledge.[93] He expressed wonder in order to instruct his followers to wonder at what he himself wondered, for example, his wonder at the Centurion's faith that Jesus could heal by mere command (cf. Mt. 8.10).[94] Aquinas excludes from Christ the other five types of *timor* enumerated by Damascene.

86. Cf. *STh.* III, q. 15, a. 7 *c.*
87. Cf. *STh.* III, q. 15, aa. 4–5; Aquinas, *Compendium Theologiae*, I, 232.
88. Cf. *STh.* III, q. 15, a. 7 *ad* 1–2; Busiello, 'Le Passioni in Tommaso d'Aquino', p. 98.
89. Cf. *STh.* I–II, q. 41, a. 4 *c.*
90. Cf. *STh.* I–II, q. 32, a. 8 *c* and *ad* 1; *STh.* I–II, q. 41, a. 4 *ad* 4.
91. Cf. *STh.* III, q. 15, a. 8 *ad* 2.
92. Cf. Gondreau, *The Passions of Christ's Soul*, pp. 419–20.
93. Cf. Loughlin, 'The Complexity of *timor*', p. 14; cf. *STh.* III, q. 15, a. 8 *c*; Gondreau, *The Passions of Christ's Soul*, pp. 421–7, 366–72, especially 425–6 where Gondreau analyses Aquinas' vacillation, development and ultimately incomplete position on Christ's acquired knowledge.
94. Cf. *STh.* III, q. 15, a. 8 *sed contra.*

Christ did not experience, moreover, servile, worldly or initial fear since they arise from evil or imperfection. Since Christ did not and could not sin, he does not experience that fear of punishment. He also did not experience worldly fear since it too arises from the imperfection of being attached to the world. Jesus most certainly did experience a perfect filial fear as a gift from the Holy Spirit far beyond any other person thereby giving Christians an example to imitate and for which to hope.[95] Jesus exemplifies the perfection of fear as filial fear, the holy form of fear.

Christ's timor *in Gethsemane*

In his commentary on the agony in the Garden, St. Thomas further delineates the appropriation and redemption of human fear by the Lord Jesus. His agony in the Garden manifests in a fundamental way his true human nature expressed in his human will and his *timor* as a natural propassion. St. Thomas argues that Jesus truly suffers fear in Gethsemane: 'there is the text of *Mark, Jesus began to be greatly distressed and troubled*'.[96] The word *timor* does not appear in the Gethsemane accounts in the Vulgate; rather Christ's fear is expressed in the terms *taedere* (Mk. 14.33), *pavere* (Mk. 14.33) and *turbata* (Jn. 12.27). The emotions expressed in the Garden indicate for the Angelic doctor Jesus' true human nature and are not suffered by his divinity. In fact he explicitly states in his comments on the Matthean account that Christ did not say, '*I* am sorrowful' indicating his Person, but that his *soul* is sorrowful thereby indicating his human soul.[97]

St. Thomas emphasizes in Christ's fear in Gethsemane the apprehension of his imminent passion and death. Jesus could apprehend the sensitive pain of brutal crucifixion. He could suffer interiorly in the apprehension of humanity's sins which he ascribes to himself, of the sins of those who conspired in his death and of the apostles, and of the loss of his own bodily life.[98] His fear was intensified by his perfect human nature because of its unparalleled sensitivity in both body and soul, and also due to the voluntary nature of his fear. Finally Jesus' fear is magnified by his innocence which makes the suffering all the more undeserved.[99] The role of imagination, moreover, ought not be overlooked in Jesus' agony in the Garden since fear stems from a future evil. With his perfect knowledge Jesus could have sharply focused images come to his imagination.[100]

While noting that some of the Fathers, namely St. Hilary, hold that Christ was not sorrowful for himself but for the disciples, St. Thomas sides with

95. Cf. *STh.* III, q. 7, a. 6 *c.*
96. *STh.* III, q. 15, a. 7 *sed contra*; Eng., XLIX, 213 (editor's italics).
97. Cf. Aquinas, *Super Evangelium S. Matthaei Lectura* (http//: www.corpusthomisticum.org) 26, 5.
98. *STh.* III, q. 46, a. 6 *c.*
99. Cf. *STh.* III, q. 46, a. 6 *ad* 4.
100. Cf. Gondreau, *The Passions of Christ's Soul*, p. 411.

Damascene who stated that Christ did suffer *pro seipso* in his human soul.[101] Damascene rejects Hilary's anaesthetized view of Christ's sufferings which allowed physical but not psychical suffering. This suffering in his human soul occurs on the level of his sensitive appetite, and the natural shrinking of his human nature from suffering and death. This interior agony, therefore, involved the sensible and not the rational faculty of his human soul, while the higher power of his soul did not suffer by virtue of the beatific vision which was a source of joy and delight, not grief. Aquinas notes, however, that, due to the hylomorphic quality of Christ's human nature, 'all the powers of Christ's soul did suffer according as any faculty is said to be affected as regards its subject, because all the faculties of Christ's soul were rooted in its essence, to which suffering extended when the body, whose act it is, suffered'.[102]

St. Thomas' interpretation of Jesus' agony on the Mount of Olives hinges upon a distinction within the intellective will between a spontaneous movement of the will (*voluntas ut natura*, θελησις) and a more deliberated or reflective movement of the will (*voluntas ut ratio*, βουλησις).[103] Jesus prays that the Father's will (βουλησις) be done, and that his will (θελησιζ) not be done. Jesus' agony, therefore, can be taken as a manifestation of his natural fear, but not an indication of a reflective, deliberated fear. Jesus' agony reveals his spontaneous, non-deliberative intellective human will; and therefore, an expression of his complete human nature.[104] This non-deliberate activity of his human will naturally shrinks from suffering while the deliberate activity of his human will chooses suffering in order to save us.[105] Though his non-deliberate will wished something other than the divine will, Jesus was not torn by contradictions for his non-deliberate will did not reject the higher will of his human reason and the divine will. Moreover, the will of his human reason and the divine will were not impeded by either this non-deliberate will or his sensitive appetite.[106] Aquinas writes,

> His mental agony was not such that his will suffered a conflict of reasons, as with us when we are caught with a divided mind. This comes from our weakness and inability to discern what is simply for the best. Such was not the case with Christ, whose reason was quite decided that the best course for him was to suffer if we were to be saved. The conflict lay in his sensitive appetites, which as Damascene notes dreaded the coming ordeal.[107]

101. Cf. Aquinas, *Super Evangelium S. Matthaei Lectura*, pp. 26, 5.
102. Cf. *STh.* III, q. 46, a. 7 *c*.
103. Cf. *STh.* III, q. 18, a. 3; Gondreau, *The Passions of Christ's Soul*, p. 311. The distinction has its source in St. Maximus the Confessor and finds its way to St. Thomas via St. John Damascene. Damascene classifies the terms as two different things which allows in Jesus a natural fear (*timor naturalis*) but not a reflective fear (*timor cogitationis*). Cf. Id., *The Passions of Christ's Soul*, p. 311.
104. Cf. *STh.* III, q. 18, a. 1.
105. Cf. *STh.* III, q. 18, a. 3; Eng., L, p. 73.
106. Cf. *STh.* III, q. 18, a. 6 *c*.
107. *STh.* III, q. 18, a. 6 *ad* 3; Eng., *Theological Texts*, pp. 319–20.

In addition to the two-fold distinction in the intellective will, St. Thomas also posits in Christ 'the will of sensuality' (*voluntas sensualitatis*) which represents the will from the sense appetite. This term is similar to the non-deliberative will (*voluntas ut natura*) and expresses the natural, instinctive aversion to sense evils, especially the perception of a violent death. Thus Jesus in both the non-deliberative will and the sensitive will expresses his natural repugnance to death. St. Thomas in his *Compendium Theologiae* explains this natural movement of the lower appetite in Christ away from death (remove this cup from me), and the movement of his higher reason (not my will, but yours be done).[108]

This spontaneous movement of his intellective and sensitive will ought in no way to be confused with a type of rebellion in Jesus' passions. None of these movements involve resistance to his higher reason, as his prayer in Gethsemane shows. The following passage from St. Thomas illustrates his position:

> Similarly his allowed all the powers of his soul to function according to their nature. Now it is apparent that it is natural for the sensuous will (*voluntas sensualitatis*) to shrink from physical pain and bodily injury. Likewise the will acting by natural instinct (*voluntas ut natura*) rejects whatever is contrary to human nature and intrinsically evil, such as death and what is connected with it. Nevertheless, as modified by judgment, the will (*voluntas rationis*) may sometimes choose to undergo such evils in order to attain its goal.[109]

Thus, St. Thomas terms Jesus' emotional suffering in Gethsemane a propassion, that is, the beginning movement of a passion which then goes no further because of the perfect ordering of the passion by reason and virtue. Therefore, in Gethsemane he *began* to experience the passion of fear in his sensitive appetite, but it went no further to affect his intellect and will.[110] His lower soul was naturally repulsed by suffering and death, but was perfectly ordered by the higher part of his soul. The Dominican master, furthermore, holds that Christ's suffering is united to his joy, and that joy and suffering are not opposed because they do not have the same object.[111] A coincidence of fear and joy occur in Gethsemane, but not in the same way.[112] The Lord's joy flowed from his uninterrupted beatific vision of the Father throughout his suffering, while his fear operated in his lower soul. In other words, Aquinas understands Christ's joy more in terms as over and above his sufferings rather than flowing from his sufferings.

108. Cf. Aquinas, *Compendium Theologiae*, I, p. 233.

109. *STh*. III, q. 18, a. 5 *c, ad* 1; Eng., L, p. 79.

110. Cf. Aquinas, *Super Evangelium S. Matthaei Lectura*, 26, 5; *STh*. III, q. 15, a. 4 *c*.

111. Cf. *STh*. III, q. 46, a. 8 *ad* 1.

112. Cf. *STh*. III, q. 46, a. 7–8.

Christ's timor *and his beatific vision*

The consideration of the type and intensity of negative *timor* in Christ necessitates a deeper look at the relationship between Jesus' affective sufferings and the beatific vision he had as man. Reconciling Christ's beatific vision with his terrible suffering in Gethsemane is a challenging mystery for the theologian. Yet the issue merits some consideration in this study because Jesus' beatific vision during his earthly life is a primary factor in determining both his capacity to experience *timor/Angst* as well as the degree to which he could experience it.[113] The question of his beatific vision has its roots in the interpretation of 1Cor. 13.13,[114] and the relationship between Christ's divine and human knowledge. How can Christ simultaneously be a *comprehensor* and *viator*? How can he simultaneously *possess* full beatitude and also *tend* towards beatitude? This question burned in the thirteenth century mind as much as it does now, and St. Thomas, Gondreau observes, concludes his treatment of Christ's passions precisely on this question.[115] The difficulty lies not only in reconciling how Jesus can truly suffer with such a vision, but also reconciling that knowledge with Aquinas' hylomorphic understanding of human nature in which body and soul mutually affect each other.

The primary reason for attributing the full, explicit beatific vision to Christ during his earthly life, and thus beatific knowledge in his human intellect, seems to be *soteriological* for St. Thomas. Christ must have the beatific vision himself in order to lead others to it, and to effectively function as the mediator between God and man. The beatific vision also seems demanded by Jesus' human perfection in holiness and grace. Thomas White argues that the beatific vision is necessary in order to preserve the unity of Christ's actions as the God-man.[116] Only by preserving his perfect humanity, which is perfect through his perfect *knowledge*, and its subsistence in his divine Person, can Christ atone for human sin as well as provide us with an example of virtue. In this view, the more perfectly Jesus as man knows, the more his human perfection is preserved. In order to maintain Christ's perfect human nature,

113. A complete treatment of Christ's beatific vision on earth merits a full study of its own. What follows is a summary of the basic problem in theology as posed by St. Thomas and contemporary scholarship on St. Thomas with some conclusions in order to make a comparison with Balthasar's position at the end of Chapter 7.

114. The interpretation hinges upon whether faith and hope abide from now into eternity, or if they abide only in this life. Both interpretations exist in Catholic theology. The first is that man's faith and hope are only for earthly life and these are overtaken by the vision and comprehension of God in Heaven. The second current emphasizes the aspect of trust, which would allow a certain 'faith' and 'hope' in heaven in the exercise of creaturely freedom in the giving and receiving of love.

115. Cf. *STh.* III, q. 15, a. 10; Gondreau, *The Passions of Christ's Soul*, p. 441. Gondreau adds that Aquinas makes a similar allusion in every major work treating Christ's human affectivity: *Sentences*, *De veritate*, *Compendium Theologiae*, and *Summa Theologiae* (cf. Id., *The Passions of Christ's Soul*, 441n).

116. Cf. T. White, 'The Voluntary Action of the Earthly Christ and the Necessity of the Beatific Vision', *The Thomist* 69 (2005), pp. 497–534.

soteriologically essential for us, Jesus as man *must* have the perfection of knowledge. Thus it is right for St. Thomas to attribute the highest kind of knowledge – beatific knowledge – to the human soul of Jesus. This knowledge comes to him from his beatific vision.

Yet Christ's psychosomatic suffering is also soteriologically important. How can Christ experience both? Aquinas holds that Christ was both a *comprehensor* and *viator* during his earthly life but not in the same manner.[117] He was a *comprehensor* 'having the beatitude characteristic of the soul' and a *viator* 'proceeding towards beatitude *in the areas in which he still lacks it*'.[118] In what way did Christ lack beatitude?

According to St. Thomas, the earthly Jesus was a *viator* due to the passibility of his body and soul from a divine dispensation (*dispensationem divinae*). According to the divine arrangement or economy of salvation, and out of a free and loving decision, Jesus' mind (*mens*) 'was prevented from suppressing the capacity for suffering in both his body and soul'.[119] St. Thomas characterizes this ability in Christ in terms of a suspension of the joy of the higher reason (*superior ratio*) from reaching the lower powers (*vires inferiors*). Thus, in his human nature, the normal *redundantia* between soul and body is voluntarily suspended. The divine dispensation did not interrupt Christ's beatific vision but 'blocked the redounding effects of the vision on the lower powers of the soul'.[120] The consummate joy within the higher part of the soul, therefore, did not redound into the lower part of the soul and the body thus allowing the coincidence of affective suffering and spiritual joy. Jesus' lower powers are subject to the movements of disagreeable passibililty while his higher reason remains in the beatific vision.[121]

Thus Jesus is a *comprehensor* in his higher reason and *viator* in his lower powers. Gondreau elaborates that this distinction implies no schizophrenia in Jesus. It is a formal not a material distinction of objects.[122] Jesus as man, therefore, was simultaneously 'pilgrim and beholder, sufferer and seer, enjoying the beatific vision of his Father, and yet feeling a sorrow surpassing all the suffering endured or endurable by men in this present life'.[123] Out of his unimaginable compassion, our Lord's human will to suffer which ruled his non-deliberative will in Gethsemane 'prevented happiness flowing from the summit of his soul, where he looks on the face of his Father, down to its relatively lower slopes, where he is assailed by the storms of agony'.[124] This

117. Cf. *STh*. III, q. 15, a. 10.

118. *STh*. III, q. 15, a. 10 *c*; Eng., XLIX, p. 221 (author's italics).

119. Gondreau, *The Passions of Christ's Soul*, p. 445.

120. Ibid., p. 449. Cf. *STh*. III, q. 46, a. 8 *c*.

121. Cf. *STh*. III, q. 46, a. 7–8.

122. Cf. Gondreau, *The Passions of Christ's Soul*, 447; *STh*. III, q. 46, a. 8 *ad* 1.

123. J. Saward, *The Mysteries of March: Hans Urs von Balthasar on the Incarnation and Easter* (Washington D.C.: Catholic University Press, 1990), p. 55.

124. Ibid., p. 55.

state of Christ's is simultaneously 'supreme and ineffable spiritual joy and unspeakably intense affective suffering'.[125]

It can be observed, however, that the joy and suffering do not occur in Christ in the same way. Christ's joy does not come from his suffering but from the beatific vision. God incarnate suffered *timor* in his human nature, according to Aquinas, as part of his Passion in making satisfaction for man's sins. It is a limited suffering circumscribed by his divinity and perfect human nature. Christ's constitution excludes the possibility of his suffering the *timor gehennalis* which in Aquinas' view would require setting aside his beatific vision and thereby compromise his sinless human nature.

The difficulty remains, however, that Aquinas' Christ does not suffer in his entire soul. Gondreau states the difficulty in the following manner:

> [I]f the penetration of reason into Christ's sensibility was so radically extensive that every movement of his affectivity was instinctively and innately oriented to reason's *imperium*, it remains unclear how this holds true for the instinctive impulse of affectivity that Jesus experienced in the Garden of Gethsemane, even if this impulse occurred before his reason had determined what was best to choose. It is not out of the question that the penetration of reason into Christ's sensibility leaves sufficient room for an instinctive impulse of affectivity, that, no matter its initial inclination to its own sentient object, becomes forthrightly subsumed and finalized by reason.[126]

On this position, Aquinas is forced to set aside, in Gondreau's view, his position on human affectivity in general within which the notion of *redundantia* is central, as well as the descriptions given by Holy Scripture.[127] It is difficult to reconcile Christ's beatific knowledge and his intense affective suffering as well as supreme spiritual joy in St. Thomas' position.

In addition to maintaining the unity of Christ's natures, an adequate accounting of the *crucifixus etiam pro nobis*, how Christ was 'made sin' for us (2 Cor. 5.21), in St. Thomas' doctrine of redemption is also soteriologically important.[128] This dimension, which affects how Christ can appropriate human fear to himself, is not immediately clear in St. Thomas' position. According to Jacques Servais, Christ was made sin for us in Aquinas' theology in terms of 'merit', 'satisfaction', 'sacrifice' and 'redemption'.[129] Servais argues that the interpreter of St. Thomas must not fail to account for this dimension of the Angelic doctor's position. St. Thomas holds that Christ's Passion was not undergone out of necessity in an absolute sense, but by a free, loving choice, and that he describes the sufferings of the Passion as expressions of self-emptying love.[130] It is out of love that the Lord Jesus freely hands himself

125. Gondreau, *The Passions of Christ's Soul*, p. 450.

126. Ibid., p. 317.

127. Cf. Gondreau, *The Passions of Christ's Soul*, p. 451; cf. pp. 36–9.

128. Cf. Servais, 'Le *pro nobis* dans la conscience de Jésus', in H. U. von Balthasar, *Au cœur du mystère rédempteur* (repr. 2, Magny-les-Hameaux: Socéval, 2005), pp. 167–99.

129. Cf. Servais, 'La doctrine thomiste de la Rédemption', in Balthasar, *Au cœur du mystère rédempteur* (repr. 2, Magny-les-Hameaux: Socéval, 2005), pp. 145–65.

130. Cf. *STh.* III, q. 46, aa. 5–6; Servais, 'La doctrine thomiste de la Rédemption', pp. 150–2.

over to be made sin for us and to suffer on behalf of us sinners.[131] St. Thomas distinguishes between the *sensus poenae* and the *vis poenae* in Christ's sufferings in that he took upon himself our punishment, not our sin.[132] Servais observes that Christ's sufferings remain extrinsic to his Divine Person in St. Thomas' position.

Before leaving this section of our study, we should mention that Christ's full and explicit beatific vision during his earthly life, which guides Aquinas' interpretation of Christ's *timor*, has found expression in certain statements of the ordinary Magisterium.[133] Servais argues that the teaching articulated by the Magisterium on this question need not be interpreted in a unilateral manner, and that an acceptable range of opinions can exist within the boundaries established thus far.[134]

Aquinas' position regarding the Lord's beatific vision in his earthly life, furthermore, has been challenged in recent decades by some Catholic theologians, Balthasar among them, who nevertheless adhere to the orthodox conciliar formulations regarding Christ. They find the scholastic explanation inadequately expressive of the biblical data and in danger of compromising Christ's full humanity and/or the hypostatic union,[135] or does not adequately express that Jesus suffered *pro nobis*.[136] On the other hand, some formidable

131. To merit salvation for us, Christ, in his preeminent charity, took upon himself the punishment for our sin (cf. *Summa contra Gentiles*, III, p. 158; *STh*. III, q. 48, a. 2; Id., 'La doctrine thomiste de la Rédemption', pp. 150–6. This satisfaction, moreover, is not only sufficient, it is superabundant. The superabundant satisfaction, reasons Servais, is due to Christ's preeminent charity, the efficient value because of the divinity of the Incarnate Son who undergoes the suffering and the penalty associated with his sufferings (cf. Id., 'La doctrine thomiste de la Rédemption', pp. 155–6).

132. Cf. Servais, 'La doctrine thomiste de la Rédemption', p. 161.

133. The Magisterium's intervention on this issue has been infrequent, but when it does, it points the theologian toward the position of an uninterrupted, explicit beatific vision. The first intervention came in 1918 when the Holy Office responded that a thesis which denies the beatific vision of the historical Christ 'cannot be taught with safety' (DS 3645) (cf. F. Ocáriz, L. F. Mateo Seco and J.A. Riestra, *The Mystery of Jesus Christ* (Dublin: Four Courts Press, rev. edn, 2004), p. 156. The teaching surfaces again in Pope Pius XII's *Mystici corporis* (1943) and *Haurietis aquas* (1956), and appears also in the teaching of Pope John Paul II and in the CCC, n. 473. Liam Walsh states that although Christ's uninterrupted beatific vision in his human soul has found its way into the ordinary Magisterium (and mentions DS 3645, 3812) it 'is not a defined teaching of faith' and thus a 'challenge to St. Thomas's position would seem to be dogmatically permissible' (*STh*. Eng., LXIX, 89n).

134. He writes, 'quand le premier dit que l'âme du Christ, durant la Passion, jouissait *toute entière* de la vision béatifique, cela ne signifie pas, nous précisent-ils subtilement, que pareille vision était *entièrement* béatifique' (Servais, 'Le *pro nobis* dans la conscience de Jésus', p. 169) (author's italics).

135. Perhaps the most forceful and developed argument against the scholastic interpretation of the beatific vision during Christ's earthly life, and recognized by scholars on St. Thomas as such, is made by the Jesuit Christologist Jean Galot. Cf. Galot, 'Le Christ terrestre et la vision', *Gregorianum* 67 (1986), pp. 429–50. The Franciscan theologian, Thomas Weinandy, offers a more recent challenge which echoes that of Galot: Weinandy, 'Jesus' Filial Vision of the Father', *Pro Ecclesia* 13 (2004), pp. 189–201.

136. Cf. Servais, 'Le *pro nobis* dans la conscience de Jésus', p. 170.

scholars on St. Thomas argue strongly against positions such as Galot's and for the necessity of the beatific vision in Jesus' earthly life.[137] The issue at stake for Thomas White is not so much Jesus' full humanity, but rather the unity of his human operations from his human nature's subsistence in his divine person.[138] But then how are we supposed to understand Christ's sufferings? White follows a similar line as Gondreau in stating that Jesus suffers by divine dispensation in which the *redundancia* between the higher and lower parts of the soul is suspended.[139] He reasons further that the beatific vision, in a way, contributes to the experience of Jesus' suffering in that it brings, in White's words, 'existential dissatisfaction', that is, 'the desire for something known to be in the future but as yet unattained'.[140]

The important point to be made for the purposes of this study is that arguments exist within orthodox Catholic theology, even within Thomism itself, on whether a direct, immediate terrestrial beatific vision in the Lord Jesus is necessary to adhere to the statements given by the ordinary Magisterium thus far. Some propose a different *mode* of the beatific vision which need not be explicit in Christ's human consciousness, and which also need not threaten Jesus' consciousness of his divine Personhood or his salvific mission. Perhaps there is more than one way to characterize the filial mode of being in the historical Christ.

Possible existential stretching in Christ's appropriation of timor?

Is it possible to admit a 'stretching' of Christ's experience of fear in Aquinas' position to allow a more adequate account of his psychosomatic suffering? It appears that such a possibility presents itself based upon three aspects of his interpretation. First his hylomorphic understanding of Christ's affectivity means that reason penetrates affectivity, and this must happen in a preeminent way with Christ. As Loughlin argued earlier in this chapter, 'when someone fears, it is the *person* himself who fears'.[141] Although man's appetitive 'directedness' is distinguished from his apprehensive powers, these apprehensive powers play a large role in the generation of emotion because one must judge the thing itself as good or bad for the one perceiving it in order for an emotion

137. Cf. White, 'The Voluntary Action of the Earthly Christ', pp. 497–534. He also mentions the work of R. Cessario, J.M. Garrigues, M. Levering and G. Mansini.

138. Ibid., p. 498.

139. Ibid., 531n.

140. Ibid., pp. 532–3. As forcefully as White argues for the beatific vision, he nevertheless recognizes in St. Thomas' position that the *mode* of beatific vision can vary according to the demands of the salvific economy. His description of Christ's suffering as 'existential dissatisfaction' does not seem to account adequately for the biblical data of Jesus' intense suffering, and the term is left unexplained in his article. I agree with White when he writes that 'theologians who wish to reconsider this classical teaching of the Church must face the real challenge of explaining how, in the absence of this vision, the unity of the theandric acts of Christ may properly be maintained' (see also, p. 534).

141. Loughlin, 'Complexity of *timor*', 2 (author's italics).

to be generated (see I.a). St. Thomas' view of human emotional life expands beyond the movements of the sensitive appetite to involve the entire person including the higher parts of the soul as well as the élan of one's life towards happiness. What can be said about Christ's *timor* within the élan of his life as the incarnate Son and his happiness at our redemption? It does not appear that the hylomorphic dimension of Aquinas' interpretation is developed into its full implications.

Secondly, a more nuanced understanding of the object of Christ's fear could allow a greater experience of it. A distinction can be made by the proper objects of Christ's instinctive aversion to death and his propassion of fear. Gondreau writes, 'the object of Jesus' instinctual desire to avoid his fate is the preservation of his life (a sense good), an object that stands in the way of what the Father commands, while the object of his passion of fear is his approaching torture and death (a sense evil), an object that, in fact, *accords* with the Father's will'.[142] This distinction, according to Gondreau, is given insufficient explicit insistence by Aquinas. By giving this dimension more explicit insistence Jesus' fear in Gethsemane is 'more than a simple "instinctive retreat" at the thought of the horrifyingly tortuous execution that he knew loomed before him'.[143] Therefore a greater experience of fear can be granted to Christ's propassion of fear. It is a 'fully elicited passion' with an 'intense quality' but did not impede his intellect and will. Christ's fear, in this view, is more than an instinctual reaction yet less than a full-blown, second stage passion which clouds reason.

Thirdly, St. Thomas does attribute *compassio* to Christ's suffering as seen earlier in Servais' emphasis on the *pro nobis* character of the Thomistic doctrine of salvation. St. Thomas writes, 'The soul of Christ could indeed stand fast against emotion, and not let himself be overwhelmed by it, especially by his divine power. But by his own choice he let himself be affected, both physically and emotionally'.[144] St. Thomas attributes the source of Christ's sufferings to his love. This love leads him to embrace suffering.

Finally, some scholars on St. Thomas propose alternatives to an explicit beatific vision in Christ during his earthly life that would grant a greater experience of affective suffering in the earthly Christ without making soteriological compromises. Gondreau advances the proposal of his mentor Jean-Pierre Torrell in which the beatific and infused knowledge of Christ is transposed into the special knowledge of prophesy known not from a 'prophetic' but a 'Christic' light. This would allow the relinquishment of Christ's beatific vision during his earthly life while fulfilling the exigency of Christ needing the beatific vision in order to bring others to it by attributing it to him in his resurrected state.[145] However Torrell's view is not without criticism.[146]

142. Gondreau, *The Passions of Christ's Soul*, p. 412 (Gondreau's italics).

143. Ibid., p. 412.

144. *STh.* III, q. 15, a. 4 *ad* 1; Eng., XLIX, pp. 203, 205.

145. Cf. Gondreau, *The Passions of Christ's Soul*, pp. 451–2.

146. West, Review of *The Passions of Christ's Soul in the Theology of St. Thomas Aquinas*, p. 627; White, 'The Voluntary Action of the Earthly Christ', pp. 516–20.

Pope John Paul II has suggested this existential stretching in General Audiences and in *Novo Millenio Ineunte*.[147] He reasons that Jesus' cry of abandonment is a profound mystery of faith, whose suffering is intensified *because* of his union with the Father, and asks, 'Is it possible to imagine a greater agony, a more impenetrable darkness'?[148] Jesus' cry of abandonment is not without hope but a prayer in which the Incarnate Son offers himself in love to the Father. The Holy Father directs his reader to the 'lived theology' of the saints to seek an explanation of the mysterious union of beatitude and suffering of the Cross. He writes, 'Not infrequently the saints have undergone *something akin to Jesus' experience on the Cross* in the paradoxical blending of bliss and pain',[149] and cites the examples of Sts. Catherine of Siena and Thérèse of Lisieux. He writes that St. Thérèse 'lived her agony in communion with the agony of Jesus, "experiencing" in herself the very paradox of Jesus's own bliss and anguish: "In the Garden of Olives our Lord was blessed with all the joys of the Trinity, yet his dying was no less harsh. It is a mystery, but I assure you that, on the basis of what I myself am feeling, I can understand something of it" '.[150]

Conclusion

According to St. Thomas, the Divine Son assumed a perfect human nature in his Incarnation, and he understands Christ's human perfection in terms of knowledge. This concept of human perfection excludes certain types of negative *timor* from the Lord Jesus including any *timor* from ignorance, sin, concupiscence or disordered passions. St. Thomas holds that the *timor* experienced by Christ is perfect filial fear and a pro-passion of his human soul. Aquinas also holds that God incarnate suffered *timor* in his human nature as part of his Passion in making satisfaction for human sin. It is a limited suffering circumscribed by his knowledge and uninterrupted beatific vision. Christ's constitution excludes the possibility of his suffering the *timor gehennalis* which, in Aquinas' view, would compromise his sinless human nature. St. Thomas' position, moreover, has found expression in the ordinary Magisterium.

It is difficult, however, to reconcile in St. Thomas' position of the historical Christ's beatific knowledge with his intense affective suffering indicated by the

147. Cf. John Paul II, *General Audience* (30 November 1988) in *L'Osservatore Romano* (*English edition*) [5 December 1988] p. 1; quoted in Saward, *The Mysteries of March*, p. 56. Cf. John Paul II, *Novo Millenio Ineunte, AAS* 93 (2001) nn. 25–7. White places this passage of Pope John Paul II in support the traditional scholastic doctrine (cf. White, 'The Voluntary Action of the Earthly Christ', 497n). I suggest a more nuanced position to the Holy Father's teaching in paragraphs 25–27, in observing that his is not a simple repetition of the tradition but that he extends the traditional teaching into the existential dimension of Christ's suffering.

148. John Paul II, *Novo Millenio Ineunte*, n. 25.

149. Ibid., n. 27 (John Paul II's italics).

150. Ibid., n. 27.

biblical data as well as the *pro nobis* of the Creed. Scholars of St. Thomas are not univocal about the traditional scholastic teaching of Christ's earthly beatific vision, and indicate the possibility for various interpretations of Christ's uninterrupted, direct vision of God during his earthly life without compromising defined magisterial teaching. It seems possible to admit an existential 'stretching' of Christ's ability to appropriate negative *timor* in Aquinas' position based upon his hylomorphic understanding of Christ's affectivity, a more nuanced understanding of the object of Christ's fear, and his attribution of *compassio* to Christ's suffering. This existential 'stretching' of Christ's ability to appropriate negative *timor* is suggested by the Thomistic positions of Gondreau, Loughlin, Torrell and Pope John Paul II. The purpose for exploring Aquinas' position on *timor* and especially Christ's *timor* is to make a comparison with Balthasar's which will be done at the conclusion of the next chapter.

Chapter 7

Balthasar's Interpretation of Angst and its Redemption

On the Mount of Olives it is a final, precipitous plunge into the abyss of anxiety . . . vicariously for every sinner and every sin.

(H.U. von Balthasar)[1]

We continue our theological analysis of anxiety which brings the anthropological discussion (part two) to the Word of God in Balthasar's thought. An immediate observation can be made between Balthasar and Aquinas on this topic is that Balthasar's explicit treatment of the theme is neither exhaustive nor systematic, and he does not intend it to be so. Instead he moves immediately to a biblical-theological investigation of the topic. Divine Revelation, according to our author, is the ultimate authority and measure of human anxiety. He begins his treatment with the following calm observation: 'When one surveys even from a distance how often and how openly Sacred Scripture speaks about anxiety, one arrives at an initial conclusion: the Word of God knows no anxiety about anxiety'.[2] Divine Revelation, in Balthasar's view, neither exalts nor debases anxiety, but recognizes it as a fundamental given in life that has been redeemed and revalued from God's point of view – the Cross.[3]

In order to construct Balthasar's understanding of anxiety and its redemption, we first present his own treatment of anxiety in Sacred Scripture given in *Der Christ und die Angst*. In this way, Balthasar's own mode of inquiry is respected, namely, Sacred Scripture is the foundation of his theological interpretation. Yet because our author wrote that work before articulating many of his positions on Christology and soteriology, especially as expressed in his volumes of the *Theodramatik*, we then summarize relevant aspects of his Christology and soteriology from subsequent works in order to apply them to the theme of anxiety. This application can offer a more ample picture of Balthasar's view of the redemption of anxiety. At the end of this chapter a comparison is then made between Balthasar and Aquinas on the redemption of anxiety and some conclusions are drawn.

1. *CA*, p. 37; Eng., p. 74.
2. CA, p. 13; Eng., p. 39 (translation adapted by author).
3. Cf. *CA*, p. 13; Eng., p. 40.

The Evaluation of Anxiety by Sacred Scripture According to Balthasar

Balthasar's observations on the phenomenology of anxiety in Sacred Scripture were given in the first chapter of this study. So we proceed directly to his interpretation of the biblical data. Balthasar does not seem to intend to offer a systematic treatment of anxiety in Sacred Scripture, but rather to glean a selection of passages which distill essential points which can serve as a foundation for his interpretation.[4] He further focuses the beginning of his reflection within the wisdom literature. The first observation he makes is that biblical revelation acknowledges anxiety as a fundamental given of human life, and neither minimizes nor exaggerates its presence or intensity in the world.[5] He identifies three basic categories of human anxiety as revealed by God in the Old Covenant: natural, sin and righteous anxiety.

Natural anxiety

The Old Testament initially presents, according to Balthasar, a general and neutral anxiety (*Angst des Daseins*)[6] that is both universal and constant in the fallen human condition. Because the world is fallen, and therefore dangerous, man must contend with anxiety. The believer in the Old Covenant, immersed as he was in this natural and existential anxiety, found himself squeezed by a 'terrible paradox' between his own finitude, now circumscribed by birth and death, and the divine command to stand in God's light and rejoice in expectation for the coming Messiah.[7] This paradox leaves the believer 'convulsed by anxiety', since through the course of his life the jaws of death continually widen while the object of his hope, the Messiah, does not yet arrive. The natural anxiety revealed by God in the Old Testament, however, does not remain neutral. Instead it bifurcates into two modes: the anxiety of the wicked (*Angst der Bösen*) and the anxiety of the good (*Angst der Guten*). One's natural anxiety takes on a specific character depending on one's orientation towards or away from God.

4. Cf. Costacurta, *La Vita Minacciata*, for a more ample treatment of fear in the Old Testament. Even a brief comparison between Costacurta's study and Balthasar's remarks in *Der Christ und die Angst* indicate that he could not intend them to be a comprehensive treatment of all the passages in Sacred Scripture in *Der Christ und die Angst*.

5. Our author's tone in *CA* remains deliberately calm and measured in direct reaction against the tone he perceived characterized the writing on anxiety at the time. Tourenne makes the same observation: cf. Tourenne, 'Un théologien et son temps', p. 15; Eng., pp. 11–12.

6. *CA*, p. 16.

7. Cf. *CA*, p. 15; Eng., p. 42.

Sin-anxiety

Sin-anxiety (*Sündenangst*) is the term that Balthasar associates with the anxiety of the wicked.[8] Sin-anxiety is the modality of anxiety of the one standing away from, and in opposition to, God. Our author appeals, especially to the passage from Wis. 17 which interprets this anxiety as an imprisonment in darkness and a shadow life within an unreal world, actually a counter-world in opposition to God's reality. The choice to live in evil is, therefore, to live outside of God's reality, and this counter-world becomes for the wicked man an *Angstkosmos* in which he is both 'driven' and 'paralyzed'.[9] One loses the ability in this counter-world to understand the origin and goal of his existence. The sinner's choice for evil is an abandonment of reason which results in the meaninglessness of his own life and cowardice in facing God's reality. The wicked individual's sin-anxiety intensifies, according to Balthasar, to the point where the sinner becomes anxious about everything – even imaginary things and nothing at all.[10]

The darkness that envelops the wicked individual and causes his sin-anxiety is identified by our author as an emanation from Sheol, the ultimate origin of the sinner's 'primal anxiety' (*Urangst*) in the Old Testament.[11] The sinner in the act of sin strives to avoid the divine light even to the point of being forgotten by God and his Providence which leaves him no sense of security. The sinner's existence becomes a shadow existence in which he can no longer see the difference between what is real and what is not, and to stand up to the threats he perceives. The divine light, moreover, constantly disturbs his self-enclosed prison and serves as a foretaste of divine punishment.[12] Further personal sin increases his inability to face God's reality and continues the descent of his mind into insanity. Phrased in more psychiatric terms, sanity means rationality, the ability to live in and cope with reality. Evil corrupts and can even destroy one's relationship with God, the source and sustainer of reality. Sin thus drives the human mind in anxiety towards insanity.[13]

8. In the *CA* text Balthasar uses the terms *Sündenangst, Angst der Sünde*, and *sündigen Angst* to denote the anxiety due to sin (cf. *CA*, pp. 53–5, 57, 59–61, 65–6, 90).

9. *CA*, pp. 20–1; Eng., p. 50.

10. Cf. *CA*, p. 22; Eng., pp. 52–3.

11. *CA*, p. 16; Eng., p. 44.

12. Cf. *CA*, p. 19; Eng., pp. 47–8.

13. Balthasar is not arguing that all anxiety is rooted in the choice for sin, but rather that the choice for sin causes sin-anxiety. On this point our author connects with St. Thomas' position that one cannot properly interpret human emotional life without recourse to the moral life and the final end of human life. When contending with anxiety, one's relationship with God via moral action is essential.

Righteous anxiety

The opposite side of natural anxiety's bifurcation is the anxiety characteristic of the righteous believer (*Angst der Guten*).[14] Although still anxiety, the good individual's anxiety is completely different from that of the wicked in Balthasar's read of Sacred Scripture. In fact, the good person is commanded not to be afraid.[15] God forbids him to know or to enter natural or sin-anxiety. Instead, he is commanded to live in a state of freedom from anxiety (*Angstlosigkeit*).[16] The divine prohibition to be free from anxiety is founded on the intimacy and security of the Covenant. God is with the good man and so he need not be anxious, and the exercise of biblical faith within the Old Covenant not only protects him from anxiety but is even opposed it.[17] The reason for freedom from anxiety is that the choice for good binds the believer to God. The Old Covenant brings intimacy and the promise of protection from one's enemies, and imbues one's life with meaning and security. *Angstlosigkeit* in the Old Covenant even possesses geographical dimensions because of its intimate connection with dwelling in the Promised Land. Faith, freedom from anxiety and living in the Promised Land rise and fall together.

Although God calls the believer to dwell in *Angstlosigkeit*, the believer must still live into that reality, which may entail anxious struggle. Balthasar identifies three reasons for the continued struggle with anxiety: God's proximity, man's continual fall into sin and the absence of the Messiah. In the Old Covenant, man comes into unparalleled proximity with Almighty God 'who is himself surrounded by fear and trembling'.[18] This anxiety stems not from Sheol but from the narrow space which the Old Covenant grants him. The good man is squeezed on one side by God's intense proximity without the 'protective covering' of the Incarnation, and on the other side by his own sinfulness within a framework of a future redemption that has been promised but has not yet arrived.[19] Balthasar writes, 'The devouring purity in which he is invited to live only uncovers more and more profoundly his failure, his apostasy, his stubborn inability and unwillingness'.[20] The believer in the Old Covenant must fight for *Angstlosigkeit.* He oscillates between his own sin-anxiety and freedom from anxiety. Thus the decision to remain in the Old Covenant entails a righteous anxiety, yet the choice to abandon the struggle within the covenant would entail entering the *Angstkosmos* of sin-anxiety.

14. Cf. *CA*, p. 24; Eng., p. 55.

15. Cf. *CA*, pp. 22–3; Eng., p. 53.

16. Cf. *CA*, pp. 23–4, 26–7, 45, 59. The English translator renders the term 'freedom from anxiety' or 'fearlessness'. The other terms that Balthasar uses to denote the same state is *Nichtangst* (*CA*, pp. 31, 90) and *Furchtlosigkeit* (*CA*, pp. 27, 58).

17. Cf. *CA*, p. 23; Eng., p. 53.

18. *CA*, p. 24; Eng., p. 55. He writes, 'Open the Old Testament to whatever page you want: it will always mention the *good man's anxiety* about his relationship with God' (*CA*, p. 24; Eng., p. 55). It seems that the term is comparable to the biblical term 'fear of the Lord' and St. Thomas' filial fear.

19. Cf. *CA*, p. 25; Eng., p. 56.

20. *CA*, p. 26; Eng., p. 58.

The righteous man's anxiety, furthermore, is intensified by God's testing, for example, in Ps. 107. The curse of the Old Covenant, and all its anxieties, which originally stood behind man to push him further into the Covenant stands in front of the good man being tested in the Old Testament. During this testing, which is intended to increase the good man's dependence and trust in God, he cannot distinguish between his own personal guilt and God's positive will. Righteous anxiety in the Old Covenant is constituted by a dialectic oscillating between deciding for God (and *Angstlosigkeit*) and living in anxiety from sin and lack of faith. Often the anxiety due to sin and the anxiety due to God's testing are indistinguishable.

Intensification of anxiety in the Old Covenant

As the Old Covenant presses forward towards fulfilment, Balthasar observes an intensification of anxiety. The threats become more terrible. The anxiety of the believer in the Old Covenant becomes intensified to unsustainable proportions in Job. His anxiety operates within his subjective inability to distinguish between guilt and God's testing, and the objective dialectic operating between Job and his friends and between Job and God. Balthasar writes, 'Job stands in the nakedness of fear [*Angst*] before God. Every earthly covering is ripped away from him at the start, all his worldly supports are removed, so that later, when the real tribulation begins, nothing remains but for him to be the abandoned one, the man delivered over to anxiety'.[21] The narrow field of the Old Covenant into which man was squeezed is 'inundated and submerged' in Job's life.[22] God removes the finite border protecting the righteous man as the New Covenant begins to dawn upon the horizon. The anxiety of both the wicked and righteous intensifies as the Old Testament comes to a close, manifested in the 'great and terrible' Day of the Lord in the later prophets.

An irresolvable dialectic

In the Old Testament, according to Balthasar, God's reveals anxiety as 'a multivalent, malleable phenomenon, which, in the hand of God, is capable of serving the most varied purposes'.[23] Balthasar's interpretation of anxiety in the Old Testament shows two diametrically opposed types of anxiety, that of the wicked and that of the good. He notes that the anxiety of the wicked is a 'lasting condition' while righteous anxiety is a 'process' or 'passage'.[24] Yet both types are circumscribed in the Old Covenant by their provisionary nature. Jörg Splett comments, 'neither is the wicked man already irretrievably

21. *CA*, pp. 30–1; Eng., p. 65.
22. *CA*, p. 31; Eng., p. 66.
23. *CA*, p. 33; Eng., p. 68.
24. *CA*, p. 32; Eng., p. 67.

lost, nor is the good man surely saved'.[25] It seems, therefore, that righteous anxiety, while described as a process of moving into freedom from anxiety, is constrained by the unfulfilled Covenant and his own sin so that it functions as an irresolvable dialectic. The Old Covenant does not truly deliver man from sin, but rather reveals it. Righteous anxiety, therefore, has a dialectical shape in the Old Covenant. Balthasar, moreover, rejects any attempt to establish some sort of equilibrium between anxiety and hope in the Old Covenant which would 'oversimplify its unprecedented drama'.[26] The prohibition of anxiety and the command to hope given to the righteous are fixed coordinates for an unwavering course. The apparently irresolvable dialectic is nevertheless met with the command to hope.

Recapitulation and intensification of anxiety in the New Covenant

The anxiety of the Old Covenant, argues Balthasar, is recapitulated and intensified as it is brought to fulfilment in the New Covenant. The Day of the Lord finds its fulfilment in final judgement upon sin and the world as Sheol takes on the terrifying dimensions of Hell. Sin-anxiety takes on these new dimensions.[27] Righteous anxiety also intensifies from the divinely willed *Angstschrei* in Ps. 107 to that of Jesus' disciples in the storm on the Sea of Galilee (Mt. 14.24–27) in which God himself seems ghostlike.[28] The narrow space created by God's proximity and man's unworthiness continues in the many disciples. Yet all the human anxieties which swirl around the Incarnate Son are appropriated and take on new meaning in his own anxiety (*Angst Christi*), the topic of the next section.

In Balthasar's view, Sacred Scripture affirms the natural anxiety of finite existence in the face of eventual death (*Angst des Daseins*), indicates its split into sin-anxiety (*Sündenangst*) and righteous anxiety (*Angst der Guten*), and its continual intensification towards the anxiety of the Incarnate Son. Sin-anxiety comes from one's opposition to God and living in the counter-reality of evil. Righteous anxiety is constituted by dialectic between freedom from anxiety and relapse into sin-anxiety. Anxiety then intensifies in either mode from the Old Covenant to the New Covenant. Sacred Scripture also indicates, in Balthasar's view, that anxiety was part of the redemption wrought by Jesus, God incarnate, who took it all upon himself through his agony in the Garden and own death on the Cross. *How* Jesus Christ redeems anxiety is the topic of the next section. Since Balthasar had not yet articulated his Christological and soteriological positions at the time of writing *Der Christ und die Angst*, we first summarize these positions and then apply them to our theme.

25. Splett, 'Der Christ und seine Angst', p. 317 (author's translation).
26. *CA*, p. 32; Eng., p. 67.
27. Cf. *CA*, p. 35; Eng., pp. 70–1.
28. Cf. *CA*, p. 36; Eng., p. 72.

Relevant Aspects of Balthasar's Christology and Soteriology for Interpreting Christ's Anxiety

A Trinitarian perspective

The first fundamental aspect of Balthasar's Christology to aid our interpretation of anxiety's redemption is that Balthasar looks at Jesus Christ through a Trinitarian lens in which heavy emphasis falls upon the *Person* of the Divine Son.[29] This fundamental point of departure was taken from the influence of St. Maximus the Confessor.[30] Balthasar writes, moreover, that 'the Trinity, and not Christology, is the last horizon of the revelation of God in himself and in his dramatic relationship with the world'.[31] The entire life and Paschal Mystery of Jesus is both an act of the Trinity and a revelation of the Trinity:

> [T]he revelation of God that takes place in Jesus Christ is primarily a trinitarian one: Jesus does not speak about God in general but shows us the Father and gives us the Holy Spirit. Thus it is on the basis of Jesus' trinitarian relationship with God that we should construct a picture of the divine 'essence' and 'being'; for the latter manifests itself, in the historical 'happening' of Jesus himself, as an eternal 'happening'.[32]

The divine nature as kenotic love

A second relevant point of Balthasar's Christology is his emphasis on the divine nature as kenotic love. The Blessed Trinity is revealed in the kenosis of the Son from his Incarnation all the way through his death on the Cross and descent into hell. The economy of salvation reveals the Trinity through the Son's kenosis (cf. Phil. 2.5–11) which alone grants man access to the Trinity.[33] The Divine Son's surrender of the *forma Dei* in order to take up the *forma servi* reveals the kenotic life within the Trinity and the divine nature as self-giving love.[34] The kenotic love which characterizes the divine nature signifies that

29. Cf. Marchesi, *La Cristologia Trinitaria di Hans Urs von Balthasar*, p. 618. Even the title of Marchesi's study is suggestive of this perspective.

30. Balthasar writes, 'In the midst of the complexities of the Christological debate, Maximus always took his refuge in trinitarian theology'. Balthasar then quotes Maximus' phrasing of his insight in his dispute with Pyrrhus: 'The Logos, having once become human, still remains, as Logos, one of the three who are God, and therefore a proposition in Christology may not contradict a proposition about the Trinity' (*KL*, p. 210; Eng., p. 213). Like St. Thomas, Balthasar is a staunch proponent of the Chalcedonian formula and Constantinople III. Balthasar sees in Maximus that Trinitarian truths can help to elucidate Christological questions (cf. *KL*, pp. 207–13; Eng., pp. 212–6).

31. *TDV*, p. 48; Eng., p. 56.

32. *TDV*, p. 58; Eng., p. 67. The same point is made by Marchesi (cf. Marchesi, *La Cristologia Trinitaria di Hans Urs von Balthasar*, pp. 331–2).

33. Cf. Marchesi, *La Cristologia Trinitaria di Hans Urs von Balthasar*, p. 329.

34. The movement from the *forma Dei* to the *forma servi*, reasons Balthasar, is not expressing the two natures of Christ, 'but rather the "succession of different phases in the

divinity is divinity by its not-clinging-to-itself. In order to characterize the divine nature in this way, Balthasar posits 'an incomprehensible freedom in God that allows him to do more, and to be other, than the creature would suppose of him on the ground of its concepts of "God" '.[35]

This fundamental understanding of the divine nature as eternal self-emptying love begins with the Father's primal kenosis (*Ur-kenose*) in the generation of the Son as consubstantial with himself.[36] Balthasar describes the kenotic life within the Blessed Trinity in many places of his writing, but the following can suffice as a clear formulation of his idea:

> The Father strips himself, without remainder, of his Godhead and hands it over to the Son; he 'imparts' to the Son all that is his. . . . The Father must not be thought to exist 'prior' to this self-surrender (in the Arian sense): he *is* this movement of self-giving that holds nothing back. This divine act that brings forth the Son, that is, the second way of participating in (and of *being*) the identical Godhead, involves the positing of an absolute, infinite 'distance' that can contain and embrace all the other distances that are possible within the world of finitude, including the distance of sin. Inherent in the Father's love is an absolute renunciation: he will not be God for himself alone. He lets go of his divinity and, in this sense, manifests a (divine) God-lessness (of love, of course). The latter must not be confused with the godlessness that is found within the world, although it undergirds it, renders it possible and goes beyond it.[37]

In order to avoid any confusion of his idea with any type of process theology, Balthasar adds, 'the Father, in uttering and surrendering himself without reserve, does not lose himself. He does not extinguish himself by self-giving, just as he does not keep back anything of himself either. For, in this self-surrender, he *is* the whole divine essence'.[38] This paternal kenosis reveals divine omnipotence in the apparent powerlessness of love.[39]

The Father's primal kenosis in the generation of the Son sets the pattern for all other kenotic acts by Persons of the Godhead. The Son for his part gives himself to the Father in complete selflessness and thanksgiving (*eucharistia*), thereby receiving 'this unity of omnipotence and powerlessness from the Father'.[40] The infinite distinction between the Father and the Son in their mutual self-emptying is united by the Holy Spirit who is the 'pure communication and gift of love between the Father and the Son',[41] and who maintains,

continuity of the one drama of salvation", or, as P. Henry says, the temporal succession of "conditions"' (*HIII/2/2*, p. 196; Eng., pp. 211–12). The self-emptying of the Son in the salvific economy is the temporal expression of his eternal self-emptying in Love.

35. *HIII/2/2*, p. 197; Eng., p. 213.

36. Cf. P. Martinelli's summary of Trinitarian kenosis in Martinelli, *Il mistero della morte in Hans Urs von Balthasar: Il mistero pasquale come rivelazione dell'amore trinitario di Dio* (Milano: Jaca, 1996), pp. 342–51.

37. *TDIII*, pp. 300–1; Eng., p. 323.

38. *TDIII*, p. 303; Eng., p. 325.

39. Cf. *TDIII*, p. 303; Eng., p. 325.

40. *TDIII*, p. 303; Eng., p. 326.

41. Marchesi, *La Cristologia Trinitaria di Hans Urs von Balthasar*, p. 357 (author's translation).

seals and bridges the distinction between the Persons.[42] Self-emptying love is the foundation for both the distinction and unity of the three Divine Persons.[43] Balthasar's emphasis on the divine nature as kenotic love shows his preference for understanding divinity in terms of the Good: the eternal 'movement' of kenotic love between the Divine Persons.

The revelation of divine love in the economy as Hinterlegung and obedience

The intra-Trinitarian life of kenosis is manifested in the salvific economy through the Incarnate Son's Kenosis from the Incarnation to the Cross. This conception of the Trinity allows Balthasar to link the divine nature to the suffering of the Incarnate Son, and attempt to overcome the hiatus of God's 'impassibility' and his nature as kenotic love. Balthasar notes, 'Only God himself can go right to the end of the abandonment by God. Only he has the freedom to do this'.[44] By virtue of his divine kenotic love, the Son is able to empty himself of the *forma Dei* and take up the *forma servi* which entails no contradiction of his nature as God but rather precisely corresponds to, and reveals, this divine nature.[45] The Son's eternal procession from the Father (*forma Dei*) is manifested in the world through his mission (*forma servi*); mission thus provides the continuity between the two states. Balthasar agrees with St. Thomas that the Son's obedient *missio* in the world perfectly reveals his divine *processio* from the Father.[46] The Son's mission in the economy is for Balthasar the 'modality', 'translation' and 'economic form' of the Son's eternal procession.[47] Thus there remains a distinction between *processio* and *missio* in that *missio* is the *Gestalt*, the expressive form in human terms of his *processio*. His mission, therefore, becomes the measure of his existence and consciousness as man.

42. *TDIII*, p. 301; Eng., p. 324.

43. Marchesi observes, 'Balthasar loves to repeat with St. Bonaventure: *Inaequalitates oriuntur ex aequalitate*. ... The differences (*inaequalitates*) between God and the world, that is the other of God, the infinitely other from Him, are hidden or have their origin from the distinction or difference between the Father and the Son, which is not another "thing" from God, but, as the Holy Spirit, is the Other in God' (Marchesi, *La Cristologia Trinitaria di Hans Urs von Balthasar*, pp. 338–9) (Marchesi's italics; author's translation).

44. *HIII/2/2*, pp. 195–6; Eng., p. 211.

45. Cf. *HIII/2/2*, p. 199; Eng., p. 215.

46. Cf. *TDIV*, pp. 53–7; Eng., pp. 61–5. Balthasar cites St. Thomas for support (*STh*. I, q. 43, a. 2). Even more explicit is St. Thomas' passage from his commentary on the Sentences: *Scriptum super Sententiis* (http//:www.corpusthomisticum.org) I, d. 16, q. 1, a. 1 sol; d. 15, q. 4, a. 1 sol (cf. *TDIV*, p. 55; Eng., pp. 62–3; Marchesi, *La Cristologia Trinitaria di Hans Urs von Balthasar*, p. 348). Meiattini observes that Balthasar 'transcribes into aesthetical (*proportio, Einstimmung*) and dramatic (*Person, Sendung*) categories that which St. Thomas speaks of in purely metaphysical terms' (Meiattini, *Sentire cum Christo*, p. 91) (Meiattini's italics; author's translation).

47. Cf. *TDIV*, pp. 218–22, 224; Eng., pp. 242–6, 248; Meiattini, *Sentire cum Christo*, p. 92.

Given the divine nature as essentially kenotic love and Jesus' mission in the world as the perfect manifestation of his divine procession from the Father, Balthasar introduces a new term to describe the Incarnate Son's kenosis in the economy: *Hinterlegung*.[48] By this term, he seeks to interpret the revelation in human terms of the divine nature as kenotic love in the movement of the Son's condition from *forma Dei* to *forma servi*. When the Son surrenders the form of God to take up the form of a slave, the divine Son 'deposits' his divine prerogatives with the Father so that he is able to suffer and die in the condition of a slave all the way to experiencing the abandonment of the Father on the Cross. The Son empties himself of these divine prerogatives, not thereby ceasing to be divine but in fact to reveal his divinity. By *Hinterlegung* Balthasar wishes to show that what appears as *separation* between the Father and the Son in the economy is in fact an act of their eternal *unity* of love revealing the *distinction* of their Persons. Even the abandonment of the Son during his passion is a mode of his union with the Father in the Holy Spirit. Nevertheless it remains true that even in what subjectively appears to be separation of Jesus from the Father because of the Son's *Hinterlegung* is objectively a function and expression of his supreme intimacy of love with the Father and of his reciprocal union in the Holy Spirit.[49]

The depositing of the Son's divine prerogatives in the Incarnation reveals the Son's mission in terms of *obedience*. The Incarnate Son's eternal kenosis of thanksgiving to the Father takes the form of loving obedience in the economy.[50] His filial obedience is the mode of his eternal love for the Father. In fact, our author states that obedience, more so than suffering, is emphasized in the kenosis of the Philippians hymn.[51] Obedience is the human expression of the Son's eternal procession from the Father, and expresses the unity of his eternal procession and his mission in the world.[52] Since obedience, in Balthasar's view, is the most fundamental aspect of Jesus' mission and the most revelatory of his eternal procession as Son, then obedience will figure prominently in Balthasar's understanding of the Incarnate Son's human perfection. Obedience to the Father more than knowledge constitutes the Son's human perfection. Therefore, the Incarnate Son's surrendering of his form of

48. The term is usually rendered 'depositing' in English. It is also translated as 'left in safekeeping' (*TLII*, p. 262; Eng., p. 288). The term is translated into Italian as *reposizione* ('repositioning'). It seems that Balthasar's term is an intensification of St. Thomas' idea in his commentary on the *Sentences* which Balthasar quotes favourably: 'So when the Son becomes man, he "comes forth from paradise like an aqueduct", and "though he does not lose the paradise of the Father's glory, *he conceals it*"' (*TDIV*, p. 53; Eng., p. 61) (author's italics). Balthasar's concept also suggests influence from St. Bonaventure's understanding of *compassion* (cf. *TDT*, pp. 99–100; Eng., pp. 103–4).

49. The role of the Holy Spirit is indispensable for Balthasar in this concept of *Hinterlegung* for the Holy Spirit maintains the unity between Father and Son throughout the economic 'distance' in the Son's suffering Godforsakeness.

50. Marchesi, *La Cristologia Trinitaria di Hans Urs von Balthasar*, p. 357. The central place that Balthasar gives obedience in the life of the incarnate Son is inspired, according to Marchesi, by the mystical intuitions of von Speyr. See also, p. 519).

51. Cf. *TDT*, p. 90; Eng., p, 94.

52. Cf. Marchesi, *La Cristologia Trinitaria di Hans Urs von Balthasar*, p. 618.

God and being obedient unto death is the highest revelation of the divine nature. The kenosis of the Incarnate Son is the revelation, taking into account the sin of the world, *par excellence* of the Triune God.[53] Jesus' kenotic existence is a scandal because it can only be explained by Triune love.[54]

Redemption as vicarious representation (Stellvertretung)

Having sketched the fundamental lines of Balthasar's Christology in its Trinitarian and kenotic emphases, attention must also be given to his concept of redemption. The Incarnate Son redeems man from sin, according to our author, through 'vicarious respresentation' (*Stellvertretung*).[55] With this concept Balthasar seeks to overcome the shortcomings of previous theories, and to chart a course to unite the best aspects of St. Anselm's theory of substitution (developed by St. Thomas) and what he calls Luther's 'radicalism'.[56] The Anselmian line of thought, in his view, does not allow a sufficient identification of Jesus with sinful man's condition.[57] It is sin, and not just the consequences of sin that the Suffering Servant takes upon himself. On the other hand, he seeks to avoid Luther's exaggerations and lapses into contradiction, especially in understanding God's wrath in an overly punitive way.[58]

Balthasar situates the work of atonement in the economy of salvation within the intra-Trinitarian life. The Son's distinction from the Father consists

53. Cf. *HI*, p. 444.

54. Cf. *HIII/2/2*, p. 204; Eng., p. 221.

55. His word in German is difficult to render in English, and roughly means 'vicarious substitution' or 'representation'. Servais writes that Balthasar's term signifies a true exchange of places and suggests the gesture of someone who takes something on himself in order to remove it from another (cf. Servais, 'Mérite substitution, sacrifice de l'Église', p. 211). H. Saward in her article on *Stellvertretung* in the work of Le Fort writes, 'The words "substitution" or "representation" cannot convey the complete sense of the German, hence the need for paraphrase such as "vicarious sacrifice", "atonement", "expiation", or "reparation"' (H. Saward, 'A Literature of Substitution', p. 179). Several studies offer summaries of the concept of *Stellvertretung* in Balthasar's soteriology: Marchesi, *La Cristologia Trinitaria di Hans Urs von Balthasar*, pp. 546–69; Nichols, *No Bloodless Myth*, pp. 157–71; J. O'Donnell, *Hans Urs von Balthasar* (London: Geoffrey Chapman, 1992), pp. 99–114.

56. Cf. Balthasar's summary and analysis of the theological tradition in *TDIII*, pp. 212–94; Eng., pp. 231–316. He charts his course by using critically the insights of a few contemporary writers: Galot, S. Bulgakov, A. Feuillet, and R. Girard (cf. Nichols, *No Bloodless Myth*, pp. 163–4; O'Donnell, *Balthasar*, p. 106).

57. Cf. *TDIII*, pp. 225–45, 252, 265; Marchesi, *La Cristologia Trinitaria di Hans Urs von Balthasar*, p. 556; Nichols, *No Bloodless Myth*, pp. 160–3; O'Donnell, *Balthasar*, pp. 102–3.

58. Cf. Balthasar's treatment of Luther's theory of atonement in *TDIII*, pp. 263–9; Eng., pp. 284–90. Balthasar stays clear of Luther's concept of 'penal substitution' whereby the Father's wrath is diverted from us and strikes the Incarnate Son, and the doctrine of *simul iustus et peccator* in which Jesus is simultaneously justified and damned. Jesus bears the contradiction of holiness and sin within himself, but in such a way that the separation in the act of abandonment is so stressed that he ends up with a type of Nestorian dualism.

in infinite nearness and distance. Each Divine Person makes 'room' for the others through each Person's respective kenosis, which is always bridged by their mutual love. The possibility for the Incarnate Son to experience 'Godlessness' (*Gottlosigkeit*) lies in the God-lessness of the intra-Trinitarian kenosis where no Person retains the divinity for himself.

The primal drama of kenotic love within the Godhead enables one to see the contours of Balthasar's concept of *Stellvertretung*. Since God is love he must reject sin. Sin cannot be incorporated into the Trinitarian life of love. Divine wrath is God's fully real and categorical No to the world's rejection of his love.[59] A God who loved but did not hate evil would contradict himself. God's love and his wrath, therefore, are not mutually exclusive terms if understood in the correct way. This love, Balthasar continues, must be both that of the Father and of the Son.[60] Only a unique subject could submit himself to this wrath so that sin may be expiated. This unique subject cannot be the sinner since the sinner incites God's wrath. Rather he must be the Sinless One, understood not 'from a juridical doctrine of imputation' or 'a doctrine of physical solidarity' but from 'the New Testament's idea of the divine love that *out of love* takes upon itself the sins of the world'.[61] Only the Son, in Balthasar's view, could be this unique subject who can expiate the sin of the world.

The primal drama, combined with the unity of the Incarnate Son's procession and mission and the *Hinterlegung* of his divine prerogatives, enables him to vicariously represent guilty man in a true and deep way by 'an *inner* appropriation of what is ungodly and hostile to God'.[62] The eternal distinction of the Persons of the Godhead is 'transposed' into the economy to include man's distance from God opened up by sin in order to reveal 'that the God-forsakenness of the Son during his Passion was just as much a mode of his profound bond with the Father in the Holy Spirit as his death was a mode of his life and his suffering a mode of his bliss'.[63] Economic 'separation' is a mode of eternal union-in-distinction of the Divine Persons. Jesus bears the contradiction of sin without inner division to himself for he remains in his perfect surrender to the Father.[64] The Incarnate Son is 'distant' from the Father insofar as he is made sin. He is in union with the Father insofar as this

59. Cf. *TDIII*, pp. 315–27; Eng., pp. 338–51 for more on divine wrath as an expression of covenantal love.

60. *HIII/2/2*, p. 192; Eng., p. 207. Balthasar writes, 'The only right approach to the mystery is to see the whole momentum of "God's wrath" in the Old Testament over the broken covenant as taken up into the far greater momentum of the love of God in the New Testament – the love of the Father, as well as of the Son – and therefore, to guard against both extremes, that of interpreting the suffering of Christ as a punitive raging of divine anger against the innocent victim (as the Reformers tended to do), and that of seeing this suffering as merely the manifestation of the superabundance of divine love' (*HIII/2/2*, pp. 189–90; Eng., p. 205).

61. *HIII/2/2*, p. 192; Eng., p. 207 (Balthasar's italics).

62. *TDIII*, p. 311; Eng., pp. 334–5 (Balthasar's italics).

63. *TDIV*, p. 232; Eng., p. 257.

64. O'Donnell comments on Balthasar's position, 'The cross signifies not contradiction but love in the midst of contradiction' (O'Donnell, *Balthasar*, pp. 103–4).

'distance' represents his loving obedience. God's wrath and mercy are united in God's pure unbounded love. Through the deep, inner appropriation of man's sinful condition the creaturely No in sin is assumed into the infinite distinction between the Father and the Son, and is assumed into the Incarnate Son's total Yes. Therefore, Balthasar grants the Incarnate Son a free acceptance of experiencing the wrath of God on our behalf, but not in Luther's sense. Jesus experiences divine wrath, but not divine punishment because he is innocent. Objectively the Cross was not punishment for Jesus although on the level of subjective experience it felt like punishment.[65] Balthasar writes:

> Whether or not the concept of 'punishment' is to be applied to Christ's sufferings on the Cross is largely a matter of language. If we say that an innocent man as such cannot be 'punished', even if he is atoning for the guilty, we shall avoid the term. It is possible to distinguish, like Hilary, between the *sensus poenae*, which Christ experienced, and the *vis poenae*.[66]

Through the concept of *Stellvertretung*, Balthasar reasons that Jesus suffers in a unique and unrepeatable way the experience of abandonment of the Father because he is, and always remains, the Son who also has experienced to the very end the deepest intimacy with the Father. It is thanks to this intimacy that the Incarnate Son can suffer and overcome the abandonment of God.

Christ's vicarious representation, according to Balthasar, assumes man's sinful condition into the relationship between the Father and the Son, and by the Incarnate Son's suffering of the divine wrath on our behalf in loving obedience, expiates it. The novelty of Balthasar's position is to situate the entire distance created by man's sin within the intra-Trinitarian distinction of Persons.[67] Balthasar's grounding of the drama of redemption within the inner divine life helps him to avoid the double pitfall of identifying God and the suffering of the world as in Hegel and others, or to exaggerate God's immutability in a manner that would prevent him from sharing meaningfully in the tragic human condition.

65. Balthasar writes, 'The Son bears sinners within himself, together with the hopeless impenetrability of their sin, which prevents the divine light of love from registering in them. In himself, therefore, he experiences, not their sin, but the hopelessness of their resistance to God and the graceless No of divine grace to this resistance' (*TDIII*, p. 325; Eng., p. 349; cf. Marchesi, *La Cristologia Trinitaria di Hans Urs von Balthasar*, p. 558; Nichols, *No Bloodless Myth*, p. 170).

66. *TDIV*, p. 314; Eng., p. 337.

67. The positive meaning of 'otherness' that the distinction of the Divine Persons gives, along with Balthasar's location of the finite realm within the distinction of the Divine Persons suggests a response to Kierkegaard's concept of anxiety. According to Kierkegaard anxiety is the finite creature's dread in the face of the Absolute, that is, contingent man's fear at the realization that he is wholly other than God who is. This anxiety is met in the Triune God who shows that being 'other' than God is not an unmitigated disaster.

The human knowing and 'Faith' of Christ

In order to investigate both the type and intensity of Jesus' anxiety, and given the primary role cognitive factors play in anxiety, it is important to determine Balthasar's position on Jesus' human knowing during his earthly life. St. Thomas holds that Jesus' experience of anxiety was limited in his earthly life because of the full and uninterrupted beatific vision he possessed in his human nature, although we also noted the possibility of an existential stretching of Jesus' appropriation of fear in St. Thomas' position. Balthasar holds, via his principle of *Hinterlegung*, that the Son at his Incarnation is permitted in the salvific economy to deposit with the Father his full and explicit beatific vision as an expression of eternal Triune Love. Part of the Son's laying aside the form of God and depositing it with the Father entails a not-knowing in the economy. In other words, as man the Son does not want to know that which he knows as God so that he can be entirely dedicated to suffering.[68] With this position, our author does not outrightly reject St. Thomas' position, but seeks to ease the tension between 'faith' and vision.[69] Balthasar's position on Jesus' terrestrial beatific vision reveals his dissatisfaction with aspects of the traditional scholastic interpretation.[70]

How then does Balthasar construe Christ's human knowing without compromising his divinity or the unity established by the hypostatic union? Balthasar casts Jesus' human knowing in terms of 'mission consciousness'

68. Cf. *TDIV*, pp. 232–40; Eng., pp. 256–65 ('Separation as a mode of union').

69. He writes, 'In Adrienne von Speyr's entire work, perhaps no mystery of the faith appeared harder to her than an adequate formulation of the relation between vision and faith in the lived experience of the God-man. . . . On the one hand, von Speyr maintains almost always that on earth the Son possessed the vision of the Father. It is rare that she speaks of Christ's faith. But we also find her saying that Jesus' obedience existed despite this vision or that as *comprehensor* he had vision and as *viator* faith or that vision could veil itself into obedience' (*TLII*, p. 261; Eng., pp. 286–7).

70. The following are two of the more sharply phrased passages from our author about his dissatisfaction: 'Any theology (including present-day echoes) which says that Christ on the Cross suffered only in the "lower" part of his soul, while the "peak of his [created] spirit" continued to enjoy the heavenly beatific vision, breaks the top off the drama of redemption. It does not see that the Son, as a whole, takes on himself the situation of the sinful world that has turned away from God; indeed, by his absolute obedience he has "infiltrated" it and rendered it impotent. The Triune God is capable of more than pious theologians imagine. At the same time, it is absolutely true that this "dereliction" between Father and Son (made possible through their common Spirit) is a most extreme form of their mutual love and of God's Triune love for the world' (Balthasar, 'Ist der Gekreuzigte "selig"?', *Internationale katholische Zeitschrift Communio* 16 [1987], pp. 107–9 [108]; cited by J. Saward, *Mysteries of March*, pp. 56–7 [Saward's translation]). He makes a similar point in his *Theologik*, 'The idea of Jesus enjoying the beatific vision of God at the "summit" of his soul, while the "lower parts of the soul" experience Godforsakenness, nowadays seems quite incredible and cannot be salvaged by the arguments adduced' (*TL*, 261n; cited by Saward, *Mysteries of March*, p. 166 [Saward's translation]).

(*Sendungsbewußtsein*).[71] Jesus' mission consciousness is the earthly expression or temporal extension of the eternal consciousness that the Son has of himself. Jesus' consciousness of his mission coincides with his eternal self-consciousness as the divine Son. Mission is the principle that regulates the knowing and not knowing of the Incarnate Son without compromising his divinity or the unity of his knowing.[72] The Incarnate Son, according to Balthasar, 'deposits' his divine prerogatives with the Father, 'as much of it as the obedience of his mission on earth requires',[73] and receives the concrete details of his mission moment-by-moment from the Holy Spirit.[74] Balthasar characterizes this depositing as a freely chosen 'non-use' of his beatific vision.[75] The Holy Spirit thus plays an indispensable role in Jesus' earthly life as the guarantor that his moment-by-moment direction he gives to the Incarnate Son is always the Father's will. Balthasar holds, according to Becker, that Jesus knew about his approaching hour but surrendered the knowledge of its content into the hands of the Father in order to exercise even greater obedience.[76]

At the foundation of Jesus' human consciousness, according to Balthasar, is his primal intuition (*Urintuition*) of his identity as the Son sent by the Father which begins *in utero*. The Incarnate Son never ceases to know as man that he is the Son of the Father, and that he has been sent to do the Father's will. This primal intuition unfolds explicitly as Jesus' human nature matures until full human consciousness is reached at his Baptism.[77] The Blessed Virgin Mary plays an important role for our author in bringing Jesus in his human nature to an explicit knowledge of his divine origin and mission in his human consciousness. What Jesus knows more intuitively as an infant he eventually knows in a reflective manner, although in a way utterly unique from any other human nature because his psycho-experiential life is inseparably divine and human. Although described with different terms Balthasar's fundamental idea is not opposed St. Thomas' position on Jesus' discursive and acquired knowledge. At no moment in Jesus' life, even in his abandonment on the Cross, is he confused about who he is or what he is supposed to do. No dualism exists between his 'I' and his role, between who he is and what he represents.

Jesus' not-knowing during his earthly mission is an expression of his *Hinterlegung*. Balthasar connects Christ's terrestrial human knowledge with his poverty. Because the Incarnate Son assumes a perfect human nature, his human life is characterized by the evangelical counsels, as shown in Chapter 5

71. Cf. Balthasar's treatment in *TDII/2*, pp. 149–85; Eng., pp. 163–202, and Becker's interpretation of Balthasar's position in Becker, *The Historical Jesus in the Face of His Death*, pp. 241–4.

72. Cf. Meiattini, *Sentire cum Christo*, p. 94.

73. *TLII*, p. 262; Eng., p. 288.

74. Cf. *TDII/2*, pp. 175–85; Eng., pp. 191–202; Meiattini, *Sentire cum Christo*, p. 94; *TDII/2*, p. 179. In Balthasar's pneumatology, the Holy Spirit not only proceeds from the Son, he drives the Son in his earthly mission.

75. *TLII*, p. 262; Eng., p. 288.

76. Cf. Becker, *Historical Jesus*, pp. 277–80, 286–7.

77. Cf. Meiattini, *Sentire cum Christo*, p. 121.

of this study. His human knowing exists between his evangelical poverty and his authority and rights as the divine Son.[78] In this way, Balthasar is not forced to attribute to the terrestrial Christ a vision that is always explicit and thematized.[79]

If our author does not attribute the beatific vision to the Lord during his earthly mission, how does he characterize Jesus' human knowledge? He calls it 'faith'.[80] His understanding of Jesus' terrestrial 'faith' does not mean intellectual assent to propositions as it indicates the interior 'attitude' (*Haltung*) of obedient trust.[81] Faith in this sense emphasizes the volitive aspect of faith, that is, 'reliability, trustworthiness, fidelity, conviction, warranty and trust, both in the active sense (having trust) as well as in the passive (enjoying the trust of another)'.[82] It also entails the fidelity (*emet*) of God towards the Covenant, fidelity to which Israel must attain as a proper model. Jesus is the perfect human expression of divine fidelity. The totality of this attitude, that obliges all of man, is also an experience (*Erfahrung*), insofar as it is a 'total act' (*Gesamtakt*).[83]

Jesus exemplifies this biblical attitude of faith perfectly, and in this way faith is attributable to him. His attitude of faith is also understood by Balthasar in terms of 'indifference' (in the Ignatian sense) and selflessness (*Selbstlosigkeit*).[84] Jesus' faith as indifference and selflessness is a temporal expression of the eternal, gratuitous relationality within the Trinity in which every hypostasis makes itself poor in order to enrich the other.[85] The only part of this attitude which our author excludes from the incarnate Lord is the aspect which adheres to the content of the kerygma since the content coincides with his own person which places Christ above faith.[86]

It is not difficult to see that Balthasar's concept of faith in Christ is understood much more in personal-biblical categories than in Hellenistic inspired concepts. He nevertheless integrates the Hellenistic into the biblical perspective. Consequently it is not the 'non-vision' aspect that is emphasized, but the *knowing as interpersonal relationship and fidelity*. In this way the strain between *fides* and *visio* is eased since faith is no longer a transitory act ending with the beatific vision but a true *inchoatio gloriae*. Faith is always more than knowledge (*Wissen*) and vision (*Schau*) for Balthasar.[87]

78. Cf. Meiattini, *Sentire cum Christo*, pp. 124–6; *TLII*, pp. 201–55; *HIII/2/2*, p. 124.

79. He writes, 'Once we recognize this unity of theory and practice, contemplation and action, in Jesus' mission-consciousness, we shall no longer need regretfully to banish "direct vision" in Jesus' consciousness to the "uppermost region of the soul", lest it should endanger the life of his normal human soul' (*TDII/2*, p. 179; Eng., p. 196).

80. He sets out his position on Christ's faith in several places including *SV*, pp. 45–79; Eng., pp. 43–79; *SC*, pp. 51–75; Eng., pp. 57–83; *TLII*, pp. 261–5; Eng., pp. 286–90.

81. Cf. *SV*, p. 45.

82. *SV*, p. 52; Eng., p. 51.

83. Cf. Meiattini, *Sentire cum Christo*, p. 130; *HI*, p. 211.

84. Cf. *SV*, p. 54; Eng., p. 53.

85. Cf. *HI*, p. 316; Eng., p. 328.

86. Cf. *SV*, pp. 52–3; Eng., pp. 51–2.

87. Cf. *TG*, p. 37.

Our author concludes it is not contradictory to recognize in Jesus the measure of vision inscribed in faith which would not exclude a possible obscuring of vision. As man, Christ experiences the Father in his mission, that is in a coming-going from and to the Father which he does both as *comprehensor et viator*, to use St. Thomas' terms. Jesus as man is a *comprehensor* in his appropriation of his mission, and a *viator* in his walking on his path with the depositing of the complete view of this mission.[88] The complete view is maintained by the Holy Spirit and as communicated to Jesus' human knowing step-by-step in his mission. In Balthasar's view, therefore, it is not necessary to attribute to Jesus' human consciousness an immediate beatific vision in the higher part of his soul in order to maintain the hypostatic union. In fact, Meiattini holds that it is not necessary for Balthasar to attribute to this vision any other content than that of the mission.[89] Faith and knowing, the object and personal adherence converge in Balthasar's position which we find in everyday life: one cannot know without interpersonal trust.[90]

Our author also holds that one can attribute 'hope' to Christ. He argues that the exclusion of hope from Christ stems from 'a peculiarly narrow Augustinian definition'.[91] He further comments that Aquinas was the only theologian to oppose this view arguing that if one was united to another in love, that person 'could also hope for good things for the other person – as it were for one's other self'.[92] Our author reasons, therefore, that Christ could hope on earth and in heaven for the redemption of every member of his Mystical Body. Christ's foreknowledge is no obstacle to his hope for uncertainty is in fact detrimental to hope: 'infallible hope is the most perfect hope'.[93]

Balthasar's position on Christ's earthly beatific vision is not a radical departure from that of St. Thomas but one that attempts to ease the tension between faith and vision. Our author emphasizes the interpretation of 1 Cor. 13.13 which allows for the continuance of faith and hope in the beatific vision.[94] He understands faith and hope in the beatific vision as an essential part of the enduring creativity of freedom, divine and creaturely, in Heaven.

88. Cf. *TDII/2*, pp. 157–8, 166–7; Eng., pp. 172, 182.

89. Cf. Meiattini, *Sentire cum Christo*, p. 133; *TDII/2*, p. 152.

90. Pope John Paul II develops the same point that all knowing is based upon interpersonal trust. Cf. John-Paul II, *Fides et Ratio, AAS*, p. 91 (1999), pp. 1–88 (n. 32).

91. *SV*, p. 67; Eng., p. 67.

92. *SV*, p. 67; Eng., p. 67; cf. *STh*. II-II, q. 17, a. 3.

93. *SV*, p. 68; Eng., p. 67.

94. Cf. *TDIV*, pp. 368–76; Eng., pp. 402–10. The two strands he identifies are represented on the one hand by Gregory of Palamas, St. John Chrysostom, the Cappadocian fathers, Diadochus, Dionysius and Maximus the Confessor, and on the other by Origen, St. Bernard, John XXII and Benedict XII (cf. *TDIV*, p. 371; Eng., p. 405). Balthasar supports his position with reference to God's infinite possibilities. He writes, 'we must hold fast to the paradox that God, precisely in the trinitarian event that he always *is* . . . ever more mysterious; the trinitarian event that he *is* remains beyond freedom and necessity. . . . In the abstract contemplation of essence (essential energies, *visio essentiae*), this interplay of vision and non-vision does not emerge with due clarity; only when God's trinitarian reality is revealed as event do we see that the two aspects can be reconciled' (*TDIV*, p. 373; Eng., pp. 407–8).

The faith and hope that are part of the life in Heaven is constituted by the limitless trust in the activity of other creaturely freedoms.[95] Thus our author writes, 'the word "trust" leaves the field open for "faith" and "hope": in the interpersonal sphere these two are most at home where two people know each other so well that they can take the risk – without fear – of depending on the other'.[96] Understood in this manner, it is possible that Jesus as man was able in his earthly life to have 'faith' and 'hope' without compromising the unity of his two natures. It is the Incarnate Son's mission 'that also decides the modality of his vision of the Father'.[97]

Three conclusions for interpreting Christ's anxiety

From the summary above three interconnected conclusions emerge for the interpretation of Christ's anxiety. First, Balthasar's Trinitarian lens, not surprisingly, refracts more attention to the *person* of Christ than to his respective natures, and he admits this emphasis.[98] The accent of Balthasar's Trinitarian Christology falls on the *subject* of the Philippian's hymn: the pre-existent Son and his change of 'conditions'.[99] Balthasar's emphasis on the person of the Son will make his analysis of the Incarnate Son's sufferings different than St. Thomas whose emphasis tends to fall on the Son's two natures.

Balthasar's view of the divine nature as self-giving love and the mission of the Son as the perfect human representation of his procession from the Father in love converge upon a second conclusion: Christ's entire human nature becomes a perfect representation not only of the world's sin but also of his divinity. Our author's concept of *Stellvertretung* places the Person of the Incarnate Son in deep involvement with his human suffering. In fact, Christ's suffering as man is the expression in human terms of his eternal self-emptying love as the Divine Son. Our author, therefore, sees no separation between Christ's Divine Person and his human nature in suffering since his suffering is divine love transposed into a human key. Divinity does not have to be viewed as inimical to human suffering when it is understood in its essence as self-emptying love. Therefore, the more Jesus' human nature suffers, the more Trinitarian love is revealed. Balthasar avoids limiting the sufferings of Jesus' human nature to the lower part of his soul.

Third, if the divine life is characterized by self-giving love, then this self-giving love sets the pattern for the assumption of human nature. It can be argued that Christ's human perfection is also characterized by this love.

95. Meiattini argues that Balthasar's position on the beatific vision stands in contrast to that of P. Galtier and closer to that of P. Parente and Rahner (cf. Meiattini, *Sentire cum Christo*, p. 95; *TDII/2*, p. 158; *TG*, p. 25).

96. *TDIV*, p. 370; Eng., p. 404.

97. *TLII*, pp. 264–5; Eng., p. 290.

98. Cf. *HIII/2/2*, p. 198; Eng., pp. 213–4.

99. Cf. *HIII/2/2*, p. 196; Eng., p 212; Marchesi, *La Cristologia Trinitaria di Hans Urs von Balthasar*, p. 524.

Christ's human perfection, in other words, can be based not on his *knowledge* but on his *self-emptying love* expressed in *obedience*. Jesus' human knowledge is more the knowledge of interpersonal relationship than intellectual vision. Divine perfection is seen in the ability to give oneself away completely in love. Human perfection follows the same pattern: to give oneself away entirely in love through obedient fulfilment of one's divinely given mission. Such a position grants the possibility of surrendering an explicit beatific vision, and thus a greater flexibility for Christ to suffer in his human nature. In the ability to deposit his beatific knowledge and live his earthly life in 'faith' and utter obedience, his human nature can become a much deeper experiential representative of divine love in a world of sin by allowing this perfect human nature to suffer death in Godforsakenness. Balthasar grants to Jesus' human nature a much greater ability to experience suffering without violating, in his view, dogmatic boundaries that would compromise his divinity or eviscerate the soteriological import of Christ's sufferings.

Balthasar's Interpretation of Christ's Anxiety

Christ's appropriation of anxiety via Hinterlegung and Stellvertretung

These fundamental principles of Balthasar's Christology and soteriology give us the ability to construct a more complete picture of how he understands Jesus' intense anxiety described in Chapter 2 of this study. His interpretation of Christ's anxiety is explicitly theological. He does not intend to construct a psychology of Jesus which he thinks is impossible.[100] The Son's *Hinterlegung* of his divine prerogatives, including his full and explicit beatific vision of the Father, allows his human nature the ability to appropriate anxiety 'to the utmost degree'.[101] He writes 'God could not become man in any other way than by coming to know human fear [*menschlische Angst*] and by taking it upon himself'.[102] We observed in Chapter 2 that Balthasar notices a crescendo of intensity in the way the Lord appropriates all human anxiety in his Incarnation and his shuddering before the tomb of Lazarus and in the Temple at hearing the Father's voice about the inevitability of his 'hour'. Jesus moves towards his hour in absolute vulnerability knowing it will be a terrible moment. The 'cup of wrath' he must drink and the 'baptism' he must receive constantly loom on the horizon of his earthly mission.

Our author, however, excludes certain types of anxiety from Jesus' human knowing that would compromise his divinity or the unity of his two natures. The not-knowing of Jesus is never ignorance of who he is and what he has to accomplish. Christ did not experience the anxiety that we do in coming to know who we are and our proper role in life. No conflict exists between Christ's 'I' and his mission. Jesus never wavers in his obedience in the

100. *TDII/2*, p. 151. 2n; Eng., 166n.
101. *CA*, p. 37; Eng., p. 74.
102. *CA*, p. 37; Eng., p. 73.

accomplishment of his mission. He exhibits no uncertainty or vacillation with regard to the Good.[103] Moreover, Jesus does not experience anxiety as necessity. Christ was not compelled to undergo anxiety by necessity, but rather freely chose to undergo it by love. Kenotic love allows the Lord to undergo what he by nature is not compelled to undergo.

A dimension of human anxiety that surfaced in our examination of St. Thomas' work is the role of the virtues and how they shape or eliminate anxiety. What does Balthasar say about Christ's virtues? He notes, 'the attempt to delimit those "virtues" that Christ had and must have had from those that he "cannot have had" is difficult and elusive'.[104] One does not find a treatment of Christ's human virtues such as courage or fortitude in Balthasar's work. He remains focused on Christ's faith and hope, which St. Thomas excludes from Christ.

Christ's anxiety in Gethsemane and on the Cross

The Lord's appropriation of anxiety comes to its climax, according to Balthasar, in the Garden of Gethsemane and the Cross. In the Garden, therefore, an abyss of anxiety [*Abgrund der Angst*] breaks over him as he vicariously suffers for sinners. The incarnate Son is able to experience anxiety a manner that is totally unique and far surpasses that which any human being could experience. Therefore, all the types of anxiety in the Old and New Covenants described in Sacred Scripture are in Gethesemane 'gathered together and infinitely surpassed, because the person who in this human nature is frightened [*ängstigt*] is the infinite God himself'.[105]

Chapter 2 of this study described the phenomenology of Christ's sufferings in Gethsemane. Yet what is driving this phenomenon? How is anxiety operating in the Incarnate Son given his unique constitution? Our author does not offer an explicit reflection about the operation of the Lord's human will in Gethsemane outside of his favourable treatment of St. Maximus the Confessor's position.[106] Balthasar notes that Maximus excludes from Christ any anxiety from intellectual uncertainty or volitional wavering. Any 'gnomic' choosing (changing opinions, vacillation towards the Good), which Kierkegaard describes well in his concept of anxiety, is excluded from the Lord Jesus because his human intellect and will operate at a higher level, the level of love which is beyond the indifference of freedom of choice. Any tension between

103. Balthasar explores this aspect of Christ's anxiety in the Garden in his study on Maximus. (cf. *KL*, pp. 263–9; Eng., pp. 265–71).

104. *SV*, p. 67; Eng., p. 67.

105. *CA*, p. 37; Eng., p. 74.

106. Cf. *KL*, pp. 263–9; Eng., pp. 265–71. According to St. Maximus, writes Balthasar, 'Christ, who possessed our nature ontologically as his own, had our natural human capacity to will in himself in the same way that we do and put it to use. . . . But since he could not make our sinful manner of willing his own ontologically, he assimilated it to himself through "relative appropriation"' (*KL*, p. 265; Eng., p. 267).

the human and divine wills is borne and resolved by virtue of the absolute freedom of his Person. It seems that Maximus' appropriation by relationship in a way anticipates Bonaventure's notion of *compassio*.

Jesus' unsurpassable merit lies in the fact that in his human will he always remained beyond any vacillation before the Good because of his utter obedience to the Father's will. Balthasar writes, 'The drama on the Mount of Olives is the ultimate price and the ultimate proof of this obedience. "Physically", the "appropriation" of our rebellious will, and the healing that results from it, has saved the human race by restoring to it an incorrupt, naturally functioning faculty of self-determination'.[107] Balthasar's interpretation of Christ's actions in Gethsemane easily connects with Adam's actions in the Garden of Eden in which his mind fell from orientation towards the Good to the vacillation between good and evil and the tendency to choose evil. Jesus in his perfect human will re-conquered what Adam had lost in his will through original sin.

Christ's anxiety on the Mount of Olives is constituted by three aspects according to Balthasar. First his anxiety is 'the suffering of the infinitely Pure One, the infinitely Righteous One (who is also God) when confronted with all that God abhors and that can reveal its full hideousness only to the Pure One (who is also God)'.[108] This aspect manifests the uniqueness of Christ's anxiety. He is the totally innocent and infinitely Pure One. His unique origin and divinity means that he experiences sinful man's impurity all the more acutely, a point St. Thomas makes as well. The Pure One in experiencing the burden of human sin 'produces absolute nausea in the one who loves God, who is nourished by God (Mt 4,4; Jn 4,34); the fact that it is God who prescribes what is absolutely opposed to God, awakes absolute dread in him'.[109]

Second Jesus' anxiety is a vicarious suffering (*stellvertretenden Leiden*) for every sinner and every sin. He writes, 'It is the vicarious suffering of this Pure One for all the impure, that is, experiencing that anxiety which every sinner by right would have to go through before the judgement seat of God and in being rejected by him'.[110] What is the anxiety that every sinner by right would have to undergo? It is the ultimate anxiety of being separated from God for eternity, the *timor gehennalis*. This ultimate intensification of sin-anxiety far surpasses any natural or sin-anxiety. It also far surpasses any anxiety from death, ego-consciousness, discursive reasoning or disordered passions, discussed in part two. These anxieties find their ultimate expression in the natural fear of physical death, but the *timor gehennalis* is anxiety over the second death – to be eternally damned in Hell. Our author holds that the Lord's vicarious suffering on our behalf entails his suffering the *timor gehennalis*. How could Jesus really experience this if at all times he is aware that he is the Divine Son of the Father and accomplishing his mission for him? How could Jesus fear Hell if he knows that he is the totally Innocent One? The only way Christ could

107. *KL*, pp. 268–9; Eng., p. 271.
108. *CA*, p. 37; Eng., pp. 74–5.
109. *HIII/2/2*, p. 193; Eng., p. 209.
110. *CA*, pp. 37–8; Eng., p. 75.

experience this in a real way is through his *Hinterlegung* of his divine knowledge and by living his mission moment by moment in 'faith'. Balthasar proposes, therefore, that in the Garden 'Christ was not certain of his salvation by any other means than his prayer of supplication'.[111]

Our author appeals to a line of thinking from the *Sententiae Divinitatis* through Alexander of Hales to St. Bonaventure to support his position and indicate how the divine and sinless Lord could experience the *timor gehennalis*. He first quotes the *Sententiae Divinitatis*: 'Some say that he knew it [*timor gehennalis*] in his (ecclesial) members. But we say, to the contrary, in his own person – not for himself, but for his members'.[112] Alexander of Hales' position, according to Balthasar, draws out the uniqueness and freedom of Christ's suffering. In fallen human beings, the possibility of suffering is bound up with the necessity of suffering, the will not to suffer but without the ability to avoid it. In the Lord Jesus, by contrast, the possibility of suffering is not bound to the necessity of suffering. He has the will to suffer and the power not to suffer.[113] He indicates, in our author's estimation, the uniqueness of the hypostatic union and the voluntary nature of the Son's kenosis 'which conditions and structures his human nature, and allows it to house a quite different measure of suffering than that of the sinner whose suffering is constrained'.[114]

St. Bonaventure provides, in Balthasar's view, 'a more penetrating light' which overcomes the boundary of Christ's beatific vision in suffering through his distinction between *passio* and *compassio*. Balthasar quotes the Seraphic doctor: 'In what concerns the pain of suffering, *passio*, Christ suffered more intensely in his sensibility; in what concerns the pain of co-suffering, *compassio*, he suffered more intensely in his spiritual nature. But the pain of co-suffering was greater than the pain of suffering'.[115] Therefore, Christ's *compassio* allows the most spiritual part of his human soul to suffer and not just the lower through a free choice to do so. This insight is developed by St. Bernard Clairvaux and Hugh of St. Victor in which Jesus' physical pain 'drew his soul into co-suffering, while the psychic pain occasioned by our sins took along the body with it'.[116] Our author concludes, 'The stronger the love is, the more painful are the wounds of co-suffering'.[117] This line of thought indicates a much greater suffering than a propassion. This suffering is not the beginning of *timor*, but a deep psychic and somatic suffering. This line of thinking leads our author to formulate his interpretation of Christ's anxiety in Gethsemane:

> [O]n the Mount of Olives, Christ's anguish was a co-suffering with sinners, of such a kind that the real loss of God which threatened them (the *poena damni*) was assumed by the incarnate Love of God in the form of a *timor gehennalis*. Since the sin of the

111. *TDT*, p. 98; Eng., p. 103.
112. *TDT*, p. 98; Eng., p. 102.
113. Cf. *TDT*, p. 99; Eng., p. 103.
114. *TDT*, p. 99; Eng., p. 103.
115. *TDT*, p. 99; Eng., p. 104.
116. *TDT*, p. 99; Eng., p. 104.
117. *TDT*, p. 99; Eng., p. 104.

> world is 'laid' upon him, Jesus no longer distinguishes himself and his fate from those of sinners – the less so, according to Bonaventure, the more the love is – and thus in that way he experiences the anxiety and horror which they by rights should have known for themselves.[118]

Balthasar reasons, in other words, that if Jesus experiences sin on our behalf, he also endures 'genuine fear of death and hell'.[119] The Lord Jesus places himself in vicarious representation of sinful man and thus allows the divine wrath to fall upon him. The wrath is not only that from the sinful Gentiles, but most of all from the broken covenant and the terrible Day of the Lord. Balthasar writes that Christ's anxiety extends beyond that of the righteous man exemplified in the prophets and even the anxiety of Job.[120] Jesus 'experiences both at once, God's utter absence in everything that is loaded on to him, and the yet more terrifying presence of a God who "hedges him in" (Job 3.23), who "hunts" him (10.16) and "hounds" him (10.17); and because the sufferer is in a state of complete powerlessness, he is "oppressed" by God and "robbed of his dignity" (10.3)'.[121] The inconceivable unity of the world's sin and God's will come together in a way which renders any relationship with God or the world impossible.

The Son's *Stellvertretung* means that all human anxiety, even every sinner's anxiety before God in judgement, is appropriated by him. Our author gives three reasons in *Theologie der drei Tage* to make sense of his position. First, Jesus' entire human consciousness is entirely determined 'by the Logos and his eternal attitude of love toward the Father'.[122] Second, Jesus' complete readiness opens his human nature up to co-suffer in absolute obedience. Third, the Son truly identifies his fate as man to the eschatological fate of the sinful human race. Christ's anxiety goes deeper than a *passio animae* to a deeply physical and psychic pain all the way to suffering the *timor gehennalis*. The difference that Balthasar posits is between the objective and subjective levels, between the logical and experiential levels. Jesus can vicariously experience subjectively what is objectively foreign to him. The Incarnate Son plunges in anxiety to the far side of man's anxiety created by his distance from his No to Father through sin. This distance is taken by force into the distinction between the Father and the Son, is blown open by the Son's eternal, obedient Yes, and is consumed in the fire of the Holy Spirit of love burning between Father and Son.

This point leads us to the third aspect of Christ's anxiety in Gethsemane, its revelation of Trinitarian love. His anxiety is a revelation in human terms

118. *TDT*, p. 100; Eng., p. 104.

119. *TDIII*, p. 266; Eng., p. 287.

120. He writes, 'Jeremiah and Ezekiel must experience and proclaim the inevitability of the punitive judgment; and Lamentations call in the devastated sanctuary to the God who has vanished and is absent; Job experiences in his own body, during the exile, how the righteousness of God has been withdrawn – without his understanding the sufferings he must endure, his existence symbolizes the broken covenant' (*HIII/2/2*, pp. 190–1; Eng., p. 206).

121. *HIII/2/2*, pp. 193–4; Eng., p. 209.

122. *TDT*, p. 100; Eng., p. 105.

and by analogy of 'God's own anguish' for the world.[123] Our author writes that it is 'the anguish [*Angst*] that God (in human form) suffers on account of his world, which is in danger of being lost to him – which, indeed, at that moment *is* an utterly lost world'.[124] This divine 'anxiety' demonstrates in human terms and in an analogous way how much the world matters to God. Christ's anxiety is a revelation of the glory of the Lord, and Balthasar draws out the strong connection between the glory manifested on Mount Tabor and that manifested on the Mount of Olives.[125] Christ's anxiety in the Garden of Gethsemane, in all three of its aspects, 'is, in the proper and strict sense of the word, the absolute anxiety, which undergirds and surpasses every other anxiety and thus becomes the standard and tribunal for all'.[126]

All the anxiety Christ experiences in the Garden of Gethsemane culminates in his Cross, where this absolute anxiety is 'drained to the dregs . . . in the actual abandonment of the Son by the Father'.[127] Based upon the uniqueness of the Incarnate Son, Balthasar holds that this is 'an absolute forsakenness [*absolute Verlassenheit*] and, therefore, the absolute measure of the abyss (ἄβυσσος) and of every other abysmal experience'.[128] This absolute anxiety is so intense that it produces an 'eclipse' of his faith and hope reaching the apex of his abandonment in his cry from the Cross. Nevertheless this 'eclipse' is a mode of his supreme intimacy of love with the Father in the Holy Spirit. Balthasar summarizes, 'the Son of Man has known anxiety and therein, as in everything he was, did, and suffered, he has translated something incomprehensible and divine into human language. . . . God's fear and trembling for the world, for his creation, which is on the verge of being lost'.[129] The revelation of the Triune God in anxiety means that 'man's fear of God has become God's anxiety for man'.[130]

From objective constriction to objective dilation

What does Christ's appropriation and redemption of anxiety mean exactly according to our author? First, Jesus has appropriated all human anxiety into the Trinitarian life and in doing so has made it his and through it revealed Triune love. Man's anxiety, all the way to its ultimate form in the *timor gehennalis*, is appropriated into the relationship of eternal love between the Father and the Son. As a result of Christ's vicarious substitution in anxiety,

123. *CA*, p. 37; Eng., p. 73; cf. *TDII/2*, pp. 202–10; Eng., pp. 220–9, and Martinelli's treatment of Balthasar's use of analogy in Martinelli, *Il mistero della morte*, pp. 112–18.

124. *CA*, p. 38; Eng., p. 75 (Balthasar's italics).

125. Cf. *HIII/2/2*, pp. 321–2; Eng., pp. 345–7.

126. *CA*, p. 38; Eng., p. 75.

127. *CA*, p. 38; Eng., p. 75.

128. *CA*, p. 38; Eng., p. 75.

129. *CA*, p. 89; Eng., p. 146.

130. *TDIII*, p. 467; Eng., p. 502.

'Human anxiety thus becomes the material, as it were, by which Jesus restores the fallen creation to the Father and imparts to it God's absolution'.[131]

In Christ's redemption of human anxiety, Balthasar distinguishes between the subjective and objective levels of our Lord's experience. The subjective level of his experience is what one would expect – the horrible psychosomatic experience of constriction. Christ's subjective experience of anxiety is how man experiences anxiety except that Christ's far surpasses it. Subjectively he experiences the fruitlessness of such suffering, a suffering even devoid of the feeling of joy. Our author links Jesus' subjective experience with the Old Testament image of labour pains without giving birth.[132] Balthasar writes, 'The anguish of Eve and of her curse (Gen 3:16) resounds from the Old Testament image, in which fecundity seems to have no part. Anxiety as contraction, constriction, cramping: that is all that the image of birth in the Old Covenant yields. If any fruit is mentioned it is merely "wind" '.[133]

The newness of anxiety's redemption appears on the objective level. Jesus' appropriation and redemption of anxiety changes the objective structure of anxiety. The objective level of Christ's anxiety is a revelation of Trinitarian love. Therefore, the objective motion of Christ's anxiety moves in the opposite direction of the subjective motion. The subjective experience is constriction while the objective reality is expansion. Christ's human nature objectively undergoes not a constriction but a *dilation* in love. Our author links the objective reality with that mysterious passage in Psalm 4: '*In tribulatione dilatasti mihi*'.[134] Thus the objective structure of anxiety is changed from constriction to dilation. Anxiety in Christ can now dilate human nature by love rather than simply constrict and harm it. The following passage from Balthasar illustrates his point:

> [T]he basis for the anxiety of the Cross is nothing other than the love of God, who takes this entire world of anxiety upon himself in order to overcome it by suffering, a love that is in all respects the opposite of the sinner's experience of anxiety: it is instead a turning toward, an availability, life, fruitfulness, security and support, expansiveness, liberation. The first set of properties ['a turning away, flight, a rigidity in life, sterility, desolation, the plunge into the abyss, constriction, incarceration, withdrawing into self, banishment'] appears as a function of the second. This is true to such an extent that these properties, as anxiety that is *borne*, are not like a compact bundle that is moved externally while remaining unaffected inwardly; rather, the properties in and of themselves, and even as they are experienced, undergo a profound transformation.[135]

131. Tourenne, 'Un théologien et son temps', p. 19; Eng., p. 16. Torralba-Roselló proposes that Balthasar's understanding of anxiety's redemption recovers Kierkegaard's Christology presented in *Practice in Christianity* (1850), and grants a central, living role to anxiety in Christian faith (cf. Torralba-Roselló, 'Prefacio', p. 21).

132. Cf. Isa. 13.8; 26.17–8; Jer 4.31; 49.24; 50.43; 22.23; Mic. 4.9–10.

133. *CA*, p. 40; Eng., p. 78.

134. *CA*, p. 41; Eng., p. 79.

135. *CA*, pp. 48–49; Eng., p. 90 (Balthasar's italics).

Joy out of anxiety

Because of this objective dilation in love, Christ's anxiety brings together suffering and joy in a unique way. Joy breaks forth from *within* anxiety. The two are not mutually exclusive due to the objective structural change of anxiety wrought through the redemption. Balthasar writes, Jesus' suffering 'follows from and actually expresses his eternal, triune joy'.[136] Because Jesus made anxiety the vehicle of revelation of Triune love, anxiety now also can be an objective expression of Triune joy. Balthasar supports his position with St. Paul: 'Throughout his entire letter to the Philippians, written in suffering, he expresses pure joy and exhorts his readers to nothing but joy'.[137] Christ's anxiety is a revelation of his eternal love, and thus the joy flowing from his eternal love flows in the midst of his anxiety. Joy is the fruit of self-surrender and self-giving, and flows from his total obedience to the Father. Balthasar quotes von Speyr, 'The truer the love is, the more joyful it is in all its suffering'.[138] Joy and suffering are not mutually exclusive but both together become expressive of the reality of triune love.

Balthasar acknowledges, however, that the subjective experience of joy that the Incarnate Son possesses can also be part of his *Hinterlegung*. During his Passion he can lay aside even the subjective experience of joy.[139] His joy does not lessen the suffering since the suffering itself is the human expression of his love of the Father. Paolo Martinelli writes of it as a mystery of *objective* joy through *subjective* anxiety.[140] In fact, the abandonment of the Son by the Father on the Cross is done precisely to increase the joy of the Son: 'For his part the Father "cannot give any answer, because he desires to give the Son perfect joy, namely, the joy of having died for him in the experience of forsakenness"'.[141] The greater the self-surrender is, the greater the love, the greater the joy. This perspective of our author and the revelation of the Son's 'I' in extreme self-surrender 'explodes the self-reference of an egoistic "I"; it *is* perfect self-surrender'.[142] The appropriation and redemption of anxiety by the Incarnate Son then reveals the provisionary nature of the darkness of abandonment. The darkness is transitory; the joy remains.

136. *TDIV*, p. 228; Eng., p. 252 (cf. the entire section entitled 'Death/Life; Sorrow/Joy', pp. 226–32; Eng., pp. 250–6, in which Balthasar constantly quotes from von Speyr on this topic of the unity of suffering and joy).

137. *TDIV*, p. 228; Eng., p. 253.

138. *TDV*, p. 229; Eng., p. 254.

139. Balthasar writes, 'It is by no means suggested that, while he bears sin, the Son can actually feel this glory, this joy; but it does not alter the fact that joy is the consistent presupposition for all experience of forsakenness. On the Cross, the lived reality of death, objectively, is life; so extreme suffering, objectively, is joy' (*TDV*, p. 230; Eng., p. 254).

140. Cf. Martinelli, *La Morte di Cristo come Rivelazione*, p. 358.

141. *TDIV*, p. 230; Eng., p. 255.

142. *TDIV*, p. 231; Eng., p. 255 (Balthasar's italics).

Redeemed anxiety, freedom from anxiety and salvific anxiety

What does Christ's redemption signify for man in his anxiety? What kind of effect does the redemption have on human anxiety? Jesus' archetypical anxiety has redeemed and revalued anxiety, and so becomes the measure and norm of the authenticity and depth of all experience including anxiety.[143] Christ's anxiety becomes the archetype for how anxiety is transformed in his members. All human anxiety now exists within the life of Trinitarian love. The suffering of anxiety no longer lies 'outside' the experience of the God-man. Moreover, his redemption of anxiety opens up an entirely new modality of being for the human race. It does not abolish the void that was opened by original sin in the human mind. Rather, Christ's presence comes into the void through the redemption. This presence, however, is not the same as the immediate presence in the evening breeze of Eden, but rather as a fullness being communicated in the void. Christ's redemption has not abolished all anxiety just as it has not abolished suffering and death, but rather anxiety has been revalued in the believer through the changing of its objective structure by Jesus.[144] The experience of anxiety remains, but it has been transformed from within. Jesus redemption of anxiety can change man's natural and sin-anxiety into 'redeemed' anxiety.

Redeemed anxiety, in Balthasar's view, gives rise to two new realities with regard to human anxiety. The first new reality from redeemed anxiety is that for the first time since the Fall man is given the real possibility of being free from anxiety (*Angstlosigkeit*). Redeemed anxiety gives rise to freedom from anxiety because the Lord Jesus has overcome anxiety. One can be freed from natural and sin-anxiety. Man was commanded to be free from anxiety in the Old Covenant, but this prohibition was challenged in various ways. Now the command to 'Be not afraid' reaches its greatest and truest force. Balthasar writes, 'The first thing that must be said, and which can never be said powerfully and triumphantly enough, is that human fear has been completely and definitively conquered by the Cross'.[145] Through Christ's death and resurrection, the power of death is destroyed and so the one in Christ no longer need fear death. It is now the doorway into eternal life. The 'world', understood as a kingdom of darkness, has also been conquered and has no more claim on the believer. Natural anxiety is conquered. Christ has also suffered man's anxiety in sin and achieved reconciliation and mercy for man. Therefore, the one in Christ no longer need fear divine judgement since mercy and forgiveness are possible for him. Sin-anxiety is conquered. Even the righteous anxiety of the Old Covenant is transformed since through the Incarnation, Passion and Resurrection, God's proximity is completely human. God's proximity and judgement, death, the devil, the world, and sin are no longer sources of anxiety for the Christian. The example our author gives is St. Peter: 'On Easter

143. Cf. Martinelli, *La Morte di Cristo come Rivelazione*, pp. 415–8; Meiattini, *Sentire cum Christo*, p. 390.

144. Cf. Martinelli, *La Morte di Cristo come Rivelazione*, p. 415.

145. *CA*, p. 42; Eng., p. 81.

day Peter can no longer fear the One whom he has betrayed three times. His anxiety has been taken away, and confident love has been granted him in its place'.[146] Even the terrible Day of the Lord can be met in confidence.[147]

The second new reality from redeemed anxiety is that a new type of anxiety is brought into being by Jesus. Redeemed anxiety gives rise not only to freedom from anxiety but also 'salvific anxiety', that is, a positive anxiety that contributes to man's salvation. Our author calls this new anxiety a 'salvific' or 'redeeming anxiety' (*erlösenden Angst*),[148] a 'Christian anxiety' (*Christliche Angst*),[149] and even a 'catholic anxiety' (*katholische Angst*).[150] A participation in Christ's anxiety is now possible for man. Christ's death is exclusive in that only he could do it. His death is inclusive in that he allows the members of his body to participate in that act not only by receiving the fruits but by sharing in his suffering of it.[151] Though all are invited to have their anxiety redeemed and embrace an anxiety-free life, the Lord may lead a member of his body to participate in his salvific anxiety. This new anxiety is predicated upon a participation in Christ's anxiety which enables one to enter into his anxiety (*Mitängstigen*)[152] and to establish a true 'shared anxiety' (*Mit-angst*)[153] with him and through him with all sinners. The Lord invites the members of his Mystical Body to share in the wonderful exchange possible in the communion of his mystical body.

Christ's redemption of anxiety, in Balthasar's view, thus gives a new quality to filial *timor* which St. Thomas does not explicitly treat. Christ establishes the ultimate righteous anxiety: those in Christ can now participate in Christ's anxiety on behalf of sinners. Filial *timor* or righteous anxiety now can be the vicarious suffering of anxiety for sinners. Anxiety no longer has to be a fruitless suffering. Balthasar writes, 'Now it is possible for anxiety to participate in the fruitful anguish [*fruchtbare Angst*] of the Cross'.[154]

Conclusion

This chapter examined Balthasar's interpretation of Angst and its redemption. Balthasar offers a unique interpretation of Christ's anxiety based upon his positions in Christology and soteriology, especially his concepts of *Hinterlegung, Stellvertretung* and the divine nature understood as kenotic love. Basing

146. *CA*, p. 43; Eng., p. 83.
147. Cf. *CA*, p. 44; Eng., p. 84.
148. Cf. *CA*, pp. 54, 59.
149. Cf. *CA*, pp. 49, 51–5, 57, 62, 64–5, 90–1.
150. Cf. *CA*, p. 50.
151. Cf. Servais' summary of Balthasar's position on the inclusive nature of the redemption in Servais, 'Mérite substitution, sacrifice de l'Église', pp. 212–16.
152. Cf. *CA*, pp. 48, 66. He also uses the term 'shared concern' (*Mit-Sorge*) in connection with *Mit-angst* (*CA*, p. 50).
153. Cf. *CA*, p. 50.
154. *CA*, p. 40; Eng., p. 79. Balthasar sees it in the life of St. Paul (2 Cor. 6.4; 1 Cor. 4.15; 2.3; 2 Cor. 11.29; 12.9; Rom. 8.19–27).

his interpretation on the mystical experience of Adrienne von Speyr and the more Bonaventurian line of thinking in the tradition, Balthasar holds that Jesus appropriated human anxiety to its ultimate extreme in the *timor gehennalis*. This requires the 'depositing' of a full and uninterrupted beatific vision in Jesus during his earthly life. Anxiety is appropriated and redeemed through Jesus' suffering in Gethsemane and on the Cross. This redemption actually changes the objective structure of anxiety so that it no longer has to be an objective constriction. Rather it can become an objective dilation of human nature in love even if the subjective experience feels like a constriction. Finally the redemption of anxiety brings to man the possibility of being free from anxiety as well as the possibility of a salvific anxiety in which a member in the mystical body shares in Christ's anxiety.

Part Three Conclusion

With the positions of Aquinas and Balthasar having been presented, we are now in a position to draw some conclusions about the redemption of anxiety in Balthasar's theology of anxiety. We will first note their agreement regarding anxiety's redemption, and show why Balthasar is ultimately dissatisfied with St. Thomas' position. Then we will note Balthasar's achievement in treating Christ's anxiety, and finally the challenges found in his interpretation.

Balthasar's Agreement with Aquinas on Christ's Anxiety

Several points of agreement can be identified between Aquinas' and Balthasar's interpretation of Christ's anxiety. Both agree that the human nature the Son assumed in his Incarnation was complete and perfect as formulated at Constantinople III. The fact that they differ on the *mode* of Christ's human perfection is explained below. Neither theologian has any intention of compromising this perfection since it would destroy the soteriological value of Christ's atoning Passion.

Both, therefore, exclude certain types of anxiety from Jesus' appropriation of it. Both would agree that anxiety from personal sin, concupiscence, or ignorance (at least of his personal identity as the divine Son and of his mission) is excluded from Christ. Servile, worldly and initial fear, moreover, would also be excluded for the same reason. In Balthasar's theology, Jesus possesses the constant awareness that he is the Son of the Father and is unwaveringly steadfast in his obedience to the mission the Father has given him. Thus throughout Jesus' earthly life he as man would express perfect filial *timor* in his relationship to the Father expressed in the total and constant obedience to the mission the Father gave him. Furthermore, both writers argue that Christ's experience of anxiety is absolutely unique based upon his unique constitution as the God-man and the unique human nature he assumed in the Incarnation.

It is also evident that both authors would agree that Christ was not subject to intellectual anxiety but for different reasons. Aquinas excludes intellectual anxiety from Christ based on his perfect knowledge. Balthasar would exclude intellectual anxiety from Christ based on his 'mission consciousness' and his nuanced understanding of Jesus' 'faith' and 'hope'. The ontological difference poses no threat to Jesus' human intellect and his human will is never in a position of wavering before the Good.

Furthermore, both agree that Jesus did appropriate certain types of anxiety. Both thinkers indicate that Jesus expressed the emotion of fear during his earthly life, including astonishment (*admiratio*). Both would also agree that Christ did suffer anxiety in Gethsemane, and that this suffering coincided with his joy. How the anxiety and joy coincidence, however, differs between the two writers. St. Thomas locates Christ's joy in the higher part of his human soul which is immersed in the beatific vision, while the lower part of his human soul and his body would experience his unique *timor*. The joy and suffering are going on at the same time but not in the same 'location'. Balthasar's view on the other hand maintains that Christ's joy actually breaks forth from within the suffering. Since suffering is the human expression of divine love, the joy flows out of the suffering. They are going on in the same 'location'.

Aquinas and Balthasar, however, conceive of Jesus' anxiety quite differently. St. Thomas allows a limited appropriation of negative *timor*, a propassion, given Jesus perfect knowledge and consummate virtue. Balthasar allows from a much greater appropriation of anxiety, all the way to the *timor gehennalis*, given Jesus' perfect love and obedience. St. Thomas excludes the possibility of the *timor gehennalis* in Jesus' experience. Both the Angelic doctor and Balthasar would agree that Christ's appropriation of anxiety is not necessary but rather a free act of love on his part. Jesus is not compelled in his human nature to suffer as we are. He freely chooses suffering by assuming in his Incarnation certain defects – to use St. Thomas' term – in his human soul and body which enable him to suffer. Balthasar explains this reality in terms of the Son's kenotic love in *Hinterlegung* and *Stellvertretung*.

From the discussion in Chapter 6, it seems that there is room in Aquinas' position for some existential stretching in Jesus' appropriation of *timor*. The Angelic doctor's acknowledgement of the suspension between the higher and lower parts of his human soul in Christ's suffering marks a point of contact between the two positions. Balthasar, however, wants to expand such a notion in a radical manner through the Son's ability to lay aside his divine prerogatives in order not to threaten Christ's divinity and the hypostatic union, but in fact to *demonstrate* his divinity. To phrase Balthasar's position in more Thomistic terms, the love that suspends the glory of Jesus' divinity from flowing into the lower part of his soul and his entire body (St. Thomas' view), suspends the glory from flowing into Jesus' *entire* human nature so that his suffering forms a perfect correspondence with the total, self-emptying love of his divinity. His entire human nature given over to suffering, the *forma servi*, to be the perfect revelation of the *forma Dei*.

Balthasar's Dissatisfaction with Aquinas' Interpretation

Despite such agreement Balthasar finds Aquinas' view of Christ's suffering in general, and thus *timor* in particular, dissatisfying. The initial, and perhaps foundational, reason for our author's dissatisfaction is due to the lack of resonance the traditional scholastic interpretation has with the mystical experience of A. von Speyr in which Christ's *totale Angst* extends far beyond the sensitive appetite. The dissonance between the scholastic interpretation and von Speyr's experience serves as a goad to Balthasar to find a theological interpretation that more adequately accounts for her experience, which he never doubted. Our author's interpretation of anxiety's redemption attempts to give adequate voice to the 'lived theology' of the saints, to quote Pope John Paul II.

The inadequacy Balthasar finds with St. Thomas' position is the lessening of Christ's suffering. Our author would not think that St. Thomas' position gives an adequate account of the data from Sacred Scripture or of the *pro nobis* proposition of the Creed. Balthasar's position on the *Hinterlegung* of the Incarnate Son's divine prerogatives and the *Stellvertretung* of his atoning Passion attempts to show, in human terms, the unfathomable depths of Jesus' suffering. That Christ was 'made sin' for us, I would suggest, is a foundational principle of Balthasar's soteriology. Balthasar's nuanced position argues for an easement of the tension between vision and the exercise of faith and hope (properly understood) in the beatific vision allows him to grant a greater existential range of suffering to Jesus.

Balthasar also disagrees with the Angelic doctor on that which constitutes Christ's human perfection. Aquinas envisions human perfection in terms of knowledge. Balthasar views human perfection as obedience and self-surrender. St. Thomas' position on human perfection emphasizes the intellective aspect; Balthasar's the volitive. St. Thomas emphasizes perfection in terms of Truth while Balthasar emphasizes perfection in terms of the Good. Both positions have their roots in the tradition. A final difference between St. Thomas and Balthasar on Christ's anxiety is that Aquinas gives greater attention to Christ's natures while Balthasar's emphasis falls most heavily on his Person.

Balthasar's Achievement in Interpreting Anxiety's Redemption

The primary achievement in Balthasar's interpretation lies in his ability to give a deeply existential account of Christ's anxiety, and to manifest the fundamental reality of God as self-giving love. He is able to show in an original way how anxiety has been taken up within the life of God himself, has been redeemed, and has become a vehicle by which he reveals himself as love to sinful man. Balthasar's treatment of anxiety's redemption, moreover, manifests the open nature of Christ's redemption, that is, the ability for the Christian to share in it. Balthasar's theology of anxiety shows how Jesus' redemption of anxiety creates 'salvific anxiety', an anxiety that is totally unique and redemptive for the world, and the possibility for man to share in it.

By taking human perfection in terms of the Good, specifically obedience, Balthasar forges a theological path that grants a much greater existential experience of suffering to Jesus, and a deeper representation with sinful man without compromising either his natures or their hypostatic union. Christ's obedience in his mission can demonstrate his perfect human nature while allowing for a more flexible position on his terrestrial beatific vision which in turn allows for a greater appropriation of anxiety. In his account of Christ's anxiety, our author is able to unite more closely the coincidence of anxiety and joy.

I would also suggest that Balthasar's interpretation carries heavy apologetical weight in an age when existential concerns are so prominent.[1] A theology of anxiety developed with attentiveness to the existential dimension can reach into the very heart of the contemporary drama of human anxiety. Although Balthasar's Christology does not lend itself to forming a 'psychology' of Jesus' anxiety, Balthasar's theology of anxiety can have a psychological impact on his reader, especially in the cognitive dimension of anxiety. God indeed does care about human anxiety, and has gone so far as to appropriate it to himself, including the worst anxiety of the *timor gehennalis*. His experience of anxiety reaches far beyond any anxiety we could suffer. Human anxiety is now interior to divine love and, therefore, the Lord is not absent from it. He even offers the possibility of not only relief of anxiety, but also that our anxiety can be transformed in a way that we begin to share in Jesus' redemption of anxious sinners. One's anxiety can become salvific in Christ.

When comparing two writers like Aquinas and Balthasar, separated as they are by several centuries, it is important to recognize the differences in their approach in thinking.[2] The existential state of man seems of much greater concern in the twentieth than in the thirteenth century; yet medieval theologians like St. Thomas were also intimately acquainted with the existential reality of fallen human nature, especially through their priestly ministry. It is, therefore, important in this existentially sensitive age to interpret the Angelic doctor both in light of the whole of his work and in light of how it can be fleshed out existentially. Because of the great metaphysical confidence of the Middle Ages, St. Thomas' thought naturally rises above the existential to the essential level. A consideration of how St. Thomas' position could be stretched existentially in Chapter 6 is an attempt to flesh out the existential dimension of his treatment.

Challenges in Balthasar's Interpretation of Anxiety's Redemption

Balthasar's interpretation has its challenges. An initial read of the last two chapters shows that Balthasar's position does not systematize as easily as Aquinas'. I agree with John Saward and Giulio Meiattini that Balthasar could

1. Meiattini writes, 'Balthasar's experiential Christocentrism is able to show all its particular and critical sensibility to modernity's plea, recovering and founding the subjective in the heart of the objective norm' (Meiattini, *Sentire cum Christo*, pp. 391–2) (author's translation).

2. I am grateful to Stephen Loughlin, PhD. and Jacques Servais, S.J. for providing the insight on this point.

be more precise in his language.[3] Our author's poetic style and use of paradoxical language, surrounded by quotations, risks overwhelming theological precision at times.

It is also not clear in Balthasar's interpretation how anxiety operates within Christ's perfect human nature in its relationship to the natural virtues. Although Balthasar treats Christ's 'faith' and 'hope', we do not find a consideration of the natural virtues such as courage and fortitude. Is there a place in Christ's human nature, in Balthasar's view, for the natural virtues which shape human anxiety? Perhaps here is where Balthasar's Christological emphasis on the Person of the Son falls short in giving a more complete account of the specific properties of his human nature.

Finally, Balthasar appeals to God's unfathomable freedom and the experience of the saints to ground his position. By taking a position on the logic of divine love that transcends the grasp of the human intellect, Balthasar's position is vulnerable to the charge that his position risks the rationality of his discourse. To use a recently suggested phrase, 'does love trump reason'?[4] At least it can be said from the point of view of our theme that reason without love, which precipitated the Fall, is the origin of all negative anxiety. A loveless reason ought to be trumped.

3. Cf. Saward, *Mysteries of March*, p. 55; Meiattini, *Sentire cum Christo*, p. 393. For example, Saward writes that Balthasar distinguishes 'insufficiently between the *feeling* of abandonment and its *reality*' (Saward, *Mysteries of March*, p. 55) (Saward's italics).

4. This phrase framed three of the papers presented at 'Love Alone Is Credible: Hans Urs von Balthasar as Interpreter of the Catholic Tradition. A conference honouring the work of Balthasar on the 100th Anniversary of his birth' (Lansdowne, Virginia; 14–17 April 2005). At the time of publication only D.C. Schindler's paper has appeared in published form: D.C. Schindler, 'Toward a Non-Possessive Concept of Knowledge: on the Relation between Reason and Love in Aquinas and Balthasar', *Modern Theology* 22 (2006), pp. 577–607. The first volume of this conference was been published: D.L. Schindler (ed.), *Love Alone is Credible: Hans Urs von Balthasar as Interpreter of the Catholic Tradition* (Grand Rapids: Eerdmans, 2008). The second volume, presumably with the articles by L.P. Hemming, 'The Nature of Reality: Does Love Trump Reason?' and C. O'Regan, 'Reason in Ecstacy: Truth and Being True in Balthasar', has not yet been published. I agree with Schindler's conclusion that the charge that Balthasar's thought tends towards voluntarism or irrationalism come from an overly narrow construal of the intellectual act with the soul's act of internalization. Balthasar does not reject this view but seeks to integrate it into a more comprehensive view. A non-possessive concept of reason means that one can know without subordinating what is known to oneself. Schindler writes, 'Balthasar avoids both horns of the dilemma by making intelligence an act that preserves the difference of analogy and thus leaves room for an eternity of wonder and surprise as a restful *end* rather than as a ceaseless chase. It is this view of the understanding that lies behind Balthasar's making service the form of beatific vision, 108 and we can affirm this form even while retaining the superiority of reason over the will' (Schindler, 'Toward a Non-Possessive Concept of Knowledge', p. 598).

Conclusion

Our author preserves the intimacy of the Son with the Father, that they are never objectively separated. His nuanced position on Christ's terrestrial beatific vision, principles of *Hinterlegung, Stellvertretung* and 'mission consciousness', our author charts a theological course that permits a greater experience of suffering for the Incarnate Son and therefore, account for the demands of the biblical data and the *pro nobis* of the Creed. Balthasar's soteriology, deliberately cast in dramatic categories, is so shaped by his initial point of departure, the Good, that it inevitably leads him to form a position divergent from St. Thomas.

I suggest, moreover, that Balthasar's interpretation of Christ's anxiety carries greater apologetical weight in the post-modern age. Balthasar's attentiveness to action, existence and the Good has an appeal for the post-modern listener. Anyone suffering from anxiety can find in Balthasar's position that the Incarnate Son in Gethsemane and on the Cross appropriated it all, even it its ultimate end, and redeemed it. All human anxiety now lies within the relationship between the Father and the Son in the love of the Holy Spirit. Divine love is able to do 'far more abundantly than all that we ask or think' (Eph. 3.20).

Part Four

The Garden of the Church: Anxiety Transformed by Anxiety Redeemed

Chapter 8

The Shape of Christian Anxiety

What kind of new life is this we are now beginning?

(St. Ignatius of Loyola)[1]

The previous section showed how Balthasar understood the redemption of human anxiety by Christ's anxiety. Christ has redeemed, conquered and revalued all human anxiety. If the Lord has redeemed anxiety, then how does this redemption of anxiety reach the believer? What shape does it possess? What is the specific quality of the transformation of the believer's anxiety? Is the Christian supposed to be completely anxiety free? If not what sort of anxiety is the Christian to bear in this life and how ought it be borne? This chapter seeks to answer these and similar questions by developing Balthasar's interpretation of the nature of Christian anxiety. Our author indicated in general terms that human anxiety undergoes a qualitative change through the Lord's redemption, and that it is transformable in two fundamental ways: freedom from anxiety is possible, and that the believer's anxiety can participate in Christ's.

The present chapter seeks to clarify and develop Balthasar's position on Christian anxiety by placing his thought in dialogue with Martin Luther, whom he primarily engages on the theme of Christian anxiety. We will first present Luther's position on Christian anxiety, and then proceed to examine more closely Luther's position through the eyes of Balthasar noting his agreement and critique of Luther's interpretation. Finally, we will present Balthasar's proposal concerning Christian anxiety.

The Dialectical Shape of Christian Anxiety According to Luther

The genesis of Christian anxiety in simul iustus et peccator

The source of Christian anxiety in Luther's thought can be traced to his doctrine of justification encapsulated in his famous two-part formula *simul iustus et peccator*, that is, the Christian is at the same time both righteous and a

1. *UA*, 98n; Eng., 102n. Cf. Ignatius of Loyola, *A Pilgrim's Journey: The Autobiography of Ignatius of Loyola*, (Wilmington: Michael Glazier, 1985), pp. 25–6. Balthasar cites this line in reference to the beginning of von Speyr's mystical anxiety. St. Ignatius made the observation in his autobiography when desolation begins to descend on him.

sinner.[2] This central doctrine of Luther arose in response to what he saw as a lived Pelagianism in the way many Christians approached their salvation. The Pelagian heresy holds that man is able to do good independent of divine grace thereby inculcating a false security about the believer's justification before God. The Church's doctrine of justification and especially as taught in scholastic theology, in Luther's view, encouraged such heresy.[3] He writes in his *95 Theses* in the norms for good preaching on the need for lifelong repentance: 'Christians should be exhorted to concentrate on following Christ their Head in penances and enduring death and hell. So they seek to enter heaven more through many tribulations than by trusting in any present security of peace'.[4] Luther argues that following his doctrine of the *simul* formula is the correct way of viewing the Christian's justification in Christ, and of preventing Pelagianism from infecting the Christian life. Both parts of the formula are relevant for our theme of anxiety.

The first essential realization is that man is a sinner. One must acknowledge his radical sinfulness, make his *confessio peccati*, and admit that he can do nothing to justify himself before God. The preaching of the indulgences, in Luther's view, undermined the need for the believer to make this confession thereby eliminating a necessary anxiety about his state before God. Christians, according to Luther, need to be reminded continually of sin's pervasive infection so as to imbue the Christian life with penitence and the imploring of the Divine Mercy.

Man's radical sinfulness is so important for Luther that he argues that its presence remains even after forgiveness and justification. This position is founded upon his equating of sin with the drive of concupiscence,[5] and the essential bondage of the human will even after justification.[6] Thus human

2. Cf. *WA*, pp. 56, 272, 17 (*LW*, pp. 25, 260). Citations are given in volume, page and when appropriate, line. Luther's position on justification underwent development in his lifetime, and has been subsequently developed and interpreted by many. To treat such complexity in an adequate manner extends beyond the scope of this thesis, and so I will remain focused on Luther himself. What is attempted in this section is not to give an exhaustive treatment of Luther's formula, but rather to give a fair exposition of the doctrine for the purposes of our theme. The following presentation of Luther's doctrine follows closely that of J. Wicks in 'Justification and Faith in Luther', *Theological Studies* 44 (1983), pp. 3–29, and 'Living and Praying as *Simul Iustus et Peccator*', *Gregorianum* 70 (1989), pp. 521–48.

3. Cf. A. McGrath, *Iustitia Dei: A History of the Christian Doctrine of Justification* (Cambridge: Cambridge University Press, 2002), p. 197.

4. *WA*, pp. 1, 238, 18; translated and cited by Wicks in 'Living and Praying', p. 524. The *LW* edition reads, 'Christians should be exhorted to be diligent in following Christ, their head, through penalties, death, and hell. And thus be confident of entering into heaven through many tribulations rather than through false security of peace' (*LW* 31, 33).

5. Cf. *WA*, 56, 287, 18–24 (*LW*, pp. 25, 274–5).

6. Cf. Wicks, 'Justification and Faith in Luther', p. 20. Its bondage is threefold according to Luther: its inability to change its aversion to God's law (cf. *WA*, pp. 18, 709, 21–710, 7–8 [*LW*, 33, 176–7]; *WA*, 18, 685, 10–17; *WA*, pp. 18, 768, 17–26; *WA*, pp. 18, 774, 19–775, 18; *WA*, pp. 18, 786, 7–14), its inability to consent to divine grace and comply with its justification (*WA*, pp. 18, 634, 37–635, 7 [*LW*, pp. 33, 65]), and finally its inability to act freely within God's preordination of all things (*WA*, pp. 18, 615, 25–616, 12 [*LW*,

autonomy before God is walled off in order to preserve divine initiative and sovereignty. Luther's position excludes any dynamic cooperation between divine grace and human freedom, between man's inability and God's superability. Because of his enslaved will, the unjustified sinner can only will and do what is evil, and for Luther this enslavement continues even in the justified sinner.

To help clarify his position on the *peccator* side of the formula, Luther introduces two terms to distinguish between the presence of sin before and after justification: *peccatum regnans* ('sin ruling/reigning') and *peccatum regnatum* (literally, 'sin having been ruled'). Before justification man is under the dominion of sin which incites God's wrath against him. Sin reigns in him, and his sins are judged by God unto condemnation and the punishment of Hell. The *peccatum regnans* understandably produces sin-anxiety in the unbeliever. After justification the believer remains a sinner, but since he clings to the righteousness Christ won for him, his sinfulness does not incite divine wrath but rather Divine Mercy.[7] This is the *peccatum regnatum*. Though his sin remains, it is ruled by Christ. In justification Christ reigns over the believer's sin.

The continued infection of sin in the Christian's soul, however, means that he must then contend and struggle against it. Luther writes

> When someone comes forth out of baptism, he is truly pure, without sin, and wholly guiltless. Still, there are many who do not properly understand this. They think that sin is no longer present, and so they become remiss and negligent in the killing of their sinful nature, even as some do when they have gone to confession. For this reason, as I have said above, it should be properly understood and known that our flesh, so long as it lives here, is by nature wicked and sinful. . . . But although not pure in all things, he has begun to grow into purity and innocence.[8]

The continuance of sin in the believer as *peccatum regnatum* is the proper antidote against complacency and negligence in the Christian life for Luther. The use of terms devised by scholastic theology such as *fomes* is an innovation, according to Luther, which minimizes sin's reality and the dramatic struggle Christians must wage against it. Softening the impact of sin through a concept like *fomes* leads to the pastoral consequence that people cease to make war on their concupiscence. Luther writes, 'Those who deny this sin make people rest apathetically and carelessly in the gift they have received. In this way they cheapen Christ's grace and minimize God's mercy, from which necessarily follow coldness in love, slackness in praise, and lukewarmness in gratitude'.[9] The anxiety that is produced from the *peccator* side of the *simul* formula resembles somewhat St. Thomas' understanding of servile *timor* insofar as it works against presumption.

pp. 33, 37–38]; *WA*, pp. 18, 618, 19–619, 21; *WA*, pp. 18, 714, 18–19; *WA*, 18, 714, 38–722, 29; *WA*, pp. 18, 752, 12–15; *WA*, pp. 18, 753, 28–33).

7. Cf. *WA*, pp. 1, 168, 11–29 (*LW*, pp. 14, 149); *WA*, pp. 5, 76, 12–14.

8. *WA*, pp. 2, 729, 19–25 (*LW*, pp. 35, 32); *WA*, pp. 2, 730, 7–10 (*LW*, pp. 35, 33).

9. *WA*, pp. 8, 114, 39–115, 1 (*LW*, pp. 32, 240); cf. *WA*, pp. 8, 103, 19–25 (*LW*, pp. 32, 223).

The second aspect of the *simul* formula is that the one who confesses his sinfulness and believes receives God's mercy and is thereby justified. By confessing himself a *peccator*, and making an act of faith, the believer can be *iustus* before God. God in his infinite mercy then does not impute one's sins unto damnation. The believer confesses his sinfulness while at the same time God judges him righteous. Luther exclaims, 'And if he made his righteousness mine, then I am righteous in the same righteousness as he. But my sin cannot swallow him up, but is swallowed up in the infinite abyss of his righteousness, for he is God Himself, to whom be praise forever'.[10] The *iustus* side of the formula means in the words of Luther, 'Now, since God has taken my salvation out of my hands into His, making it depend on His choice and not mine, and has promised to save me . . ., I am assured and certain both that He is faithful and will not lie to me, and also that He is too great and powerful for any demons or any adversities to be able to break Him or to snatch me from Him'.[11] Luther's view of the righteousness given to the believing sinner is *iustitia Christi aliena*, meaning that the righteousness that the believer receives through faith is not and may not ever be considered his own.[12] The good works which Luther nevertheless recognizes is the *result* of justification by God rather than a *cause* of justification.

In order to clarify the *iustus* side of the formula, Luther introduces another distinction between what he terms *gratia* ('grace') and *donum* ('gift'). This distinction explains God's two-fold action in the life of the believer, and helps Luther explain both the simple relationship between God and the believer-made-righteous, and the dramatic and lifelong struggle against sin in the believer's life. The first divine action is *gratia* whereby the Lord brings the complete remission of guilt, and frees the believer in his conscience from the domination of sin. *Gratia* is an unmerited, extrinsic, one-act event by God upon the believer protecting him from divine wrath. *Gratia* is not, therefore, a quality inhering in the believer's nature, but a divine act of forgiveness. It changes the *peccatum regnans* which overwhelmed the conscience with condemnation and sin-anxiety to the *peccatum regnatum* in which Christ dominates sin in the believer's conscience and breaks sin's power to condemn. Since God's merciful grace has wiped away all guilt, the relationship established by

10. *WA*, pp. 56, 204, 8–29, citing lines 19–23; translated and cited by Wicks in 'Justification and Faith in Luther', p. 14.

11. *WA*, pp. 18, 783, 28–39 (*LW*, pp. 33, 289). Cf. Wicks, 'Justification and Faith in Luther', p. 17.

12. On this point I recognize that certain Lutheran scholars, especially in more contemporary times, reject the forensic justification interpretation of Luther's position, and argue that Christ really does become one with the person who has faith. Some has taken this view even further and argue that Luther is a 'metaphysical realist' and taught the doctrine of theosis (cf. C. Braaten, 'The Finnish Breakthrough in Lutheran Research', *Pro Ecclesia* 5 [1996], pp. 141–43, and R. Saarinen, 'Salvation in the Lutheran-Orthodox Dialogue', *Pro Ecclesia* 5 [1996], pp. 202–13). However, these positions are not without criticism. I am grateful to Prof. Rodney Howsare, PhD., for helping me appreciate the breadth of views within contemporary Lutheran scholarship.

gratia brings assurance, courage, peace and joy to the conscience of the believer.[13]

By the *donum*, the Lord begins the incremental, laborious and lifelong purification of the ongoing presence of sin as *peccatum regnatum* in the life of the believer.[14] *Donum* opposes the believer's daily sinful and corrupt self-seeking, any merit-mentality, and doubts about God's mercy and promises.[15] The believer must struggle daily to grow in purity and innocence because 'all is not yet completed and he still lives in sinful flesh'.[16] Luther writes, 'Here the works begin; here a man cannot enjoy leisure; here he must indeed take care to discipline the body by fasting, watchings, labors, and other reasonable discipline and to subject it to the Spirit so that it will obey and conform to the inner man and faith and not revolt against faith and hinder the inner man'.[17]

The *iustus* side of the formula, then, is comprised of the simultenaity of state (*gratia*) and process (*donum*). *Gratia* constitutes the relationship and *donum* the process of living out of the relationship. Grace protects the believer from God's wrath, and thus effects in the believer peace, consolation and courage, and seemingly eliminates any reason for anxiety. Grace then instils in the believer a courageous heart to embark on the process of gift. God's gift then opposes the sinful inclinations from the operation of the *peccatum regnatum*.

Access to justification in Luther's doctrine is through faith. The first aspect of justifying faith in Luther's doctrine is a confessing faith, that is, a faith that accepts and confesses the truth of human sin. This aspect of faith is formed by the *peccator* side of the formula and receives more emphasis by Luther in the years 1513–1516. Confessional faith ushers in a change of perspective in the believer from his own to God's,[18] and transforms self-assessment from false security to true self-accusation. Justifying faith can only enter into the one who accepts God's judgment of human sin.

13. Cf. In the *Antilatomus* (1522), *WA*, pp. 8, 88, 25–9 (*LW*, pp. 32, 202); *WA*, pp. 8, 94, 8 f.; *WA*, pp. 8, 106, 10–15; *WA*, pp. 8, 106, 37–107, 4; *WA*, pp. 8, 107, 13–23, 32–6. In the prefaces to Romans (1522, 1529), *WA Deutsche Bibel*, pp. 7, 8, 10–22; *WA Deutsche Bibel*, pp. 5, 622, 17–41; *WA Deutsche Bibel*, pp. 5, 623, 26–32 (*LW*, 35, 369–370). In the exposition of Ps 51 (1532, printed 1538), *WA*, 40II, pp. 350, 33–7 (*LW*, pp. 12, 327); *WA*, pp. 40II, 351, 23–25; *WA*, 40II, pp. 352, 21–3; *WA*, 40II, pp. 352, 35–353, 21; *WA*, 40II, pp. 353, 36–354, 20; *WA*, 40II, pp. 357, 35–358, 19. In a disputation on justification (1536), *WA*, 39I, pp. 99, 18–27 (*LW*, pp. 34, 168–9).

14. Cf. *WA*, 2, 414, 14–9; *WA*, 2, 536, 3–4; *WA*, 2, 570, 16–7; *WA*, 5, 299, 30–4; *WA*, 39I, 113, 20–114, 4 (*LW*, 34, 182f.); *WA*, 39I, 394, 13–19; *WA*, 39I, 395, 22–396, *WA*, 39I, 1; 398, 11–20.

15. Cf. *WA*, pp. 8, 107, 13–23, 32–6; *WA Deutsche Bibel*, pp. 5, 622, 18–24, 34–7; *WA Deutsche Bibel*, pp. 5, 623, 17; *WA*, 40II, pp. 351, 26–352, 17; *WA*, 40II, pp. 352, 33–6; *WA*, 40II, pp. 354, 21–32; *WA*, 40II, pp. 355, 16–24; *WA*, 40II, pp. 356, 19–23; *WA*, 40II, pp. 357, 20–31; *WA*, 40II, pp. 358, 19–26. First Antinomian Disputation (1537), *WA*, 39I, pp. 383, 3–12. Third Antinomian Disputation (1538), *WA*, 39I, pp. 495, 11–26; *WA*, pp. 1, 593, 12–28 (*LW*, pp. 31, 190).

16. *WA*, pp. 2, 730, 7–10 (*LW*, pp. 35, 33).

17. *WA*, pp. 7, 60, 2–6 (*LW*, pp. 31, 358–9).

18. Cf. *WA*, pp. 56, 229, 11–14.

This first movement of faith in the confession of sins gives rise to the second movement – a *fides apprehensiva*. This movement of faith which stresses the joyful certitude of forgiveness began to receive greater emphasis in 1518 in his writing on the Sacraments and to those with troubled consciences. Because the justification imputed onto the believer is foreign (*aliena*) to the believer, his faith must be a *fides apprehensiva*, that is, a faith that continually lays hold of Christ and adheres to him so that the believer can exchange continually his sin for Jesus' righteousness. A *fides apprehensiva* is also fiducial. Justifying faith seizes hold of the redemptive work of Christ which alone justifies him, and allows him to approach God in complete trust without being consumed in divine wrath. The entirety of his certitude rests upon Christ's word communicated to the believer through the proclamation of the Gospel especially in the sacraments and received in faith.[19] The believer's *fides apprehensiva* allows the proclamation of the Gospel to break up and overthrow *Anfechtung* ('temptation') which can torment his conscience.[20] Thus justifying faith for Luther is self-accusatory and confessional as well as *apprehensiva* and fiducial. Through his justifying faith, the believer seizes his redemption in bold confidence and lives in penitential purification.

With his *simul* formula, Luther thus sums up the believer's situation in Christ. It first conveys the fact that man's salvation does not arise from his nature or moral achievements since these bring forth only sin. Rather justification comes from the righteousness of Jesus Christ which is completely extrinsic to the believer.[21] The cause of justification is the work of Christ; however, Luther does allow the believer's confession of sin to serve as a *causa secunda* or *causa sine qua non* of justification.[22] On the basis of the *peccatum regnans-peccatum regnatum* distinction, the justified believer should see the *iustitia* constituting his justification more in terms of his *relationship* with God rather than as an *inherent quality* in his nature. The believer's relationship with God is just, though his inherent quality remains sinful. The believer remains intrinsically a sinner though he is extrinsically justified. The *peccator* side of the formula indicates that the believer standing in his justification cannot rest secure. He must strive and struggle daily to work against sin's power in his life. Luther writes, 'Once a Christian is righteous by faith and has accepted the forgiveness of sins, he should not be so smug, as though he were pure of all sins. For only then does he face the constant battle with the

19. Cf. *WA*, 40I, pp. 591, 16–30.

20. The German word *Anfechtung* is used by Luther to describe the experience of overwhelming spiritual trial, temptation, affliction, and religious crisis which he suffered throughout his life. *Anfechtung* is the terrifying feeling that God is about to judge and condemn the sinner at any moment, and results in feelings of deep sorrow that the Lord has forsaken the believer.

21. Cf. *Ennaratio Psalmi LI*, 1538; *WA*, 40II, pp. 327, 31 (*LW*, pp. 12, 311); *WA*, 40II, pp. 352, 36 (*LW*, pp. 12, 328). Luther writes, 'He [the Christian] is righteous and holy by an alien or foreign holiness' (*LW*, pp. 12, 328).

22. Cf. Wicks, 'Living and Praying', p. 523; *WA*, 40II, pp. 358, 35–359, 25 (*LW*, pp. 12, 332).

remnants of sin'.[23] The *iustus* side of the formula reminds the believer that he constituted into this saving relationship with Christ and is given the power to strive against sin and sinful inclinations in his life. The believer stands in this present justification believing that in time God will complete the cure he has begun. Luther summarizes

> Those therefore who are truly righteous not only yearn for and implore the grace of God because they see that they have an evil will and so by this are sinful before God, but as well because they see that they can never fully grasp how deep is the evil of their will and how far it extends. They thus always believe that they are sinners, as if the depth of their evil will were infinite. Thus they humble themselves, thus they plead, thus they yearn, until at last they are perfectly healed – which takes place in death.[24]

The *simul* formula, therefore, not only describes the believer's situation in justification, it also gives him a task. Without the *peccator* side the believer would abandon a truly Christian life; without the *iustus* side he would despair of salvation. Both sides of the formula are necessary for Luther to protect against both presumption and despair.

The existential and dialectical shape of the simul formula

Two hallmarks of Luther's interpretation of justification expressed in the *simul* formula are its strong existential quality and its dialectical structure. Experience plays an essential role in Luther's thinking. Neither the sense of sin nor faith can be simply concepts for Luther. The existential dimension of faith receives even greater emphasis through Luther's constant insistence that Christ stands before the Father *pro me*. Experience is so central to Luther's thinking that he even uses it to test the veracity of doctrines. Based upon experience, Luther formulates his doctrine that sin remains after baptism since saying that it does not would lull believers into a false sense of security about their salvation.[25]

A second characteristic of the *simul* formula is its strong dialectical shape. Luther's insistence on man's radical sinfulness, the identification of concupiscence and sin, and the extrinsic character of Christ's righteousness drives this dialectic. The believer's nature is not qualitatively changed in this life through justification according to Luther. Rather the believer must hope, amid appearances to the contrary, that God will deliver on his promise to save. The dialectic oscillates within the believer between what he is *in re* and *in spe*. He remains a sinner *in re*, yet longs for his final and actual justification after death *in spe*.

23. *WA*, 40II, pp. 352, 33–5 (*LW*, pp. 12, 328).
24. Wicks, 'Living and Praying', p. 529; cf. *WA*, pp. 56, 235, 31–7 (*LW*, pp. 25, 220–221) (translation adapted by Wicks).
25. Wicks, 'Justification and Faith in Luther', p. 17; cf. *WA*, pp. 18, 632, 30–633, 3 (*LW*, pp. 33, 62). Another example is one of Luther's last arguments against Erasmus on the bondage of the will was an argument based upon experiential outcome of the doctrine.

Christian anxiety and angstlosigkeit from the simul formula

From the aforementioned summary of Luther's central doctrine, the lines of anxiety's operation within the Christian begin to appear. Both anxiety and freedom from anxiety constitute the Christian life for Luther. Yet in what way is the Christian anxious and in what way is he supposed to be free from anxiety?

Before justification the non-believer swims in the natural and sin-anxiety inherent in the fallen human condition. The beginning of justification begins with the intensification of one's sin-anxiety in the realization of one's radical sinfulness, bondage of will and total inability to work any good, and thus the conclusion that one deserves God's condemnation and the eternal punishment of Hell. This intensification of anxiety is salutary since it helps to cure one of Pelagian tendencies, and to lead one to confess his sinfulness. The Lord brings this salutary sin-anxiety to the one who is smug in order to shake him out of his complacency and bring him to conversion. Luther writes, 'Christ would comfort those whom the devil wants to frighten and dishearten, and, on the other hand, He would intimidate those whom the devil makes smug and presumptuous'.[26]

Next, this intensified sin-anxiety is relieved through justifying faith. The believer's faith which connects him with Christ's redeeming work assuages the conscience with the assurance of forgiveness and healing. Justifying faith, in other words, is supposed to produce *Angstlosigkeit* in the believer. Luther writes on the Sacrament of Baptism, 'No one should be terrified if he feels evil lust or love, nor should he despair if he falls. Rather he should remember his baptism, and comfort himself joyfully with the fact that God has there pledged himself to slay his sin for him and not to count it a cause for condemnation, if only he does not say Yes to sin or remain in it'.[27] The one who believes is made firm against all hostile threats and dangers. Luther continues in the *Freedom of a Christian*:

> If the knowledge of sin or the fear of death should break in upon it [the Christian's heart], it is ready to hope in the Lord. It does not grow afraid when it hears tidings of evil. It is not disturbed when it sees its enemies. This is so because it believes that the righteousness of Christ is its own and that its sin is not its own, but Christ's, and that all sin is swallowed up by the righteousness of Christ.[28]

Sin-anxiety is swallowed up by Christ who is reigning over sin in the believer. The anxiety produced by the *peccatum regnans* is overcome by the Lord's *gratia* and the believer's *fides apprehensiva*. This distinction within man's sinful condition (*peccatum regnans-regnatum*) marks off the difference between anxiety in the unbeliever and the believer. Justifying faith is the bulwark against the incursion of anxiety in the believer's life, especially

26. *WA*, pp. 45, 473 (*LW*, pp. 24, 15).
27. *WA*, pp. 2, 731, 29–37 (*LW*, pp. 35, 35).
28. *WA*, pp. 7, 59, 10–15 (*LW*, pp. 31, 357).

the anxiety of sin, guilt and death. When the disciple is anxious he should cling to Christ's words through the *donum*. Luther concludes, 'Christ says that the victory has been won, that all peril and anxiety have vanished. It is no longer necessary for us to wrestle and fight. All this has already taken place'.[29]

If the believer suffers from anxiety, it is a temptation from the devil, and therefore what is needed is a stronger faith. Luther writes, 'He [the Christian] must learn to resist the devil, who frightens and saddens him, and to say: "You lie, you wicked devil. . . . I am baptized in His name and I believe the Gospel . . ." '.[30] Luther writes in the same vein to an unknown person who was anxious about his salvation in a letter dated 8 August 1545:

> To be sure, it is a serious thing to be so troubled. But you should know that we are forbidden to concern and worry ourselves about this question. . . . In him [Christ] we shall find our election to be sure and pleasant, for without Christ everything is peril, death, and the devil, while in Christ is pure peace and joy. Nothing but anxiety can be gained from forever tormenting oneself with the question of election. Therefore, avoid and flee from such thoughts, as from the temptation of the serpent in paradise, and direct your attention to Christ.[31]

To his wife, Catherine, who was anxious about his well being, Luther responds in a similar way.[32] In his last letter to his wife, dated 10 February 1546, a week before his death, Luther writes, 'Pray, and let God worry. You have certainly not been commanded to worry about me or about yourself'.[33] Justifying faith ushers in *Angstlosigkeit* into the Christian's life filling him with joy, peace, confidence and courage.

However, the dialectic operating within Luther's doctrine of justification begins to shape the movements of anxiety and freedom from anxiety. The believer cannot rest content in freedom from anxiety but enter the struggle with the *peccatum regnatum*. The continued presence of sin in the believer's life gives him reason to be anxious about sin, since it remains, and thus the need for a daily renewal in his justifying faith.

The *simul* formula, therefore, establishes two basic poles between which the Christian's life oscillates. The first, established by *gratia*, is the fundamental relationship of the person to God in justifying faith and the overcoming of the *peccatum regnans*, and the second, established by the *donum*, is the

29. *WA*, pp. 46, 109 (*LW*, pp. 24, 421). Cf. Luther's lectures on the Sermon on the Mount in *LW*, pp. 21, 196–206. He writes in his introduction to Ecclesiastes that Christians are to 'live contentedly in the present without care and yearning about the future and are, as Paul says, without care and anxiety (Phil 4,6). It is useless to plague oneself with anxiety about the future' (*WA*, pp. 20, 9 [*LW*, pp. 15, 7]). Cf. *WA*, pp. 20, 12–14 (*LW*, pp. 15, 10–11).

30. *WA*, pp. 45, 473 (*LW*, pp. 24, 15).

31. *WA Briefwechsel*, pp. 11, 165–6; Eng., M. Luther, *Letters of Spiritual Counsel* (trans. T.G. Tappert; Philadelphia: Westminster, 1955) pp. 137–8.

32. Cf. *WA Briefwechsel*, pp. 11, 286–7 (*LW*, pp. 50, 302).

33. *WA Briefwechsel*, pp. 11, 291 (*LW*, pp. 50, 306).

believer's intentional activity in his Christian life purifying the *peccatum regnatum*. The second pole can be seen as the daily grasping of the first, a daily laying-hold-of divine mercy. Anxiety and freedom from anxiety follow this same oscillation within the believer in Luther's position. The fundamental relationship of *gratia* brings freedom from anxiety while the daily grasping of this relationship in the *donum* necessarily involves anxiety. The pole of anxiety contains both a positive and negative dimension: positive in that it prevents smugness and spurs the believer to seize the *donum* and reconnect with the *gratia*, negative in that it can indicate a faith that is still weak or attempting to take refuge in the goodness of one's own works. The negative aspect of anxiety in this case, however, indicates a less than Christian anxiety. It is anxiety from a weak faith.

If we examine more deeply the anxiety operating within the believer, we can find in Luther's view that even a strong faith is characterized by anxiety, even the cause of anxiety. Anxiety arises from the believer's inherent sinfulness which in fact never actually changes in this life. Luther's doctrine holds that the believer's nature remains unchanged in this life, but must live in the promise of a changed nature that has not yet arrived. The anxious position in faith is intensified when combined with Luther's position that the believer does not participate in Christ's redemptive work. Thus Christian anxiety according to Luther, though different from that of the unjustified sinner, is not a sharing in Christ's anxiety but remains the believer's own sin-anxiety. Faith necessarily places the believer in a life threatened by destruction and alienation from God yet sustained by the divine promise of mercy. This anxiety from a strong faith is what can be properly termed Luther's 'Christian anxiety'. Luther observes that the saints were constantly begging for grace and afraid of doing evil.[34]

Christian anxiety, in Luther's view, serves a purpose much like the righteous anxiety in the Old Testament. The Lord allows trials in the life of the Christian which make him anxious in order to bring him to a deeper faith.[35] In his commentary on Jn. 16.33, in Jesus' words about tribulation for the apostles, Luther writes in the voice of Jesus, 'For I am giving you clear information in advance that you will surely experience anxiety and distress. You must be resigned to this, and you should be prepared for it, in order that you may not lose courage and your comfort. But be of good cheer and unafraid, for I tell you that the battle is already won'.[36] He continues writing in the voice of Christ,

> Consequently when I say that you shall have peace, you must understand this to mean that you will have to experience anxiety in the world. You must realize that in German peace means fear in the world. This is the connotation of My words: peace means discord; good fortune means misfortune; joy means anxiety; life means death in

34. Cf. *WA*, pp. 56, 503, 18–22.

35. Luther offers the examples of the adversity encountered by Abraham and Jacob (cf. *WA*, pp. 42, 578–80 [*LW*, pp. 3, 42–4]; *WA*, pp. 44, 75–7 [*LW*, pp. 6, 102–4]).

36. *WA*, pp. 46, 104 (*LW*, pp. 24, 415).

> the world. Conversely, what the world calls discord, fear, and death, I call peace, comfort, and life.[37]

The believer, therefore, must contend with anxiety as an essential part of his life of justification, oscillating in a dialectic between anxiety and freedom from anxiety. Faith thus combats anxiety, yet anxiety remains internal to the life of justification and not simply because of a weak faith but from an inherent sinfulness that remains. Luther sees this anxiety as nevertheless something good since it helps to preserve the believer from presumption and lukewarmness.

Luther's instructions on prayer give voice to the oscillation of the dialectic of anxiety established by the *simul* formula. He exhorts believers to meditate on Christ's passion in which the believer is brought to terror over the sins which caused Jesus' suffering, followed by meditations to open the believer for a greater acceptance of divine grace. Anxiety is needed for a vibrant prayer life. Luther writes, 'This violence decreases and disappears, to be sure, whenever the Spirit draws and carries our heart upward by grace, or surely, when a present and major anxiety compels us to take refuge in prayer. And without these two factors, prayer becomes a most difficult and tedious thing'.[38] Furthermore, he changes the traditional four-fold prayer of *lectio divina* which follows the progression of *lectio, meditatio, oratio* and *contemplatio* to a three-fold version of *oratio, meditatio* and *tentatio*.[39] This different progression begins with the believer's prayer to the Holy Spirit for guidance and instruction, moves to simple meditation to internalize what is read in Holy Scripture, and ends in the painful daily experience of trials involving anxiety whereby one arrives at deeper grasp of what was prayed. Instead of a culmination in joyful, consoling *contemplatio*, Luther emphasizes *Anfechtung* by which the believer is instructed in confession of sin, renewed trust and patient endurance that he is being brought to complete righteousness despite appearances to the contrary.[40] This change follows the logic of living as *simul iustus et peccator*. The justified person's faith remains threatened by sin and the danger of loss throughout his earthly life.

Balthasar's Catholic Interpretation of Luther's Formula

It is admittedly not easy to examine Balthasar's thoughts about Luther. Howsare identifies three major difficulties in presenting Balthasar's view of Luther. The first is that Balthasar never confronts Luther in the meticulous way he treats Barth, and never seems to concern himself with understanding Luther's thought in and of itself. Second, when Balthasar does engage Luther, he relies heavily on the work of two Luther scholars, P. Hacker and T. Beer

37. *WA*, pp. 46, 108 (*LW*, pp. 24, 419–20).

38. *WA*, pp. 46, 468 (*LW*, pp. 25, 460).

39. Cf. Wicks, 'Living and Praying', p. 545; *WA*, pp. 50, 658, 29–660, 16 (*LW*, pp. 34, 285–7).

40. Cf. *WA*, pp. 50, 658, 29–660, 16 (*LW*, pp. 34, 285–7).

whose work is not universally accepted.[41] A third difficulty lies in the pluriform way Luther's work can be construed by scholars. Perhaps our author's clearest treatment of the *simul* formula is found in several dense pages in his study of Barth's theology.[42] Balthasar first identifies what he sees as Luther's two-fold intent in the formula which emphasizes the eschatological thrust of the believer's status in the world, and the completely unmerited gratuity and extrinsic character of justification. Then Balthasar offers a Catholic interpretation of the formula which he delineates in seven points.

First, Balthasar points out that the believer is a *homo viator* in this world. His temporal existence in faith is always moving towards a final goal in which he is called 'to spurn the past and turn toward what is coming (Phil 3:13) by dying each day to the outer man and being renewed inwardly day by day (2 Cor 4:16) and by an ever-renewed act of repentance' (Heb 3:7f.).[43] Man's final, definitive redemption is *in spe*, and in this world the believer lives in a world of sin as a sinner with other sinners, and so must continually confess his sinfulness and implore the Divine Mercy. Balthasar points out, however, that the believer's *homo viator* status proclaimed in Holy Scripture must be joined to other equally important passages of Holy Scripture which proclaim that he 'has already been freed from past sin in this very aeon and partakes of God's life in grace and thus is freed from the pressure to sin further'.[44] Therefore the *in spe* of man's temporal status does not exclude or oppose the *in re* of already beginning to partake of the divine life. Grace understood in the Catholic sense as a real participation in God's nature already in this life means that the *in spe* and *in re* constitute neither a dialectic nor a contradiction.

Second, Balthasar agrees with Luther that God's grace offered to man in justification is an 'absolutely unilateral and unmerited gift'.[45] God's grace precedes any act of human cooperation. Yet human cooperation is possible, and justification does begin a process of real sanctification in this life. Our author writes, 'One must actively allow God to act in us that we may become coworkers, not only reflecting but actively radiating the real light given to us.

41. Cf. Howsare, *Hans Urs von Balthasar and Protestantism: The Ecumenical Implications of His Theological Style* (London: T&T Clark, 2005) p. 42; P. Hacker, *The Ego in Faith: Martin Luther and the Origin of Anthropocentric Religion* (Chicago: Franciscan Herald Press, 1970). Cf. Wicks' criticism of Beer's work in his review: Wicks, Review of *Der fröhliche Wechsel und Streit. Grundzüge der Theologie Martin Luthers*, *Gregorianum* 63 (1982), p. 163. The following exposition of Balthasar's interpretation of Luther recognizes the difficulties raised by other scholars in Balthasar's treatment of Luther.

42. Cf. *KB*, pp. 378–86; Eng., pp. 369–78. In this section I summarize Balthasar's direct comments on Luther's formula without entering into, as far as possible, Barth's positions. For though Barth, in Balthasar's estimation gives Protestantism '*for the first time* its most completely consistent representative', Barth modifies or drops entirely 'crucial points of Luther's doctrine' (*KB*, pp. 31–2; Eng., p.22) (Balthasar's italics).

43. *KB*, p. 381; Eng., p. 372.

44. *KB*, p. 381; Eng., p. 372.

45. *KB*, p. 381; Eng., p. 373.

The gift of grace should become such an intimate part of ourselves that we can bring forth its fruit as if it were our own'.[46]

Third, the fact that the believer can already begin to share in the divine life does not resolve but only serves to deepen the paradox of the Christian's life in this world. The more the believer tries to live his life the more aware he becomes of divine grace operating within him. This paradox which began in the order of creation between the infinite, free Creator and the finite, free creature, is intensified dramatically in the order of redemption. Balthasar writes,

> Now in the order of sin, man's awareness of this abyss [between Creator and creature] is even sharper: this consciousness is so acute that he draws back in shame when he encounters graciousness: 'Lord, depart from me. I am a sinful man!' And the more worthy a person becomes to share in the gracious works of the Lord, the more evident it becomes how unworthy he is (all the saints say so!), all the more sober becomes his humility, all the more realistic his view of himself.[47]

This leads our author to his fourth point about the *simul* formula. It is only by already beginning to share in the divine life that one can then begin to have a deep grasp of the fallen world and his own fallen nature. Luther's insight that the world is the place of the *peccatum regnans* is quite true. Sin reigns in the fallen world, and this world is pregnant with an 'active potency' ready at any moment to give birth to sin.[48] Although the line dividing actual sin and this active potency is real, expressed in the difference between sin and concupiscence, Balthasar also admits the many connections between them. Concupiscence continues to draw the believer towards sin. The task of distinguishing and untangling the complexity of actual sin, concupiscence and the world cannot be accomplished on a merely psychological level. Rather faith brings the believer into a new type of experience, the spiritual sense and the discernment of spirits, which incorporate and transcend psychological factors. The discernment of spirits leads the believer to this deeper understanding of sin, which often drives the saints 'to a kind of despair about themselves' and desire 'to separate themselves totally from the "monstrous corpse" they are, so that only God's own life might live within them'.[49] Though Balthasar offers a Catholic voice to the *peccator* side of the formula, he nevertheless clearly distinguishes himself from Luther's position by adding that this experience of the believer's own sinfulness is only possible with a true and intrinsic sanctification.[50]

The paradox of the Christian's situation in the world intensifies in Balthasar's fifth point. In the new experience that faith inaugurates, the believer finds it increasingly difficult to distinguish between his sin and the sins

46. *KB*, pp. 381–2; Eng., p. 373.
47. *KB*, p. 382; Eng., pp. 373–4.
48. Our author directs his reader to 1Jn. 1.16 and Jas 1.14–15 (cf. *KB*, p. 383; Eng., p. 374).
49. *KB*, p. 383; Eng., p. 374.
50. Cf. *KB*, p. 383; Eng., pp. 374–5.

of others and the rest of the world. For sin, even personal sin, has a communal dimension. Balthasar argues that the paradox which Luther's formula exposes does not go deep enough. Our author writes,

> [T]he Catholic paradox is far superior here to Protestant interpretations, for it insists that the just man, to the extent that he shares an active portion in the holiness of the Redeemer, also receives a more active portion in the task of bearing a guilt not his own, thereby sharing in the very work of redemption. This finally reaches the point where he can no longer distinguish whether he is suffering for his own sins or that of others.[51]

In his Passion, the Incarnate Lord did not wish to distinguish his innocence from the world's guilt according to Balthasar. Jesus reveals in his suffering and death that the more one is innocent (or in the believer's case, justified), the greater share he has in bearing the world's guilt.

The trajectory of the paradox of grace and sin finds full expression in Balthasar's sixth point about the experience of temptation which figures so prominently in Luther's understanding of the Christian life. It lays bare the 'yawning chasm between Being and Ought, between what is and what should be'.[52] It heightens the drama inherent in the order of redemption, for in temptation the believer sees 'not an empty and speculative possibility, but a very real one: we realize that God *could* very well have dealt with us out of pure justice'. Balthasar continues, 'In temptation, we come to appreciate how much of a dead-end sin really is. . . . And even though it has been given especially to the saints to stare most intently at this naked truth, something of this insight lies within every Christian conscience.[53] The believer's experience of temptation drives home the reality of the fallen world, and how tainted, even distorted, are his good works. The fires of temptation reveal his good works as so much straw. In temptation the believer teeters over the abyss of sin and would fall if grace were lacking, a grace neither to which he has right nor upon which he may presume.

In these six points, Balthasar draws out the existential and subjective aspects of a Catholic assessment of the *simul* formula. His seventh point relates these subjective aspects to their objective and dogmatic counterpart. Only in Christ crucified and risen can the Christian find the solution to the paradox of sin and grace in the *simul* formula, and not in himself. He writes, 'It is *Christ on the Cross* who is *simul justus et peccator*; he is the sinless one who was made sin for our sake (2 Cor. 5:21) and who was turned into a curse (Gal. 3:13) so that we might be redeemed from sin and its curse'.[54] Only in the Paschal Mystery can the Christian understand, on the one hand, temptation, suffering and death, and on the other hand, the extraordinary power of grace. Jesus himself is the final, decisive form of the *simul iustus et peccator*.

51. *KB*, p. 384; Eng., p. 375.
52. *KB*, p. 384; Eng., p. 375.
53. *KB*, pp. 384–5; Eng., p. 376 (Balthasar's italics).
54. *KB*, p. 385; Eng., p. 376 (Balthasar's italics).

A distinction, however, always remains between Christ and the Christian. Christ remains always and forever the totally Just and Innocent One; the Christian is still a sinner although to the degree lives into his salvation has truly ceased sinning.[55]

Balthasar summarizes his Catholic interpretation of the *simul* formula by stating that the believer truly participates in God's inner life through grace, and this participation is 'neither purely forensic nor purely eschatological, rather it is real, internal and present' transforming the very nature of the believer.[56] At the same time this grace 'leaves room for all real events and phases that make up man's way to God: conversion, progress, backsliding, cooperation and obstacles'.[57] Redemption is effected incrementally in the believer who remains a *viator* while in this world. Each step that the Christian makes in his life within the realm of Divine Providence is thus pregnant with drama and meaning.

Balthasar offers no explicit presentation of Luther on Christian anxiety. When he writes about Luther on the theme, our author enters immediately into an evaluation of Luther's position noting agreement and disagreement. Thus we proceed directly to such a discussion.

Balthasar's Agreement with Luther on Christian Anxiety

Our author recognizes Luther's 'unfathomably profound' understanding of Christian anxiety, and finds in Luther points of agreement on the interpretation of the Christian's anxiety.[58]

The Christian's freedom from anxiety

Balthasar agrees with Luther that Christian faith is supposed to free one from anxiety. In a way not dissimilar to some of Luther's statements quoted above, Balthasar writes, 'The first thing that must be said, and which can never be said powerfully and triumphantly enough, is that human fear [*menschliche Angst*] has been completely and definitively conquered by the Cross'.[59] Christ's redemption opens the possibility for true freedom from anxiety for the Christian. Anxiety, like all suffering and even death, now lies in the hands of the Lord Jesus, is subject to him and used for his purposes.

The Old Covenant prohibition to anxiety ("Fear not!") now can actually be fulfilled. Balthasar notes that this prohibition was challenged in the Old Covenant in four ways: by the narrowness of the graced area of *Angstlosigkeit*

55. Cf. *KB*, pp. 385–6; Eng., p. 377.
56. *KB*, p. 386; Eng., p. 377.
57. *KB*, p. 368; Eng., p. 377.
58. *CA*, p. 57; Eng., pp. 101–2.
59. *CA*, p. 42; Eng., p. 81.

given the righteous man, by the fact that the grace offered was in the form of hope for what had not yet arrived, by the constant threat of darkness overwhelming the graced region of *Angstlosigkeit* despite God's promises, and finally by the righteous man's continual relapse into sin within the Covenant.[60] Thus the righteous man in the Old Covenant never truly attains freedom from anxiety. His faith may be able to free him from natural anxiety, but it cannot completely free him from sin-anxiety. This four-fold challenge to *Angstlosigkeit* is overcome by Jesus in the New Covenant. Through Christ's redemption the finitude of the graced region of *Angstlosigkeit* is taken away as well as its modality of hope.[61]

Christ is the King of all creation and so the believer has no more reason to be anxious from any perceived threat in creation including 'the world', the devil or death. Our author argues that anxiety is not only no longer necessary, it is ontologically no longer *possible* to the degree that the believer possesses the life of faith.[62] Sin-anxiety is banished from the believer. Balthasar writes that the believer's guilty conscience which makes him anxious is overtaken by 'a love against which all the self-accusation of the sinner cannot prevail'.[63] Not even the terrible Day of the Lord, the day of final judgment, need be a cause for anxiety (1 Jn. 4.17–18). Love casts out fear. In fact, Balthasar observes, the believer is even supposed to rejoice and consider himself blessed when suffering any affliction in the world.

Anxiety from a weak faith

Like Luther, Balthasar also holds that the Christian can be subject to anxiety due to a weak faith. A weak faith prevents the believer to enter into the *Angstlosigkeit* that Christian faith brings. Both see this incursion of anxiety as a less-than-Christian life, a Christian life needing additional purification. Balthasar is adamant about the reality of Christian *Angstlosigkeit* to those in philosophy and psychology and to those Christians who would claim anxiety's dominance:

> If the Christian's fearlessness [*Angstlosigkeit des Christen*] before God, before the world, and before every power other than that of Christ is strictly commanded in the New Covenant, it follows that all the 'facts' set forth by modern philosophy and psychology concerning the dominance [*Herrschaft*] of anxiety are struck down by this command. . . . If he nevertheless is a neurotic and an existentialist, then he suffers from a lack of Christian truth, and his faith is sick or frail. Because *this* anxiety has been forbidden by Christ.[64]

60. Cf. *CA*, p. 42; Eng., p. 82.
61. Cf. *CA*, pp. 42–3; Eng., p. 82.
62. Cf. *CA*, p. 43; Eng., p. 83.
63. *CA*, pp. 43–4; Eng., p. 83.
64. *CA*, pp. 45–6; Eng., pp. 85–6 (Balthasar's italics).

Christian anxiety in the existential unity of faith and anxiety

A third point of agreement between Balthasar and Luther is the presence of anxiety within the act of faith. The act of faith itself, in Balthasar's view, has an agonic quality to it, not in its propositions but in its existential attitude and stance. This agonic quality stems from the fiduciary character of Christian faith, or to use Luther's term, in one's *fides apprehensiva*. The believer is called to trust and abandon himself ever more deeply in the action of Christ in his life. In this way, we could say that the anxiety functions as an existential modality of Christian faith. Balthasar writes, 'This is precisely why the act of faith can be described and maintained only by means of the paradox which it also exhibits in John. On the one hand, what is inalienable is kept inalienably; on the other hand, one must be held in suspense in the constant danger of not being oneself able to guarantee "abiding" in the Beloved'.[65] Anxiety exists in the Christian life in the constant need for self-surrender to the object of faith. The believer abides in the truth of faith to the degree that he relinquishes his own hold on his life and abandons himself to faith's object. Since the act of faith itself is comprised of the self-abandoning movement of love on the part of both object and subject, Balthasar concludes

> [T]he believer does not contain death in himself as 'anguish' (as with worldly beauty) but, rather, if he really believes, he has already left anguish behind (1Jn 4:17f.). And yet there remains a certain trembling on the part of a freedom that surrenders itself – a tremor over whether it is really giving itself, over whether it has really taken the law of the Beloved upon itself, over whether it has attained to a faith that is love. . . . John approves of this form of anguish.[66]

The unity of anxiety and faith in its fiduciary dimension is intensified if we take into account the analogy that Balthasar establishes between the act of faith and act of the perception of Beauty. In the aesthetical act, the subject is overwhelmed by the light breaking through the beautiful form. This light elicits the response of wonder which St. Thomas calls *anxietas* and categorizes it as a type of *timor*.

More direct comments on the existential unity of faith and anxiety in Balthasar's corpus can be found in his study on Bernanos. Our author writes that the boundaries of one's life, birth and death, give rise to 'that most elemental of all feelings that imparts to existence its fundamental coloring: the unity of *wonderment* and *anguish*, which is to say, of childlike self-entrusting to another and deepest shuddering in the act of surrender'.[67] He continues, 'The specifically Christian unity of wonderment and anguish, moreover, rests on the suffering that God's eternal Child underwent on the

65. *HI*, p. 228; Eng., pp. 236–7.
66. *HI*, p. 229; Eng., p. 238.
67. *B*, p. 428; Eng., p. 479 (Balthasar's italics).

Mount of Olives'.[68] Balthasar argues that Bernanos is especially adept in distilling this fundamental aspect of Christian faith.[69]

For Balthasar no contradiction exists between the believer's certainty and anxiety in the act of faith because they are not taken in the same sense. He reasons, 'What Bernanos is speaking of, therefore, is not a doubt of faith but a most inward shudder at that seam in the fabric of existence where nature and supernature blend together, that juncture where what is grace and, conjointly, innermost freedom could be lost'.[70] The anxiety felt in the act of faith comes from the possibility that what is given could be lost.

On this level Balthasar sees anxiety operating in the Christian life as inherent in the freedom of the Christian. Anxiety arises from the realization that he has the ability, and even the inclination (due to concupiscence), to turn away from Christ. Balthasar, however, notices a maturing of the concept in Bernanos by the end of his life which points towards the Catholic interpretation of Christian anxiety when the French novelist writes, 'faith really is a crown of thorns that makes us participants – most often, alas, despite ourselves! – in the Most Holy Agony'![71] Balthasar comments, 'Faith itself is here "agonic", "agony" in the most literal sense of the word, as we have seen: struggle, contest, wrestling with the angel through the night, above all an immense hunger and thirst, an emptiness crying out for the fullness of God'.[72] In this way, faith can be seen as a virtue which grows by practicing it. Balthasar summarizes: 'Here faith is considered not as the Creed of the Church – since this is unassailable – but as *an existential attitude and stance*: a nakedness before God, a will to be taken by Another precisely where one has nothing left to give . . .'.[73] An existential shuddering occurs in the act of faith, and this shuddering is good.

The uniqueness of Christian anxiety

Finally Balthasar agrees with Luther that Christian necessarily experiences anxiety within the life of faith, even a strong faith. He agrees that this anxiety is distinct from that of the non-believer and is both good and salutary. One's anxiety is qualitatively transformed when one makes the act of faith and embarks on the Christian life. For Luther, this anxiety is the continued presence of the *simul peccator* in the believer's life. This anxiety helps to humble the believer, and prevents Pelagianism from infecting his faith. Balthasar agrees with Luther on this point to an extent. From his Catholic interpretation of the *simul* formula earlier, he notes that Christian faith brings a heightened sense of one's sinfulness, and helps to expose and intensify the paradox of

68. *B*, p. 428; Eng., p. 479.
69. Cf. *B*, p. 429; Eng., p. 479.
70. *B*, p. 429; Eng., p. 480.
71. *B*, p. 429; Eng., p. 480.
72. *B*, p. 431; Eng., p. 482.
73. *B*, p. 431; Eng., p. 482 (author's italics).

grace and sinfulness operating in his life. The believer can subjectively experience a type of dialectic of his justification and his sinfulness, and along with it both anxiety and freedom from anxiety.

Our author wonders if the requirements placed upon the Christian make him endure 'a superhuman tension' and even ask the impossible of him.[74] He writes, 'Does not the Christian who takes sin and salvation seriously get lost in a dialectic with no exit, in which each increase in grace brings forth an increase in unworthiness, even guilt, so that in this tangled thicket religion becomes a real inferno? And does not all this furnish the most merciless psychoanalysis with an easy target'?[75] Christian faith does change the character of sin-anxiety, and may feel like a dialectic in the life of the believer, yet this Catholic interpretation of Luther's understanding of Christian anxiety applies to the believer's existential struggle with concupiscence and relapses into sin in the life of faith.

Balthasar's Critique: The Shape of Christian Anxiety is not Dialectical

Our author, nevertheless, distances himself from Luther's position which holds that the objective shape of Christian anxiety is constituted by a dialectic. The great difference between Luther and Balthasar on Christian anxiety lies in the objective structure of anxiety operating within the believer. The difference seen in the objective structure of Christian anxiety flows from the divergent doctrines on the operation of grace in justification. Our author rejects the objective dialectical shape that Luther gives to Christian anxiety while acknowledging that Luther had to come to such a conclusion from his distortion of two primary concepts: the believer's status as *viator* and his real participation in the divine life in this life.

Luther's 'exaggerated eschatologism'

Luther's *simul* formula is skewed, in Balthasar's view, by 'an exaggerated eschatologism' which distorts the Christian's status as *viator*.[76] In Luther's view, justification is ascribed to the Christian only as a hope, and not as a present reality since this justification remains foreign and never intrinsic to him. With this view of justification *in spe*, Luther abides too closely to an Old Testament understanding of eschatology according to Balthasar. The believer's justification never truly arrives to his nature in this life, which makes his anxiety resemble that of the righteous man in the Old Covenant who did not possess the strength to overcome completely his sin-anxiety in the face of the divine prohibition.

74. *CA*, p. 55; Eng., p. 99.
75. *CA*, pp. 55–6; Eng., p. 99.
76. *KB*, p. 379; Eng., p. 370; cf. *CA*, pp. 57–8; Eng., pp. 101–2.

Balthasar admits that the Old Covenant perspective seems to continue in the New insofar as the believer, as *viator*, still journeys towards the accomplished salvation and perfect righteousness. He observes that 'something like vertigo' comes over the believer in the movement between anxiety and hope. Yet Balthasar is adamant that this movement is only a transition and not a definitive state. Christianity, he writes, 'offers man, not a bottomless pit, but solid ground – grounding in God, of course, and not in self'.[77] The Christian life means to relinquish one's own sinful ground in order to stand on the Lord's ground through faith, hope and love. The theological virtues constitute the firm ground that the Christian walks as a *viator*. Through Christian faith, man is not thrown back upon himself but cast forward into God. Even if the believer should stumble in sin, 'a momentary loss of footing does not necessarily intervene. Whoever believes, whoever reaches out for faith, takes a real step'.[78] Our author argues that Christian experience, and we could say even the experience of anxiety, 'implies a *progressive entrance* of the believing person into the total reality of faith and the *progressive "realisation"* of this reality'.[79]

In order for the sinner to make his stand in God, he must leave behind the place he had been standing previously. Any attempt to straddle the two places will necessarily cause anxiety. It means the Christian has stopped walking which does not indicate a living faith. Luther situates Christian anxiety in the inevitable 'inbetween' space established by the dialectic of his *simul* formula. This 'inbetween' space, in Balthasar's view, is forbidden to the Christian, and instead is under the domain of Christian *Angstlosigkeit*. Therefore, the anxiety that Luther argues is constitutive of the Christian life is, in Balthasar's view, an indication of an immature faith at best which is still making the passage from one's own ground onto God's solid ground, or at worst a sick and weak faith. Balthasar thus concludes

> The uneasy conscience that many Christians have, and the anxiety based on it, do not come about because they are sinners and backsliders but because they have stopped believing the truth and efficacy of their beliefs; they measure the power of faith by their own weakness, they project God's world into their own psychological makeup instead of letting God measure them. They do something that Christians are forbidden to do: they observe faith from the outside; they doubt the power of hope; they deprive themselves of the power of love; and they lie down to rest in the chasm between the demands of Christianity and their own failure, in a chasm that, for a Christian, is no place at all. Is it any wonder that anxiety seizes them on account of this placelessness?[80]

The Christian, therefore, as a *viator* must take firm steps away from the anxiety of sin onto the solid ground of faith, hope and love. To wallow in sin-anxiety is not Christian living. Christian faith is 'genuine movement, a firm

77. *CA*, p. 56; Eng., p. 100.
78. *CA*, p. 56; Eng., p. 100.
79. *HI*, p. 230; Eng., pp. 238–9 (author's italics).
80. *CA*, p. 57; Eng., p. 101.

stride – in the same way that faith is described in the New Testament as something tangibly sure, giving rest and security – certainly not as a flickering dialectic between sin-anxiety and assurance of salvation, trembling before the devil one minute and triumphing over him the next'.[81] Consequently, Luther's 'exaggerated eschatologism' never grants the believer a real deliverance from sin-anxiety, and therefore his position never attains to a Christian *Angstlosigkeit* that is deeper than that of the righteous man of the Old Testament. In other words, the uniqueness that Luther ascribes to Christian anxiety is not unique enough for Balthasar. True Christian *Angstlosigkeit*, according to Balthasar, is far deeper than Luther allows. True Christian anxiety is located not in the 'inbetween' space of the *simul* dialectic within the believer, but it is located in Christ and in whose life the believer may participate here and now.

Lack of participation in Christ's anxiety according to Luther

Secondly Luther's *simul* formula is distorted, according to Balthasar, by his doctrine that Christ's work remains foreign to the believer.[82] Luther is unwilling to accept a Christian's real participation in Christ's anxiety. Christian anxiety in his view is never a *Mit-angst* with Christ's, but rather his own, stemming from his *peccatum regnatum*. In contrast, Balthasar goes much further to demonstrate the absolute and unparalleled uniqueness of Christian anxiety precisely because it is a participation in Christ's own anxiety.[83] Because justification in Catholic doctrine means participation in Christ's justice, his anxiety is also a share in Christ's. The believer is inserted into Christ's justification. The real participation means that Christ's redemption brings to the believer the possibility of 'Christian redemptive anxiety' (*christliche Erlösungsangst*).[84] He writes, 'The Catholic cannot view salvation merely as an objective fact accomplished on the Cross, which the believer then notes together with its effect; rather, between objective and subjective redemption he sees the requirement of participatory appropriation. Consequently, the path from sin-anxiety to redeeming anxiety is for him a real pathway'.[85] How the Christian participates in this redemptive anxiety must be understood properly, and is explained in the next section of this chapter.

81. *CA*, p. 57; Eng., p. 101.

82. Luther's lack of sufficient emphasis on the believer's participation in Christ seems rooted in the influence of nominalist metaphysics. Cf. Howsare's summary of Luther's relationship to nominalism in Howsare, *Balthasar and Protestantism*, pp. 44–54.

83. The term that Balthasar most often uses to denote Christ's anxiety is *Kreuzesangst* ('Cross anxiety' or 'anxiety from the Cross'), cf. *CA*, pp. 48, 57, 59–61, 66. This term is often used in contradistinction with his use of 'sin-anxiety'.

84. *CA*, p. 59; Eng., p. 104. Other terms that Balthasar uses to describe this qualitatively unique anxiety of the Christian in his participation in Christ's *Kreuzesangst* are *christliche Angst* ('Christian anxiety'), *CA*, pp. 49, 51–5, 57, 62, 64–5, 90–1; *Mit-angst* ('shared anxiety'), *CA*, p. 50; *katholische Angst* ('catholic anxiety'), *CA*, p. 50; *mystische Angst* ('mystical anxiety'), *CA*, pp. 61, 63; and *übernatürliche Angst* ('supernatural anxiety'), *CA*, p. 64.

85. *CA*, p. 59; Eng., p. 104.

For these two primary reasons, Balthasar rejects Luther's position that Christian anxiety possesses an objective dialectical structure with the believer's oscillation between anxiety and freedom from anxiety. Balthasar understands that Luther was led inevitably to his dialectical position. Luther intended to bring freedom from anxiety to the Christian. Balthasar reasons, however, 'the vertigo of reflection that seizes them [Luther and Calvin] prevents the aspect of present reality from becoming effective alongside the eschatological aspect'.[86] Because Catholic doctrine affirms the effectiveness of grace in the present reality alongside the eschatological aspect, the objective shape of Christian anxiety is not a dialectic but a trajectory.

Balthasar's Proposal to Luther: Christian Anxiety is a Trajectory

Luther understands the objective shape of Christian anxiety as a dialectic; Balthasar argues that the shape of Christian anxiety is actually a trajectory, and this objective trajectorial shape makes Christian anxiety absolutely unique. This trajectory moves from the anxiety of the non-believer, to the back-and-forth of sin-anxiety and *Angstlosigkeit* in the life of the weak Christian, to the firm steps onto the ground of the theological virtues of the believing Christian, and to an actual participation in Christ's anxiety for the more mature Christian. Balthasar receives inspiration for this insight into the trajectorial nature of Christian anxiety from the *Spiritual Exercises* of his spiritual father, St. Ignatius of Loyola (1491–1556). St. Ignatius in his experience in Manresa observed a transformation that happened to his anxiety when he himself experienced the difference between sin-anxiety and Christian anxiety, and which prompted him to wonder, 'What kind of new life is this that we are now beginning'?[87]

The trajectory of anxiety in the Spiritual Exercises

The first week of the *Spiritual Exercises* focuses the exercitant on the reality and horror of sin.[88] The first exercise focuses on three sins of others: the angels, Adam and Eve, and the soul which went to Hell for one mortal sin. The second exercise considers one's own sin in its manifold expressions. The first week continues with a repetition of the first two exercises and then a summary. Finally one makes a meditation on Hell. The intent of the first week is to cultivate a deep awareness of sin and to intensify one's sin-anxiety. But this intensification of sin-anxiety has a purpose: to lead the exercitant not towards despair but towards a 'cry of wonder' at God's mercy. After considering the number and gravity of one's sins, the deep corruption of his nature and

86. *CA*, p. 59; Eng., p. 104.
87. *UA*, 98n; Eng., 102n.
88. Cf. Ignatius of Loyola, *Spiritual Exercises* (New York: Harper, 2000), n. 4.

how opposed one's nature is to God, the believer is lead to see God's mercy in a deeper and new way as *pro me*. Thus described, the dynamic of the first week is not unlike the dynamic leading to the *confessio peccati* of Luther's position.

St. Ignatius, however, leads the exercitant further and envisions a transformation of the believer's sin-anxiety by the third week of the *Exercises*. The meditations of this week are devoted to the consideration of the Lord's Passion and petitioning the Lord to give a kind of emotional resonance and participation in what Christ is feeling in his Passion.[89] At first glance it seems that the *Exercises* are repeating what transpired in the first week. Upon deeper examination, however, we find that St. Ignatius foresees something else taking place. Each exercise leads the exercitant to an identification with Jesus' sufferings, and a willingness to enter into them. The Spiritual Master writes, 'In the Passion it is proper to ask for sorrow with Christ in sorrow, anguish with Christ in anguish, tears and deep grief because of the great affliction Christ endures for me'.[90] Thus the Christian is led from the anxiety about his own sins to share in the anxiety of Christ in his Passion, to feel and experience interiorly through prayer all that Christ experiences, as well as the Blessed Virgin Mary and the disciples.[91] Thus the very dynamic of the *Spiritual Exercises* moves from the believer's sin-anxiety to freedom from that anxiety and into a participation in Christ's.

The 'three laws' governing the trajectory of Christian anxiety

Governing this trajectory of Christian anxiety, according to Balthasar, are three 'laws' which flow from the logic of the Cross.[92] The first law is that Christ's redemption delivers a true liberation from natural anxiety and sin-anxiety, and grants a share in Christ's redemptive anxiety. Our author formulates his first law in the following way:

> *Christianity is intent upon and capable of delivering man from sin-anxiety, provided that he opens himself up to that redemption and its conditions. In the place of sin-anxiety, it provides him with anxiety-free access to God in faith, love and hope – which, however, because they stem from the Cross, can in and of themselves put forth a new, grace-filled form of anxiety that stems from catholic solidarity and shares in Christ's work of atonement.*[93]

Only when Christian *Angstlosigkeit* is firmly established, by stepping away from sin-anxiety and into the theological virtues, can Christian anxiety be

89. Ibid., n. 193.
90. Ibid., n. 203.
91. Cf. Ignatius of Loyola, *Spiritual Exercises*, n. 208.
92. Cf. *CA*, p. 65; Eng., p. 113. Cf. Martinelli's summary in Martinelli, *Il mistero della morte in Hans Urs von Balthasar*, pp. 416–17.
93. *CA*, pp. 53–4; Eng., pp. 96–7 (Balthasar's italics).

properly understood as a share in the anxiety of the Cross. Balthasar continues, 'When sin-anxiety [*Sündenangst*] in all its forms . . . has been fundamentally removed from a man and hence has been forbidden him, then from the Cross opens up something completely different: grace, and, in the measure granted by grace, permission to suffer anxiety [*mitängstigen*] as a share in Christ's anguish [*Angst Christi*]'.[94]

The grace that comes to the believer from the Cross, and in the form of the Cross, transforms the objective nature of his anxiety. Anxiety outside the Cross is marked by constriction, isolation, making a person withdrawn and diminished in ability. Anxiety from the Cross brings this same subjective suffering with it. *Kreuzesangst* feels and appears much like the constriction and isolation inherent in natural or sin-anxiety. However, the grace of the Cross transforms the objective structure of anxiety into its opposite – a dilation of his nature in love. The believer's objective dilation in love by anxiety is an image of the archetype established in Christ's own dilation in love as man in Gethsemane and on the Cross. As was mentioned at the beginning of this study, Balthasar conceives Christian experience as the participation in Christ's own experience. The Christian's experience becomes progressively attuned and shaped by Christ's. Thus by participating in Christ's anxiety, the Christian is objectively expanded in love, even if the subjective experience has all the appearances of natural and sin-anxiety.

This new objective structure that the Cross brings to anxiety is set in complete opposition to the objective structure of sin-anxiety both that of the non-believer and also that produced by Luther's dialectic. The dilating effect that *Kreuzesangst* anxiety has on the Christian is nothing other than a mode of Divine Love acting upon him. The objective structure of Christian anxiety is not a constriction or a turning away, but a turning towards and a casting oneself into God. The felt constriction of redeeming anxiety is objectively sharing in the labour pains of the new creation. All the phenomenological symptoms of anxiety that the Christian bears becomes a function of this new objective structure and serves it. Since access to all beatitude comes through the Cross, beatitude will only be gained through anxiety from the Cross. Balthasar's first law preserves the uniqueness of Christian anxiety.

This first law, which trenchantly separates the Christian from natural and sin-anxiety, leads to his second law. Balthasar's second law of Christian anxiety focuses on the nature of the Christian's participation in Christ's anxiety. He writes

> *Insofar as we are sinners and even as believers can always become sinners anew, the anxiety of sin is not simply taken away from us by the objective act of redemption on the Cross but rather is set before us even in the New Testament. We are permitted to leave sin-anxiety behind us to the degree that we appropriate in truth the living faith offered to us from the Cross, that is, a faith active in our lives. However, even when the grace of sharing in the*

94. *CA*, p. 48; Eng., p. 89.

> *anxiety of the Cross is granted, the distance between the one who suffers in compassion and the Redeemer who originally suffered is maintained in it entirety, and the anguished soul is aware of it.*[95]

In other words, freedom from anxiety is also a task set before the believer. In this law, it seems as if our author seeks to maintain a truth that Luther's formula also seeks to preserve: 'no Christian stands on any sort of equal footing with Christ in matters of justification, and no one who is drawn close to him by grace is tempted to mistake himself for Christ'.[96] The image can never mistake itself for the archetype. Balthasar holds that the believer can never equate his Christian anxiety with Christ's precisely because the Catholic still can fall into sin and that his Christian anxiety is a participation in Christ's. The Christian, moreover, cannot identify himself with Christ in order to separate himself from sinners. The Christian must make the move from sin-anxiety to Christ's anxiety, which the Master never had to make for he is like us in all ways but sin. Thus within the justifying and sanctifying relationship with Christ, the believer maintains 'at the point where grace calls him "friend", he acknowledges himself to be "servant", and not merely servant but sinner'.[97] Christ alone redeemed the world. Balthasar's second law protects the uniqueness of Christ's anxiety, even from one of his members participating in it.

While distinguishing the believer's anxiety from that of Christ, Balthasar then relates the two by showing how the believer begins to participate in Christ's anxiety. Balthasar writes, 'New Testament anxiety is always and fundamentally a catholic anxiety, in which the boundaries of the individual are transcended and blurred, with respect both to the origin and to the goal and effect of anxiety'.[98] This solidarity again follows the simple logic of the Cross. Since the Lord Jesus 'made the anxiety of each and every sin – indeed, the oneness of the whole world's anxiety – merge into the oneness of his anxiety as God-Man, an isolated penance for an isolated, personal guilt is, for a Christian, no longer conceivable'.[99] Christian anxiety finds its genesis in the Lord's new commandment to love. The Christian's walk of faith into the divine life does not abandon sinners in the world, but rather snatches them up and brings them along, even making the walk on their behalf.

This true participation in Christ's anxiety and this true solidarity with sinners means that Christian anxiety can participate in the incongruity of the Cross in which the participation, its fruit and even the objective structure of Christian anxiety may be hidden subjectively from the one experiencing it.[100] According to Balthasar, the *Hinterlegung* principle can apply to

95. *CA*, p. 60; Eng., pp. 105–6 (Balthasar's italics); cf. Martinelli, *Il mistero della morte in Hans Urs von Balthasar*, pp. 416–17.
96. *CA*, p. 59; Eng., pp. 104–5.
97. *CA*, pp. 59–60; Eng., p. 105.
98. *CA*, p. 50; Eng., p. 92.
99. *CA*, p. 50; Eng., p. 92.
100. Cf. *CA*, p. 48; Eng., p. 89.

the Christian as well. The believer may not be able to see that his anxiety is participating in Christ's, or that his suffering in anxiety is accomplishing anything. The Christian hands over his own strength and vision into the Lord's hands so as to suffer in deprivation, following the Lord's own example. Christian anxiety arises when faith, hope and love 'overlook their own presence, indeed, renounce any further recognition of themselves' in order to suffer in love.[101] In order to participate in Christ's suffering of anxiety, the Christian also can experience an 'eclipse' of faith, hope and love in the soul. However, this eclipse is actually an expression, a mode of one's faith, hope and love, just as Christ's was. Therefore, the experience of the eclipse of the theological virtues in the awareness of the believer does not objectively cross over into despair of their operation, as in the experience of St. Thérèse. The image-coming-to-greater-likeness of God becomes veiled to the person's awareness in Christian anxiety, which is objectively different than in sin-anxiety where the image is actually damaged. Any objective participation in Christ's anxiety will necessarily have a subjectively fractured quality, and bear the anxiety. This law enables the participant's anxiety in a mysterious way to follow the pattern of Christ's, and enter into an isolation and loneliness that even seems removed from Christ and his anxiety.

The third 'law' of Christian anxiety emerges from the second, and protects Christian anxiety from the rejected interpretation of the *simul* formula. Balthasar formulates it in the following way:

> *God grants a (mystical or even usual) participation in the anxiety of his Son on the Cross to no believer unless he has first granted to him the entire strength of the Christian mission and joy and the entire light of faith, love and hope – that is to say, unless he has first taken from him the anxiety of sin. To consider a 'synthesis' of both to be possible, or even worth striving for, does not conform to sound Christian doctrine.*[102]

For Balthasar there can be no admixture of sin-anxiety and Christian anxiety in the objective nature of Christian anxiety. One cannot be led directly from sin-anxiety into Christian anxiety, but rather must pass through the theological virtues whereby sin-anxiety is purged.

Christian anxiety is derived from faith, hope and love, not from sin-anxiety. Thus one can be led into Christian anxiety only after knowing God's light. The mystical night, explains Balthasar, is given only to one who knows the divine light of faith, hope and love in his soul, since the mystical night is the eclipse of precisely this light. The suffering of abandonment in the mystical night is predicated on that soul's intimacy with God.[103] Sin-anxiety is borne

101. *CA*, p. 53; Eng., p. 96.

102. *CA*, p. 66; Eng., p. 114 (Balthasar's italics); cf. Martinelli, *Il mistero della morte in Hans Urs von Balthasar*, p. 417.

103. Cf. *CA*, pp. 62–6; Eng., pp. 108–14. Christian writers, he warns, must therefore be cautious in portraying Christian anxiety. Our author thinks that Georges Bernanos is the

from the darkness of sin; Christian anxiety from the divine light. Balthasar drives a strict dividing line:

> In God there is no darkness, and in guilt there is no light. The Son of God became like us in all things except sin, and this 'except' is the prerequisite that enabled him to take each and every sin upon himself and to atone for it completely. Whoever deviates a hairsbreadth from that rule entangles everything. A Christian can share burdens and be in solidarity precisely in the measure that he has separated himself from sin. He can enter into anxiety on behalf of the sinner precisely in the measure that he has, objectively, been freed from the anxiety of sin.[104]

Three unique qualities of Christian anxiety: joy, indifference and patience

This transformed Christian anxiety is imbued with three new qualities that are not usually associated with the phenomenon of anxiety: joy, indifference and patience. The first quality of Christian anxiety, to which Balthasar devotes the most attention, is joy. Like all suffering in the Cross, Christian anxiety is characterized by joy, but joy understood in a uniquely Christian manner. Joy is defined for the Christian, according to Balthasar, by the subject's relationship to Christ through the Cross whereby the philosophical category of joy in suffering and self-renunciation is stretched to unforeseeable dimensions and is inwardly fulfilled.[105]

On one level Christian joy resembles that of the Old Testament and secular understandings: the joy that is found on the *other side* of suffering, or the joy that is found by knowing that the suffering will bring joy in the end.[106] But for the Christian the endurance of suffering in order to attain joy is changed to possessing joy in the midst of suffering in love. The alienating aspect of suffering, which seems to push the believer away from joy, in fact becomes 'the pledge, and even the hidden presence, of eschatological joy'[107] when suffered as love. Therefore, St. Paul writes that suffering becomes relativized both by its temporal character and when measured against the 'eternal weight of glory' (2 Cor. 4.17).

Furthermore, the experience of suffering is not a private affair for the Christian, but is destined for the communion of saints in which suffering vicariously can bring consolation to others who are suffering.[108] The life of the Church follows the life of her Divine Spouse. The Church, and those in the

best at portraying it. Le Fort is more questionable since she less clearly distinguishes what is natural and mystical in Blanche de la Force's anxiety. Paul Claudel and Reinhold Schneider push its limits, while Graham Greene is simply wrong by attempting to make a direct connection between sin-anxiety and Christian anxiety in a kind of 'sin mysticism'.

104. *CA*, p. 66; Eng., p. 114.
105. Cf. *W*, p. 139; Eng., p. 161.
106. Cf. *W*, p. 140; Eng., p. 162; Heb. 12.11; 2 Cor. 2.3, 7.8–9.
107. *W*, p. 141; Eng., p. 164.
108. Cf. *W*, p. 142; Eng., p. 165.

Church, are not exempt from suffering to bask in Easter joy, but rather are called to share in the joy of the Cross. Thus the Church, standing between the Ascension and the Parousia, lives in the unity of joy and the Cross because the Cross, as a divine act, is not simply an accomplished fact of past history, nor is the sinfulness of the Church's members a closed issue.[109] Easter joy never relativizes the Cross. Jesus refers the suffering of the Cross to that of a woman in childbirth where the joy before and the joy after are submerged in the pain of the present moment. The Christian, therefore, can be mystically led into all kinds of desolation in following Christ so long as the Christian lives in time.[110]

The Christian thus can share in the *Hinterlegung* of the experience of joy in suffering: 'Those who love bear suffering "joyfully, although the feeling of joy remains hidden"'.[111] The believer may possess joy objectively while subjectively not feel joy. Though experientially the believer may feel crushed and mortally terrified, the objective movement of the anxiety expands him. It is 'a fruitful *dilatatio* of the birth canal, an interior trembling that expands faith, hope, and love', and draws him further into the ecstasy of the Trinitarian life.[112] We can say, then, that Christian anxiety moves in the opposite direction of natural and sin anxiety for joy is the movement of *ek-stasis*.[113] Thus Christian anxiety is characterized by joy since this anxiety is 'fundamentally an intensification of light and of joy, a "darkness bright as day", because it is suffering *out of* joy, anxiety *out of* exaltation: it is a sign of God's ever-greater confidence in the one who believes'.[114]

Secondly, Christian anxiety possesses the quality of 'indifference', understood in the Ignatian sense, that is, a surrender and readiness to undergo whatever is for the greater glory of God. Indifference is the Christian's unqualified Yes to the will of God. It is 'that trusting gift of self that, "in every state and way of life", wants and chooses only what God wants and chooses',[115] and 'the untroubled readiness of soul to receive the divine will in whatever form it may make itself known'.[116] This quality of indifference in Christian anxiety is how redeemed anxiety heals the anxiety caused by the wound in the human mind inflicted by original sin. Original sin ripped open a void in the human mind which had been previously filled by the presence of God. The

109. Cf. *W*, pp. 144–5; Eng., pp. 166–8.

110. Our author observes this in the experience of the mystics like St. Thérèse (cf. *W*, 133n; Eng., 154–5n).

111. *TDIV*, p. 231; Eng., p. 256.

112. *CA*, p. 90; Eng., p. 148.

113. Cf. D.C. Schindler, *Hans Urs von Balthasar and the Dramatic Structure of Truth*, p. 407.

114. *CA*, p. 90; Eng., pp. 147–8.

115. *CS*, p. 389; Eng., p. 475.

116. *CS*, p. 325; Eng., p. 400. Servais clarifies the paradox and inner unity of indifference to created things and loving engagement with the world in St. Ignatius' understanding of Christian indifference in Servais, 'Should We Engage Ourselves in the World, or Make Ourselves Indifferent to All Things?', *Communio: International Catholic Review* 32 (2005), pp. 472–91.

anxiety producing void opened up by original sin in the human mind, described in Chapter 3 and 5, means that God is not the first thing known to man and that reality is rendered abstract by suspending man between absolute Being and contingent being.

Positive Christian indifference helps to heal the negative indifference from original sin. Christian indifference does not do away with the void created by original sin, but begins to allow the Lord to fill it again with his presence. Balthasar explains, 'through the abiding void in man (the *indifferentia intellectus et voluntatis ad omne ens*) God's fullness reveals itself as presence in such a way that God as the first thing demands from man a total Yes to his invisible totality and in-difference. This Yes . . . is in the same way characterized as Christian indifference'.[117] The natural, fallen indifference of the intellect and will to all being is taken up into the supernatural, grace-filled indifference of Christian faith. Christian indifference is the total self-offering of the believer, with his void and anxiety, to the fullness of God's Totality.

Christian indifference implies an act of tremendous vulnerability, and relies heavily upon the fiduciary dimension of faith which casts the believer forth into the life of God. Such an attitude does not originate in the self, and evaporates when clung to. Our author elaborates using the example of St. Peter walking on the water, 'reflection on this belief ("How can I be doing this?"), Peter is already back in unbelief and sinks, and within transcendence is uncovered what had been swallowed up and drowned while transcendence was advancing step by step: anxiety. One cannot simultaneously let go and cling to the letting go'.[118] Walking in the theological virtues always involves for the finite creature a leap, a risk because only an act in which everything is risked is worthy of God. The believer in his indifference places everything in the Father's hands to be used according to his will, 'his emotional disposition as well: faith that loves and hopes is ultimately indifferent even to anxiety and nonanxiety'.[119] The believer's anxiety and sense of security are at the disposal of the divine will, and a truly indifferent faith will view both Christian *Angst* and *Angstlosigkeit* as a gift from God.

Just as the natural, fallen indifference has a two-fold movement (*abtractio* and *conversio*), supernatural indifference has a corresponding two-fold movement. Corresponding to natural *abstractio* is Christian *detachment* from all created reality; corresponding to natural *conversio* is Christian *mission* which sends him into all created reality in order to bring it to God. Thus in the Christian life detachment necessarily precedes mission if the mission is going to be genuinely Christian. Arriving at one's mission from God involves anxiety, in the searching, deliberating and groping for clarity, that is, before the mission. However, the choice to embrace the mission, according to our author, brings certainty, serenity and *Angstlosigkeit*, unless anxiety is necessarily part of the mission. The act of being sent by God on mission is anxiety free. This aspect of how Christian mission transforms anxiety is not given much explicit

117. *CA*, p. 87; Eng., p. 143.
118. *CA*, p. 88; Eng., pp. 144–5.
119. *CA*, pp. 89–90; Eng., p. 147.

development by Balthasar, and will be developed in greater detail in the following chapter.

This quality of indifference in Christian anxiety leads to the third characteristic: patience. Balthasar calls this quality 'the fundamental attitude of the Christian within time'.[120] It is not stoical endurance through time. Christian patience rather is the attitude that 'expresses itself as faith, love, hope and as indifference directed toward the Father'.[121]

Martha and Mary are singled out by Balthasar as examples of this unique Christian anxiety at work, and show its qualitative difference from that of the righteous man of the Old Testament. Their much beloved brother, Lazarus, falls ill and dies, while the Lord delays in coming. Their suffering is comparable to Job's yet is qualitatively different since theirs 'is an anxiety within incarnate love; anxiety in patient, albeit uncomprehending, surrender; anxiety without rigidity or rebellion; anxiety without pathos'.[122] All the stormy questions which characterized Job's anxiety fall away, and what remains in them is 'readiness and trembling without seeing'.[123] Moreover, the sisters' anxiety is not focused on themselves but on their neighbour. Their anxiety springs from their mission of joy with the Lord. Balthasar writes, 'From their joy in the Lord they have been led to share with the Lord a concern for their neighbor, and this shared concern [*Mit-Sorge*] leads to shared suffering [*Mit-Leiden*] and shared anxiety [*Mit-Angst*]'.[124] Their Christian anxiety is characterized by joy, indifference and patience.

The ecclesial shape of the trajectory

We cannot depart from Balthasar's interpretation of Christian anxiety without referring to the Church. He himself draws attention to the ecclesial shape of the trajectory of anxiety in the Christian life at the very end of *Der Christ und die Angst*. He writes, 'on all these pages there has been much talk about the Christian but little about *the Church*'.[125] The trajectory of Christian anxiety takes place within the Church. The Church in her concrete and immediate presence to the Christian always appears to make an excessive demand on natural, fallen man to imitate her Divine Bridegroom. Her desire, according to Balthasar, is to continually push man beyond his nature and continue in the leap of faith, hope and love.

120. *CA*, p. 89; Eng., p. 146.
121. *CA*, p. 89; Eng., p. 146.
122. *CA*, pp. 49–50; Eng., p. 91.
123. *CA*, p. 50; Eng., p. 91.
124. *CA*, p. 50; Eng., p. 92.
125. *CA*, p. 91; Eng., p. 149 (Balthasar's italics). Torralba-Roselló makes the point that the ecclesial dimension of anxiety is also important in Balthasar's response to Kierkegaard's more solitary view of man in anxiety (cf. Torralba-Roselló, '*Teologia de l'Angoixa*', p. 454).

At the same time, the Lord has placed in the Church an abundance of grace and visible aids to respond to the demands and to persevere in his walk.[126] These form the supports, the 'handrails', which help the Christian to make his leap. The coincidence of the handrails and the leap away from the handrails indicate for our author the paradox of the Church which is patterned on the paradox of the God-man. It is important to recognize this paradox, in Balthasar's view, in order to respond to Nietzsche's or Freud's charge that Christianity is a religion of anxiety. Balthasar admits that the believer who does not see this paradox or rejects it will use the supports in the Church as a kind of defence mechanism to keep him from making the leap. He writes, 'The Christianity of the Church as such is not a "religion of anxiety" – arousing anxiety through its claims and threats, then numbing anxiety through its forms and rites – but, because existence in the Church is the most vulnerable kind of human existence, everything about the Church is a hairsbreadth away from anxiety'.[127]

The handrails offered by the Church are there to help the believer move outward further into the Trinitarian life in Christian detachment and mission. Thus to live in the Church requires courage, the supernatural courage that Balthasar calls Christian fortitude. Because of the objective structural change in anxiety, Christian indifference, therefore, combines both the virtue of courage and the experience of anxiety for Balthasar.[128] Balthasar again draws the parallel between the natural and supernatural realm. In the natural realm, the mind's courage to think is based upon its innate knowledge of its own ability, and so even when anxiety enters the mind through its functioning, it does not destroy the primal knowledge of the mind's ability. Balthasar reasons, 'anxiety ultimately takes its measure from that primal feeling; anxiety can only be the anxiety of this courage itself'.[129] Natural courage develops into fortitude in its habitual non-wavering in the face of anxiety. This natural fortitude becomes supernatural Christian fortitude through grace when the believer's indifference takes the 'form of the courage to say Yes in every instance to every word of God that may affect my life'.[130]

Thus a paradox grows within the life of the believer through the trajectory of Christian anxiety. As the vulnerability increases so does the divine power indwelling that vulnerability. Our author appeals to the saints to illustrate this reality. The saint is the most vulnerable and exposed person towards God, and therefore most susceptible to anxiety. Yet it is precisely this stance towards God that is the pinnacle of courage and strength. The 'armament' that St. Paul

126. Our author mentions ecclesial office, Sacred Scripture, the Sacraments, Tradition and the example of the saints (cf. *CA*, p. 92; Eng., p. 150).

127. *CA*, p. 93; Eng., p. 151.

128. He writes, 'genuine Christian fear can spring from courage alone, just as the Cross itself of the Son of God sprang from his extreme courage in braving as a solitary man all the powers of hell. The courage of a Christian, which can be loaded with anxiety, is in turn nothing other than his act of faith, in which he dares to place himself and the whole world in the hand of the One who can dispose of him for death and for life' (*CA*, p. 49; Eng., p. 90).

129. *CA*, p. 94; Eng., p. 153.

130. *CA*, p. 95; Eng., p. 154; cf. 2 Cor. 4.7–9; 12.9–10.

speaks of (Eph. 6.10–17; 1 Thess. 5.8) are precisely those things that open up man to God in vulnerability. This vulnerability and exposure to anxiety is how the Christian conquers the world. Yet the Christian is not facing the world as an individual but is sent into the world after being inserted into Christ and his Church. This insertion will be taken up and expanded in the next chapter.

Conclusion

In this section we have presented Balthasar's understanding of how the redemption of anxiety by Christ affects the life of the Christian. We placed his thought in conversation with Luther. The shape of Christian anxiety, Luther argues, is essentially dialectical based upon his doctrine of *simul iustus et peccator*. Balthasar affirms certain aspects of Luther's *simul* formula, understood correctly, such as the intent to deliver man from sin-anxiety and the existential unity of faith and anxiety in the fiduciary dimension of the act of faith. The Council of Trent gave Luther a dogmatic response; however, Luther's concerns were very much existential. It perhaps can be argued that Luther's challenges finally receive a Catholic existential response in Balthasar. Our author, however, rejects the objective shape of Luther's interpretation of Christian anxiety because of its roots in Luther's distorted doctrine on justification, specifically in its eschatological and participatory dimensions, and argues that Christian anxiety is far more unique than Luther grants.

Instead of a dialectic Balthasar proposes a trajectorial shape to Christian anxiety, in which the believer firmly walks away from natural and sin-anxiety into the divine life on the pathway of faith, hope and love according to Balthasar's 'three laws'. As he walks away from sin-anxiety and further into the divine life, the Christian is able to participate in Christ's own redeeming anxiety in union with him and in solidarity with sinners. In this way Christian anxiety transforms man's anxiety, and through grace imbues this new anxiety with joy, indifference and patience. On the existential level, it can be very difficult for the believer to distinguish between sin-anxiety needing purification by faith, hope and love and the believer's sharing in Christ's anxiety, because the joy of Christian anxiety may be obscured in the believer's self-awareness. Often only a proper discernment of spirits can distinguish non-Christian anxiety from Christian anxiety since the subjective experience can appear so similar. The trajectory of Christian anxiety, moreover, takes place within the Church. Balthasar develops his theology of Christian anxiety this far, and himself admits that much more could be said. In the final chapter we will bring the lines of his theology of anxiety to bear on other aspects of his thought in order to develop even further how anxiety is transformed in the Christian life.

Chapter 9

Anxiety Transformed by the Church

In each individual case, one must demonstrate the superiority of mission over 'psychology'.

(Hans Urs von Balthasar)

Balthasar admits towards the end of his book on anxiety that the work still needed a fourth part in which his ideas could be developed further by an ecclesially focused reflection.[1] What part does the Church play in the transformation of human anxiety into Christian *Angstlosigkeit* and Christian salvific anxiety? How does this transformation occur in the Church? This chapter attempts to develop Balthasar's interpretation of Christian anxiety following the indications given by him at the end of *Der Christ und die Angst*, and by bringing relevant aspects of Balthasar's ecclesiology to bear on his theology of anxiety. The redemption of anxiety by Christ, Balthasar argued, changed the objective structure of anxiety and creates the real possibility for man to be free from anxiety and to participate in Christ's redemptive anxiety. What is the ecclesial shape of the trajectory of Christian anxiety outlined in the previous chapter which transforms the anxiety that diminishes and even destroys man's life to the fruitful, joyful and even salvific anxiety of the Cross?

Before proceeding to such a consideration, however, it is helpful to summarize the types of anxiety that present themselves for transformation by the *Kreuzangst* of the Redeemer. Man suffers from natural, existential anxiety. He is finite and destined for death, and the world has been a dangerous place for him ever since the Fall. His life is constantly threatened by the possibility of suffering and the inevitability of death. Because of his fallen nature, man also stands in a 'placelessness' in his alienation from God and others. The discussion with Kierkegaard opened up the dimension of anxiety within the fallen human mind. Man's fallen intellect opens up a 'placelessness' in his mind. The functioning of his intellect and will gives him no footing either in Being itself or in the world of created beings. All becomes abstract to his thinking and willing. This state of the fallen intellect can continue its fall into the lack of courageous thinking expressed, for example, in the anxiety of Bernanos' *imbeciles*. Freud puts into relief the anxiety that flows from being conscious of oneself and the world around him, one's role in this world, and how that role

1. Cf. *CA*, pp. 91–2; Eng., p. 149.

is assigned. Balthasar's reflection on the original state emphasized man's original mission in the world and how that mission was damaged by original sin. There is also the sin-anxiety that comes from committing evil, which alienates one from God and elicits his just condemnation. Finally the good man's anxiety, whether it stems from his continued sinfulness, lack of faith or proximity to God, begs for transformation.

The anxiety from discursive reasoning, ego-consciousness and original sin, the ultimate origin of all anxiety, can be transformed by Christ via the Church according to Balthasar. At the end of the previous chapter, we indicated the initial transformation of man's anxiety by Christ's redemption in the life of faith, hope and love exercised within the Church. But our author did not explain further the ecclesial shape of the trajectory of Christian anxiety. In order to see how the Church transforms human anxiety, we first present, in summary form, our author's view of the nature of the Church. After identifying these primary principles of his ecclesiology, we then apply them to the process of anxiety transformation. I suggest that Balthasar's ecclesiology can offer a more specific and detailed explanation of how the organs of the Church transform human anxiety into freedom from anxiety and initiate one into the salvific anxiety of Christ.

Relevant Aspects of Balthasar's Ecclesiology for Interpreting Anxiety's Transformation[2]

From the outset it is important to mention that our author does not intend to offer a systematic ecclesiology in his writing. Instead he forms his reflections around a constellation of persons who as a whole embody the Church as the transparent mediation of the Christ-event. These figures are those 'who were closest, who found themselves involved in this mystery so that they became an

2. Balthasar's ecclesiology is treated at length by several scholars, the details of which extend beyond the context of this study. What follows is a summary gleaned from the consonant perspectives of the following scholars: S. Ackermann, 'The Church as Person in the Theology of Hans Urs von Balthasar', trans. E. Rielley, *Communio: International Catholic Review* 29 (2002), pp. 238–49; L. Chapp, 'Who is the Church? The Personalistic Categories of Balthasar's Ecclesiology', *Communio: International Catholic Review* 23 (1996), pp. 322–38; B. Leahy, *The Marian Principle in the Church according to Hans Urs von Balthasar* (European University Studies, p. 558; Frankfurt: Peter Lang, 1996); and *The Marian Profile in the Ecclesiology of Hans Urs von Balthasar* (New York: New City Press, 2000); Servais, 'Giovanni, fra Maria e Pietro: L'identità ecclesiale del consacrato', in A.M. Jerumanis and A. Tombolini (eds), *La missione teologica di Hans Urs von Balthasar: Atti del Simposio internazionale di Teologia in occasione del centesimo anniversario della nascita di Hans Urs von Balthasar* (Lugano: Eupress FTL, 2005), pp. 347–63; Id. 'Maria, Pietro e Giovanni, figure della Chiesa', *Communio: Rivista internazionale di teologia* 203–204 (2005), pp. 117–32; A. Sicari, 'Maria, Pietro, Giovanni: Figure della Chiesa. L'ecclesiologia di H.U. von Balthasar', *Communio: Rivista internazionale di teologia* 120 (1991), pp. 80–94; 'Mary, Peter and John: Figures of the Church', trans. M. Waldstein, in *Communio: International Catholic Review* 19 (1992), pp. 189–207.

essential part of its historical event': the Blessed Virgin Mary, St. Peter and St. John.[3]

The incarnational, personal and sacramental nature of the church

Before treating these three figures, it is first important to expose the Church's deeply incarnational, personal and sacramental dimensions in Balthasar's thinking, that is, the deep union the Christ has with his Church as his Body and Bride. Our author contends that the Church understands herself to be the work of her Divine Bridegroom, Jesus Christ, and the one who mediates the form of his revelation to the world.[4] She is created 'purely from the being of Christ himself',[5] possessing 'the highest possible similarity to the archetype itself'.[6] Thus the Church is the visible manifestation of her Divine Spouse in the world and is patterned upon his own being as both divine and human. 'The Church', he writes, 'is not Christ, but she can claim for herself and for the world no other figure than the figure of Christ, which leaves its stamp in her and shapes her through and through as the soul shapes the body'.[7] The Church is established in her essence through a twofold relationship with Christ: identity (the Body of Christ) and non-identity (the Bride of Christ). As the body of Christ, the Church 'is, and cannot be other than an extension, a communication, a partaking of the personality of Christ'.[8] The identity of Christ and the Church as Body, however, is not such that the Church dissolves into the identity of Christ. Christ's spousal relationship to the Church founds her non-identity with Christ. This non-identity is important so that the relationship between Christ and his Church can be constituted as love. The non-identity of the Church as Bride also allows the existence of personal subjects in her.

The foundation for understanding the Church is the event of the Incarnation itself. The Church, according to Balthasar, is not simply predicated from the Incarnation or an extension of it, but more deeply she is a constitutive part of the Incarnation event itself, manifested in the Blessed Virgin Mary. The event of the Incarnation for Balthasar signals not only the arrival of the Son

3. A. Sicari, 'Mary, Peter and John: Figures of the Church', p. 190. Leahy also identifies St. Paul and St. James in the constellation of persons forming the Church. He categorizes these archetypical ecclesial principles of Petrine, Pauline, Johannine and Jacobine under the all-embracing Marian principle (cf. Leahy, *The Marian Principle*, pp. 98–100; Servais, 'Giovanni fra Maria e Pietro', p. 351). It can be argued that the Pauline and Jacobine principles do not figure as prominently in Balthasar's ecclesiology as the Marian, Petrine and Johannine.

4. *HI*, p. 535; Eng., p. 556.

5. *HI*, p. 536; Eng., p. 557.

6. *HI*, p. 538; Eng., p. 560.

7. *HI*, p. 538; Eng., p. 559. Chapp comments, 'the inner orientation and essence of the Church is the very being and substance of Christ himself' (Chapp, 'Who is the Church?', p. 324).

8. *SV*, p. 151; Eng., p. 145.

into the world, but the establishment of the Church.[9] The Church is 'this living ecclesial chain that guarantees the reference to the Son of God *as incarnate, as true man*'.[10] Then in the establishment of the community of the apostles with Jesus she 'represents *in nuce* all the ecclesial relationships and structures of the later Church'.[11] This conception of the Church prevents any docetic characterization of the Church; the real flesh of these disciples preserves the incarnational reality, the bodiliness of the Church. This grounding in actual historical and human persons in a nuptial relationship with Christ, moreover, prevents the Church from being reduced to a mythology. Thus the Church as the Body of Christ mediates the proximity of Christ to the world here and now and is able to bring the form of Christ to bear on her every member.

At the same time, the Church is the Bride of Christ and as such is a person. But in what way is the Church a person? Who is the subject of the Church? In a pre-eminent sense, Balthasar holds that the subject of the Church is Christ himself.[12] She is the Body of Christ. Nevertheless, the mystery of the Incarnation has forged a union between the divine Son and his human nature, and his human nature is not dissolved into his divinity which thus creates the possibility of the spousal relationship of the Church. The Church is a person in this second sense as the Bride of Christ. The Church is a person in the second sense in the persons of Mary, Peter and John, and all the others who have been 'personalized' by Christ.[13]

In addition to the incarnational and personal qualities of the Church, mention must be made concerning the sacramental nature of the Church which flows from those first two qualities. The sacramental nature of the Church and in particular the seven Sacraments find their origin in Christ himself. Our author writes, 'If, according to Catholic teaching, the sacraments "contain and confer the grace they visibly signify," (DS, 1606), then Jesus Christ – in his Incarnation, in his hidden and public life, in his death on the Cross and in his Resurrection – is the primordial sacrament'.[14] Balthasar continues, 'There can be no *res* (*gratia*) which would not, in Christ, already be *res et sacramentum*. For this reason, every ecclesial *sacramentum* must adhere both interiorly and exteriorly to this archetype'.[15] Therefore, the Church as the Body of Christ and Bride of Christ is capable of touching the human senses and the human body.[16]

9. Cf. Sicari, 'Mary, Peter and John', p. 192.
10. Sicari, 'Mary, Peter and John', p. 194.
11. *CS*, p. 235; Eng., p. 290.
12. Cf. *SV*, p. 150; Eng., p. 144.
13. A 'person' in the philosophical sense, which Balthasar calls a 'spiritual subject' becomes a 'person' in a full, theological sense when they accept their mission from Christ in the Church. The embracing of one's mission conforms him to the pattern of personhood of the Divine Persons of the Blessed Trinity.
14. *AA*, p. 113; Eng., p. 133.
15. *HI*, p. 554; Eng., p. 576.
16. The concreteness of the Church's form can produce anxiety (*Formangst*) in the believer because of its demands in such proximity. Balthasar observes that two behaviours can result to avoid this anxiety: flight from the form, for example, in Gnosticism and a certain liberal Protestantism and Catholicism, and flight into the form, for example, in a type

The Marian principle

Balthasar continues to delineate the subjectivity of the Church according to three primary subjects: the Blessed Virgin Mary, St. Peter and St. John. These three persons ground the personal mission for every member of the Church. The Marian principle in the Church is the most fundamental according to Balthasar. Our author writes, 'The Church is not, purely and simply, Christ. She is not hypostatically united to God who dwells in her. In this opposition, therefore, she is receptive to her Head and so has a feminine role. She is Marial'.[17] This principle lies not only at the temporal beginning of the Church but remains an active source in her. She is the 'image of the Church' (*Urbild der Kirche*) since she is the actual, historical location of the Word's incarnation and since she is perfectly receptive spiritually with her whole being to live in conformity with the Word.[18] The Blessed Virgin Mary is the Church's 'deepest origin and unsullied kernel'.[19]

Our author believes that the objective power in the Church which gives the Church her objective holiness is founded upon the subjectivity of Christ himself. This objective holiness provided by God himself is seen most clearly in how the Sacraments function *ex opere operato*. It is an objective holiness not dependent on the subjective holiness of a particular minister of the Sacrament. Balthasar reasons, however, that such an objective spirit in the Church implies a subjective spirit capable of receiving such a gift.[20] Therefore, reasons Balthasar, Christ must reproduce in his Body and Bride the same identity of objective and subjective holiness. The subjective holiness that is capable of receiving the objective holiness that Christ brings into the Church must be holiness free from all sin. Thus the subjective spirit in the Church capable of receiving the objective holiness of Christ is the Blessed Virgin Mary.[21] Without

of Pharisaism within the Church (cf. *SC*, p. 444; Eng., p. 502). But such a flight in his view actually intensifies the anxiety. By fleeing the concrete form of the Church, one loses also the 'protective covering' of the Incarnation in one's relationship with God. One's relationship with God slips back into the Old Covenant, or it can become more remote by making God in one's own image. By fleeing into the form, one exhibits a type of behavioural avoidance of the anxiety of living in the ambiguity of one's fallen nature in such proximity to God. Fleeing into the form can be seen as a way of keeping God at a distance and attempt to control him.

17. *SV*, p. 198; Eng., p. 187.
18. Cf. *BG*, p. 22; Eng., p. 27; *TDII/2*, pp. 322–4; Eng., pp. 351–2.
19. *K*, p. 69; Eng., p. 108.
20. Cf. *SV*, pp. 167–8; Eng., pp. 160–1.
21. Balthasar writes, 'Mary is the subjectivity that, in its womanly and receptive manner, is enabled fully to correspond to the masculine subjectivity of Christ, through God's grace and the overshadowing of his Spirit. The Church flowing forth from Christ finds her personal centre in Mary as well as the full realization of her idea as Church' (*SV*, pp. 168–9; Eng., p. 161). The Church in her most fundamental sense is feminine, and our author makes frequent use of masculine and feminine archetypes to describe the structure of the Church. The masculine principle is represented in the objective structures in the Church and in Christ himself, while the subjective, receptive side of the Church is portrayed as feminine. The feminine receptivity is far from an inert passivity, but a fully active receptivity which constantly appropriates all that her Divine Bridegroom communicates to her.

Mary's perfect subjective holiness grounding the Church's subjective holiness, 'the empirical nature of the subjective holiness of the Church could be called into question'.[22] Subjective holiness in the Church is not a Platonic form which is never concretely, historically and personally realized in the Church's earthly existence. It has already been realized and grounded in Mary's perfect holiness.

The Marian principle of the Church guarantees that the Church will perfectly mediate between Christ and the world despite the sinfulness of her members. The Blessed Virgin Mary as the principle of the Church's subjective response guarantees that the Christ form that the Church reveals to the world is the true Christ form taken from her very body. Mary's form is the model of the believer's being formed in Christ.[23] Therefore, our author reasons that 'the image of her interior reality stands before the eyes of Christians and should stand before their eyes whenever the conditions for their becoming conformed to Christ are being considered'.[24] Every believing subject receives this feminine form. Balthasar writes, 'we can hold fast to the assertion that the Church, as subject, is inchoately present in Mary and that she can also be called the personal center of the Church insofar as she fulfills her personal mission by surrendering her Son'.[25] The Marian principle is the mission of being-at-the-disposal-of-the-other, the mission of all the baptized to first of all receive from Christ. Mary is the 'Church in origin' (*Kirche im Ursprung*).[26]

The Petrine principle

The person of St. Peter in the constellation of persons forming the Church represents the 'objectively complete holiness' of the Church.[27] If the Marian principle guarantees the Church's spousal reality as Bride, the Petrine principle guarantees that the Church's spousal reality is always united to her Divine Spouse as Bridegroom.[28] The offices of the Church, patterned on Peter's vocation form the Church in the service of love; the Petrine mission is responsible for the visible unity of the Church and the infallibility in the exercise of her functions.[29] The building-up of this Body by means of the different offices involves a dynamic process whereby the Christ-form is further implanted in the Body. Office is established by and at the service of love. Office ensures that all those down through the ages have access to the original

22. Chapp, 'Who is the Church?', p. 334.
23. Cf. *HI*, p. 541; Eng., p. 563; Rom. 8.29; Phil. 3.10, 21.
24. *HI*, p. 541; Eng., p. 563.
25. *TDII/2*, p. 324; Eng., p. 352.
26. Ackermann, 'The Church as Person', p. 246.
27. Sicari, 'Mary, Peter and John', p. 199; cf. Servais, 'Giovanni fra Maria e Pietro', pp. 353–5.
28. Leahy observes that the Petrine principle of the Church is just as original as the Marian, though the Petrine is exercised within the Marian (cf. Leahy, *The Marian Principle*, p. 193).
29. Cf. Servais, 'Giovanni fra Maria e Pietro', p. 353.

event. Balthasar writes, 'the event in which the Church is "born" from Christ is a continual event, happening here and now. The abiding structure of offices in the Church (the "institution") means that we are guaranteed the possibility of participating in the original event at any and every time'.[30]

The Bride and the Bridegroom are concretely represented in Our Lady and St. Peter, and both are necessary in order for the new life to be generated in the Church. Just as Mary personifies the subjective holiness of the Church; Peter personifies the Church's objective holiness. The immaculate nature of Mary's subjective holiness finds an analogue in the 'immaculate' nature of Peter's objective holiness, his infallibility. The Marian principle, however, remains primary since Mary's infallible profession of faith guarantees Peter's infallibility. This primacy nevertheless does not eliminate the immediacy with which Jesus institutes ministry in the Church. The Petrine mission embodies the objective and official dimension of the Church. Leahy asserts that Balthasar 'sees the Church as founded both on the hierarchy and charism, on objective and subjective sanctity'.[31] Institution and charism can be distinguished but not separated for institution itself is a charism given by the Holy Spirit, and the incarnational quality of the Church, which has historical and visible form, does not allow such a separation. Nevertheless, the Petrine principle of the Church does not encompass all the vitality in the Church. The Marian and Petrine principles together manifest the nuptial reality of the Church.

The Johannine principle

The Blessed Virgin Mary establishes and guarantees the subjective holiness of the Church and her reality as Body and Bride of Christ. St. Peter guarantees the objective holiness of the Church and the presence of the Bridegroom to the Bride. St. John the Beloved, for his part, provides the link between the two.[32] This principle preserves the unity and mediation of the subjective with the objective holiness of the Church. St. John 'stands under the Cross in place of Peter and on his behalf receives the Marian Church'.[33] Balthasar sees in St. John the 'office of love'.[34] He is the one whose mission ensures that the objective holiness of institution is constantly filled with the love from the subjective holiness of the Church. The Johannine mission represents 'all those whose mission is one of contemplative love', especially in the evangelical counsels.[35] St. John's mission 'indicates a new way of living which is through and beyond the cross' as the son of Mary.[36] The Johannine principle is linked to the Marian principle 'primarily in the inner bridal heart of the Church' and

30. *TDII/2*, p. 326; Eng., p. 355.
31. Leahy, *The Marian Principle*, p. 192.
32. Cf. *AA*, pp. 186–7; Eng., pp. 224–5.
33. *AA*, p. 187; Eng., p. 225; cf. Servais, 'Giovanni fra Maria e Pietro', pp. 355–6.
34. *CS*, p. 229; Eng., p. 283.
35. Leahy, *The Marian Principle*, p. 100.
36. Ibid., p. 143.

constitutes the original cell of the Church.[37] The Johannine principle is also linked to the Petrine by 'not only outlining and highlighting Peter's office but also humanly and lovingly accompanying this office'.[38]

The communio of the Church

The Church, therefore, is for Balthasar 'a medium, as a system of relations, whose form becomes comprehensible when it brings together in a coherent manner the elements that the medium must communicate and unite'.[39] The three persons constituting the primary archetypes of the Church form an inclusive and interpenetrating *communio* of missions. Christ's universal mission is unique, yet he opens it to be inclusive of all the members of his Body. Balthasar writes, 'The Church's unity of life comes about through the self-emptying and externalizing of God's unique spirit-life *beyond*, *in* and *through* the individuals integrated in it. Their creaturely uniqueness is neither limited nor endangered; on the contrary, by grace it is put in touch with the uniqueness of God and thus opened to perfection'.[40] This inclusion is seen first in Our Lady, St. Peter and St. John, and then expands to include the particular mission of every member of the Church, every member who is personalized by Christ in mission. Balthasar understands the missions in the Church as mutually interpenetrating in an analogous way to the circumincession (*perichoresis*) of the Divine Persons. The interpenetrating communion of the Church is patterned on the interpenetrating communion of the Divine Persons. The Church is constituted by a unity, not of monism, but of interpenetrating communion which has no adequate analogue outside the Godhead itself.[41] Christ's Church is inconceivable without personal distinction within the unity of love. The nuptial relationship between Christ the Bridegroom and his Bride the Church is continually realized in the living persons of the Church.

The personalization of man by divine mission in the Church

It is through the activity of Christ in his Church, according to Balthasar, that a human being is changed from a 'spiritual subject' into a theological

37. Ibid., p. 190.
38. Ibid., p. 191.
39. *HI*, p. 537; Eng., p. 559.
40. *BG*, p. 83; Eng., p. 94 (Balthasar's italics). Ackermann comments, 'The total identity between consciousness of self and consciousness of mission in Jesus opens up "room ... for others to have analogous, unique, personal missions". These missions do not, as in Christ's case, constitute an *a priori* synthesis with [one's] person, but are synthesized *a posteriori* along with the created, chosen persons [*Geistpersonen*]' (Ackermann, 'The Church as Person', p. 241).
41. Cf. *SV*, pp. 179–80; Eng., p. 171.

'person'.[42] When a believer gives his Marian Yes of faith and is incorporated into the Body of Christ, he is expropriated out of the narrowness of his finite and sinful condition, and expanded to the dimensions of the mission of Christ and the Church. Christ personalizes a human being by addressing him, expropriating him, taking him out of himself and giving him a mission. This conferral of meaning and role does not come from one's own self, from parents or from society, but from God himself.[43] The believer by embracing and living his mission, according to Balthasar, brings his non-identity into an ever closer approximation to identity with Christ. The believer's 'I' is to be increasingly conformed to his mission, even to become his mission. The divinely conferred mission brings with it both the personal and social dimensions of the I's own identity.

An example of this personalization is found in St. Peter. He is called into the Church through the mysterious election of Christ whereby 'Simon' is re-made and personalized in 'Peter'. Before being able to personify office in the Church, Simon must be personalized by Christ. Balthasar describes such a personalizing of St. Peter:

> Simon the fisherman could have explored every region of his ego prior to his encounter with Christ, but he would not have found 'Peter' there; for the present, the 'form' summed up in the name 'Peter', the particular mission reserved for him alone, is hidden in the mystery of Christ's soul. Then Christ confronts him with it, unyielding, demanding obedience, and it will be the fulfillment of everything that, in Simon, vainly sought a 'form' that would be ultimately valid before God and eternity. In the form of Peter [*Petrusform*], Simon will be able to understand Christ's word, since the form itself proceeds out of the words and incorporates its addressee into the Word. Each time Simon follows the understanding native to 'Simon' he will go dangerously astray, whereas he will always hit the mark when, refusing to 'confer with flesh and blood', he attends only to his commission, which reveals the Father's will to him.[44]

St. Peter 'is projected forthwith out of the personal ("Thou art Simon, son of John") into the official dimension ("Thou shalt be called Cephas" [John 1: 42])'.[45] The call of Simon illustrates in a dramatic way, our author's understanding of 'person': the identification of one's 'I' with his mission. A person is the one who becomes his mission.

Through this expropriation by Christ, the individual begins to discover his true personal self, his 'I' which is no longer an isolated, monadic-I but an ecclesial-I, a wholly relational-I, an 'I' that is 'no longer I but Christ' (Gal. 2.20). Through his personalization in the Church, the believer is no

42. Balthasar's central insight of mission as the mediating principle of 'person' in both his trinitarian theology and Christology, also characterizes his view of the Christian's place in the Church (cf. Balthasar, 'On the Concept of Person', p. 18).

43. Here Balthasar's 'theological person' stands in striking contrast to Freud's 'psychological man' whose role is a compromise worked out by the ego, negotiating between the demands of the id and social reality. Balthasar's notion of mission offers no hint of such a compromise.

44. *BG*, p. 52; Eng., p. 60.

45. *CS*, p. 221; Eng., p. 273.

longer alone. He lives within the interpenetrating communion of Divine Love with the Trinity and all those in the Body of Christ. He no longer understands himself simply in terms of himself or any role given him by the world. He understands himself now in terms of Christ and the Church. He is no longer an isolated individual, but one who lives and acts within the 'We' of the Trinity and the Church.

In the appropriation of the mission, the believer's consciousness begins to interpenetrate with the Church's consciousness, and 'thinking *with* the Church' [*sentire cum ecclesia*] becomes increasingly the 'thinking *of* the Church' [*sentire ecclesiae*], and 'love *for* the Church' becomes the 'love *of* the Church'.[46] This interpenetration continues to expand the person's ecclesial-I beyond itself to be poured out in loving service of God and neighbour so that it becomes increasingly an *anima ecclesiastica*, 'a soul conformed to the Church'.[47] Balthasar writes, 'the individual person, suffused by God, is elevated and heightened in its personality and, at the same time, opened and distributed in the sense of community'.[48] To the degree that a person shares in Christ's universal mission, he himself becomes universalized. Personalization means de-privatization. Balthasar writes, 'If the mission is accepted and carried out, it de-privatizes the "I" causing the latter's fruitful influence (through grace) to expand into the whole "Mystical Body" of Christ. In this way, there is a mutual interpenetration of the diverse missions and the persons who identify themselves with them: this is what is meant by the *communio sanctorum*'.[49]

The paradox of theological personhood is the more one gives himself away in his mission, the more he becomes himself. In the mystery of Divine Personhood, self-identity grows in proportion to self-giving. The believer's person takes on increasingly ecclesial features. Without ever ceasing to be himself, and in fact becoming increasingly himself and increasingly unique, the believer begins to resemble increasingly the Incarnate Son. The believer's new personality, whose uniqueness is actually heightened by his incorporation in the Church, cannot be adequately measured, according to Balthasar, by the

46. Ackermann, 'The Church as Person', p. 245.

47. Cf. Ackermann, 'The Church as Person', pp. 244–5. Ackermann quotes Balthasar, 'the more selflessly and un-egotistically a Christian serves and commits himself to God's work in the world in Christ, the more he is at the disposal of God, the Church, and his neighbour, the more his heart is open to the needs of others, the more Christ's desire to save all becomes important to him, even outweighing his own personal salvation and well-being, the more universally his prayer to God includes all humanity, even the most "reprobate," the more he presents himself to God and places his life, and perhaps his death, if necessary, at the disposal of the saving will of God, by that much more will he be fruitful in the kingdom of grace . . . by that much more will he grow to the dimensions of the Church and identify himself with her intentions, becoming, as the Fathers say, a "man of the Church," an "anima ecclesiastica"' (Balthasar and J. Ratzinger, *Maria – Kirche im Ursprung* [Freiburg: Verlag, 1997], p. 121).

48. *SV*, p. 180; Eng., p. 171.

49. *TDII/2*, p. 321; Eng., p. 349. He also calls this interpenetration of missions 'the eucharistic "permeability" of all subjects to one another' (*TDV*, p. 350; Eng., p. 383).

tools of the 'psychological sciences'.[50] The Church bears within herself 'the "I" of mission, not that of psychology'.[51]

The Marian principle underlies each and every interpenetrating mission in the Church. Our Lady and her perfect response lie at the foundation of the response of every member of the Body. The believer's imperfect act of faith and imperfect response in mission is encompassed by Mary's perfect act of faith and perfect response in mission. In embracing his mission, the believer is upheld in his Yes by Mary's Yes. He is not alone is giving his imperfect Yes, and even more, her perfect Yes will help to ensure that he will not fail in his mission.

Because the Church is the transparent mediation of God's self-revelation, she possesses the fullest and most adequate measure of man. Balthasar suggests that this measure is found in Christ personalizing man through mission in the Church. Out of this conviction, he would make such a statement as 'in every individual case we must demonstrate the superiority of mission over "psychology"'.[52] The Church is able to measure man from the perspective of God, and therefore, evaluate man in his truest and deepest sense. In the Christian perspective such a transpsychological approach also entails that it is ultimately Christ, the God-man, who gives man his fullest measure. If this is true, then it falls to 'Christians to assume responsibility for the true measure of and proportions of man in this world'.[53]

The Church as Casta Meretrix

We would not give an adequate portrait of Balthasar's ecclesiology and its impact upon the transformation of anxiety without also mentioning the sinfulness of the Church in her members. The Church is not only Beatrice, the spotless bride, but Dante in his confession before Beatrice at the summit of the mountain of Purgatory.[54] Balthasar writes,

> [T]he Church is both eternal and temporal, infallible and fallible, immaculate in herself and yet sinful in her members. In her first aspect, the Church requires the most childlike obedience and an open love for the truth entrusted to her, a truth she freely

50. Chapp summarizes, 'Just as the "I" of Christ is part of the circumincession of the trinitarian "We", so too the "I" of the individual believer is not negated in the new ecclesial consciousness, but is raised to a new level through participation in the "we" of the Church with its "constellation" of missions (ET II, p. 168). Thus, it is fruitless to try and write a "psychology of Paul" that begins by ignoring the force of this new spiritual reality in transforming Paul's personality. "The personal reality", states Balthasar, "that drives forward with such impetus cannot, by its very nature, be contained in these [psychological] categories, although it does not destroy them but makes sovereign use of them" (ET II, p. 168). Paul's personal "I" has not been destroyed, but transformed into the new *anima ecclesiastica*' (Chapp, 'Who is the Church?', p. 332).

51. *SV*, p. 177; Eng., p. 169.

52. *ZSW*, p. 29; Eng., pp. 31–2.

53. *B*, p. 23; Eng., p. 31.

54. Cf. *SV*, p. 203; Eng., p. 193.

> dispenses and simply is – in her deepest identity as Bride and Body of Christ, as communion of saints, and as 'love'. In her second aspect, the Church requires open judgment, criticism, and even humiliation, things the Christian cannot spare the Church provided he lays claim to his part in the burden of guilt.[55]

Balthasar observes, 'All Christians are sinners, and if the Church does not sin as Church, she does sin in all her members, and through the mouths of all her members she must confess her guilt'.[56] Thus the Church in her earthly reality has constant need of purification in her members.

The only way the Bride of Christ is preserved as *casta* is by her Divine Bridegroom.[57] Our author writes, 'she has consciousness only in the human beings who form her. Now these human beings are nature, not grace. As human beings, they have been brought into unity and elevated above and beyond themselves in order to form the Church. Left to themselves, they can fall back again on themselves and become sinners'.[58] The sinfulness of her members will remain a source of anxiety for the believer, especially his own.

Christian Freedom from Anxiety from the Incarnational and Sacramental Nature of the Church

From the earlier exposition of the relevant aspects of Balthasar's ecclesiology, we can now apply them to the transformation of anxiety into freedom from anxiety and into Christian salvific anxiety. First, the Incarnational-Sacramental nature of the Church has a transforming effect on anxiety. The Church's incarnational character brings the presence of the triune God into the immediate here and now of the believer's life. Through the Church's concrete, visible and historical reality, the Incarnate Son's closeness to human beings remains just as close. The proximity of the Lord gives a sense of security to a human life threatened by suffering and death. Even more, the Sacraments of the Church bring the concrete immediacy of the Incarnate Son to each individual believer at particularly significant points in the cycle of human life. Because sacramental grace is conferred through matter, the human body also is involved in the encounter with Jesus. The Sacraments in particular address the physiological dimension of anxiety, for the body as well as the soul is affected by anxiety. The body and soul can be calmed in their anxiety through sacramental contact with Jesus. All of the Sacraments in their own way have this transformative effect on anxiety.

At the source of the seven Sacraments is Baptism. The Sacrament of Baptism plays an indispensable role in the transformation of anxiety because it establishes the life of faith, hope and love in the believer which, according to Balthasar, figure prominently in bringing the believer into Christian

55. *B*, p. 96; Eng., pp. 109–10.
56. *SV*, p. 257; Eng., p. 245.
57. Cf. *SV*, p. 251; Eng., p. 238.
58. *SV*, p. 251; Eng., p. 238.

Angstlosigkeit. Closely linked to Baptism is the Sacrament of Confirmation whereby the Christian is strengthened by the Holy Spirit to live out his Baptismal promises in Christian mission.

Those Sacraments which the believer can receive in his daily life bear further mention. The pre-eminent Sacrament in this regard is the Blessed Sacrament, Jesus' own Body and Blood coming into vital contact with the believer's own body and blood. This summit of sacramental encounters is one of security and intimacy, where one is known and loved by God himself in a most immediate and concrete way. Sacramental communion helps to transform the anxiety of isolation and abandonment. Christ is with the believer in his Real Presence. Another Sacrament figuring prominently in the transformation of anxiety, especially in converting sin-anxiety into *Angstlosigkeit*, is the Sacrament of Penance. This sacramental encounter brings the believer into immediate and concrete contact with the mercy and forgiveness of the Lord. The penitent is told by Christ himself, through the Petrine mission represented in the priest, that he is forgiven, that his sins are no more. The penitent, moreover, is also given grace to avoid those sins in the future. The anxiety of being alienated from God through sin, and the anxiety over divine judgement of sin, is washed away by Divine Mercy flowing upon the penitent in sacramental confession.

The power of the sacramental nature of the Church to transform anxiety into *Angstlosigkeit* is also found in the conferral of one's mission in the Church as in Holy Orders, Holy Matrimony, as well as the sacramental of religious profession. In these instances, the believer's mission is conferred by solemn rite in a visible and concrete manner involving both body and soul. The believer is aware not only of his own choice to embrace the mission, but the Church is also present choosing the candidate for such a mission. The mission, which transforms the anxiety of meaninglessness, is embraced by the person who is also reminded that he has the promised help of the Church. The Church is there not only as witness but as helper in her Marian principle to assist the believer in the fruitful living out of the mission. Finally, the anxiety of death can be transformed by the Sacrament of Anointing, especially when death is imminent. The believer's soul and body come into immediate and concrete contact with Jesus Christ who confers his grace through the sacramental signs. The seven Sacraments confer and the sacramental dispose to receive sacramental grace which brings the believer into vital contact in soul and body with Christ the Redeemer, and help deliver the believer both psychically and physiologically from anxiety.

Christian Freedom from Anxiety from the Marian Principle

The Marian principle as spiritual childhood

The Marian principle of the Church is characterized by feminine receptivity, which is an active receptivity, a constant disposability to the will of God. Another way to characterize the Marian principle for our author is spiritual childhood. Spiritual childhood is that ecclesial attitude of receptivity and vulnerability on the part of the believer. How does Balthasar characterize the spiritual childhood latent in the Marian principle?

Spiritual childhood is patterned on the Incarnate Son's attitude towards the Father.[59] Therefore, spiritual childhood is not infantilism but the fullness of Christian maturity. The first childlike attitude of Jesus, described by Balthasar, is his gazing upwards with wonder to the Father and recognizing that the Father is greater (Jn. 14.28). The Son is never threatened by the Father's greatness, nor does he try to compete or attain to it. Rather he knows himself to be total Gift from the Father as the only Begotten Son, and the One who has received all that the Father is in love. He opens himself to receive the full brunt of the Father's love and shares fully in the divine nature with the Father and the Holy Spirit. He is the eternal 'Thou' of the Son's 'I'. The believer is to adopt the same attitude which is not servile but filial. The Father is not someone to fear, as in Freud's theory, because the Father has given all not only to generate the Son but also to hand him over that we might be generated anew: 'the Father loves you himself' (Jn. 16.26).

Balthasar's view of the father stands in stark contrast to a view like Freud's. In Freud's theory, the child sees in the father a competitor for the mother's love. The child overcomes his wish to kill the father through his stronger fear that he will lose his father's love (or worse, that his father will castrate him), and his realization that his father is stronger than he. The Oedipus complex is overcome according to Freud only after a new equilibrium between anxieties is established. Anxiety from the unconscious wish to kill the father (which is repressed) and anxiety from the 'reality principle' which in this case shows the child that killing the father for the mother's exclusive love is neither possible nor really desirable. Anxiety, in any case, is not truly overcome. It becomes repressed in order for the child to function. The love that the child has for the father in Freud's view arises from the child's *servile* fear.

The Son's wonder of the Father is translated into his earthly existence 'beginning with the existence of his loving Mother, then passing on to his own existence, finally going from both to all the forms offered by the surrounding world, from the tiniest flower to the boundless skies'.[60] All his wonder as man is derived 'from the much deeper amazement of the eternal Child who, in the absolute Spirit of Love, marvels at Love itself as it permeates and transcends all that is'.[61] The possibility of recognizing that the Father-is-greater-than-I lies in every human experience. Every act of authentic love can move a person into childlike wonder. Imitation of the Incarnate Son's wonder is not an easy task for the believer since we are taught to master and to control rather than to

59. What follows is taken primarily from *Unless You Become like this Child*. Balthasar also explores this theme throughout his study on Bernanos, especially the section 'Childhood and Hope' (*B*, pp. 291–307; Eng., pp. 322–40), and in his essay 'Faith of the Simple Ones' (*SC*, pp. 51–75; Eng., pp. 57–83).

60. *WdK*, pp. 59–60; Eng., p. 46.

61. *WdK*, p. 60; Eng., p. 46.

wonder and to surrender. Moreover, the wonder present in our rational faculties creates anxiety.

The second attitude flowing from his wonder of the Father's love is the Son's receptivity and indifference to the Father's will even unto death on a Cross. Our author characterizes Jesus' suffering in Gethsemane as the suffering in spiritual childhood. He writes, Jesus 'suffers as the Son. In his own prayer, the child's word, "Abba!" ("Papa") is first heard on the Mount of Olives (Mk 14:36). Even though the Father can now no longer respond, still all Jesus' suffering – even the cry of abandonment on the Cross – is suffered in the spirit of childhood'.[62] Spiritual childhood is 'a repetition of the eternal Son's loving readiness to obey the "command" (*mandatum*) of the Father: we must persevere, together with Christ, in fleeing to the Father, in entrusting ourselves to the Father, in imploring and thanking the Father'.[63] Thus the believer strives in spiritual childhood to dispose himself to the Father's will. The disposability of spiritual childhood '*consists of being perfectly pliable in God's hands and permanently available to his good pleasure*'.[64] Yet the believer's pattern follows that of the Incarnate Son. Spiritual childhood also opens up the believer to receive the full brunt of the Father's love, especially when it entails a participation in the Son's Cross.

The third attitude of spiritual childhood is one of gratitude and thanksgiving. 'Thanksgiving, in Greek *eucharistia*', writes our author, 'is the quintessence of Jesus' stance toward the Father'.[65] Thanksgiving is the proper response to one who has received, one who is dependent. By a life of gratitude, the believer not only recognizes his status as creature but also as redeemed, and thus depends on the Lord for everything. Therefore, even as an adult, we never outgrow the need to be thankful to the Father for our life and salvation. Thanksgiving forms the basis for the Lord Jesus' prohibition against anxiety in the Sermon on the Mount. All has been received and will continue to be given; thus we can freely and joyfully give to others.

The Blessed Virgin Mary embodies the clearest and most perfect expression of the believer's spiritual childhood. She manifests wonder at the Father's love and is completely disposed to the divine will. Being preserved from original sin, she never outgrows her condition of spiritual childhood in her own human process of maturing. When St. Gabriel appears in the Annunciation, her response 'presupposes a pure childlike attitude that entrusts everything to the Father, even when he wills to interfere in her relationship with Joseph, to whom she is engaged'.[66] Her childlike attitude enables her mission to be fruitful. Her mission also takes her into the separation from her Son which participates in the 'distance' of the Father and Son in the Cross. Spiritual childhood is the gateway to holiness, according to Balthasar, and is the true fountain of youth. Balthasar refers to St. Thérèse of Lisieux, St. Joan of Arc as well as

62. *WdK*, p. 81; Eng., p. 61.
63. *WdK*, p. 52; Eng., pp. 40–1.
64. *B*, p. 287; Eng., p. 317 (Balthasar's italics).
65. *WdK*, pp. 62–3; Eng., p. 47.
66. *WdK*, p. 91; Eng., p. 69.

Bernanos' characters of Chantal, Donissan and the Curé of Ambricourt as examples of spiritual childhood.

The transformation of sin-anxiety and the anxiety from danger, helplessness and self-hatred

Spiritual childhood flows from the fiducial aspect of the act of faith and is nurtured by the Marian principle in the Church. The wonder, trust, indifference and thanksgiving that characterize spiritual childhood help to transform sin-anxiety as well as the anxiety of danger, helplessness and self-hatred. Through spiritual childhood, the believer grows in his unconditional trust of the Father that despite all the threats and dangers in the world, including suffering and death, the Father will provide. The dangerous world, which elicits feelings of helplessness, does not have to be feared since the Father will take care of the believer, and even suffering and death can be part of the Father's love and care leading the believer more deeply into the saving mystery of his Son's Cross.

The acceptance of the Father's love transforms the anxiety of self-hatred since the Father's love creates the new consciousness of the believer. This attitude in the believer helps him to let go of his self-hatred from falling into sin and failing at his mission, and instead to accept himself as little, weak and totally dependent on the Lord. Furthermore, the acceptance of the Father's love transforms the anxiety from one's self-identity that has been damaged by the failure of love in one's parents. Spiritual childhood cultivates self-forgetfulness and leaves the self in the hands of the Father as the self seeks to accept the Father's love and live out his mission. Self-hatred is transformed into the acceptance of God's view of the self in which he views the believer as imminently loveable, good and capable of all sorts of goodness with the help of divine grace.

The transformation of anxiety from discursive reason

The Marian principle of the Church also has a transformative effect on the anxiety produced by discursive reasoning. One of the dimensions of the transformative power that the exercise of faith, hope and love has upon anxiety, especially faith, is their effect on the exercise of reason, both in the intellect and the will. This dimension is not explicitly developed by Balthasar, yet a connection can be forged with his work on Bernanos. Ever since the Fall, reason's tendency has been to act in a cowardly manner, that is, to shrink away and withdraw from both Being and beings because of their abstract quality in the human mind.

First, spiritual childhood moves reason to relinquish its stance of adjudicating good and evil, the very stance which first created anxiety. It does this in two ways: by helping reason surrender itself and by helping it becomes more committed to the truth. Balthasar writes:

> Believing reason which is this writer's [Bernanos'] organ to attain to knowledge, is therefore characterized by two things: first, it is a wholesale casting of oneself into God . . . second, with regard to the world, it is a personal and solitary decisiveness and commitment. And the freedom of reason consists in the unity of these, its two aspects. Thinking is self-surrendering trust. Thinking is solitary decisiveness.[67]

It is by self-surrender and commitment that reason begins to regain the freedom it lost in the Fall. The Church is not only able to assist reason in this manner, but has a mission to assist reason since she is the one who bears the Incarnate Logos to the world. Balthasar writes, 'the Church must take upon herself the responsibility for freedom and also, inseparable from it, the responsibility for reason'.[68]

Faith helps to restore reason's receptivity to truth by self-surrender. One can only know by giving himself to the truth. Reason is helped in its self-surrender to God by being brought to the two weakest points in human life: 'poverty of childhood' and the 'denudation of the dying', birth and death.[69] These are the places where God's transcendence breaks forth most clearly in the human condition and shows the need for reason to surrender itself to something greater. Faith, moreover, keeps reason from attaining knowledge without love, the cold knowledge that is the source for the worst kind of evil in the world.

The self-surrender of Christian faith to God also helps restore courage to human reason. The virtue that most every writer from Aristotle to St. Thomas and even Luther agrees helps to overcome anxiety is courage. Faith is not only the assent to propositions, but the decision to stake one's life on the truths believed. It aids reason to commit itself to the truths it knows. Balthasar writes that 'Thinking authentically requires courage',[70] and 'Self surrender to God contains within itself the commitment to the truth at all costs'.[71] Christian faith gives reason its prophetic and Catholic character, which helps the thinking person move out of intellectual anxiety into intellectual *Angstlosigkeit*. Balthasar summarizes: 'to the openness of existence, to its adventure beyond death and the abyss, ending in life eternal, corresponds the prophetic character of reason, which has as both prerequisite and result the attributes of commitment, audacity, and freedom. The Church, moreover, is the place where reason attains its denudation, completeness, and catholicity'.[72] Through spiritual childhood, faith takes the anxious intellect and will and transforms them into courageously operating faculties in the human person. Commitment, like surrender, also comprises reason's freedom. Freedom is attained in 'the bold risk taken by thought, as the commitment of the person to the truth it has discerned, as that total personal stance that is the result of a certain worldview and makes reason clear-sighted'.[73] Constituting reasons'

67. *B*, p. 79; Eng., p. 91.
68. *B*, p. 94; Eng., p. 107.
69. *B*, p. 72; Eng., p. 83.
70. *B*, p. 83; Eng., p. 95.
71. *B*, p. 83; Eng., p. 95.
72. *B*, p. 106; Eng., p. 120.
73. *B*, p. 89; Eng., p. 102.

freedom is 'total trust in God', and 'is paid for in the world with the solitary commitment to God's unabridged truth'.[74] By surrendering to truth and being committed to truth, reason becomes courageous and free.

Balthasar observes, however, that such a transformation of reason by which it becomes courageous 'is not a virtue acquired once and for all that may be activated at will'.[75] This is a grace that is given moment by moment, in the same 'walking' in faith, hope and love as outlined in Chapter 8. Therefore, reason-being-transformed in this way means that on the existential level such a transformation can be accompanied by 'the sting of anguish and fear'.[76] Courage develops as a virtue by being practiced in difficult circumstances.

Faith and transformed reason begins the restoration of the childlike vision we lost in the Fall by filling the abstract quality of our knowing with surrendered, committed and concrete knowing in love. Faith directs reason's gaze away from the abstract to see the infinite God in the concrete face of Jesus of Nazareth. Balthasar suggests that the transformation of the anxiety in human reason occurs through 'childlike thinking': wonder and gratitude, courageous and secure since the child does not set himself up as the measure of truth. Childlike thinking allows God to ground one's reality. Thinking in this way is also thinking with Christian indifference, not the indifference stemming from abstraction, but from the active disposability of the will. Childlike thinking is our author's more complete response to Kierkegaard.

The transformation of anxiety about the future

Anxiety could not be transformed for Balthasar without reference to Christian hope. This fundamental attitude for our author figures importantly in the transformation of anxiety since it is a suffering in anticipation of a future suffering. How does Christian hope, operative in spiritual childhood, transform anxiety? Christian hope for our author is founded both upon God's saving deeds in history, ultimately in his Cross and Resurrection, and upon his utter faithfulness to his promises. Through his Resurrection, Jesus Christ brings his eschatological reality to the world's time.[77] He is the Lord of all time, past, present and future, and is present now in each moment of time. Balthasar writes, 'the *memoria* and the *spes*, are already embraced by the real presence of God in the Eucharist'.[78] Because the eschaton has already begun to be present in time, due to Christ's risen presence in his Church, 'all that remains for Christianity, therefore, is the *present*'.[79] The Christian does not immerse himself in a timeless realm through his hope. Rather in the grace of God present in each particular moment of time, and 'has the courage to affirm

74. *B*, pp. 89–90; Eng., p. 102.
75. *B*, p. 84; Eng., p. 96.
76. *B*, p. 84; Eng., p. 96.
77. Cf. *W*, pp. 160–1; Eng., p. 186.
78. *W*, p. 165; Eng., p. 191 (translator's italics of Balthasar's quotation marks).
79. *W*, p. 164; Eng., p. 190 (Balthasar's italics).

the present, because God has affirmed it, and imparted his grace and truth to it'.[80]

Christian hope flows from the Marian principle and thus also belongs to the constitution of spiritual childhood. A consequence of the wonder of spiritual childhood is its effect on the Christian's relationship to time. Our author writes, 'A child that knows God can find him at every moment because every moment opens up for him and shows him the very ground of time: as if it reposed on eternity itself. And this eternity, without undergoing change, walks hand in hand for the child with transitory time'.[81] Spiritual childhood is the attitude by which the Christian lives his hope. Childlike wonder and Christian hope bring one to live in the present moment and not the anxieties about the past or the future.[82] Since the Christian does not have to depend on his own resources to change his own life or the world around him, he does not have to get lost in the past or the future, but remain with his crucified and risen Lord who is present in the moment of *here* and *now*.[83] By immersion in the grace of the present, the child of the Father is grasped and possessed by divine grace. Balthasar states, 'It is not possession, but a being possessed, that lends wings to Christian hope'.[84] By appropriating this grace and cooperating with it, the Christian is opened up to an unimaginable future – the advent of Christ, the Incarnate Son coming towards his Bride in all the ardour of his love.

The Christian's hope gives him the power to engage the world and shape it according to God's salvific will. The Christian, according to Balthasar, is commanded in his mission to labour for the salvation of man and the world without trying to accomplish it himself or hasten its fulfilment, knowing that 'there will never be enough room for the Kingdom of God in the strained conditions of time'.[85] The manner in which the Christian gives shape to the world follows the pattern set by Christ's crucified love. Therefore, the Christian is also necessarily one who is handed over. The hope present in spiritual childhood is equally necessary so that the Christian can consent to such a *traditio*. The Christian shares in the way in which Christ wins victory over the world and evil: by a 'resoluteness in handing himself over to the clutches of evil persons, this ultimate courage to immerse love in hatred and to let it hold out therein until it outlasts hatred, this patience in allowing all opposition to exhaust and

80. *W*, p. 164; Eng., p. 190. Christian hope, therefore, does not have simply a future oriented perspective such as found in Hegel's theory, Marx's praxis, Jewish hope, or certain theologies of liberation.

81. *WdK*, p. 74; Eng., p. 55.

82. This relationship to the present underlies Jesus' prohibition to anxiety in his Sermon on the Mount. Thus the Christian can say with St. Paul, 'Not that I have already obtained this or am already perfect; but I press on to make it my own, because *Christ Jesus has made me his own*. Brethren, I do not consider that I have made it my own; but one thing I do, *forgetting what lies behind and straining forward to what lies ahead*, I press on toward the goal for the prize of the upward call of God in Christ Jesus' (Phil. 3.12–14) (author's italics).

83. Cf. *W*, pp. 162, 165; Eng., pp. 188–9, 192.

84. *W*, p. 165; Eng., p. 191.

85. *W*, p. 162; Eng., p. 188.

perish'.[86] The task appears impossible but Balthasar assures the Christian with an assurance flowing from the receptivity of spiritual childhood: 'The Lord gives the disciples a share in his own courage that lets him be handed over; more than this, he promises them – as the highest of all the promises for the earthly future – that they will be handed over in genuine reality in him and through him'.[87] The power of the Cross and Resurrection is in the present moment, and the Christian who shares in Christ's cross is at the height of action.[88]

The Christian's being handed over on behalf of the world exposes the other aspect present in Christian hope: that the present moment has not reached definitive fulfilment. 'Christian hope', writes Balthasar, 'springs from the fulfilment attained in Christ and is shot through with the painful lack of fulfilment in man and the world'.[89] The painful lack of fulfilment is manifested in St. Paul's words about being in anguish and the mystics' and martyrs' longing for death. Balthasar writes,

> Because we are redeemed beings in an eschatological sense – that is, already in the midst of time – for that very reason is it so unbearable for creation and God's children to have to sigh at possessing their redemption only in hope. But this unbearable sighing itself, which is continually bursting us open, is the pledge and guarantee of the Spirit.[90]

The very act of being handed over in fact testifies to the new age in Christ. He writes, the Christian's love 'poured out in every act of being handed over is already the new aeon in Christ'.[91]

The Christian attitude of hope lived in spiritual childhood transforms the anxiety about the future (and the past) since it keeps the believer in the present, time's root in eternity. All of the believer's time can be redeemed by Jesus the Lord of all time and history. The transformation of one's anxiety about the past or future seems, especially important in healing anxieties that come from abuse and traumatic events, which bring many to therapy. The one suffering, for example from sexual abuse or abortion, can be built up in Christian hope that Christ has already redeemed the horrible memories of the past which can now be recalled in the safety of the Lord's redemption. He has made every moment of time his, as well as provided for the future, for example in the case of abortion, that the child is not definitively lost.

Anxiety Transformed by the Petrine Principle

We have seen earlier how Christ personalizes a human being in the Church by conferring on him a mission. This personalization gives one a new 'I' that is

86. *SC*, p. 439; Eng., p. 497.
87. *SC*, p. 440; Eng., p. 498.
88. Cf. *W*, p. 163; Eng., p. 189.
89. *W*, p. 159; Eng., p. 176.
90. *B*, p. 73; Eng., p. 84.
91. *SC*, p. 447; Eng., p. 506.

wholly and intimately related to the Persons of the Trinity and the persons in the Church. Since this aspect of Balthasar's ecclesiology has already been explained, we proceed to a more specific examination of how Christian mission operates in the transformation of anxiety.[92] We place this examination under the Petrine principle since the conferral or confirmation of one's mission occurs through the Petrine principle. The Church is indispensable in the believer's mission, according to Balthasar, because the Church is the one who mediates the mission from the Trinity to the believer, and who mediates between the general call to holiness among the baptized and the particular call to a vocation within the Body of Christ. Because of the historical nature of God's election, his historical Church is the place wherein the individual believer finds his calling. The formal aspect of the believer's intensely personal call is predicated on Christ's Incarnation and the establishment of the Church. God always reveals himself to man in a concrete, chosen form. This mediation can range from actually calling an individual, as in the secular priesthood, to confirming a call communicated interiorly to him, as in the life of the evangelical counsels.[93]

The transformation of anxiety from ego-consciousness and meaninglessness into Christian freedom from anxiety by mission

Mission, according to Balthasar, answers the question, 'Who am I?', the question of personal identity and meaning. Consequently it helps to transform the anxiety stemming from ego-consciousness and the confusion, frustration or lack of meaning it brings to one's personal identity.[94] Original sin damaged the human stand in God. The original mission to cultivate the Garden was lost along with a commensurate loss of meaning. The loss of a proper stand in God through original sin is the ultimate source of all anxiety, and so its recovery is essential in order to arrive at freedom from anxiety. Christ's mission restores man's ability to stand in God. Through his redemption he gave us a new stand in God, a share in his own stand. Mission is a place in which the believer stands securely in the world in the Father's will. Original sin, conceived in

92. To examine how anxiety is transformed through Christian mission, we turn our attention to *Christlicher Stand*, our author's work on the Christian state of life. *Christlicher Stand*, I suggest, is the concrete application of the ideas expressed in volume three of the *Theodramatik* to the individual Christian. It is how his anthropology is inserted into his Christology. *Christlicher Stand* shows how the Christian is inserted concretely and ecclesially into Christ's mission via his own particular mission.

93. Cf. Balthasar's discussion of the Church's role in testing, confirming and calling: *CS*, pp. 360–6; Eng., pp. 440–8.

94. Tourenne suggests that the ecclesiological dimension of Balthasar's theology of anxiety is extended in *Der antirömische Affekt* and *Katholisch* (cf. Tourenne, 'Un théologien et son temps', p. 28; Eng., p. 27). However, since the theme of mission emerges so strongly in the transformation of anxiety in Balthasar's thought, the central importance of *Christlicher Stand* ought not to be overlooked.

terms of place, means to stand *outside* the Father's will, and opens up an *Angstkosmos* for the sinner.[95]

Christ, through his Church, confers a mission on the believer which gives him a concrete, secure place from which to stand in the world *inside* the Father's will. In mission, Christ incorporates the Christian into his mission. The mission that is given to the Christian encompasses and determines one's entire life, imbuing it with the deepest identity and meaning, a meaning conferred not by parents, society or anything else in the world, but by God himself concretized in his Church. Every Christian mission inserts the believer into the foundational 'state of Christ' (*Stand Christi*) through the initial act of justification (baptism).[96] This taking-a-stand-in-Christ at the beginning of justification is part of the transformation of human anxiety into Christian *Angstlosigkeit*. The question 'Who am I?', however, cannot be fully answered in the general vocation to holiness. Thus, one's general mission to holiness is further concretized and made permanent in a specific state of life: marriage, priesthood or some form of consecrated life either in the religious life or in the lay state.[97] This more specific divine call comes to the believer in his ego-consciousness. The believer's 'I' is addressed by the loving 'Thou' of the Father whose call comes through the Son in the Holy Spirit within the life of the Church. 'The call to a divine mission', writes Balthasar, 'is an act of the personal elective love of God, an act of unique and singular predilection that fits into no secular category'.[98] Christ summons a new 'I' from the believer in his mission. The believer's 'I' is expropriated and brought into the 'I' of Christ. This event does not destroy the believer's individuality, since this insertion is into the communion of love, but rather brings it to fulfilment.

The mission bestows upon the believer his deepest 'I' and binds him to God in a particular way. There is no more reason for him to be anxious about the meaning of his life. His life is Christ; his 'I' is now united to the 'I' of Christ. Mission rather than depth analysis is the solution that Balthasar offers Freud as the transformation of the anxiety from ego-consciousness. God, as man's absolute horizon, offers man his mission as the concrete form of his destiny. Mission is what gives the individual believer his concrete and ultimate measure by God. For this reason our author writes that mission is superior to 'psychology'. The meaning of one's life is not attained by means of depth analysis and psychotherapy, but by hearing, accepting and appropriating one's divinely conferred mission in the Church. The Christian's mission transforms the human anxiety of meaninglessness and insecurity into freedom from anxiety.

Christian mission helps to heal the anxiety from original sin for it is the recovery of Adam's and Eve's original mission to cultivate the Garden. But now that preternatural mission is taken up into Christ's supernatural mis-

95. Cf. *CA*, p. 21.
96. *CS*, p. 124; Eng., p. 158.
97. Cf. *CS*, p. 398; Eng., p. 486.
98. *CS*, p. 340; Eng., pp. 418–19.

sion of saving the world. Christian mission, because it addresses the question of identity and meaning, helps to accomplish the transformation of this anxiety into freedom from anxiety. Here in the post-lapsarian, post-redemption time, the conferral of a divinely sanctioned mission gives the believer access to that dimension of anxiety-free living that characterized man's life before the Fall.

The call to mission brings one into *Angstlosigkeit*, furthermore, because it is by accepting and living one's mission that he becomes a person in the deepest sense. Christic personalization by mission far surpasses any sort of role that can be assigned to one's 'I' by society, family or even one's own choice. The one in Christian mission stands on much more solid ground because it is given by God himself and thus not subject to the finitude and sin which marks the role-assignment of society, family or self. The self is not thrust back upon itself to figure out its meaning and purpose. A foreign role is not thrust upon him by an outside force that does not know him or know him completely. Rather Christian mission is given by the Creator and Redeemer who knows supremely the perfect mission for a given individual.

Christian mission, therefore, does not reduce the ego but rather expands it into the freedom and life of God. Mission confers an unsurpassed ego-strength since its source is not found in the self, of having explained the self in terms of the self, but rather by God. Through mission the human 'I' is transformed into the ecclesial 'I' of Christ and granted a share in his mission of redemption. Therefore, Christian mission gives the 'I' its inner coherence and strength. One's mission is a life lived in God and in personal relationship with him who gives the grace not to fail in the mission. Christian mission is our author's more complete response to Freud and psychiatry.

The process of anxiety transformation in the recognition and the acceptance-rejection of the call

The Christian's path to an awareness and either acceptance or rejection of his particular mission, however, can be fraught with anxiety. The process of discernment of one's particular vocation, the second movement in Christian mission, is a process whereby the anxiety from ego-consciousness is progressively purified into Christian *Angstlosigkeit.* Freedom from non-Christian anxiety is a consequence of appropriating one's mission, but arriving at the acceptance often involves struggle with non-Christian anxiety. Therefore, the process can involve contending currents of anxiety and freedom from anxiety. In other words, the discernment of one's particular mission is a concrete way of bringing faith, hope and love to bear on anxiety. *Agonia* understood in terms of struggle, or an athlete's exertion, is part of discovering and appropriating one's mission. Christ's agony in the Garden where his sweat 'became like great drops of blood' (Lk. 22.44), can characterize the Christian's embrace of his own particular mission. The importance of one's mission for finding his identity and meaning, combined with our author's view – based on the parable of the sower – that only one in four attain to their proper vocation, indicates that anxiety is present in the three different moments of the call: before the act, the moment of the act and after the act.[99]

God's particular call is free and unpredictable. 'There are no psychological tests', writes Balthasar, 'for predicting who will hear and follow the divine call',[100] and he offers the example of St. Peter. No one could have deduced from an analysis of his character that he would be called to be the rock of the Church. The believer cannot directly infer his particular mission from his natural ability or inclinations. Before the call, therefore, the believer must strive to be attentive, vigilant and indifferent (in the Ignatian sense) to the divine will.

Such indifference is paramount in the transformation of anxiety since such indifference relinquishes the stance of holding one's personal freedom distinct from God, which is the essence of original sin. Christian indifference, predicated on one's spiritual childhood, works against the void in the intellect and will that original sin ripped open. Balthasar writes, 'In the renunciation of every desire to realize the possibility of human freedom as an autonomous freedom independent of God and in the perfect binding of oneself, in obedience, to God's call, his grace and his mission, Ignatius sees man's highest opportunity of sharing the absolute freedom that is in God'.[101] Christian indifference and obedience allows man to live in the boundlessness of God's freedom, which in turn can give meaning to man's action that is unparalleled by anything in the world. Moreover mission functions in the life of the believer as the seeking of the Lord's will in the present moment. The void in the believer's mind left by original sin is progressively filled with the moment-by-moment presence of the Lord in the form of the Father's concrete will for the believer in that particular moment and place of his life. The moment-by-moment seeking of the Father's will in mission helps to bring the presence of God back into the void in the mind left by original sin. Ignatian indifference is the new 'walking in the garden in the cool of the day' (Gen. 3.8) for man and God.

Before the call, moreover, the believer must battle against the obstacles to living in vigilance, patience and indifference without doing anything that would preempt the Lord's freedom in calling. He must develop his spiritual attentiveness by sharpening his intellectual powers of perception and to prevent them from being blunted by, for example, lust.[102] 'Neglect of this requirement [of attentive indifference]', writes Balthasar, 'is a principal reason why so few of God's calls are heard and accepted today'.[103] In the time of preparation for the call, ample room exists for anxiety and its purification by faith, hope and love. Our author also leaves open the possibility for the believer to suffer in Christian anxiety during the time of seeking his vocation. He writes, 'perplexity [in discernment] can itself be a form of the Passion and

99. Cf. *CS*, pp. 381–2; Eng., pp. 466–7.
100. *CS*, p. 321; Eng., p. 396.
101. *CS*, p. 325; Eng., p. 400.
102. Cf. *CS*, p. 400; Eng., p. 488; *STh*. II–II, p. 46, 3, *c*.
103. *CS*, p. 398; Eng., p. 486.

night of agony into which Christ was led by sin and to which he voluntarily surrendered himself'.[104]

The vigilance and indifference during the time of preparation is absolutely necessary because, Balthasar argues, there comes a single moment of decision for or against the mission which determines the meaning or lack of meaning for his existence. Upon recognition of the call, one must respond. When one recognizes the call that God is offering to him, he either accepts or rejects it. No third way exists since the postponement of a decision is a form of rejection. The one who refuses at that moment loses the mission forever. The Christian's response to the call can involve anxiety due to the ecclesial mediation of the call either in calling or confirming. Perhaps the Church is calling a man for priesthood yet the man interiorly has not sensed a strong interior calling to the priesthood, or perhaps one interiorly senses a call for religious life yet the superior or bishop do not see it or confirm it. Anxiety producing struggle can ensue between the interior and exterior aspects of the vocation.

Anxiety can arise or be intensified when one begins to recognize one's particular mission if it runs against his natural talent, inclination or expectation. There can be a yawning chasm between one's nature and the mission to which he is called. God may reveal this to the awareness of the Christian intentionally in order to show him that grace alone can bridge the gap. The awareness of one's weakness, which creates the abyss between one's nature and mission, and unworthiness can intensify sin-anxiety. One may become anxious in the realization that the Lord is asking for a response that is intensely personal and totally self-giving. God's call asks for a response of total self-giving, a complete and unreserved Yes without the slightest condition. Balthasar does not hesitate to call Christian mission a kind of knighthood, suggesting all the courage that knighthood calls forth from an individual.

The act of choice itself, constituted by the convergence of divine and human choice, brings an end to some anxiety and leaves room for other forms. The moment brings an end to the anxiety of expectation, of ignorance of one's mission, of not having a purpose in life. Yet the call itself can bring a twinge of anxiety as the believer becomes aware of the proximity of God in the call, for although ecclesial mediation precedes and follows the act of choice, the moment of the choice itself, in Balthasar's view, is an unmediated relationship between God and the soul.[105] Additional anxiety can stem from awareness of the greatness of the mission and the weakness of the believer where the task always seems to overtax and exceed the ability and strength of the person. The moment of the call is the event in which the believer's seeking becomes a finding, which in turn initiates a new life of seeking in love. Finally anxiety can stem from the drama of the moment of decision: one's life will be forever altered because of this moment. Acceptance of the call will shape, even definitively stamp one's life forever; rejection of the call will definitively stamp one's

104. *CS*, p. 374; Eng., p. 458.
105. Cf. *CS*, p. 402; Eng., p. 491.

life in no less a manner. Balthasar writes, 'God does not hesitate to compress the whole meaning of the life of his elect into this single hour of choice'.[106] The moment of choice also requires renunciation, the renunciation of other choices and other possibilities, however, good. Arriving at the moment of choice may not be clearly perceptible to the believer. It may be a discernable moment or it may dawn on a person over time in a seamless flow of saying Yes to God in one's life. Christian anxiety remains a possibility in the call for all Christian vocations are a call to share concretely in the Lord's act of redemption. Balthasar writes, 'the call itself takes on the form of crossed beams. It becomes a call to the Cross and is itself a crucified and suffering call'.[107] In the paradox of the Cross, our author even allows room for the Lord to call his elect to a non-state. Balthasar explains:

> We must not conclude, from the broken and crucified form of a particular call, that it is not, from God's point of view, a true and unified call, for its unity is, in fact, actually achieved in and through the form of the Cross, acquiring thereby, in a way we cannot understand, a share in the integral wholeness of Christ's call as it exists in the Father. And if the course of one so called seems to lead through all the perils of this world to a 'place outside' every classical concept of a state of life; if such a one is compelled by circumstances and complexities beyond his control to take his stand where, to the human eye, there is no place to stand, then the Lord himself, who came to take his stand in that total 'outside' that is beyond all states, will understand this non-state, too, as true discipleship (Heb. 13:11–14).[108]

God in his call also calls the believer to courage and responsibility in making the choice. Balthasar writes, 'whoever shares, *by obedience to mission* in this truth and freedom of God *shares also in the choice*, the plans and the providence of God himself'.[109] Here is an unassailable unity of obedience and freedom. In the choice for one's mission, the believer is asked to identify his self with the mission, to become his mission. Our author locates the non-contradiction of obedience and freedom in the relationship between the Father and the Son where the complete mutuality of their exchange does not destroy the personal freedom of the Son.[110] Love guarantees the finite autonomy of the one chosen by God.

The recognition and acceptance of one's mission requires courage. In this way, we can observe a point of contact between our author and St. Thomas and the rest of that tradition which sees courage as the natural virtue which is perfected by overcoming fear. Mission is related to the courageous and committed reason above since it requires the Christian to make a definitive choice about his life, one that affects his identity and destiny. One's reason needs the transformation by the Marian principle to make its courageous stand, especially if the will of God calls him into a mission which does not

106. *CS*, p. 403; Eng., p. 492.
107. *CS*, p. 375; Eng., p. 459.
108. *CS*, p. 376; Eng., p. 460.
109. *CS*, p. 325; Eng., pp. 400–1 (Balthasar's italics).
110. Cf. *CS*, p. 326; Eng., p. 402.

seem to fit his natural ability. Courage is required to give an unqualified Yes to God in mission. It takes courage to live out one's divine vocation in a world that is hostile and in rebellion to God.

Yet when God calls, '*It is as if God himself assumed the responsibility for the one he has called*'.[111] This fact brings one into Christian *Angstlosigkeit*. No matter how taxing or incongruous the mission may seem to one's ability, God takes responsibility for the fruitfulness of the mission. One is guaranteed the fruitfulness of his mission even if he will never be able to see it in this life, or even if the mission demands that his own life be crushed in order for it to be accomplished. Since it is God who has planted the seed, it will bear the fruit he desires. Our author reasons,

> That night that is but the nadir of mission; that trembling 'no' that is but the other side of the fearless 'yes' that the God who calls has accepted and has in his safekeeping so that, in the breaking of the human vessel, no harm may befall the mission itself. Once the one called by God has uttered his elective 'yes' to the mission entrusted to him, he moves into a final state within that mission from which God will not allow him to fall – unless he himself chooses to do so.[112]

Thus one is brought into the realm of freedom from anxiety in the recognition and acceptance of his divinely conferred mission. Mission transforms his anxiety about identity and the meaning of his life into freedom from anxiety, also the path arriving to the moment of decision is one of struggle between anxiety and freedom from it, and even the possibility of suffering Christian redemptive anxiety. Now the believer's life possesses a specific, concrete shape. His future is now a future of living his mission in which he continues to walk further into the Trinitarian life. He no longer faces the confusion of what he is supposed to do with his life, or ask himself if it has meaning. If such questions arise, and anxiety follows, it is due to a weak faith that requires greater purification, perhaps the believer has been brought into Christian anxiety, or he may be suffering for one who has rejected his call.

If mission is Balthasar's response to psychiatry, then what about the believer's sexual drive, which figures so prominently in Freud's theories regarding anxiety? Every mission, Balthasar would argue, asks for a life of total self-giving. Self-giving love encompasses his eros and much more. The more he gives himself in love through his mission even unto death, the more any anxiety from his eros is relieved. Thus, we are back to Servais' critique of Freud's metapsychology: Freud does not see love and death in unity. The daily dying to self in one's mission is the path to greatest ego development, not in the diminishment of the 'I' but the expansion of the ecclesial 'I' in the life of God.

One may also wonder about the fragmentation of the states of life after the Fall. Does this mean that the separation of virginity and fecundity brings a continual anxiety into any of the missions? Does the lack of virginity in

111. *CS*, p. 330; Eng., p. 407 (Balthasar's italics).
112. *CS*, p. 331; Eng., p. 408.

marriage create anxiety? Does the lack of biological fecundity create anxiety in the celibate? Our author does not give a clear answer. However, I think a response can be made from Balthasar's understanding of the interpenetrating communion of missions in the Church. The states of life are not united in an individual believer, but they are in the Bride of Christ, personified in Mary. Therefore, any anxiety an individual believer may experience in his state of life can be relieved to the degree that his mission interpenetrates the other missions in the Church. In the communion of the Church, the states of life are brought back into unity.

The dramatic relationship between God and man in the Church also means that one may reject the mission God gives him. This rejection can be made in varying degrees of knowledge and freedom, and therefore, entail varying degrees of culpability. Balthasar distinguishes between a rejection of the call and the impossibility in following it, yet regardless of culpability both share certain similarities.[113] How does anxiety function in the one who either refuses or is unable to respond to his call?

At the lowest level of the failure to embrace one's mission, Balthasar identifies the category of Christians who do not respond to the Lord's choice through no fault of their own. It can be the case that following the call is not possible due to external reasons, such as the sinfulness and negligence, on the part of those charged with fostering vocations, rejection of the candidate on the part of ecclesial authority, family obligations or sickness. The obstacles can also be internal due to natural character flaws, instability or a lack of spiritual strength. The inability to respond to the call leaves room for both human and Christian anxiety. They may hear the call but know not how to interpret it. This may be partly due to the 'objective weakness' of the call,[114] that is, the Lord may call quietly at first. But if it is the Lord's call a quiet beginning will always lead to objective clarity. Balthasar allows room in addition for the awareness of a mission in the consciousness of the believer and the impossibility of following it, a kind of holy 'thorn in the flesh' which can serve a useful purpose in God's plan.[115] In this case, the anxiety he may experience from the frustration of living life outside of one's mission can be a fruitful Christian anxiety.

Actual rejection of the call, however, is different than being unable to respond. Rejection has its roots in a lack of Ignatian indifference, a lack of faith, and a habit of choosing the self over God. The more natural talent one possesses the greater the possibility of a rejection.[116] Balthasar warns, 'the

113. Cf. *CS*, p. 404; Eng., p. 493.

114. *CS*, p. 393; Eng., p. 480.

115. *CS*, p. 395; Eng., p. 482.

116. Our author describes such a situation: 'The more talent and intellectual ability he possesses, the more urgently these gifts demand their own natural development and, in doing so, hold out the false promise of a natural mission and foster in him a corresponding awareness of such a mission; the more distinction he enjoys by reason of his natural endowments, the greater will be his temptation to say "no" to God's call and the deeper will be the loss he incurs with the loss of his divine calling and mission' (*CS*, p. 405; Eng., p. 494).

magnitude of one's failure to respond will be in proportion to the greatness of the mission to which one is called'.[117] Since a mission is given within the communion of the Church, refusal of one's mission involves many more than the particular individual. Rejection of the mission results not only in an absence of meaning for that person's life, but perhaps outright spiritual harm to others.[118] Missions are unique and irreplaceable, like the persons to whom they are entrusted.

Another way of rejecting the call is through a lack of surrender of the 'I' to Christ out of anxiety. Afraid of the demands of the mission or of relinquishing his own idea of mission, the Christian withdraws into himself for the sake of self-preservation instead of casting oneself into God. He thinks that surrendering his personal identity to Christ will result in the loss of identity, and may 'take refuge in sickness or neurosis'.[119] This anxiety is similar to St. Thomas' servile fear in which one fears to offend because of just punishment. All such fears – celibacy, difficult mission, obedience, the call itself, living according to the unpredictable voice of God – may culminate in a withdrawal from God.

All these anxieties, observes Balthasar, are ultimately due to a lack of faith. They are not Christian but are natural and worldly and needing purification by faith, hope and love. What is needed to overcome such fears is spiritual childhood 'that casts itself into the arms of God and expects from him all its strength and help'.[120] Here is where the childlike nature of Christian faith is so important. Spiritual childhood develops the habit of self-surrender in trusting faith; it spurs growth in Christian indifference. Spiritual childhood maintains the vitality of faith, keeping it a living faith.

The rejection of the call need not be made in full awareness. In the current climate of religious indifference and lukewarm Christian living, one may reject his call in a kind of half-awareness. The rejection of one's mission can incur sin (and sin-anxiety) or it may not. Regardless of one's culpability, such a person lives in anxiety due to the lack of meaning in his life from his missed mission. For the one whose rejection is only semi-conscious or unconscious and thus without guilt, his life feels forever unfulfilled. 'He remains a stranger among men', writes Balthasar, 'and feels himself such'.[121]

Finally there is the Christian who rejects his call in full consciousness, and consequences are drastic. Those who reject the call in full consciousness do not simply feel unfulfilled, but feel on fire because they know and sense the loss of their true life and must endure in a vain and sterile existence. In order to cope with the anxiety from such a lifelong position, Balthasar states that

117. *CS*, p. 408; Eng., p. 497.

118. Our author writes, 'many who will now remain forever in their sins might have been drawn to confession; many who will now be left in ignorance might have accepted the word of God; many who will now be forever cold might have been inflamed by the fire of faith, hope and charity. As it is, a part of God's field will be forever uncultivated' (*CS*, p. 408; Eng., pp. 497–8).

119. *CS*, p. 406; Eng., p. 495.

120. *CS*, p. 406; Eng., p. 496.

121. *CS*, p. 410; Eng., p. 500.

they can become 'convinced Stoics' or 'hardened cynics', and through the cracks of this façade 'one can see their burning and despairing spirit'.[122] The situation of the one who consciously rejects the call is extremely dangerous because their No often takes the same proportions as their Yes would have taken. Instead of surrendering the ego to Christ, their lives are characterized by an ego-centeredness. In a perversion of personhood, they substitute their ego for their mission and try to expand the ego by feeding it rather than casting it into the life of God. They attempt to collect disciples and manifest a 'compulsive desire for frequent association with what they have rejected'.[123] It is all an attempt to construct a meaning, in a type of anxiety avoidant behaviour, to replace the meaning that was offered, rejected and lost.

However, the fact that such individuals are 'condemned to burn' does not necessarily entail their doom since the Lord always offers the grace of salvation. Their tragic destiny rather is earthbound; they missed their mission on earth. They are still invited to accept the fire that burns within as purification and place it at the disposal of God's will. Our author also identifies within this category those who accept their call, live it for a while and then fall away either through negligence or a lack of courage to make a total surrender to the mission. Instead of burning they are constituted by 'a withering of the spirit'.[124] Their No to mission remains an emptiness in their soul, 'and leads them to many a guilty action that would otherwise have been left undone'.[125] Regardless of one's culpability, the rejection of one's mission makes it such that the believer will live out his earthly life with a permanent human anxiety which is not Christian anxiety, and also may not be able to be brought fully into Christian *Angstlosigkeit*. Certainly God always gives the grace for salvation, yet for the one who misses his vocation, the meaning of his life will remains elusive and frustrating.

What sort of remedy might exist for the anxiety of one who rejects his mission? Balthasar does not go much further about what is possible for such people. He indicates that they may live with an enduring non-Christian anxiety in this life. Perhaps we can speculate that the one repenting from rejecting his mission may be brought into some sort of spiritual fruitfulness even if it is not the same fruit that would have been borne in his mission or to the same degree. Balthasar alludes to such a remedy in his concluding lines of *Christlicher Stand*: the one with care for souls 'must [. . .] see that they are "gathered up" (cf. Jn 15:6) not into a community based on their "no", but into a communion of repentance for sin that, despite everything and in a way we cannot understand, will be able to become, by the power of God's grace, the beginning of a new fruitfulness'.[126]

The dramatic manner in which our author describes the rejection of the mission must be coupled with his insistence on the responsibility that the

122. *CS*, p. 410; Eng., p. 501.
123. *CS*, p. 411; Eng., p. 501.
124. *CS*, p. 412; Eng., p. 503.
125. *CS*, p. 412; Eng., p. 503.
126. *CS*, p. 413; Eng., p. 504.

Church's has in helping believers discover and accept their call. If many today are unaware of their mission, or who lack sufficient indifference to know and accept it, then perhaps it is due to the lack of attention among members of the Church, especially those holding office, in giving adequate direction to her members, especially in spiritual direction and discernment.

The role of the Petrine principle in Christian anxiety

The Petrine principle of the Church in particular can be a cause of Christian anxiety in one's mission and can give a Christian mission an intense and particularly tragic quality. He writes, 'the hierarchical office always produces anxiety, openly or secretly, in the fragile human being'.[127] Balthasar understands this anxiety-producing effect of the Church's office in its very nature as love, but also in the failures of love in those who hold office in the Church. The clearest example in Balthasar's work of the anxiety caused by the sinfulness of those in ecclesial office is St. Joan of Arc. It seemed that part of her mission in the Church was to suffer at the hands of those in the Church. Sinful members bearing office in the Church defy the divinely conferred vocation and in doing so actually help to accomplish the special mission. Her martyrdom is an example of the Church as *meretrix* accomplishing the divine plan of salvation. Suffering at the hands of those holding office in the Church is a particularly intense form, perhaps the most intense form, of Christian anxiety. St. Joan of Arc is told that her mission is actually not an ecclesial mission that it does not come from God but in fact from the devil. It appears to her that she has failed in her mission, and that she is the worst kind of outcast, no longer wanted by anyone including the Church.

Balthasar expresses his own experience of mission in the Church the year after the publication of *Humani generis*, 'To be a Christian in the Church requires courage'.[128] Such a statement, when one considers the difficulties he was experiencing during that part of his life, for example, the silencing of de Lubac and his decision to leave the Jesuits, contains its own drama and anguish. Tourenne writes that this statement expresses not bitterness but his great love for the Church. He, though no St. Joan of Arc, also suffered at the hands of those representing the Church.

Anxiety Transformed by the Johannine Principle

Christian freedom from anxiety from the evangelical counsels

The Johannine principle also plays a part in bringing the believer out of anxiety and into freedom from anxiety. It is the Johannine principle, in

127. *SC*, p. 442; Eng., p. 500.
128. *CA*, p. 94; Eng., p. 153.

Balthasar's ecclesiology, which links the Marian and Petrine principles and is where he locates the life of the evangelical counsels. One may wonder if, among the states of life in the Church, the state of the evangelical counsels would be the state of life most conducive in bringing the believer into Christian *Angstlosigkeit* in Balthasar's view. The evangelical counsels were present in man's anxiety-free original state. Christ's own life is constituted by the evangelical counsels, and the evangelical counsels are present in man's anxiety-free final state. All the missions of the Church, moreover, eschatologically converge upon the evangelical counsels. The life of the evangelical counsels in the fallen state would be thus the closet participation, at least objectively, of the original state, Christ's state and the final state of man. The close link between the evangelical counsels and anxiety-free living suggests that a life of the evangelical counsels in the fallen state more easily leads one into *Angstlosigkeit* and Christian anxiety. Perhaps this close link is derived from the fact that the evangelical counsels are particularly adept at disposing the believer to true Christian indifference.

Christian freedom from anxiety transformed into salvific anxiety

It is in the Johannine principle of the Church where it seems the transition from Christian *Angstlosigkeit* to Christian anxiety occurs most often. The Marian and Petrine principles have an important role to play through spiritual childhood and the conferral of mission, respectively. But it is in the mission of St. John who personifies the mission of the mystics where we find most often the 'eclipse' of faith, hope and love in the believer's mystical participation in the *Kreuzangst* of the Redeemer. It is here that the believer with his redeemed anxiety can be led into the new salvific anxiety. The examples that Balthasar uses to illustrate Christian anxiety are primarily women living the evangelical counsels: St. Thérèse, Madame De Croissy, and even Adrienne von Speyr. Our author writes that the Little Flower 'loses the feeling and triumphant sense of faith but never faith itself'.[129] This eclipse which is part of the dark night of the spirit, transforms the anxiety of abandonment by experiencing it in the Cross whereby the believer vicariously suffers on behalf of anxious sinners.

The Johannine principle plays an important role in configuring the experience of the Christian to the experience of Christ; the Christian's anxiety becomes progressively a participation in Christ's anxiety. Our author observes in the development of Chantal's character that as she is brought further into Christian anxiety she 'sees and experiences her own anguish from the standpoint of God's'.[130] Balthasar observes that this special form of anxiety 'has overcome the watershed between the anguish of man as sinner as the anguish of God on the Cross'.[131] Her experience becomes more and more conformed by, and expressive of, the experience of the Incarnate Son. Such souls

129. *SwG*, p. 329; Eng., p. 341.
130. *B*, p. 437; Eng., p. 489.
131. *B*, p. 437; Eng., p. 489.

participate in Jesus' agony in Gethsemane and share in his work of the redemption of anxiety. Our author reflects on the movement to Christian anxiety of the one holding office in the Church:

> The hierarchical office in the Church has in it something awesome for its bearer; it is an abyss in him, not only of a supernatural mystery, but of being disposed of and sacrificed, an undertow, a logic that presses on toward the Cross, 'where you do not wish to go'. This anxiety in the presence of the Cross can be overcome only when it is purified and transformed into an anxiety that makes for the Cross and is lived in the Cross. 'Do you wish to flee from it? Flee to it' (Augustine).[132]

Christian anxiety can be a part of any mission in the Church since every mission is a share in the mission of the Cross. It is also possible that one's mission may wholly constituted by Christian anxiety. The call to holiness, the general call of all believers, 'is a call in grace to share in the distribution of grace and, therefore, a call to a vicarious bearing of the guilt of all'.[133] One's mission is ecclesial. It is a participation in her mission and it is given for the good of all. The mission of St. Thérèse at the end of her life and that of Adrienne von Speyr are the clearest examples in Balthasar's work of a vocation to Christian anxiety. In fact, our author writes that the Lord's suffering on the Mount of Olives is pre-eminently St. Thérèse's mystery.[134]

Christian Freedom from Anxiety from the Communio *of the Church*

Finally, anxiety is transformed into Christian *Angstlosigkeit* by the communion of the Church. One is personalized in the Church and inserted as a person into the intimate relationship with the triune God and all those who are in the Church. The interpenetration of missions within the Church, the Church's true catholic solidarity, breaks the anxiety of isolation. The believer is no longer ever alone since he is bound in the communion of saints. In this communion, each member bears the weight of another. Moreover, since every mission is ecclesial, another member is in a position to suffer vicariously for another. Solidarity and spiritual friendship in the Church transform the anxiety of feeling alone in the world. Our author intimates the transforming power of *communio* in his meditation on the fourth station of the Cross. Jesus as the new Adam is accompanied by Mary the new Eve under the Cross, the Tree of Life. Jesus draws her in to share in the suffering and actually assist him to redeem. Every ecclesial mission assists the others.

132. *SC*, p. 442; Eng., p. 500–1.
133. *CS*, p. 339; Eng., p. 417.
134. Cf. *SwG*, p. 344; Eng., p. 356.

Part Four Conclusion

The trajectory of Christian anxiety has an ecclesial shape in Balthasar's work. The Church provides necessary means to bring the believer out of anxiety into freedom from anxiety and can lead him into Christian anxiety. These means include the Sacraments, spiritual childhood, and especially mission and do indeed transform the believer's anxiety. Through the powerful transformation that anxiety undergoes by the Church, our author's presentation perhaps offers an explanation as to why psychiatrists observe that Christians tend to do better in dealing with anxiety.[1] Yet the trajectory does not end with the believer holding onto these handrails. Christian anxiety always maintains its trajectorial shape. Thus the trajectory continues in the believer's further leap in self-surrender *through* the handrails into the depths of Trinitarian life. The Church's means are not to be left behind, just as one does not leave behind Jesus' humanity to encounter his divinity. Viewing the Church as 'a religion of anxiety', and to view the handrails as immature way of relieving anxiety, comes from not understanding and using the handrails properly. Examples of the transformation of anxiety in the Church that are found in Balthasar's writings are St. Thérèse, Bernanos and Blanche de la Force whose natural anxiety is transformed into Christian anxiety, and in St. Thérèse, Madame de Croissy, and Adrienne von Speyr who seem to have had little natural anxiety but were called into a mission of Christian anxiety in the latter part of their lives.

1. Cf. Vitz's comment in Chapter 4.

Final Conclusion

A Vision of the Whole

In this study, we have attempted a systematic presentation, analysis and development of Hans Urs von Balthasar's theology of anxiety, based upon his noted work *Der Christ und die Angst* and read within the context of his entire theology. Although his short book is neither an exhaustive study nor central to the structure of his theology, it demonstrates a central feature of his thought: the fragment discloses the whole. His initial theology of anxiety leads right to the centre of his thought and opens up horizons of insight into both his theology and the thought systems of his interlocutors relating them all to the figure of Jesus Christ. This study attempted to develop this initial theology of anxiety along the lines indicated in the Introduction, namely, to provide a more detailed picture of his grasp of the phenomenon, to develop the conversation between Balthasar's theology of anxiety with psychiatry, to develop Balthasar's initial theology of anxiety within the wider context of the whole of his theology and in comparison with St. Thomas, and to construct in an initial way the ecclesial dimension of his theology of anxiety based upon his ecclesiology.

In order to obtain these objectives we adopted a thematic methodology, consonant with Balthasar's own methodology in *Der Christ und die Angst*, which placed our author in critical discussion with some of the major protagonists on the theme of anxiety.[1] A synthetic overview of this study on Balthasar's theology of anxiety is now offered followed by the final conclusions of the study. The study will close with a reflection on the relevance of Balthasar's theology of anxiety to the anxiety of contemporary man described in the Introduction.

The phenomenon of anxiety

The first part of the study delineated a more comprehensive phenomenology of anxiety than was given in Balthasar's initial theology of anxiety so that his

1. At the conclusion of this study, one cannot but notice the paucity of biblical material. Some indications for this scarcity were given in the Introduction, yet it certainly merits further study, especially since Holy Scripture figures so prominently in Balthasar's theology.

interpretation could connect more deeply with the philosophical and psychiatric approaches to anxiety. Our author offers a phenomenology that includes physiological, cognitive and behavioural symptoms, with heaviest emphasis falling upon the cognitive symptoms. His grasp of the phenomenon of anxiety is not immediately evident in *Der Christ und die Angst*, but is found primarily in the writings surrounding this work. The phenomenon of anxiety, according to Balthasar, is universal to the human condition, and that phenomenologically speaking no difference can be detected within the experience of the phenomenon save one: the growing spiritual joy that is found in the anxiety of the saints, even if that joy is obscured in their self-awareness.

In our author's description of Christ's own anxiety, gleaned from the Gospel accounts, he focuses on the fear and terror which give Jesus the experience of isolation from his disciples and from the Father. Jesus' anxiety, which encompasses the human anxiety described in Chapter 1, reaches intense proportions in his realization of standing on the brink of his hour, of drinking from the cup of divine wrath and of receiving his baptism all the way to experiencing vicariously the *timor gehennalis*. Jesus' anxiety culminates with his cry of abandonment on the Cross. Balthasar's description of Jesus' anxiety again emphasizes the cognitive symptoms. Jesus' anxiety is the deepest and most unique because it far surpasses any level of anxiety in the human realm by virtue of his being the Incarnate Son, totally innocent and most intimate with the Father. His vicariously suffered anxiety not only appropriates all human anxiety, but also reveals Triune love expressed in an analogous way as God's 'anxiety' for the world.

The origins of anxiety

The interpretation of anxiety, which constituted the rest of the study, first placed our author in critical discussion with Kierkegaard and Freud on anxiety's origins. Balthasar's response to Kierkegaard, and philosophers in general, is that anxiety may be fundamental to the human mind, but it is not original to it. Taking into account Adam's original state and the effects of original sin help to clarify Kierkegaard's position about the way in which the ontological difference registers as anxiety in the human mind. Kierkegaard's concept of anxiety does not attain to the theological level because of his lack of access to Adam's original state. Without recourse to a theological analysis which allows access to the original state, man's finitude and sin become conflated. Yet the Danish philosopher's profound ability to grope down to the origin of anxiety in discursive reasoning brings his position to the threshold of revelation, and therefore can be illuminated by divine revelation.

Freud's theory of anxiety brought the anthropological discussion to consider the anxiety produced by ego-consciousness. Our author takes Freud's theory to its underlying anthropological presuppositions. He agrees with Freud on the importance of the relationship between mother and child, the relationship between the 'I' and its role as well as its relationship to the horizon of meaning and to the future. Nevertheless, he criticizes Freud's construal of the mother–child relationship, the mythic foundation of his metapsychology, and therefore Freud's position that anxiety originates in ego-consciousness. Instead Balthasar proposes a relational anthropology, which can be supported by more recent discoveries in psychiatry and neuroscience, to undergird any psychological theory regarding anxiety. Anxiety in ego-consciousness is not produced by the structure of the mother–child relationship itself, but arises from the failure to love.

Notwithstanding Kierkegaard's and Freud's achievements in interpreting anxiety, our author finds both approaches inadequate for interpreting anxiety at the anthropological level, and seeks to orient each approach towards the theological level. These two writers fall short in explaining the deepest origin of anxiety because of the limitations of their interpretive tools. The critical discussion with philosophy and psychiatry demonstrate the necessity for both of those sciences to engage the science of theology in the search for an adequate interpretation of anxiety's origins. Balthasar argues that anxiety ultimately originates neither in discursive reasoning nor in ego-consciousness but in original sin from which springs the anxiety in discursive reasoning and ego-consciousness. In other words, anxiety is not rooted in God's creative action but in man's destructive choice for sin in the Garden of Eden. Only with an adequately theological perspective are we able to distinguish between creatureliness and sin in evaluating the origins of human anxiety.

The redemption of anxiety

We continued Balthasar's theological analysis of anxiety in his investigation of anxiety's redemption by Christ by comparing it with another Catholic theology of anxiety, namely, that of Aquinas. In Chapter 6, the Angelic doctor's theory on human *timor*, how it operates within the totality of human nature, its intrinsic connection to the moral life, and how it is redeemed by Christ, was presented in his own words with the help of scholars specialized in this area of St. Thomas' thought. The Divine Son, according to Aquinas, assumed a perfect human nature in his Incarnation with certain defects which allow him to suffer as man, including *timor*. St. Thomas understands Christ's human perfection in terms of *knowledge* which is expressed in his full, uninterrupted beatific vision throughout his earthly life. This concept of human perfection excludes from Jesus any anxiety from ignorance, sin, concupiscence or disordered passions. St. Thomas holds, furthermore, that the *timor* experienced by Christ is perfect filial fear and a pro-passion of his human soul. God incarnate suffered *timor* in his human nature as part of his Passion in making satisfaction for man's sins. It is a limited suffering circumscribed by his uninterrupted beatific vision. Aquinas' view of Christ's constitution excludes the possibility of his suffering the *timor gehennalis* which, in his view, would compromise his sinless human nature. The Angelic doctor's position, moreover, has found expression in certain statements from the ordinary Magisterium.

It is a challenge, however, to reconcile in St. Thomas' position on our Lord's full and uninterrupted beatific vision during his earthly life with the biblical evidence of his intense affective suffering in Gethsemane and on the Cross and with the fact that his suffering was done *pro nobis*. Scholars of St. Thomas are not univocal about the traditional scholastic teaching of Christ's earthly beatific vision, and indicate the possibility for various interpretations of such a vision without compromising defined magisterial teaching. It does seem possible to admit in Aquinas' position an existential 'stretching' of Christ's experience of fear based upon his hylomorphic understanding of Christ's affectivity, a more nuanced understanding of the object of Christ's fear, and his attribution of *compassio* to Christ's suffering. This existential 'stretching' of Christ's ability to fear in St. Thomas is suggested by Torrell, Gondreau, Loughlin and John Paul II.

Balthasar's interpretation of Christ's anxiety begins with his investigation of Sacred Scripture's assessment of human anxiety, in its various dimensions (natural, sinful and righteous) and its intensification, up until the coming of Christ. Balthasar offers an original interpretation of Christ's anxiety based upon his concepts of *Hinterlegung, Selbstbewußtsein, Stellvertretung* and his view of the divine nature as kenotic love. Although several points of agreement can be found between St. Thomas and Balthasar on the redemption of anxiety such as the fact of Christ's perfect human nature, the exclusion of certain types of anxiety, his perfect filial fear, the unparalleled uniqueness of his *timor-Angst*, and the coincidence of anxiety and joy, our author is dissatisfied with St. Thomas' position on the redemption of anxiety. The reasons for his dissatisfaction lie in its lack of resonance with the experience of the mystics, especially that of Adrienne von Speyr, and its lack of adequately accounting for the biblical data and the *pro nobis* of the Creed.

Our author maintains that the Incarnate Son took on a perfect human nature as formulated at Constantinople III, yet understands this perfection in terms of *obedience* more than knowledge, his emphasis falling more on the Good than the True. Shaping his interpretation on the mystical experience of Adrienne von Speyr and taking inspiration from St. Bonaventure (which connects most with the *compassio* aspect of St. Thomas' position), Balthasar holds that Jesus vicariously appropriated human anxiety to its ultimate extreme in the *timor gehennalis* by virtue of his kenotic, compassionate love. The divine nature understood as self-giving love allows for the modification of a full and uninterrupted beatific vision in Jesus during his earthly life, and thus a greater ability to appropriate and vicariously suffer anxiety.

Balthasar's carefully nuanced position on the beatific vision and the 'faith' of Christ, in which he seeks to lessen the tension between faith and vision, places greater emphasis on the fiduciary aspect of faith and hope which form part of Christ's earthly life and which perdure in the life of Heaven. Our author's interpretation of anxiety's redemption, while not following St. Thomas exactly, nevertheless adheres to Catholic dogmatic boundaries. The Angelic doctor's acknowledgement of the suspension between the higher and lower parts of his human soul in Christ's suffering marks a point of contact between the two positions. Balthasar, however, wants to expand such a notion dramatically through the Son's ability to lay aside his divine prerogatives in order not to threaten Christ's divinity and the hypostatic union, but in fact to *demonstrate* his divinity. Balthasar's interpretation of anxiety's redemption, with its emphasis of Love in terms of the Good, carries great apologetical weight in the post-modern age. His position allows for a much greater appropriation of anxiety by Christ, and is able to connect suffering and joy more intimately than St. Thomas' position. Some unanswered questions and difficulties nevertheless remain in his interpretation.

Human anxiety, in Balthasar's theology of anxiety, is vicariously appropriated and redeemed through Jesus' suffering in Gethsemane and on the Cross. Jesus' anxiety, via analogy, reveals Trinitarian love as divine concern for the fallen world. The Lord Jesus in his anxiety in Gethsemane and on the Cross, and here is where the originality of Balthasar's theology shines, actually *changes* the objective structure of anxiety so that it no longer retains its objective structure as a constriction. Rather this new, redeemed and *salvific* anxiety is objectively constituted as a dilation of human nature in love, even though the subjective experience may continue to feel constrictive. Because of its new objective structure as love, this new anxiety in Christ is intrinsically linked to spiritual joy. Finally the redemption of anxiety in Balthasar's theology brings to man the possibility both of being free from anxiety as well as of possibly being led to participate in salvific anxiety in which one suffers anxiety vicariously in union with Christ for others. Human anxiety inserted into Christ's becomes redeemed, and from there some believers may be led into salvific anxiety.

The transformation of anxiety

The final part of the study investigated such an insertion of human anxiety (the phenomenological and anthropological dimension) into Christ's redeemed and salvific anxiety (the theological dimension). The nature and shape of anxiety in the life of the Christian, that is, how the redemption of anxiety by Christ affects the life of the Christian, placed our author in critical discussion with Luther. The shape of Christian anxiety, Luther argues, is essentially dialectical based upon his doctrine of *simul iustus et peccator*. Balthasar affirms certain aspects of Luther's interpretation of Christian anxiety, properly understood, such as the intent to deliver man from sin-anxiety and the existential unity of faith and anxiety in the fiduciary aspect of the act of faith. Our author, however, rejects the objective shape of Luther's interpretation of Christian anxiety because of its roots in Luther's distorted doctrine of justification, specifically in its eschatological and participatory dimensions, and argues that Christian anxiety is far more unique than Luther grants. Balthasar maintains that Christ's redeemed anxiety can free the Christian from anxiety, and bring the Christian into a true participation in his anxiety whereby it becomes salvific.

Instead of a dialectic shape, Balthasar proposes a trajectorial shape to Christian anxiety, in which the believer firmly walks *away* from natural and sin-anxiety and *into* the divine life on the pathway of faith, hope and love according to Balthasar's 'three laws'. As the Christian walks away from sin-anxiety and further into the divine life, he is able to participate in Christ's own salvific anxiety in union with him and in solidarity with sinners. In other words, the Christian united to Christ can suffer anxiety vicariously for sinners, as in the case of St. Thérèse and Adrienne von Speyr. Moreover, it is also possible for the believer to participate in God's 'anxiety' for the salvation of the world as is apparent, for example, in the life of St. Paul (2 Cor. 11.28),[2] Bernanos and Schneider (cf. Chapter 1). Through Balthasar's concept of experience, Christ progressively impresses the form of his experience onto that of the Christian. Christian anxiety transforms human anxiety, and through grace imbues this new anxiety with joy, indifference and patience. On the existential level, it can be very difficult for the believer to distinguish between natural or sin-anxiety needing purification by faith, hope and love and one's sharing in Christ's anxiety, since the joy of Christian anxiety may be hidden from the believer's self-awareness. A proper discernment of spirits is needed to distinguish non-Christian anxiety from Christian anxiety since the subjective experience can appear so similar. Balthasar indicated in *Der Christ und die Angst* that a further development was needed in the ecclesial dimension of his theology of anxiety to show the ecclesial shape of the trajectory of Christian anxiety.

By employing the primary principles of Balthasar's ecclesiology, we attempted a development of the ecclesial dimension of Balthasar's theology of anxiety in Chapter 9. The Incarnational and Sacramental nature of the Church brings the Lord to incredibly intimate proximity. The Sacraments address the physiological dimension of anxiety in a particular way. The emphasis of this dimension of the Church falls on freeing the believer from natural and sin-anxiety. The Marian principle of the Church, understood in terms of spiritual childhood, also contributes to bringing the believer out of natural and sin-anxiety. Spiritual childhood, in Balthasar's view, frees the believer from the natural anxiety of living in a threatening world and its consequent feelings of helplessness. Spiritual childhood also frees the believer from sin-anxiety and the feelings of self-hatred and discouragement that come from living in a fallen nature. The active appropriation of the Father's love by the believer creates the new 'I' of the believer, allowing him to surrender the self-hatred from falling into sin or failing at his mission, and instead to accept himself as little, weak and totally dependent on the Lord, which is far from any Pelagian tendency.

The Marian principle of the Church at work in the believer also helps to free the human mind from the anxiety produced by discursive reasoning through Balthasar's notion of courageous reason. Spiritual childhood moves human reason to relinquish its stance of adjudicating between good and evil, to surrender itself to God and to increase its commitment to the truth. In this way, Balthasar offers a more complete response to Kierkegaard's concept of anxiety. The Marian principle also transforms the believer's anxiety about the

2. Cf. *SV*, p. 177; Eng., p. 168.

future by grounding the believer in the present moment through his hope. The more the Christian walks in the present moment, the more attune he is to eternity, and the more the future takes the beautiful shape of the advent of Christ in the second coming. One need not fear the great and terrible Day of the Lord.

Human anxiety is also transformed by the Petrine principle of the Church particularly in its role in conferring or confirming divine missions. This principle of the Church works to free one from the anxiety produced by ego-consciousness and meaninglessness. Divine mission gives unparalleled meaning to the 'I', and gives one a new stand in God which was lost in the Fall. Far from restricting the ego, Christian mission personalizes and expands the ego into the freedom and life of God himself. Balthasar holds that the process of recognizing and either accepting or rejecting one's mission can be a struggle between anxiety and freedom from anxiety. The one who gives his Yes to the mission is brought into Christian *Angstlosigkeit* which then opens up the possibility for Christian anxiety within his particular mission. Rejection of one's mission can entail a permanent type of anxiety in one's life. The Petrine principle also has a role to play in transforming Christian *Angstlosigkeit* into Christian anxiety when sinful members holding office oppose a divinely conferred mission, as in the case of St. Joan of Arc. Perhaps the greatest Christian anxiety is to suffer at the hands of those holding office in the Church. Mission is Balthasar's more complete response to psychiatry in general and Freud in particular.

The Johannine principle of Balthasar's ecclesiology emphasizes the transformation of anxiety into freedom from anxiety through the life of the evangelical counsels. It is from this principle also that the believer is brought from Christian *Angstlosigkeit* into salvific anxiety. In this principle we find the Christian anxiety of the mystics, in the dark night of the spirit, and even a vocation to Christian anxiety.

Finally the trajectory of Christian anxiety is shaped by Balthasar's understanding of the communion of the Church in which all the missions interpenetrate. Through one's incorporation into the Church and receiving a mission, he is personalized which brings him in communion with the Divine Persons of the Trinity, the communion of angels and saints, as well as all the other members of the Church. This truly catholic solidarity breaks the anxiety from isolation. Moreover, the *communio* of the Church permits the vicarious suffering of anxiety on behalf of others.

The Church, in Balthasar's view, provides necessary means to bring the believer out of natural anxiety and sin-anxiety into *Angstlosigkeit* and then to lead him into Christian salvific anxiety. All of these principles of the Church which transform human anxiety into *Angstlosikeit* and Christian anxiety, in Balthasar's view, entail the courageous casting of oneself into the divine life, not withdrawing into oneself.

Final Conclusions

This study sought to develop Balthasar's initial theology in *Der Christ und die Angst* in five ways. The following are the conclusions regarding these five lines of development in the order in which they were treated in the thesis.

An adequate phenomenology

Our author's primary intention in *Der Christ und die Angst* was to offer his interpretation of anxiety, and gave little attention to the phenomenon itself, presuming his reader was already familiar with it. This left Balthasar's theology of anxiety open to the charge that he really did not understand the phenomenon which could hinder his theology of anxiety from connecting with the psychological, philosophical and literary treatments of anxiety. Having read his theology of anxiety in light of the rest of his work, we found a more detailed presentation of the phenomenon of anxiety. It is evident that Balthasar's phenomenology of anxiety adequately expresses the 'descriptive psychopathology' offered by contemporary psychiatry. The relevant passages of our author's writings when pulled together present a phenomenology that includes physiological, cognitive and behavioural symptoms, with heaviest emphasis falling upon the cognitive symptoms.

A deepened engagement with psychiatry

A second line of development was sought in a deepened engagement of Balthasar's theology of anxiety to psychiatry. Balthasar's emphasis in his initial theology of anxiety fell more on the philosophical than the psychiatric side of anxiety's interpretation. Given the fact that most of the writing on anxiety in recent decades has been primarily done by those in the psychological sciences, both Balthasar's theology of anxiety and these other sciences can benefit from a deepened conversation. The chapter on Freud in this study developed this connection with psychiatry in a way that was not apparent in *Der Christ und die Angst*.

The negative tone Balthasar sometimes uses when referring to the psychological sciences in his writing could hinder his theology of anxiety from reaching the minds and hearts of psychiatrists, psychoanalysts and psychologists. However, these statements of Balthasar must be read in light of the significant and positive influence that the psychoanalyst R. Allers had on Balthasar's thinking, and also in light of the historical context in which he wrote in which these sciences tended to be hostile to Christian faith. Balthasar's negative tone regarding the psychological sciences must be seen not as concerning the sciences in themselves but more as a reaction to a certain approach within those sciences, that is, any approach which claims to possess the full measure of man and marginalizes the contribution of theology.

Balthasar, in his evaluation of Freud's theory of anxiety, reminds these sciences that anxiety cannot be properly treated without recourse to the full measure of man, that is, God's measure. To make the same point in St. Thomas' terms, anxiety cannot be treated adequately without recourse to morality, metaphysics and the ultimate aim and purpose of human life. Psychiatry aims to help people live in reality, and reality ultimately is that which is established by God. Although theology is not the proper object of psychiatry, psychiatry can benefit from the expertise of theology to understand reality as God made it, and consequently to be able to identify the counter-reality that evil continually seeks to bring about in the world. The theological analysis offers these sciences the tools to more accurately measure evil and sanctity. This point in no way implies that theology is served as a replacement of these sciences. It does imply, however, that the psychological sciences will be more effective in the treatment of anxiety when they are in dialogue with the science of faith and recognize the competence of the theological analysis of anxiety. Every psychological theory and therapy implies a certain view of the human person. Balthasar's theology of anxiety draws attention to the underlying anthropology of a given theory, and helps to evaluate it according the divine measure of the human person. Furthermore, theology can help psychiatry attune itself to the reality of sin-anxiety and its remedy.

Theology, for its part, can benefit greatly from the conversation with psychiatry, especially in maintaining a close connection to the phenomenon, and the intrinsic interaction of the physiological, cognitive and behavioural dimensions. This enrichment was seen in how the psychiatric description helped to identify Balthasar's phenomenology of anxiety. Psychiatry, moreover, can also aid theology in addressing the anxiety of the Christian who strives to live the Christian life yet cannot seem to enter the *Angstlosigkeit* about which Balthasar speaks. It is conceivable that even with one who is strong in faith, hope and love, who is close to the Sacraments and who is living his mission, may have a physiological reason for his anxiety that may require pharmacological intervention. A person may not have a physiological deficiency but perhaps suffers from past trauma or deficiencies in love in their foundational relationships. The person's healing may be greatly aided psychotherapy in addition to living more deeply into the life of the Church. Such situations do not lie outside of Balthasar's theology of anxiety, yet it is not immediately evident how his theology addresses such situations.

On the other hand, it may not occur to the psychiatrist that casting a patient forth into the life of the Blessed Trinity, through the handrails that the Church offers, is what is needed to address anxiety. Sacramental confession, a discernment of spirits and perhaps even an exorcism can accomplish what medication and therapeutic sessions could not. Moreover, theology may be able to aid psychiatry in its decisions surrounding the use of medications in treating anxiety. It is conceivable that one's anxiety may stem from personal sin or from not knowing or not living his mission. In such a case, medication may dull a necessary anxiety, and prevent the individual from seeking forgiveness or pursuing the discernment of his mission.

Philosophy too can aid Balthasar's theology of anxiety in giving an account of the role of the natural virtues in the treatment and transformation of anxiety. Balthasar's theology of anxiety, neither in its initial form nor when read in light of the whole of his theology, treats in depth this important area of anxiety transformation.

Balthasar's theology of anxiety in light of the whole of his theology

Balthasar authored most of his other works, including his trilogy, after *Der Christ und die Angst*. His initial theology of anxiety in its anthropological, Christological, soteriological, Trinitarian and ecclesial dimensions achieved greater clarity and depth from the reflection in these later works.

His theological anthropology helped to explain anxiety's origins in original sin, and how original sin altered the anxiety-free original state of Adam and Eve. The volumes of his trilogy, and especially those of his *Theodramatik*, help to clarify how anxiety is appropriated and redeemed by Christ, especially his concepts of *Hinterlegung, Selbstbewußtsein, Stellvertretung* and the divine nature understood as kenotic love. The reflection on Jesus' *Selbtsbewußtsein* and the concept of *Hinterlegung* helped to understand the type of anxiety Jesus could have, and how his terrestrial beatific vision could be modified from the scholastic view. The concept of *Stellvertretung* helped to explain how Jesus could vicariously suffer anxiety all the way to the *timor gehennalis* while simultaneously, and analogously, manifesting God as Absolute Love.

Moreover, his discussion with Luther reveals a strong disagreement about how the Christian's anxiety can be transformed by Christ's. Spiritual childhood, which Balthasar's theology of anxiety offers to the Christian, stands opposed both to Luther's position and to Pelagianism. Finally, without recourse to Balthasar's subsequent ecclesiology we would not be able to attempt a construction of the ecclesial dimension of his theology of anxiety.

Balthasar's theology of anxiety in light of Aquinas

As mentioned in the Introduction, our author's theology of anxiety did not explicitly engage other theologies of anxiety within Catholic theology. He addressed the psycho-philosophical concerns of his time, yet a lack of engagement with other theologies of anxiety within the Catholic theological tradition left certain aspects of his theology of anxiety unclarified as to its significance in the Catholic theological tradition.

The critical discussion with St. Thomas brought greater clarity to aspects of Balthasar's theology of anxiety. The originality of Balthasar's theology of anxiety lies in the radical way he permits the Incarnate Son to vicariously suffer anxiety unto the *timor gehennalis*, in his ability to unite anxiety and joy, in showing how Christ changed the objective structure of anxiety, and how the Christian is brought into *Angstlosigkeit* and can participate in Christ's anxiety. In imitation of Christ's *compassio*, the Christian's participation in Christ's anxiety makes his anxiety also salvific. Balthasar's theology of anxiety is able to unite more closely anxiety and joy, and to show more clearly how human anxiety can become salvific in Christ than St. Thomas' position.

Balthasar's position on the redemption of anxiety, derived from his nuanced view of the Christ's beatific vision during his earthly life in which faith and vision are not opposed, is tenable within the Catholic tradition. Our author preserves the intimacy of the Son with the Father, that they are never objectively separated, and that the historical Jesus is aware of his personal identity as the Divine Son and possesses his mission consciousness as directed by the Holy Spirit which maintains the unity of the natures in the Divine Person. Through his nuanced position on Christ's beatific vision and the principles of *Hinterlegung, Stellvertretung* and mission consciousness, our author charts a theological path that permits a greater experience of suffering for the Incarnate Son and therefore account for the demands of the biblical data and the *pro nobis* of the Creed. Balthasar's soteriology, deliberately cast in dramatic categories, is so shaped by his initial point of departure, the Good, that it inevitably led him to form a position that did not follow St. Thomas exactly. Christ's perfection, both human and divine, is seen more in terms of the Good than the True.

Most of the critical observations on Balthasar's theology of anxiety come from the conversation with the Angelic doctor, and specifically on the question of Jesus' beatific vision. Balthasar could be more precise in his language. Our author's poetic style and use of paradoxical language, surrounded by quotations, risks overwhelming theological precision at times. The conversation with St. Thomas also revealed that Balthasar is not clear about how Christ's anxiety stands in relationship to the natural virtues. Although Balthasar treats Christ's 'faith' and 'hope', we do not find a developed consideration of the natural virtues such as courage and fortitude. Is there a place in Christ's human nature, in Balthasar's view, for the natural virtues which help to shape anxiety? Perhaps on this point Balthasar's Christological emphasis on the *Person* of the Son has the unfortunate consequence of overlooking a more complete account of the specific properties of his perfect human *nature*. The same critical observation can be made regarding the ecclesial transformation of human anxiety in an individual. What is the role of courage and fortitude in the transformation of anxiety within the Christian life? Regarding anxiety and the natural virtues, St. Thomas' theology of anxiety is more comprehensive. The point of this comparison, however, is not to overcome the differences of interpretation, but to show how each are rooted in the tradition and how they may approach each other.

Finally, Balthasar appeals to God's unfathomable freedom and the experience of the saints to ground his position. By taking a position on the logic of divine love that transcends the grasp of the human intellect, Balthasar's position elicits the question, does love trump reason? At least from the point of view of our theme, we may conclude that a loveless reason is the ultimate cause of the world's anxious mess.

The ecclesial dimension of Balthasar's theology of anxiety

Although Balthasar did not develop the ecclesial dimension of his theology of anxiety, we were able to apply the major aspects of his ecclesiology to the theme in order to show how the Christian's anxiety is transformed in the Church. Each of the major principles of the Church in Balthasar's ecclesiology plays an important role in bringing the believer out of natural and sin-anxiety, into freedom from anxiety, and then into Christian anxiety – all according to Balthasar's three laws. Perhaps the strongest elements to emerge in this reflection are Balthasar's insights into spiritual childhood, manifested in the Marian principle, on mission, manifested in the Petrine principle, and the vicarious suffering of anxiety for others, manifested in the Johannine principle. All human anxiety is supposed to become *redeemed* in Christ, and then some in the Body of Christ are called to enter into the new *salvific* anxiety. Balthasar's ecclesiology suggests that the organs of the Church are essential in the transformation of human anxiety. Through this ecclesial transformation, the Christian's experience of anxiety is progressively conformed to Christ's experience of anxiety whereby the believer can begin to suffer anxiety vicariously for others.

Moreover, the ecclesial reflection gives further support to Balthasar's position that the objective movement of Christian anxiety is opposite to that of non-Christian anxiety. It involves expansion and dilation, not constriction and withdrawal. Thus, the ecclesial transformation of anxiety suggested by Balthasar's theology gives a more complete response to Nietzsche and Freud in the claim that Christianity is a religion of anxiety or that religious ritual is simply a time honoured practice of behavioural avoidance in order to relieve anxiety. The trajectory of Christian anxiety does not end with the believer holding onto these handrails. Christian anxiety always maintains its trajectorial shape and thus always requires courage. Thus the trajectory continues in the believer's further leap in self-surrender *through* the handrails into the depths of the life of the Blessed Trinity.

Balthasar's Theology of Anxiety and our Contemporaries

This study would not adequately respect Balthasar's fundamental intention in *Der Christ und die Angst* if an explicit connection with our contemporaries was not made. The final chapter of the study investigated the ways in which human anxiety was transformed in the Church. But what does the salvific anxiety purported by Balthasar mean to contemporary man in his anxious condition who may not be living in the Church, or who is living in the Church but not experiencing the transformation described in the final chapter?

In this study, we came across figures who exemplify certain types of struggles with anxiety. First are individuals like St. Thérèse and the character of Blanche de la Force who seemed to have had naturally anxious dispositions, and who struggled to overcome them. A second group is represented by someone like Georges Bernanos whose anxiety seemed to be an indistinguishable mixture of natural and supernatural anxiety. Finally there is the group of individuals like Madame de Croissy and Adrienne von Speyr who did not have anxious dispositions but who suffered intense anxiety in the latter part of their lives on behalf of others. Balthasar's theology of anxiety manifests the solidarity that Christ and Christians have with those who suffer anxiety. The purpose of freeing the believer from his natural and sin-anxiety is to lead him not *away* from those who suffer anxiety but rather *into* a vicarious participation in Christ's anxiety for them. Now no one is alone in his anxiety. Christ in his Mystical Body and Bride is ever present to those who struggle with anxiety, suffering with and for them.

Secondly, no matter what a person's anxiety may entail, it can be transformed in Christ, become redeemed and the person may be led into salvific anxiety. St. Therese is healed of her naturally anxious disposition and then is led at the very end of her life into a deep salvific anxiety to suffer for atheists. The transformation of Blanche de la Force's naturally anxious disposition at the end of her life occurs through others suffering anxiety on her behalf. Despite her '*angst*-ridden existence', she is able finally to ascend the scaffold to the guillotine singing the *Te Deum* free from anxiety because of the anxiety others suffered for her.[3] Georges Bernanos' anxiety is taken up and transformed into his mission as a Christian writer. It serves as an instrument of divine purpose. Adrienne von Speyr and the character of Madame de Croissy, though they were not susceptible to anxiety, nevertheless do not remain aloof from the problem. Instead, they are led by Jesus into his vicarious suffering of anxiety in love for others. Because of Jesus' vicarious suffering of all anxiety, no anxiety need be outside his redemption. The only type of anxiety that is not transformable is the sin-anxiety of one who refuses to repent. As long as he does not repent, such a person is doomed to an anxious existence, confined within the *Angstkosmos* of evil, and to suffer the anxiety that evil brings in and of itself. Moreover, God's merciful anger at his scorned love disturbs the unrepentant sinner making him more anxious so that he will repent.

Balthasar's theology of anxiety expresses perhaps more greatly than any other theology of anxiety that God indeed cares about this suffering and has done something about it. He took it all upon himself and suffered it to the end. One's life in Christ can go to great lengths in transforming anxiety by life in the Church, even to the point at suffering at the hands of those who hold office in her. One's experience of anxiety can become an image of Christ's archetypical experience of anxiety. Balthasar's theology of anxiety, especially in his concept of experience, shows in a deep way the necessarily experiential dimension of dogma and dogma's relevance to human experience. Christian revelation and faith are not abstract but intimately involved in the existential reality of the human condition.

Balthasar's theology of anxiety teaches forcefully that the one who is anxious is not to withdraw from the void in the mind, from relationships in the

3. Cf. *TDIII*, pp. 393–4; Eng., pp. 421–2. Those ones who suffered anxiety on her behalf were Madame Croissy, Marie de l'Incarnation, Lidoine and Sister Constance.

world or from the darkness of faith, but to cast oneself forward courageously as an *anima ecclesiastica* in faith, hope and love, in indifference, joy and patience, with all the trusting vulnerability of spiritual childhood, with a courageous reason, and with all the ferocity of Christian mission even in the blackest spiritual darkness. The Blessed Trinity and the communion of saints are there. Through the transformation of human anxiety in Jesus Christ, one can join him in the Garden of Gethsemane and participate in his undoing the disobedience in Eden, whereby one's anxiety can become truly salvific for the world sharing in the labour pains of Holy Mother Church (Rev. 12.2) in bringing the new creation to birth.

Bibliography

Works of Hans Urs von Balthasar[1]

Au cœur du mystèré rédempteur (repr. 2, Magny-les-Hameaux: Socéval, 2005).
Der antirömische Affekt: Wie läßt sich das Papsttum in der Gesamtkirche integrieren? (repr. 2, Einsiedeln–Trier: Johannes Verlag, 1989); *The Office of Peter in the Structure of the Church* (trans. A. Emery; San Francisco: Ignatius Press, 1989).
Das Betrachtende Gebet (repr. 5, Einsiedeln: Johannes Verlag, 2003); *Prayer* (trans. G. Harrison; San Francisco: Ignatius Press, 1986).
Christlicher Stand (Einsiedeln: Johannes Verlag, 1977); *The Christian State of Life* (trans. M.F. McCarthy; San Francisco: Ignatius Press, 1983).
Der Christ und die Angst (Einsiedeln–Trier: Johannes Verlag, 1951); *The Christian and Anxiety* (trans. D. Martin and M.J. Miller; San Francisco: Ignatius, 2000).
'Crucifixus etiam pro nobis', *Internationale katholische Zeitschrift Communio* 9 (1980), pp. 26–35.
Erster Blick auf Adrienne von Speyr (Einsiedeln: Johannes Verlag, 1968); *First Glance at Adrienne von Speyr* (trans. A. Lawry and S. Englund, OCD; San Francisco: Ignatius Press, 1981).
Gelebte Kirche: Bernanos (repr. 3, Einsiedeln–Trier: Johannes Verlag, 1988); *Bernanos: An Ecclesial Existence* (trans. E. Leiva-Merikakis; San Francisco: Communio Books/Ignatius Press, 1996).
Gottbereites Leben: Der Laie und der Rätestand: Nachfolge Christi in der heutigen Welt (repr. 2, Einsiedeln–Freiburg: Johannes Verlag, 1993); *The Laity in the Life of the Counsels: The Church's Mission in the World* (trans. B. McNeil, CRV with D.C. Schindler; San Francisco: Ignatius Press, 2003).
Die Grossen Ordensregeln (repr. 3, Einsiedeln: Johannes Verlag, 1974); *La Vocazione Cristiana: Un percorso attraverso la Regola di san Basilio* (trans. L. Cremaschi; Milano: Jaca, 2003).
Herrlichkeit: Eine theologische Ästhetik, vol. I: *Schau der Gestalt* (Einsiedeln: Johannes Verlag, 1961); *The Glory of the Lord: A Theological Aesthetics*, vol. I: *Seeing the Form* (trans. E. Leiva-Merikakis; San Francisco: Ignatius Press, 1982).
Herrlichkeit: Eine theologische Ästhetik, vol. III/2/1: *Alter Bund* (repr. 2, Einsiedeln: Johannes Verlag, 1989); *The Glory of the Lord: A Theological Aesthetics*, vol. VI: *The Old Covenant* (trans. B. McNeil, CRV and E. Leiva-Merikakis; San Francisco: Ignatius Press, 1991).
Herrlichkeit: Eine theologische Ästhetik, vol. III/2/2: *Neuer Bund* (repr. 2, Einsiedeln: Johannes Verlag, 1988); *The Glory of the Lord: A Theological Aesthetics*, vol. VII: *The New Covenant* (trans. B. McNeil, CRV; San Francisco: Ignatius Press, 1989).
Das Herz der Welt (repr. 4, Ostfildern: Schwabenverlag AG, 1988); *The Heart of the World* (trans. E. Leiva-Merikakis; San Francisco: Ignatius Press, 1983).

1. The following are only the works used for this study. For a complete bibliography on the work of Balthasar: C. Capol and C. Müller, *Hans Urs von Balthasar: Bibliographie: 1925–2005* (Einsiedeln-Freiburg: Johannes Verlag, 2005).

'Ist der Gekreuzigte "selig"?', *Internationale katholische Zeitschrift Communio* 16 (1987), pp. 107–9.

Karl Barth: Darstellung und Deutung seiner Theologie (repr. 4, Einsiedeln: Johannes Verlag, 1976); *The Theology of Karl Barth: exposition and interpretation* (trans. E.T. Oakes, SJ; San Francisco: Communio Books/Ignatius Press, 1992).

Katholisch (Einsiedeln: Johannes Verlag, 1975); *In the Fullness of Faith: On the Centrality of the Distinctively Catholic* (trans. G. Harrison; San Francisco: Ignatius Press, 1988).

—— and J. Ratzinger, *Maria – Kirche im Ursprung* (Freiburg: Johannes Verlag, 1997); *Mary: The Church at the Source* (trans. A.J. Walker; San Francisco: Ignatius Press, 2005).

Klarstellungen (repr. 4, Freiburg: Verlag Herder KG, 1978); *Elucidations* (trans. J. Riches; San Francisco: Ignatius Press, 1998).

Kosmische Liturgie: Das Weltbild Maximus' des Bekenners (repr. 3, Einsiedeln–Trier: Johannes Verlag, 1988); *Cosmic Liturgy: The Universe According to Maximus the Confessor* (trans. B.E. Daley, SJ; San Francisco: Communio Books/Ignatius Press, 2003).

Kreuzweg der St.-Hedwigs-Kathedrale in Berlin (Mainz: Matthias Grünewald Verlag, 1964); *The Way of the Cross* (trans. A. Albrecht and M. Sullivan; New York: Herder, 1969).

Nochmals: Reinhold Schneider (Einsiedeln–Freiburg: Johannes Verlag, 1990); *Tragedy Under Grace: Reinhold Schneider and the Experience of the West* (trans. B. McNeil, CRV; San Francisco: Ignatius Press, 1997).

'On the Concept of Person', trans. P. Verhalen OCist, *Communio: International Catholic Review* 13 (1986), pp. 18–26.

'On the Tasks of Catholic Philosophy in Our Time', trans. B. McNeil CRV, *Communio: International Catholic Review* 20 (1993), pp. 147–87.

Pneuma und Institution: Skizzen zur Theologie, vol. IV (Einsiedeln: Johannes Verlag, 1974); *Explorations in Theology*, vol. IV: *Pneuma and Institution* (trans. E.T. Oakes, SJ; San Francisco: Ignatius, 1995).

Prüfet alles das Gutet behaltet (Ostfildern: Schwabenverlag AG, 1986); *Test Everything: Hold Fast to What is Good* (an interview with Hans Urs von Balthasar, by Angelo Scola) (trans. M. Shrady; San Francisco: Ignatius Press, 1989).

Schwestern im Geist (repr. 3, Einsiedeln: Johannes Verlag, 1978); *Two Sisters in the Spirit* (trans. D. Martin; San Francisco: Ignatius Press, 1992).

'Das Selbstbewußtsein Jesus', *Internationale katholische Zeitschrift Communio* 8 (1979), pp. 30–9.

Spiritus Creator: Skizzen zur Theologie, vol. III (Einsiedeln: Johannes Verlag, 1967); *Explorations in Theology*, vol. III: *Creator Spirit* (trans. B. McNeil, CRV; San Francisco: Ignatius Press, 1993).

Sponsa Verbi: Skizzen zur Theologie, vol. II (Einsiedeln: Johannes Verlag, 1961); *Explorations in Theology*, vol. II: *Spouse of the Word* (trans. A.V. Littledale and A. Dru; San Francisco: Ignatius Press, 1991).

Theodramatik, vol. I: *Prolegomena* (Einsiedeln: Johannes Verlag, 1973); *Theodrama: Theological Dramatic Theory*, vol. I: *Prolegomena* (trans. G. Harrison; San Francisco: Ignatius Press, 1988).

Theodramatik, vol. II/1: *Die Personen des Spiels: Der Mensch in Gott* (Einsiedeln: Johannes Verlag, 1976); *Theodrama: Theological Dramatic Theory*, vol. II: *Dramatis Personae: Man in God* (trans. G. Harrison; San Francisco: Ignatius, 1990).

Theodramatik, vol. II/2: *Die Personen des Spiels: Die Personen in Christus* (repr. 2, Einsiedeln: Johannes Verlag, 1998); *Theodrama: Theological Dramatic Theory*, vol. III: *Dramatis Personae: Persons in Christ* (trans. G. Harrison; San Francisco: Ignatius Press, 1992).

Theodramatik, vol. III: *Die Handlung* (Einsiedeln: Johannes Verlag, 1980); *Theodrama: Theological Dramatic Theory*, vol. IV: *The Action* (trans. G. Harrison; San Francisco: Ignatius Press, 1994).

Theodramatik, vol. IV: *Das Endspiel* (Einsiedeln: Johannes Verlag, 1983), *Theodrama: Theological Dramatic Theory*, vol. V: *The Last Act* (trans. G. Harrison; San Francisco: Ignatius Press, 1998).

Theologie der drei Tage (repr. 3, Einsiedeln–Freiburg: Johannes Verlag, 1990); *Mysterium Paschale* (trans. A. Nichols; Edinburgh: T&TClark, 1990).

Theologie der Geschichte (repr. 4, Einsiedeln: Johannes Verlag, 1959); *A Theology of History* (trans. not given; San Francisco: Communio Books/Ignatius Press, 1994).

Theologik, vol. II: *Wahrheit Gottes* (Einsiedeln: Johannes Verlag, 1985); *Theologic*, vol. II: *Truth of God* (trans. A.J. Walker; San Francisco: Ignatius Press, 2004).

Unser Auftrag: Bericht und Entwurf: Einführung in die von Adrienne von Speyr gegründete Gemeinschaft (repr. 2, Einsiedeln: Johannes Verlag, 2004); *Our Task: a report and a plan* (trans. J. Saward; San Francisco: Ignatius Press, 1994).

Die Wahrheit ist symphonisch: Aspekte des christlichen Pluralismus (Einsiedeln: Johannes Verlag, 1972); *Truth is Symphonic: Aspects of Christian Pluralism* (trans. G. Harrison; San Francisco: Ignatius Press, 1987).

Wenn ihr nicht werdet wie dieses Kind (repr. 2, Einsiedeln–Freiburg: Johannes Verlag, 1998); *Unless you become like this Child* (trans. E. Leiva-Merikakis; San Francisco: Ignatius Press, 1991).

Zu Seinem Werk (repr. 2, Einsiedeln–Freiburg: Johannes Verlag, 2000); *My Work in Retrospect* (trans. C. Capol; San Francisco: Ignatius Press, 1993).

Works on Hans Urs von Balthasar[2]

Ackermann, S., 'The Church as Person in the Theology of Hans Urs von Balthasar', *Communio: International Catholic Review* 29 (trans. E. Rielley, 2002), pp. 238–49.

Becker, W.M., *The Historical Jesus in the Face of his Death: His Comprehension of its Salvific Meaning in the Writings of Edward Schillebeeckx and Hans Urs von Balthasar (internal, historical and systematic perspectives)* (Roma: self-published, 1994).

Bonnici, J., *Person to Person: Friendship and Love in the Life and Theology of Hans Urs von Balthasar* (New York: Alba House, 1999).

Buckley, J.T., 'Balthasar's use of the Theology of Aquinas', *The Thomist* 59 (1995), pp. 517–45.

Chapp, L., 'Who is the Church? The Personalistic Categories of Balthasar's Ecclesiology', *Communio: International Catholic Review* 23 (1996), pp. 322–38.

Daley, B.E., 'Translator's Forward', in H.U. von Balthasar, *Cosmic Liturgy: The Universe According to Maximus the Confessor* (San Francisco: Ignatius Press, 2003), pp. 11–21.

Dalzell, T., 'Balthasar's Theological Aesthetics and Lacanian Psychoanalysis', *Irish Theological Quarterly* 69 (2004), pp. 3–16.

Guerriero, E., *Hans Urs von Balthasar* (Novocento teologo, 18; Brescia: Morcelliana, 2006).

Henrici, P., 'Hans Urs von Balthasar: A Sketch of his Life', in D.L. Schindler (ed.), *Hans Urs von Balthasar: His Life and Work* (San Francisco: Communio Books/Ignatius Press, 1991), pp. 7–43.

——, 'Hans Urs von Balthasar – ein katholischer Kierkegaard?', in P. Reifenberg and A. van Hooff (eds), *Gott für die Welt: Henri de Lubac, Gustav Siewerth und Hans Urs von Balthasar in ihren Grundanliegen* (Festschrift W. Seidel; Mainz: Matthias Grünewald Verlag, 2001), pp. 304–14.

Howsare, R., *Hans Urs von Balthasar and Protestantism: The Ecumenical Implications of His Theological Style* (London: T&T Clark, 2005).

Leahy, B., *The Marian Principle in the Church according to Hans Urs von Balthasar* (European University Studies, 558; Frankfurt: Peter Lang, 1996).

2. The following are the works used in this study. A detailed and up to date secondary bibliography on Balthasar is maintained at http://www.johannes-verlag.de.

——, *The Marian Profile in the Ecclesiology of Hans Urs von Balthasar* (New York: New City Press, 2000).

Marchesi, G., *La Cristologia Trinitaria di Hans Urs von Balthasar: Gesù Cristo pienezza della rivelazione e della salvezza* (Biblioteca di Teologia contemporanea, 94; Brecia: Queriniana, 2003).

Martinelli, P., *Il mistero della morte in Hans Urs von Balthasar: Il mistero pasquale come rivelazione dell'amore trinitario di Dio* (Milano: Jaca, 1996).

Meiattini, G., 'Esperienza ed esperienza mistica nel pensiero di Hans Urs von Balthasar', *Rivista Teologica di Lugano* 4 (2001), pp. 9–31.

——, *Sentire cum Christo: La teologia dell'esperienza cristiana nell'opera di Hans Urs von Balthasar* (Tesi Gregoriana Teologia, 36; Roma: Pontificia Universitas Gregoriana, 1998).

Nichols, A., *No Bloodless Myth: A Guide through Balthasar's Dramatics* (Washington, DC: Catholic University Press, 2000).

Oakes, E., *Pattern of Redemption: The Theology of Hans Urs von Balthasar* (New York: Continuum, 1994).

O'Donnell, J., *Hans Urs von Balthasar* (London: Geoffrey Chapman, 1992).

Ouellet, M., 'Paradox and/or Supernatural Existential', *Communio: International Catholic Review* 18 (1991), pp. 259–80.

Pesarchick, R., *The Trinitarian Foundation of Human Sexuality as Revealed by Christ According to Hans Urs von Balthasar: The Revelatory Significance of the Male Christ and the Male Ministerial Priesthood* (Tesi Gregoriana Teologia, 63; Roma: Pontificia Universitas Gregoriana, 2000).

Saward, J., *The Mysteries of March: Hans Urs von Balthasar on the Incarnation and Easter* (Washington, DC: Catholic University Press, 1990).

Schindler, D.C., 'Toward a Non-Possessive Concept of Knowledge: on the Relation between Reason and Love in Aquinas and Balthasar', *Modern Theology* 22 (2006), pp. 577–607.

——, *The Dramatic Structure of Truth: A Philosophical Investigation* (Perspectives in Continental Philosophy, 34; New York: Fordham University Press, 2004).

Schindler, D.L. (ed.), *Love Alone is Credible: Hans Urs von Balthasar as Interpreter of the Catholic Tradition* (vol. 1; Grand Rapids: Eerdmans, 2008).

Scola, A., 'Nature and Grace in Hans Urs von Balthasar', *Communio: International Catholic Review* 18 (1991), pp. 207–26.

Servais, J., 'Balthasar as Interpreter of the Catholic Tradition', in D.L. Schindler (ed.); *Love Alone is Credible: Hans Urs von Balthasar as Interpreter of the Catholic Tradition*, vol. 1 (trans. S. Tan; Grand Rapids: Eerdmans, 2008), pp. 191–208.

——, 'Giovanni, fra Maria e Pietro: L'identità ecclesiale del consacrato', in A.M. Jerumanis and A. Tombolini (eds), *La missione teologica di Hans Urs von Balthasar: Atti del Simposio internazionale di Teologia in occasione del centesimo anniversario della nascita di Hans Urs von Balthasar* (Lugano: Eupress FTL, 2005), pp. 347–63.

——, 'La doctrine thomiste de la Rédemption', in H.U. von Balthasar, *Au cœur du mystère rédempteur* (repr. 2, Magny-les-Hameaux: Socéval, 2005), pp. 145–65.

——, 'Le *pro nobis* dans la conscience de Jésus', in H.U. von Balthasar, *Au cœur du mystère rédempteur* (repr. 2, Magny-les-Hameaux: Socéval, 2005), pp. 167–99.

——, 'Maria, Pietro e Giovanni, figure della Chiesa', *Communio: Rivista internazionale di teologia* 203–204 (2005), pp. 117–32.

——, 'Mérite, substitution, sacrifice de l'Église', in H.U. von Balthasar, *Au cœur du mystère rédempteur* (repr. 2, Magny-les-Hameaux: Socéval, 2005), pp. 201–23.

Sicari, A., 'Maria, Pietro, Giovanni: Figure della Chiesa. L'ecclesiologia di H.U. von Balthasar', *Communio: Rivista internazionale di teologia* 120 (1991), pp. 80–94; 'Mary, Peter and John: Figures of the Church', in *Communio: International Catholic Review* 19 (trans. M. Waldstein, 1992), pp. 189–207.

Splett, J., 'Der Christ und seine Angst erwogen mit Hans Urs von Balthasar', in P. Reifenberg and A. van Hooff (eds), *Gott für die Welt: Henri de Lubac, Gustav Siewerth und Hans Urs von Balthasar in ihren Grundanliegen* (Festschrift W. Seidel; Mainz: Matthias Grünewald Verlag, 2001), pp. 315–31.

Torralba-Roselló, F., 'Prefacio', in H.U. von Balthasar, *El Cristiano y la Angustía* (Madrid: Caparrós Editores, 1998), pp. 11–23.

——, 'Teologia de l'angoixa: Kierkegaard i Urs von Balthasar', in J. Busquets and M. Martinell (eds), *Fe i teologia en la história: Estudios en honor del Prof. Dr. Evangelista Vilanova* (Barcelona: Publicacions Abadía Montserrat SA, 1997), pp. 449–56.

Tourenne, Y., 'Un théologien et son temps', in H. U. von Balthasar, *Le Chrétien et l'angoisse* (repr. 2, Paris: Desclée de Brouwer, 1994), pp. 7–31; 'Foreward', in *The Christian and Anxiety* (trans. D. Martin and M. J. Miller; San Francisco: Ignatius Press, 2000), pp. 11–29.

Yeago, D., *Theology and Drama: A Study in the Work of Hans Urs von Balthasar* (New Haven: Yale University Press, 1992).

Other Works

Ainsworth, M., *Patterns of Attachment: A Psychological Study of the Strange Situation* (Mahwah: Erlbaum, 1978).

Allers, R., *The Successful Error: A Critical Study of Freudian Psychoanalysis* (New York: Sheed & Ward, 1940).

American Psychiatric Association, *Diagnostic and Statistical Manual of Mental Disorders-IV-TR* (Washington, DC: American Psychiatric Association, 2000).

Aquinas, T., *Compendium Theologiae* (Opera omnia; vol. 42; Romae: Editio Leonina, 1979), *Compendium of Theology (Compendium theologiae)* (trans. C. Vollert; St. Louis: B. Herder Book Co., 1947).

——, *De Veritate* (Opera Omnia; vol. 22; Romae: Editio Leonina, 1976).

——, *Summa contra Gentiles* (Opera Omnia; vols. 14–15; Romae: Editio Leonina, 1926–30).

——, *Summa Theologiae* (Opera omnia; vols. 4–12, Romae: Editio Leonina, 1888–1906); *Summa Theologiae: Latin text, English translation, Introduction, Notes, Appendices and Glossary* (London: Blackfriars, 1964).

——, *Super Evangelium S. Ioannis Lectura* (http//:www.corpusthomisticum.org).

——, *Super Evangelium S. Matthaei Lectura* (http//:www.corpusthomisticum.org).

——, *Theological Texts* (trans. T. Gilby; London: Oxford University Press, 1955).

——, *Scriptum super Sententiis* (http//:www.corpusthomisticum.org).

Argyle, A.W., *The Gospel According to Matthew* (Cambridge: Cambridge University Press, 1963).

Balz, H. and G. Schneider (eds), *Exegetisches Wörterbuch zum Neuen Testament* (vol. 2; Stuttgart: Verlag W. Kohlhammer GmbH, 1978–80); *Exegetical Dictionary of the New Testament* (vol. 2; Grand Rapids: Eerdmans, 1990).

Barbaglio, G. (ed.), *Teologia* (Milano: Edizioni San Paolo, 2002).

Barbour, R.S., 'Gethsemane in the Tradition of the Passion', *New Testament Studies* 16 (1969–70), pp. 231–51.

Barlow, D.H., 'The Nature of Anxiety: Anxiety, Depression, and Emotional Disorders', in R.M. Rapee and Barlow (eds), *Chronic Anxiety: Generalized Anxiety Disorder and Mixed Anxiety-Depression* (New York: Guilford Press, 1991), pp. 1–28.

Battaglia, V., 'I "Sentimenti" del Signore Gesú. Un Modello Cristologico per la Vita Spirituale e L'Agire Morale', *Antonianum* 81 (2006), pp. 209–55.

Bauer, W., *A Greek-English Lexicon of the New Testament and other Early Christian Literature* (rev. and ed. F. Danker), based on Walter Bauer's *Griechisch-deutsches Wörterbuch zu den Schriften des Neuen Testaments und der früchristlichen Literatur*, sixth edition (ed. K. Aland and B. Aland), with V. Reichmann and on previous English editions by W. Arndt, F. Gingrich and F. Danker, Chicago 1957, 2000.

Beck, A.T. and G. Emery, *Anxiety Disorders and Phobias: A Cognitive Perspective* (New York: Basic Books, 1991).

Bernanos, G., *Monsieur Ouine* (trans. W. Bush; Lincoln: Bison Books, 2000).

——, *The Diary of a Country Priest* (trans. P. Morris; New York: Carroll & Graf, 2nd edn, 2002).

——, *Under Satan's Sun* (trans. J.C. Whitehorse; Lincoln: University of Nebraska Press, 2001).

Bordeyne, P., *L'homme et son angoisse : La théologie morale de 'Gaudium et spes'* (Paris: Cerf, 2004).

Bott-Spillius, E. (ed.), *Melanie Klein Today*, vol. I: *Mainly Theory* (New Library of Psychoanalysis, 7; New York: Routledge, 1988).

Bowlby, J., *A Secure Base: Parent-Child Attachment and Healthy Human Development* (New York: Basic Books, 1990).

Braaten, C.E., 'The Finnish Breakthrough in Lutheran Research', *Pro Ecclesia* 5 (1996), pp. 141–43.

Brown, R., *The Death of the Messiah* (vol. 1; New York: Anchor Bible, 1994).

Bush, W., *To Quell the Terror* (Washington, DC: ICS Publications, 1999).

Busiello, G., 'Le passioni in Tommaso d'Aquino tra etica, antropologia e metafisica', *Angelicum* 83 (2006), pp. 95–120.

Buttrick, G. (ed.), *The Interpreter's Bible*, vol. VII: *General Articles on the New Testament, Matthew and Mark* (New York: Abingdon Press, 1951).

Cassarini, D., *Elementi di teologia fondamentale* (Assisi: Cittadella, 2003).

Catechism of the Catholic Church (Vatican City: Libreria Editrice Vaticana, rev. edn, 2000).

Coe, D.K., *Angst and the Abyss: The Hermeneutics of Nothingness* (Chico: Scholars Press, 1985).

Cole, J.P., *The Problematic Self in Kierkegaard and Freud* (New Haven: Yale University Press, 1971).

Colman, A. (ed.), *A Dictionary of Psychology* (Oxford: Oxford University Press, 2003).

Congregation for the Doctrine of the Faith, *Libertatis Conscientia*, *AAS* 79 (1987), pp. 554–59.

Cook, C.C.H., 'Psychiatry and Mysticism', *Mental Health, Religion & Culture* 7 (2004), pp. 149–63.

Corsini, R. (ed.), *Encyclopedia of Psychology* (vol. 1; New York: John Wiley & Sons, 2nd edn, 1994).

——, *The Dictionary of Psychology* (Philadelphia: Taylor & Francis, 1999).

Costacurta, B., *La Vita Minacciata: Il tema della paura nella Bibbia Ebraica* (Analecta Biblica, 119; Roma: Pontificia Universitas Gregoriana, 1997).

Crews, F., 'The Making of a Freud Skeptic', *Skeptic* 7 (1999), pp. 42–9.

——, 'The Verdict on Freud', *Psychological Science* 7 (1996), pp. 63–8.

—— (ed.), *Unauthorized Freud: Doubters Confront a Legend* (New York: Viking, 1998).

Denziger, H. and A. Schönmetzer (eds), *Enchiridion Symbolorum, Definitionum et Declarationum de Rebus Fidei et Morum*, Freiburg 1937[23].

Dodds, E.R., *Pagan and Christian in an Age of Anxiety: some Aspects of Religious Experience from Marcus Aurelius to Constantine* (Cambridge: Cambridge University Press, 1963).

Dunning, S.N., 'Kierkegaard's Systematic Analysis of Anxiety', in Perkins, R. (ed.), *The Concept of Anxiety* (International Kierkegaard Commentary, vol. 8; Macon: Mercer University Press, 1985).

Feuillet, A., *L'Agonie de Gethsemani* (Paris: Gabalda, 1977).

Freud, S., *The Complete Introductory Lectures on Psychoanalysis* (trans. J. Strachey; New York: W.W. Norton & Co., 1966).

Fries, H., *Fundamental Theology* (trans. R. Daly; Washington, DC: Catholic University Press, 1996).

Galot, J., 'Le Christ terrestre et la vision', *Gregorianum* 67 (1986), pp. 429–50.

Garrigou-Lagrange, R., *God. His Existence and His Nature: A Thomistic Solution of Certain Agnostic Antinomies* (trans. B. Rose, OSB; vol. 2; London: B. Herder, 1936).

——, *The Love of God and the Cross of Jesus* (trans. J. Marie; vols. 1–2; London: B. Herder, 1952).

Gondreau, P., *The Passions of Christ's Soul in the Theology of St. Thomas Aquinas* (Münster: Aschendorff, 2002).

Greenspan, S., *Building Healthy Minds: The Six Experiences That Create Intelligence and Emotional Growth in Babies and Young Children* (Cambridge: Da Capo Press, 2000).

——, *The Growth of the Mind: And the Endangered Origins of Intelligence* (Cambridge: Da Capo Press, 1998).

Gregory, R. (ed.), *The Oxford Companion to the Mind* (Oxford: Oxford University Press, 1987).

Guardini, R., *Sorge um den Menschen* (Mainz: Matthias Grünewald Verlag, 1958); *Ansia per l'uomo* (Brescia: Morcelliana, 1969).

Hacker, P., *The Ego in Faith: Martin Luther and the Origin of Anthropocentric Religion* (Chicago: Franciscan Herald Press, 1970).

Harrington, D., *The Gospel of Matthew* (Sacra Pagina Series, Collegeville: Liturgical Press, 2007).

House, S.B., 'A Martyr's Theology of Assent: Reading Thomas More's *De Tristitia Christi*', *Renaissance et Réform* 29 (2005), pp. 49–63.

Ignatius of Loyola, *A Pilgrim's Journey: The Autobiography of Ignatius of Loyola* (Wilmington: Michael Glazier, 1985).

——, *Spiritual Exercises* (New York: Harper, 2000).

Jeffrey, D. (ed.), *A Dictionary of Biblical Tradition in English Literature* (Grand Rapids: Eerdmans, 1992).

John XXIII, *Pacem in Terris*, *AAS* 55 (1963), pp. 257–304.

John Paul II, *Dives in Misericordia*, *AAS* 72 (1980), pp. 1177–1232.

——, *Evangelium Vitae*, *AAS* 87 (1995), pp. 401–522.

——, *Familiaris Consortio*, *AAS* 74 (1982), pp. 81–191.

——, *Fides et Ratio*, *AAS* 91 (1999), pp. 1–88.

——, *General Audience* (30 November 1988) in *L'Osservatore Romano (English edition)* (5 December 1988), p. 1.

——, *Laborem Exercens*, *AAS* 73 (1981), pp. 577–647.

——, *Novo Millennio Ineunte*, *AAS* 93 (2001), pp. 266–309.

——, *Sollicitudo Rei Socialis*, *AAS* 80 (1988), pp. 513–86.

——, *Salvifici Doloris*, *AAS* 76 (1984), pp. 201–50.

Johnson, L.T., *The Gospel of Luke* (Sacra Pagina Series, Collegeville: Liturgical Press, 2006).

Jones, E., *The Life and Work of Sigmund Freud*, vol. II: *Years of Maturity 1901–1919* (New York: Basic Books, 1955).

Journet, C., *The Meaning of Evil* (trans. M. Barry; London: Geoffrey Chapman, 1963).

Kazdin, A. (ed.), *Encyclopedia of Psychology* (vol. 1; Oxford: Oxford University Press, 2000).

Kierkegaard, S., *The Sickness Unto Death* (trans. W. Lowrie; Garden City: Doubleday, 1954).

——, *The Concept of Anxiety* (trans. R. Thomte; Kierkegaard's Writings, vol. 8; Princeton: Princeton University Press, 1980).

——, *Stages on Life's Way* (trans. H. Hong and E. Hong; Kiekegaard's Writings, vol. 11; Princeton: Princeton University Press, 1988).

Kittel, G., *Theologisches Wörterbuch zum Neuen Testament* (Stuttgart: W. Kohlhammer Verlag, 1967); *Theological Dictionary of the New Testament* (trans. G. Bromiley; vol. 4; Grand Rapids: Eerdmans, 1967).

Ladaria, L., *Antropologia teologica* (Casale Monferrato: Piemme, 1995).

Lane, W., *The Gospel According to Mark* (The New International Commentary on the New Testament, vol. 2; Grand Rapids: Eerdmans, 1974).

Larson, D.B., J.P. Swyers and M.E. McCullough (eds), *Scientific Research on Spirituality and Health: a Report based on the Scientific Progress in Spirituality* (Rockville: National Institute for Healthcare Research, 1998).

Latourelle, R., *Man and His Problems in the Light of Jesus Christ* (trans. M.J.O'Connell; New York: Alba House, 1983).

——, and R. Fisichella (eds), *Dizionario di teologia fondamentale* (Assisi: Cittadella, 1990); *The Dictionary of Fundamental Theology* (New York: Crossroads, 1994).

Le Fort, G. von, *The Song at the Scaffold* (Garden City: Doubleday, 1961).

Léon-Dufour, X. (ed.), *Dictionary of Biblical Theology* (trans. J. Cahill, S.J. and E.M. Stewart; Boston: St. Paul Books & Media, rev. edn, 1988).

Loughlin, S., 'The Complexity of *timor* in Aquinas's *Summa Theologiae*' in A. Scott and C. Kosso (eds), *Fear and Its Representations in the Middle Ages and Renaissance* (Belgium: Brepols, 2002), pp. 1–16.

——, 'Tristitia et Dolor: Does Aquinas Have a Robust Understanding of Depression?', *Nova et vetera* (English edition) 3 (2005), pp. 761–84.

Luther, M., *D. Martin Luthers Werke: Kritische Gesamtausgabe* (Weimar: Hermann Böhlau, 1883); *Luther's Works: The American Edition* (ed. J. Pelikan and H.T. Lehmann; St. Louis and Philadelphia: Fortress Press, 1958–72).

——, *Letters of Spiritual Counsel* (trans. T.G. Tappert; Philadelphia: Westminster, 1955).

Mann, C.S., *Mark* (The Anchor Bible, vol. 27; Garden City: Doubleday, 1986).

McGrath, A., *Iustitia Dei: A History of the Christian Doctrine of Justification* (Cambridge: Cambridge University Press, 2002).

Miller, C.H., 'The Heart of the Final Struggle: More's Commentary on the Agony in the Garden', in M.J. Moore (ed.), *Quincentennial Essays on St. Thomas More* (Boone: Albion, 1978), pp. 108–23.

Moltmann, J., *The Crucified God* (trans. R.A. Wilson and J. Bowden; London: SCM Press, 1974).

——, *Theology of Hope* (trans. J. W. Leitch; New York: Harper & Row, 1967).

More, T., *The Complete Works of St. Thomas More*, vol. XIII: *Treatise on the Passion: Treatise to Receive the Blessed Body: Instructions and Prayers* (New Haven: Yale University Press, 1976).

——, *The Complete Works of St. Thomas More*, vol. XIV: *De Tristitia Christi* (New Haven: Yale University Press, 1976).

Nestle, E. and Aland, K. (eds), *Novum Testamentum Graece* (repr. 27; Stuttgart: Deutsche Bibelgesellschaft, 1993).

Ocáriz, F., L.F. Mateo Seco and J.A. Riestra, *The Mystery of Jesus Christ* (Dublin: Four Courts Press, rev. edn, 2004).

Pannenberg, W., *Systematic Theology* (trans. G.W. Bromiley; vol. 1; Grand Rapids: Eerdmans, 1991).

Paul VI, *Evangelii Nuntiandi*, *AAS* 68 (1976), pp. 5–76.

Perkins, R. (ed.), *The Concept of Anxiety* (International Kierkegaard Commentary, vol. 8; Macon: Mercer University Press, 1985).

Peterson, C. and M. Seligman, *Character Strengths and Virtues: A Handbook and Classification* (Oxford: Oxford University Press, 2004).

Pie-Ninot, S., *La teologia fondamentale* (Biblioteca di Teologia contemporanea, p. 121; Brescia: Queriniana, 2002).

Pius XI, *Casti Connubii*, *AAS* 22 (1930), pp. 539–92.

Pius XII, *Haurietis Aquas*, *AAS* 48 (1956), pp. 309–53.

——, *Mystici Corporis Christi*, *AAS* 35 (1943), pp. 193–248.

de la Potterie, I., *The Hour of Jesus* (Middlegreen: St. Paul Publications, 1989).

Rahner, K., 'Anxiety and Christian Trust in Theological Perspective' in *Theological Investigations*, vol. XXIII: *Final Writings* (trans. J. Donceel and H. Riley; London: Darton, Longman & Todd, 1992), pp. 3–15.

Ratzinger, J., *Meditationen zur Karwoche* (Freising: Kyrios Verlag, 1969); Italian trans., *L'angoscia di un'assenza. Tre meditazioni sul Sabato santo* (Brescia: Queriniana, 1971).

Reid, J. P., 'Emotional Psychopathology', in T. Aquinas, *Summa Theologiae*, vol. XXI: *Fear and Anger* (London: Blackfriars, 1965), pp. 156–63.

——, 'Somatic Reactions', in T. Aquinas, *Summa Theologiae*, vol. XXI: *Fear and Anger* (London: Blackfriars, 1965), pp. 172–77.

Revised English Bible (Oxford: Oxford University Press, 1970).

Revised Standard Version Bible: Catholic Edition (Camden: Thomas Nelson & Sons, 1966).

Rieff, P., *The Triumph of the Therapeutic: Uses of Faith after Freud* (Chicago: University of Chicago Press, 1987).

——, *Freud: The Mind of the Moralist* (Chicago: University of Chicago Press, 1979).

Ritter, J. (ed.), *Historisches Wörterbuch der Philosophie* (vol. 1; Basel/Stuttgart: Schwabe, 1971).

Saarinen, R., 'Salvation in the Lutheran-Orthodox Dialogue', *Pro Ecclesia* 5 (1996), pp. 202–13.

Sadock, B. and V. Sadock (eds), *Kaplan and Sadock's Comprehensive Textbook of Psychiatry* (vol. 1; Philadelphia: Lippincott Williams & Wilkins, 2000).

——, *Kaplan and Sadock's Synopsis of Psychiatry* (Philadelphia: Lippincott Williams & Wilkins, 2002).

Sandkühler, H.J. (ed.), *Europäische Enyzklopädie zu Philosophie und Wissenschaften* (Hamburg: F. Meiner, 1990).

Saward, H., 'A Literature of Substitution: Vicarious Sacrifice in the Writings of Gertrud von Le Fort', *German Life and Letters* 53 (2000), pp. 178–200.

Saward, J., *The Way of the Lamb: The Spirit of Childhood and the End of the Age* (Edinburgh: T&T Clark, 1999).

Schakenburg, R., *The Gospel According to St. John* (trans. K. Smyth; vol. 3; New York: Herder & Herder, 1982).

Servais, J., 'Il dualismo Freudiano di vita e morte', *Civiltá Cattolica* (1989), pp. 240–52.

——, 'Restlessness and Anxiety: toward a Christian discernment', *Communio: International Catholic Review* 34 (2007), pp. 224–242.

——, 'Should We Engage Ourselves in the World, or Make Ourselves Indifferent to All Things?', *Communio: International Catholic Review* 32 (2005), pp. 472–91.

Siegel, D., *The Developing Mind: Toward a Neurobiology of Interpersonal Experience* (New York: Guilford, 1999).

Sims, A., *Symptoms in the Mind: An Introduction to Descriptive Psychopathology* (London: Saunders Ltd., 2003).

Speyr, A. von, *Confession* (trans. D.W. Stott; San Francisco: Ignatius Press, 1985).

——, *Johannes*, vol. II: *Streitreden* (Einsiedeln: Johannes Verlag, 1949); *John*, vol. II: *The Discourses of Controversy* (trans. E.A. Nelson; San Francisco: Ignatius Press, 1993).

Stanley, D.M., *Jesus in Gethsemane* (Ramsey: Paulist Press, 1980).

Stern, D.N., *The Interpersonal World of the Child: A View from Psychoanalysis and Developmental Psychology* (New York: Basic Books, 1985).

Terruwe, A. and C. Baars, *Psychic Wholeness and Healing: Using All the Powers of the Human Psyche* (New York: Alba House, 1981).

Tillich, P., *Systematic Theology* (vol. 1; Chicago: University of Chicago, 1973).

——, *The Courage to Be* (New Haven: Yale University Press, 1970).

Vanhoye, A., 'L'angoisse du Christ', *Christus* 18 (1971), pp. 382–89.

Vatican II, *Gaudium et Spes*, *AAS* 58 (1966), pp. 1025–1120.

Vitz, P., 'Psychology in Recovery', *First Things* 151 (2005), pp. 17–21.

Weinandy, T., 'Jesus' Filial Vision of the Father', *Pro Ecclesia* 13 (2004), pp. 189–201.

West, J.L.A., Review of *The Passions of Christ's Soul in the Theology of St. Thomas Aquinas*, *Theological Studies* 64 (2003), pp. 626–27.

White, K., 'The Passions of the Soul (Ia IIae, qq. 22–48)', in S. Pope (ed.), *The Ethics of Aquinas* (Washington, DC: Georgetown University Press, 2002), pp. 103–15.

White, T. J., 'The Voluntary Action of the Earthly Christ and the Necessity of the Beatific Vision', *The Thomist* 69 (2005), pp. 497–534.

Wicks, J., 'Justification and Faith in Luther', *Theological Studies* 44 (1983), pp. 3–29.

——, 'Living and Praying as *Simul Iustus et Peccator*', *Gregorianum* 70 (1989), pp. 521–48.

——, Review of *Der fröhliche Wechsel und Streit. Grundzüge der Theologie Martin Luthers*, *Gregorianum* 63 (1982), p. 163.

Index of Persons

www.ingramcontent.com/pod-product-compliance
Lightning Source LLC
LaVergne TN
LVHW052255200926
848481LV00002B/373

* 9 7 8 0 5 6 7 0 0 0 4 7 7 *